REAL ESTATE INVESTMENT

Analysis and Strategy

ROBERT J. WILEY, J.D., Ph.D.

A RONALD PRESS PUBLICATION

JOHN WILEY & SONS, New York • Chichester • Brisbane • Toronto

HD
1 375
W54

Preface

Not only do real estate investment decisions engage the attention of a large number and variety of investors and professional people, but because real estate represents the major form of wealth in the United States, the results of these decisions have a major impact on the nation's economy, and directly or indirectly touch the lives of all of us.

The purpose of this work is to help the reader to understand the principles and methods of analysis that are useful in making productive real estate investment decisions. The book is intended to serve not only those studying in academic real estate programs but also the practitioners of professions related to real estate, such as brokers, appraisers, lenders, architects, and others. The book is also, of course, addressed to present and potential real estate investors and can be thought of as analogous to the volumes on securities analysis that are widely used in colleges and universities as well as in the securities industry.

The author's approach is to attempt to draw together in a logically organized pattern various investment principles and techniques that have been developed by those directly concerned with real estate and by those in other disciplines, such as managerial accounting, financial management, and securities analysis. The investment principles and techniques are integrated with materials that are descriptive of the institutional setting for real estate investment. The federal income tax provisions most relevant to real estate investment are considered, including the provisions of the Tax Reform Act of 1976. The reader is advised, however, to confirm from proper authority the current status of federal income tax provisions as well as relevant state law that may affect a transaction.

Many analytical techniques are explored, ranging from the traditional gross income multiplier to discounted cash flow. The book contains unique discussions and number examples in such important areas as financial leverage, refinancing decisions, tax shelter, risk analysis, and investment planning. Illustrative applications of the analytical framework are presented in the last two parts of the book, with separate chapters devoted to undeveloped land, residential properties, shopping centers, and motels. Two concluding chapters examine the investment aspects of land sub-division and property development.

While it is assumed that the reader has a knowledge of elementary algebra, a previous course in accounting principles, or in the principles of real estate, would also be helpful. Consequently the book will find its major textbook use at the upper undergraduate and graduate level.

The author expresses his appreciation to his many outstanding former teachers and to the many real estate professionals who have contributed directly and indirectly to the development of this book. Special thanks are due to Sidney M. Robbins of Columbia University, A. Plunket Beirne, Esq., and Arthur M. Weimer of Indiana University. The author also wishes to thank the American Institute of Real Estate Appraisers, the Institute of Real Estate Management, and the Urban Land Institute for permission to use certain materials relating to apartments and shopping centers.

Robert␣J.␣Wiley

Philadelphia, Pa.
January, 1977

Contents

PART IV—PROPERTY SELECTION

PART V—REAL ESTATE DEVELOPMENT

I

Introduction

1

The Nature of
Real Estate

The process of *investing,* as contrasted to *gambling,* presupposes the gathering, forecasting, and structuring of data upon which reasoned conclusions or decisions can be based. In this respect, investing in real estate is similar to investing in other commodities, whether they be shares of common stock, agricultural commodities, or perhaps even antique furniture pieces. However, the availability and nature of the relevant data as well as the manner of handling the data vary from one investment outlet to another, depending on the nature of the basic investment commodity itself. In the present chapter the characteristics of the commodity real estate will be examined, and the markets in which real estate transactions take place. Other factors influencing the real estate investment process, such as the nature of real estate investors' goals, will be discussed in the following introductory chapter.

While the expression *real estate* is often used to refer to an industry or a business, it also refers to a commodity, and as such· can be defined as *the land and, generally, whatever is erected, growing upon, or affixed to the land.* For our purposes we shall consider the terms *realty* and *real property* as being equivalent to *real estate.*

PHYSICAL ATTRIBUTES OF REAL ESTATE

There are some general physical characteristics or attributes of real estate, that are of significance for the investor, as listed and described below. Of necessity the list is a generalized one, because there exist some outright exceptions, and for any given item there certainly exist differing degrees of applicability to various kinds of real property.

Immobility. That real estate is immobile, as contrasted with other investment commodities, has many consequences of importance to the investor. For example, property is a visible, fixed, and convenient target for taxation; as evidenced by the fast-rising level of property taxes in most communities. Because real estate cannot be moved it also makes excellent security for loans and encourages relatively high loan-to-value ratios. As another consequence of immobility, the value of a piece of real property is subject to change as its surrounding environment changes.

Uniqueness. Each piece of real estate is unique, at least to some extent, and not standardized as are, say, shares of stock in General Motors Corporation, or graded agricultural commodities. Among the consequences of this attribute is the tendency for real estate markets and real estate financing to be decentralized, or localized.

Usefulness. Real estate has the capability of being personally used by the owner while his funds are invested in the property. In this sense the real estate commodity is more closely akin to antiques or works of art than to investment securities. This atribute is enjoyed by real estate owners ranging from homeowners, to farmers, and to corporations owning their own office buildings.

Large-scale investment. While real properties often undergo subdivision, they are generally not as easily divisible as some other investment commodities, such as graded agricultural commodities. Consequently, real estate investments usually involve relatively large sums of money; this in turn fosters *group ownership* and encourages *relatively high levels of debt financing.*

Physical complexities. Real estate properties often present complexities or problems of a physical nature, such as drainage and water-supply problems. Physical complexities often require the investor to employ professional services, such as those provided by engineers, architects, and land planners.

LEGAL ASPECTS OF REAL ESTATE

While part of the increasing legal complexity attending real estate investment simply reflects the growing governmental influence over private business and investment activity, there are other legal complexities that relate to the particular nature of the real estate commodity, as discussed below.

Title Complexities

Since its founding as an independent nation, the United States has continued to accept the principle of private property ownership that was adopted from the British. Two important British contributors to the philosophical justification for private real property ownership were John Locke and Adam Smith. Almost three hundred years ago Locke wrote: "Whatsoever, then, [man] removes out of the state that nature hath provided and left it in, he hath mixed his labour with, and joined to it something that is his own, and thereby makes it his property." [1] About two hundred years ago, in 1776, Adam Smith, in his classic book, *The Wealth of Nations,* argued the existence of a beneficial link between the private ownership of property, individual freedom, and the growth of a nation's wealth.

The upholding of private ownership of property in the United States has been attended by the development of an elaborate system of real estate title registration, and the use of governmental police powers and the country's court system to help defend the titleholder's legal enjoyment of his property rights.

[1] John Locke, *Of Civil Government: Second Treatise* (1689; Chicago: Henry Regnery Company, 1955), p. 22.

The most common as well as the most complete or absolute form of private real property ownership (title) is called the fee simple estate, or simply *fee simple*.[2] The fee simple titleholder can use his property or dispose of it as he wishes, within the governmental restrictions discussed in the sections below.

Despite the thoroughness of the title protection system, legal conflicts occasionally arise over title claims; not only because of boundary disputes based on insufficient property descriptions, but also for a variety of other technical reasons, that put a cloud on the title. Thus, title problems are one source of legal complexities for the real estate investor.

Restrictions on Property Use

Other legal complexities arise because despite the fact that private ownership has been recognized and protected in this country, there has also been a continuing and growing public interest in the way real property is *used* by private owners. The restrictions on property use imposed by local governments (counties and municipalities) usually take the form of *zoning regulations,* which restrict specific land areas to specific uses, such as for single-family residences, and require minimum lot sizes for specific types of buildings; *building codes,* which set construction standards for such things as wiring and plumbing; and *health and sanitation requirements.* Some counties and municipalities have additional restrictions, such as the detailed building-design standards applied in the French Quarter of New Orleans.

State laws relate traditionally to the consideration that property be so used as to not be a nuisance to others; and recently, some states have established standards controlling the amount of pollution emission by real property users. State laws also uphold legally approved restrictions on land use contained in private deeds, such as arise in housing subdivisions where, along with other requirements regarding the use of the property, a minimum home size may be stipulated for lot buyers. States also directly

---

[2] Other titles to real estate, such as the *life estate,* are discussed in various real estate law texts. Other property interests, such as the mortgage and leasehold interests, and joint property ownership interests, are discussed in Chapters 2 and 8 in this book.

influence property ownership arrangements through their corporation and partnership laws, and other laws relating to real property interests.

While most property-use restrictions are determined at the local and state levels, the national government has increasingly been playing a direct role through the establishment of pollution standards, and an indirect role by setting construction standards for property purchasers seeking government-backed mortgage financing or government housing subsidies. Another instance of the federal government's influence on private property usage is the encouragement of investors to use their land for residential developments by allowing related favorable depreciation treatment for tax purposes.[3] Rent control is another governmental action influencing the economic use of real property. Rent controls have had a long history in New York City, and more recently have become a part of the federal government's set of economic control tools.

Eminent domain is a power held by all governmental levels and represents the ultimate restriction on property use: the taking (with compensation) of private property for public use.

From an investment standpoint, an important aspect of the various governmental restrictions on real property use is that they can significantly affect the income generating potential, and hence the value of real property. Also, the legal fees incurred in dealing with use restrictions, such as attempts to change the zoning classification for a particular piece of property, as well as in dealing with title problems and other legal complexities, can substantially increase investment outlays.

Governmental Fiscal Policy

The two aspects of governmental fiscal policy can have important consequences for the real estate investor; namely, the raising of public funds through taxation, and the spending of public monies. At the local governmental level, taxation on real estate takes the form of a direct tax on capital, with the amount of tax based on the property's assessed valuation. The so-called

---

[3] The various depreciation tax provisions are discussed in detail in Chapter 4.

property taxes, or *real estate taxes* have reached very high levels in many communities and represent the largest single operating expense for many real estate investments. At the national governmental level, the income tax is the principle source of revenue, and the application of the income tax laws and the related estate and gift tax laws can influence real estate investments in many ways. At the present time several states and some cities, including New York State and New York City, also have income taxes.

The fact that the income tax rates reach such high levels makes the consideration of tax aspects of crucial importance in maximizing investment goals. Accordingly, much of the material in this book relates to federal income tax provisions affecting real estate investment. Despite the importance of income taxes, however, it is clear that overemphasis on tax details may lead one to overlook important non-tax aspects of a real estate investment proposal. Some projects with favorable tax aspects may, of course, involve unreasonable risks of loss; while, on the other hand, some projects with unattractive tax features may still be highly profitable.

The spending side of governmental fiscal policy also influences real estate values in a variety of ways; for example, the government's decisions on the placement of roads, schools, airports, parks, landfills, and other public facilities will have a direct impact on the value of neighboring properties. More indirectly influencing the general level of real property values are the federal government's expenditures made to help support housing construction and the mortgage markets.

Governmental Monetary Policy

Monetary policy relates to the government's actions designed to influence the market rate of interest. That the government can achieve such influence over interest rate levels has been amply shown in the past. Because interest expense is one of the major expense items for most real estate investments, interest rate levels clearly have a major impact on real estate investment returns and property values. Interest rate levels also have a direct bearing on the number of people able to purchase homes, as evidenced in the high-interest-rate periods in 1969 and 1973–74.

The above introductory review of the legal aspects of real estate indicates the wide range of legal considerations involved in real estate investing, and it seems very likely that governmental influence and control in private business and investment activities will be extended even further in future years. Professional legal and tax counsel will, of course, have to be called upon by the investor in dealing with specific legal and tax questions. However, the real estate investor should have an awareness of the general legal framework, or environment, when making basic decisions as to the type of property to acquire; when making risk/return analyses; and in planning ownership, financing, and other investment strategies. Accordingly, what we have called the legal aspects, including tax aspects, will be discussed in more detail at several points in the following chapters.

REAL ESTATE MARKETS

Because of the unique physical and legal attributes of real estate, the markets for real estate differ in many ways from markets for other commodities. Some of the important market characteristics are described below.

Decentralized and unorganized. Because of the immobile or fixed character of real property its value will change with shifts in local supply and demand conditions, and with alterations in the local environment. The market for real estate, therefore, tends to be localized or decentralized, as contrasted with the national market for many corporation and government securities. Most real estate sale transactions are still conducted between local buyers and sellers, notwithstanding the increasing participation of national corporations and financial institutions in the real estate markets.

Because of their decentralized nature, real estate markets are not highly organized, as are the markets for many securities issues; and real estate markets are relatively uncontrolled, as compared to some securities markets controlled through the Securities Exchange Commission.

Private transactions. Most real estate transactions are conducted in private, or in secret. In most communities no public record is made of the dollar amounts involved in real estate transactions, and while revenue stamps placed on transfer documents can be an indication of transaction value, this is not always a reliable guide. The result is that there is relatively little available market data for investors, again as contrasted with securities and commodities markets.

Limited supply. The supply of corporate common stocks is unlimited in the sense that new corporations are formed continuously, thereby generating a continuous new supply of equity securities. In contrast, it is often stated that "the supply of real estate is fixed," and that the opportunities for price gains are therefore, especially attractive for real estate, considering the increasing demand arising from a growing population, rising incomes, and a rising interest in leisure properties. While this analysis has some merit, it must be treated cautiously. For one thing, the pressing demand for living space in some urban and recreation areas has been at least partially met by high-rise construction.

With the exception of scattered reclamation undertakings, the quantity of land itself is indeed limited. However, increased demand for land around New York City does not become immediately translated into higher prices for land in Nebraska. Consequently, the limited-land-supply concept is most relevant when applied to land in specific areas of growing demand.

Lack of liquidity. Because of the nature of the real estate commodity itself (uniqueness, large-scale, and so forth), and the characteristics of the real estate markets, there is, generally speaking, a relative lack of liquidity for real estate properties. That is, more patience would generally be required of the seller of real estate than the seller of actively traded securities or commodities.

High transaction costs. The physical and legal complexities and lengthy negotiations that attend many real estate transactions often result in substantial professional service fees for the investor. It has been estimated that real estate transaction costs usually run ten to twenty times as high as for stocks and bonds.[4]

---

[4] Peer Soelberg and Norbert J. Stefaniak, "Impact of the Proposed Tax Reform Bill on Real Estate Investments," *The Appraisal Journal,* April, 1970, p. 189.

TYPES OF REAL ESTATE

In sorting out the wide variety of different kinds of real estate, land is a logical starting point. As indicated below, the quantity of non-urban land overshadows urban land in the United States. The two largest single categories in the agricultural land total below are grazing land and crop land. The figures shown are for 1960.[5]

Agricultural land	1,192,000,000 acres
Commercial forest land	484,000,000
Urban land	21,000,000
Other land	207,000,000
Total U. S. land	**1,904,000,000** acres

The second major category of real estate (aside from the land category) relates to the ways real properties have been developed; that is, the nature of the buildings or other improvements made to the property. While there is no definitive manner of classifying *developed properties,* the following breakdown covers most important types. Although there is insufficient data available on the total quantity and value of each type of property, it can be said that residential properties form the largest single category.

1. *Residential properties—*such as:
   Single-family houses.
   Multiple-family dwellings: including duplexes, triplexes, apartments, condominiums.

2. *Business properties—*such as:
   Office buildings.
   Industrial properties—factories, warehouses, mining and utilities.
   Commercial properties—stores, shopping centers, theatres, garages, amusement places.

3. *Hotels and motels.*

4. *Large-scale communities—*such as Reston, Virginia; and Columbia, Maryland.

[5] Arthur M. Weimer, Homer Hoyt, and George F. Bloom, *Real Estate* (6th ed.; New York: The Ronald Press Company, 1972), p. 56.

5. *Special-purpose properties*—such as golf courses, cemeteries, churches, clubs, hospitals.

6. *Public properties*—such as government buildings, roads, military installations.

THE REAL ESTATE INDUSTRY

The complexities attending real estate ownership and investment, and the massive number and variety of transactions and "operations" in real estate have brought many participants into the real estate industry. The following non-exhaustive list suggests the wide range of individuals, companies, and government authorities that the real estate investor often deals with, as contrasted with the concerns of the securities investor who usually deals with only a securities broker:

1. Land planners
2. Surveyors
3. Appraisers
4. Lawyers
5. Engineers
6. Market analysts
7. Architects
8. Tax accountants
9. Property insurance agents
10. Financial institutions
11. Title insurance companies
12. Real estate brokerage firms
13. Property management firms
14. Construction companies
15. Various local governmental units (e.g., zoning boards)
16. Internal Revenue Service

The principal trade association for the real estate industry is the *National Association of Realtors,* headquartered in Chicago. This organization has over 100,000 members. The organization sets standards of business conduct and licenses brokers (realtors), and also provides an extensive data collection and distribution service, and has various educational services. Two of the N.A.R.'s various affiliated institutes are the *American Institute of Real Estate Appraisers* and the *Institute of Real Estate Management.* Members must satisfy various professional entrance requirements and members carry the titles M.A.I. (Member of the Appraisal Institute), R.M. (Residential Member of the Appraisal Institute), and C.P.M. (Certified Property Manager).

Two of the regularly appearing publications of direct interest to the real estate investor are *The Appraisal Journal,* published quarterly by the American Institute of Real Estate Appraisers, and the *Real Estate Review,* published quarterly by The Real Estate Institute of New York University. From time to time articles of direct interest to realty investors appear in the architecture, finance, law, construction, and other journals, as well as in the *Wall Street Journal* and *Barrons.* Additionally, various special-topic, real estate studies are published by the National Association of Realtors, by various universities, and by the federal income tax services.

SUMMARY

As a commodity, real estate has some general characteristics that distinguish it from other investment commodities. Among the physical attributes of real property are its *immobility, uniqueness, usefulness, large scale,* and *physical complexities.* There are legal complexities as well as physical complexities attending the commodity real estate. The ubiquitous legal aspects relate not only to property title, but to various governmental restrictions imposed on the way real property can be used. Government taxation and other fiscal and monetary policies also influence real estate investments in many ways.

Some of the distinguishing characteristics of real estate markets can be considered under these headings: *decentralized and unorganized, private transactions, limited supply, lack of liquidity,* and *high transaction costs.* The applicability of these generalizations regarding real estate markets, as well as those relating to the physical and legal attributes of real estate, will depend partly upon the particular type of property involved. The principal property types were cataloged in this chapter, as were the major participants in the real estate industry.

2

The Nature of
Real Estate
Investing

There are a great variety of ways in which an investor can be said to be investing in real estate. Real estate investing has become so flexible that on very large projects a wide assortment of investment interests is often created, with each interest tailored to the needs of a certain investor or group of investors.[1] The basic investment interests, however, are three: mortgage, leasehold, and equity interests. While we are focusing our attention in this book principally on equity investments, we shall briefly review the mortgage and leasehold investment interests because the real estate equity investor usually initiates these other interests as part of his financing arrangements. Also, in practice, an active real estate investor often finds himself holding more than one major type of investment interest, or changing from one type of interest to another.

MORTGAGE INVESTMENTS

The position of the mortgage interest holder (the mortgagee) is that of a secured creditor. The mortgage itself pledges the real

[1] An informative review of large-project financing is contained in William Zeckendorf's autobiography, *Zeckendorf* (New York: Holt, Rinehart and Winston, 1970).

14

TABLE 2–1. Mortgage Debt Outstanding, by Type of Property

	Dec. 31, 1963	Dec. 31, 1973
	(billions of dollars)	
1- to 4-family houses	$182.2	$383.8
Multi-family residences	29.0	86.9
Commercial properties	46.2	123.6
Farm properties	16.8	39.4
Total	$274.3[a]	$633.7

[a]Items do not add to total because of rounding.
Source: *Economic Report of the President* (Washington, D. C.: Government Printing Office, 1974). 1973 figures are preliminary.

property as security for a loan that is evidenced by a note signed by the borrower (the *mortgagor*). In some cases the mortgage it-self and the note are combined in one instrument. While there exists a wide array of different kinds of mortgages; for example, first and second mortgages, and wrap-around mortgages, as de-scribed in Chapter 9, the mortgage holder's interest generally has the usual characteristics of any passive, fixed-income investment.

The mortgage holder's interest is usually a lower-risk, lower-return position than that of the equity interest in the same prop-erty, and the investment goal of the mortgage investor is generally that of maximizing periodic or recurring income. A national market exists to a greater extent for mortgages (especially for government-backed FHA and VA mortgages) than exists for real estate equity interests. While mortgage investment has tradition-ally involved a fixed-interest rate of return, there has been grow-ing pressure for so-called variable mortgages, or *floating-rate mortgages,* whereby the interest rate is subject to change as some other specified variable changes, such as the commercial bank prime lending rate.

The total volume of mortgage debt outstanding at the end of 1973 amounted to almost $634 billion. Table 2–1 indicates the relative importance of the various types of properties in terms of

TABLE 2–2. Mortgage Debt Outstanding, by Type of Lender

Lenders	Dec. 31, 1963	Dec. 31, 1973
	(billions of dollars)	
Savings and loan associations	$ 90.9	$232.6
Commercial banks	39.4	118.1
Life insurance companies	50.5	80.6
Mutual savings banks	36.2	73.2
U.S. agencies	11.2	55.3
Individuals and others	45.9	73.9
Total	$274.3[a]	$633.7

[a]Items do not add to total because of rounding.
Source: Same as for Table 2–1. 1973 figures are preliminary.

mortgage debt outstanding. The first two categories of residential properties combined represented 74 per cent of the total mortgage debt at the end of 1973.

The most important mortgage investors are the private financial institutions, including insurance companies; and over 20,000 financial institutions are active mortgage investors. Table 2–2 identifies the principal kinds of financial institutions investing in mortgages, and the other major categories of mortgage investors.

The value of mortgages held by the first four categories of financial institutions shown in Table 2–2 represents 80 per cent of total outstanding mortgages at the end of 1973. The institutions have been attracted to mortgage investments because of their traditionally, though inconsistently, higher returns than government and corporate securities of similar maturities. It should be noted that in very recent years some traditional suppliers of fixed-return mortgage money such as life insurance companies have been insisting upon some form of equity participation in addition to their creditor interests.

The U.S. agencies category in Table 2–2 includes government agencies such as the Federal Housing Administration and the Veterans Administration; and the government-sponsored agencies such as Fannie Mae and the Federal Land Banks. Individual mortgage investors often invest in second mortgages that they either purchase in the market or acquire upon the sale of their property. The latter situation is a common means by which equity investors become converted to mortgage investors. Some of the other mortgage investors would include mortgage companies, trust funds, and pension funds.

LEASEHOLD INVESTMENTS

The lease contract between the *lessor* and the *lessee* creates a *leasehold interest* for the lessee. The holder of the leasehold often has the option of using the property himself; subleasing it to others; or selling his interest. Hence, the leasehold investor has opportunities for periodic income and even for capital gains through the sale of his interest. The equity investor becomes converted to a leasehold investor when he sells property and leases it back; the so-called *sale–leaseback* arrangement.

REAL ESTATE EQUITY INVESTMENTS

The real estate equity investor has legal ownership of the property. He controls the use and disposition of the property within the governmental restrictions previously discussed, and within any restrictions imposed by private contracts relating to the property. The real property title holder has a *direct* equity interest in real estate, as contrasted to the *indirect* interest of the holder of shares of an organization that, in turn, invests directly in real estate, such as real estate corporations and real estate investment trusts. The expressions *owner* and *equity investor* will be used in this book to refer to the holder of a direct ownership interest, whether the holder be an individual or an organization.

The economic returns to the equity investor are residual in nature; that is, he receives any returns, or profits, only after all expenses including the interest claims of creditors have been covered. The residual nature of equity investment returns can result in opportunities for very large returns and losses; and hence the equity investment would generally be considered to have a greater risk and greater return potential than would the mortgage investment. The extent of risk and return is determined in part not only by the type of property involved, but also by the extent of leverage, that is, the amount of debt financing used for the project. Other generalizations can be made about the nature of the equity investment interest, such as the lack of maturity or due date, and the versatility of operations associated with real estate equity investments. Some other generalizations that can be made deal with liquidity, planning, and control.

Real estate equity investment liquidity. While the degree of liquidity will vary among different kinds of properties and vary with changing market conditions, the real estate equity investment is ordinarily less liquid than actively traded securities or commodities. While the holder of treasury bills or actively traded stocks can sell on short notice, the real estate investor often must be prepared to wait for an appreciative buyer. Sustained, successful real estate investing, therefore, is often attended by patience and careful cash planning.

Planning and control. By way of generalization it can be said that real estate equity investment is an *active form of investment,* rather than passive as mortgage and securities investments tend to be. Real estate equity investments often require extensive prior planning; often with thorough market, financial, and engineering analyses. When the investor develops and holds property, then construction management and general property management tasks are called for. The nature of the investor's operations and the extent of delegation of management duties will, of course, influence the extent of the investor's own activity in relation to the property. *Planning* in real estate investing is generally of a long-term nature, with five- to twenty-year or longer projections often called for. Consequently, real estate investment analysis tends to be more akin to corporate capital budgeting analysis than to security analysis.

With the planning and management activities that often accompany real estate ownership, however, goes *control.* The fact that the investor can control many aspects of the investment is often cited as a major benefit of real estate investing—as contrasted to some other ownership forms, such as the small common stock position in a large corporation, which does not give any day-to-day control over the organization's activities. Such day-to-day control is usually present for the real estate equity investor even where the equity position represents only a small portion of total project capitalization, as when liberal debt financing is employed.

Real Estate Equity Investors

It is more difficult to gather meaningful data on the ownership of real estate equity interests than it is to find data on mortgage ownership. To measure the value of equity interests in the country would require periodic reappraisals of all properties, which is not now undertaken. Some of the general trends in the ownership of real estate equity interests can be reviewed, however. For this discussion, investors will be categorized as being either institutional investors or non-institutional; with institutional investors being the very large financial, industrial, and other organizations having substantial assets.

Non-institutional investors. In numbers of investors, home-owners represent the largest single category of real estate equity investors in this country. According to the 1970 Census, there were 63.4 million year-round occupied housing units in the U.S., of which 62.9 per cent were occupied by *owners.* The extent to which homeowners view themselves as investors seems to vary over time. In the 1920's, a period of expanding property values, there reportedly was a widespread investment attitude, with many individuals acquiring urban plots of land and small multi-family rental properties.[2]

During the 1960's, the average value of owner-occupied homes rose by almost 43 per cent; from $11,900 to $17,000. The increase in property values and the general inflation psychology prevalent in recent years have no doubt helped to bring an increase in the number of people viewing their home as an investment, and an increase in the number of individuals acquiring other real estate properties as investments. Additionally, the impact of federal income taxes on homeowners has probably brought an increased awareness of the investment features of real property ownership.

[2] Louis Winnick, "Long-Run Changes in the Valuation of Real Estate by Gross Rents," *The Appraisal Journal,* October, 1952, p. 494.

Internal Revenue Service figures indicate that 28 per cent of the total itemized income tax deductions for individuals in 1968 were directly related to home ownership; with property-tax deductions amounting to $9.4 billion, and home mortgage interest deductions totalling $9.8 billion. During the 1960's and 70's there has also been an increase in the mobility of individuals, and large numbers of individuals acquiring lots and second homes in recreation areas.

In addition to the large group of relatively small investors in real estate equities, there is a much smaller group of relatively large investors in real estate who invest alone or in small groups. These are individuals, of course, with relatively large amounts of surplus funds. They are often highly paid professional people, industrialists, and merchants who on a part-time basis invest surplus funds in apartments, motels, shopping centers, and the whole range of properties. Other equity investors would include those spending full time on some phase of the real estate business, such as property developers, promoters, and real estate brokers engaging in the formation of, and participating in investment syndicates.

Institutional investors. While historically the non-institutional investors have been the principal source of venture capital and the principal initiators of real estate investment projects, there has been a rapidly growing participation in recent years by the very large institutions. One important group of institutions is composed of the financial institutions, including the life insurance companies, that have taken equity positions in real estate projects either directly or through real estate subsidiaries. Other major institutional investors include the real estate investment trusts (REIT's) that were established as tax-sheltered investment organizations in 1961.

Another important group of institutional investors is composed of the large, well-known industrial corporations, such as Reynolds Metal, ALCOA, Chrysler Corporation, International Paper Company, Gulf Oil, and many others. Some of these corporations were drawn into large-scale real estate investing because some of the properties that had been acquired for corporate purposes had become extremely valuable for other uses, for example, the paper companies' properties in recreation areas. Some other corporations established subsidiaries to engage in large-scale residential development projects, either alone or in joint ventures with independent real estate developers.

The impact of the large institutional investors on real estate markets has been growing in importance, just as it has been in the securities markets. The large institutional real estate investors, of course, have the advantage of being in a position to marshal very large financial and human resources. This means that they can carry a large project through its early years, when cash flow demands are often very high; and it means that they can diversify their holdings and thereby better absorb occasional losses. The largest institutions also have the capacity to acquire a relatively large area for a particular development project, which allows them to take advantage of the growth in peripheral land values often attending real estate developments. At times, the large investor is in a position to change whole neighborhoods, and thereby achieve a form of *synergistic gains*.

The advantages of the very large institutional investors have led some to question whether smaller investors and developers can be expected to compete successfully in the future. However, real estate markets are still essentially local in nature; and this gives an advantage to the investor, large or small, who knows his local area intimately. Also, the smaller investor–entrepreneur has the advantage of flexibility of operation that is often a key to successful real estate investing, and is often lacking in large corporations.

In sum, it would appear that in the future there will continue to be a great variety of individuals, groups, and institutions participating in real estate equity investing. The various investment goals held by different kinds of real estate investors are described and categorized in a subsequent section of this chapter; however, in a very general way, it can be said that the basic appeal of real estate as an investment must be attractive returns.

Real Estate Equity Returns

It is common knowledge that many fortunes have been made in real estate; stories abound of speculative profits arising from dramatic increases in property values. Such stories often involve acreage that is transformed in a few years from pasture or wood-lands into premium-priced residential or commercial property. Aside from these dramatic speculative gains, what returns do investors generally expect from real estate investments? How do such returns compare, say, with common stock investments?

As will be discussed in the next Part of this book, there are various ways to compute rates of return; and the rate-of-return picture for real estate, as with common stocks, will change quite sharply when the time periods that are analyzed are altered. Another problem in making rate-of-return statements about real estate is that returns will vary with different types of properties. One final problem is the relative lack of available data for analyzing real estate returns as real estate equity investors hesitate to publicize their returns. Because of these various problems, one can only generalize about real estate equity returns. For example, one authority stated in 1968: "Generally, the after-tax return on equity investment for real estate companies ranges from 15 to 35 per cent. . . ." [3]

A 1965 study of returns during the period 1952–1962 for twenty FHA-financed apartments in San Francisco, as opposed to 76 randomly selected industrial common stocks, found the average annual after-tax cash returns on real estate equity investments to be 10.9 per cent, as compared with a 5.7 per cent average return on the stocks.[4] Of course, the assumptions used in the rate-of-return calculations; the particular time period chosen; and the particular properties covered, all influenced the results. Perhaps the following statement by Beaton best describes the general return patterns for real estate investments in recent years: "Prime real estate will yield a before-tax return on total investment, including equity and debt, of from 8 to 15 percent. Speculative real estate will show yields of up to 25 per cent or more." [5] With the favorable use of leverage, the returns on equity would, of course, be higher.

[3] Samuel Hayes III, quoted in Eleanore Carruth, "Look Who's Rushing into Real Estate," *Fortune,* October, 1968, p. 173.
[4] Paul F. Wendt and Sui N. Wong, "Investment Performance: Common Stocks versus Apartment Houses," *The Journal of Finance,* December, 1965, pp. 633–46.
[5] William R. Beaton, *Real Estate Investment* (Englewood Cliffs, N.J.: Prentice-Hall, Inc., 1971), p. 15.

INVESTMENT GOALS

The real estate investment process begins with the investor defining his investment objectives or goals. This, in turn, requires a review or inventory of the investor's resources, preferences, skills, and other factors, as discussed below.

Some investors seem to enjoy a sense of accomplishment, well-being, or perhaps prestige in being able to point as owner to an apartment house or other investment property. Others gain satisfaction in helping an area or community become more attractive. Another non-economic goal would be the enjoyment of personally using real estate properties which at the same time represent investment properties. The specific *economic goals* of the real property investor will depend upon many variables; such as the investor's tax situation, his willingness to take risks, his other holdings, his retirement plans, the amount of time he can devote to investing activities, and if the investor is a financial institution, the applicable legal constraints on real estate investment. The list could, of course, be extended greatly.

The ultimate economic goal of most real estate as well as of most other investments could probably be considered to be the maximization of after-tax returns; however, it is useful in developing a general framework for real estate investment analysis to focus on four subsumed investment goals or objectives that are commonly found among real estate investors; (1) *periodic income or cash flow,* (2) *tax shelter,* (3) *price appreciation,* and (4) *entrepreneurial profit.* Because common stock investors seek periodic income (dividends) and price gains, it is the tax shelter and entrepreneurial profit goals that distinguish real-estate-equity investing from common-stock investing.

The nature of the federal income tax provisions combined with the particular attributes of real estate operations result in substantial tax-shelter benefits, that is, tax savings, for many real estate projects. The goal of the real estate developer is often what can be called business or entrepreneurial profit, the fourth goal listed above. The nature of the development process is similar in many ways to other entrepreneurial undertakings, as it involves the gathering and coordination of various resources, in addition to money resources, in accordance with detailed plans and studies. This process, of course, differs markedly from more passive investments in income-producing or capital-gains-producing investments in real estate or other investment commodities. The third goal listed above, that of price appreciation, would perhaps suggest the concept of *speculation,* as opposed to *investment;* however, that distinction will not be observed in this book because, drawing the line between the two concepts requires highly subjective judgments.

The particular goals that an individual investor entertains would be a function of the various investor attributes and preferences as discussed previously. For example, a wealthy doctor's high tax bracket may well lead him to seek a tax-sheltered investment, while the retired school teacher may well wish to maximize periodic income.

PLAN OF THE BOOK

Having defined his investment goals, the real estate investor is then faced with the task of developing and applying standards and techniques for measuring the goal-achievement potential of particular investment proposals. A basic analytical framework for this purpose—a set of so-called *decision models*—is presented in Part II of this book. The general nature of the input data required for analyzing the profit potential of real estate projects is discussed in the next chapter of this introductory Part I.

After having defined his goals and having acquired the basic tools and standards for measuring the goal-achievement potential of particular investments, the maximization of goal satisfaction requires (1) an awareness of some basic alternative strategies regarding the organizational form, financing, and timing of investments, and regarding the disposition of properties; and (2) the selection of an appropriate type of property upon which to focus the investment analysis. Some basic investment strategies are discussed in Part III, and the investment attributes of land and some individual types of developed properties are analyzed in Part IV. In the final Part V the real estate development process is discussed, which as noted previously, is related to the entrepreneurial profit goal.

Quantitative vs. Qualitative Analysis

There exists a school of thought that successful real estate investing is based upon successful subjective, or intuitive judgments; and some would add the element of good luck. There are also occasions when quick decisions are called for that preclude a thorough quantitative analysis, as there are in other areas of business and investment decision making. It is also probably true that an overreliance on extensive quantitative analysis can lead to the overlooking of some key economic factors underlying a project.

Notwithstanding the important role of good judgment and other factors in successful investing, many real estate projects do lend themselves to financial analysis by techniques that have been developed historically in the real estate industry, and by the techniques developed more recently by securities analysts and by those concerned with corporate capital budgeting decisions. In fact, many of the mathematical models developed in recent years for use in capital budgeting analysis are ideally suited for some real estate investment analyses, because of the relative certainty of cash flow projections for certain real estate projects, such as purchase–leaseback investments. Also, the computer makes practical the application of extensive analysis, including the preparation of various schedules, which are invaluable for analyzing, planning, and controlling very large projects.

Actually, some quantitative techniques have long been used by professional appraisers and by others in the real estate industry, including the discounting or capitalizing of future benefits, which is a central part of many of the modern techniques used in corporate capital budgeting and in securities analysis. The attempt in this book will be to present *practical* real estate investment analyses and strategies, with recognition given to the rough but useful rule-of-thumb guides, as well as the more sophisticated analytical techniques that are practical for analyzing certain types of investment proposals.

SUMMARY

While there exists a wide range of real estate investment interests, the three basic forms are: the *mortgage,* the *leasehold,* and the *equity* interests. The mortgage investor generally holds a fixed-return, passive, relatively low-risk/return type of investment interest. The equity investor, on the other hand, holds a residual, non-fixed–return investment interest that is generally of a higher risk/return nature than the mortgage interest. The equity investment often involves long-term planning and active control, and the equity interest is generally less liquid than other real estate investment interests.

While individuals and small groups of individuals have traditionally been the primary suppliers of venture equity capital for real estate investments, many large financial and industrial corporations have recently become important real estate equity investors, as have the real estate investment trusts. The data are not plentiful on the economic returns received by real estate equity investors; however, observers have reported very attractive rates of return as compared with those of other popular types of investments. The existence of attractive returns on realty is also evidenced by the growing investment participation of large institutional investors.

Investment goals. While the maximization of after-tax economic returns could be considered to be the ultimate investment goal, it is convenient to focus on four subsumed investment goals or objectives: (1) *periodic income or cash flow,* (2) *tax shelter,* (3) *price appreciation,* and (4) *entrepreneurial profit.* Parts II–IV of this book are concerned with the development and application of analytical techniques and strategies for use in making investment decisions aimed at the maximization of the achievement of the first three of the listed goals. The fourth goal of entrepreneurial profit is discussed in Part V, Real Estate Development.

3

Basic Investment
Data

Before undertaking a quantitative analysis of the profit-making potential of a particular real estate investment proposal, a gathering of data relevant to the analysis is required. In the present chapter we consider the *nature* of such basic data, and an approach for gathering and organizing the data. The discussion here is limited to the situation where raw land or fully developed property is being considered for purchase at a given asking price, rather than the property-development investment for entrepreneurial profit, the discussion of which is reserved for the last part of the book.

The analysis of proposed real estate investments requires data relating to the future, and therefore the basic data to be generated will be in the form of forecasts or estimates. In some cases the future economic inflows and outflows can be predicted with some degree of certainty, such as where a long-term net lease is involved. In most cases where the major inflows and outflows are not preset by contract, however, there is bound to be forecasting uncertainty, which will increase as one predicts farther into the future. Nonetheless, the analyst must do his best to estimate future performance, as with investments made in securities and other commodities.

The forecasted future economic inflows and outflows can be considered to fall into three general categories: (1) future rental income, (2) future operating expenses, and (3) future selling price. These three categories of data requirements will be discussed in the following sections. While not included in our present discussion of basic economic data, information on the non-operating expense features of a proposed investment, including depreciation, financing, and tax features, is of course an important part of a complete financial analysis and will be considered later.

FUTURE RENTAL INCOME

Just as an estimation of sales revenue is the starting point and cornerstone of financial planning for commercial and industrial companies, an estimation of future rental income is the starting point and cornerstone of real estate investment analysis. Periodic rental income will not only be the source of funds for covering periodic expenditures and profits, but future income levels will directly influence the future selling price of the property.

The first step in the data-collection process is therefore the forecasting of future periodic, usually annual, rental income; or more precisely: gross rental income at full occupancy, less an allowance for rentals lost because of vacancies, plus any other significant non-rental income expected to be produced by the property. In the case of raw land acquired for development, a task prior to estimating annual rentals is to determine, through a *highest and best use study,* the particular use of the property that will maximize return on investment.

The usual starting point in forecasting future economic data is to study relevant past and present data and to extend observable trends into the future, with adjustments then made for any predicted future circumstances that would change the previous patterns. When a rental property with some years of operating experience is acquired, the data collection process would include a study of the historical rental performance of the property combined with an analysis of probable future conditions in the market for that type of rental space. This latter activity is generally referred to as the market study.

The Market Study

The market study for a rental property involves an analysis of expected future conditions that will influence the demand and supply for the type of rental space provided by the property in question. The factors emphasized in the study will vary with the type of property. For example, a shopping center study will emphasize information relating to the probable future number of shoppers and their buying habits and buying power. A motel market study, on the other hand, will stress factors that will influence the number of travelers arriving in the area of the motel. Additional discussion of the unique investment factors relating to individual property types is contained in Part IV.

Notwithstanding the particular type of property involved, however, there is a general market study outline that can be employed for most types of real estate properties, such as the one shown in Table 3–1.

The preparation of a market study within the general format shown in Table 3–1 will be considered further in the following sections. Where necessary for illustrative detail, the factors discussed below will be related to the market for an apartment project.

National economic conditions. As noted in Chapter .1, the market for a particular piece of property tends to be a localized market; hence, a study of demand and supply in the local area served by the property is at the heart of the market study; however, it would be hard to find a community completely insulated from the impacts of market conditions in the state and in the nation as a whole. When the national economy is in a recession or in a boom period, or when interest rates are at high levels nationally, for example, the impacts are felt in most parts of the country.

Despite the application of the federal government's fiscal and monetary policies to attempt to accomplish the declared national policy since the 1946 Employment Act of achieving consistently high employment and low rates of inflation, business cycles with alternating periods of recession and prosperity continue to persist. Cycles persist today also in the real estate markets, involving alternating periods of short-supply and over-

---

TABLE 3-1.   General Format of a Typical Real Estate Market Study

---

Demand Analysis

A. Analysis of national economic conditions.
B. Definition of the trade area.
C. Analysis of potential demand in the trade area.

Supply Analysis

A. Inventory of existing competition.
B. Analysis of potential competition.

Conclusions

---

supply of various types of real estate properties; most notably, office buildings.

There are generally more up-to-date data available regarding national economic conditions than there are for state and local economies. Monthly figures are published by the federal government with a time lag of only a few months on such general economic indicators as *gross national product, disposable personal income,* that is, after-tax spendable income, various *employment* measures, and *interest rates.* With the use of these indicators and others, an attempt can be made to forecast at least relatively short-run national economic conditions and related real estate market conditions. In addition to an analysis of economic indicator data, the market study would include a review of any other relevant and significant factors on the national level, including such things as anticipated tax-law changes, fuel-supply conditions, government interventions in the mortgage and housing markets, and the changing trends in individuals' life styles.

U.S. Census data.   The analyst should review the U.S. Census data for *population* and *housing* patterns. Population data is of prime importance in analyzing the demand for most rental property. Not only total population growth figures for the nation as a whole and for parts of the country, but also figures on the age and income distribution in the overall population, and average household size are important. For example, the younger and older age brackets have traditionally represented the major apartment population rather than those in the middle age groups. By reviewing past data and extrapolating the discernible population trends, one can help focus on national demand patterns for rental units.

For market studies related to residential properties, the U.S. Census data grouped under the heading General Housing Characteristics can be of value. These data, that are available not only for the nation as a whole but also for states and for major urban centers, cover such things as the number of people owning and renting housing units, the average value of owner-occupied homes, the average level of rental payments, and data on vacancy rates. The problem with census data is that they are up-dated every ten years rather than every month, but these data can be useful for a long-term trend analysis and they can also be used in conjunction with other, more current, information from sundry sources such as state and local housing studies.

Trade area demand analysis. The study of "local" supply and demand factors commences with the delineation of the *trade area,* that is, the geographical market area directly served by the subject property. There are no definitive criteria for defining the boundaries of the trade area; however, some possible criteria for an aparement project might include the following, listed by Anthony Downs:[1]

1. Accessibility along the same arterial roads.
2. Orientation toward the same commercial centers.
3. Orientation toward the same major employment sources.
4. Similar income and housing characteristics.
5. Coincidence with political or census boundaries where applicable.

[1] Anthony Downs, Chapter 1, *The Dynamics of Real Estate Investment* (Los Angeles: California Real Estate Association, 1966), p. 6.

Once the investor has made a judgment as to the geographical boundaries of the trade area for the project, he can proceed to collect data on that area. Information relevant to the potential demand for an apartment project would focus on expected population growth and on expected age and income-level distribution of that population. Information would also be sought on estimated employment growth in the area. Other background information would be gathered on the trade area, touching on such matters as public utilities, local tax rates, school systems, governance systems, fire and police forces, employment sources, and local transportation and recreational facilities.

The sources for local data would include, among others, census data (if the area studied conforms to census boundaries), an analysis of building permits, studies by local planning commissions, local Chamber of Commerce reports, and by personal interviews and surveys in the area.[2] A comparative analysis of the subject trade area with other nearby areas is usually appropriate in this section of the market study.

Trade area supply analysis. The market study for a particular apartment project being considerel for acquisition should include an inventory of existing apartments serving the same trade area. For each of the competing apartment projects, data should be gathered as to age, accommodations, the number of one-, two-, and three-bedroom units in the project, and the size (in square feet) and present rental rates for these three size categories in each project. Of course, information on present and past vacancies and waiting lists, if any, would also be included for each competing project.

The review of existing competitive projects will be followed up with an analysis of future competition from expected new or expanded apartment projects serving the same trade area. This analysis would be based upon such factors as the amount and cost of land available in the area for future apartments, data on recent building permits issued, any information that is available on plans for new apartment projects or expansions of present projects, the probable future availability of

[2] See Downs for an illustration of the use of building permit data in a 25-unit apartment project market study, _Ibid.,_ p. 8.

project financing, and the availability of public utilities for use by future multiple dwellings.

Market study conclusions. By analyzing the data gathered and organized in a format such as that just described, the analyst should be able to make estimates of the size of the future market for apartment units in the area, the *absorption rate,* and the number of future units available, the *supply rate.* Based thereon together with the information collected on the present and past performance of the apartment project being considered for purchase, an estimate can be made of the level of expected occupancy for each of the years during which the investor would plan to hold the property. The number of units that can be rented times the expected rent per unit will give the expected achievable rental levels. The schedule of annual rental income figures so developed will provide the starting point for the financial planning and analysis, as will be illustrated in the next chapter.

It is to be recognized, of course, that a preliminary study of the market for the space provided by the property being considered for acquisition will entail time and expense for the investor, and such costs must be considered in determining just how deep the study should go. It must be stressed, however, that this type of study is an important part of financial planning. The market study can, for example, be of help in guarding against the apparently not uncommon tendency for investors to project presently favorable demand levels indefinitely into the future without adequate consideration of possible future conditions that could reduce future rent levels.

FUTURE OPERATING EXPENSES

For our purposes we shall define *operating expenses* as being all expenses incurred to operate and maintain a real estate investment property, *except* depreciation expense, interest and other financing expenses, rent expense, and income taxes. While the exclusion of depreciation and rent expenses from the operating expense category is not generally practiced in business-enterprise accounting, the treatment of those expenses as non-operating expenses is a convenient as well as traditional practice in real estate investment analysis, as will be shown in the next chapter. Also excluded from the operating expense classification are, of course, cash outflows not treated as accounting expenses; the principal ones in real estate investment being mortgage debt amortization payments, or *principal payments,* and capital improvements made to the property.

Types of Operating Expenses

Listed below are some of the specific categories of operating expenses often associated with real estate rental properties. For undeveloped land held as an investment, the operating expense list would usually include only property taxes, liability insurance, and perhaps some minor maintenance expense.

1. *Basic Operating Expenses:*

   Real estate taxes   Administrative expenses
   Property insurance   Maintenance and repairs
   Utilities expenses

2. *Other Types of Operating Expenses:*

   Interior painting,   Pool service
      decorating, alterations   Garbage collection
   Janitorial and cleaning   Exterminator expenses
      expenses   Payroll expenses
   Advertising and   Agent's commissions
      promotion   Other operating expenses
   Supplies

The five expenses labeled as basic operating expenses in the above list were arbitrarily so categorized because they are usually associated with all types of developed properties. *Real estate taxes,* or *property taxes,* often represents the largest single operating expense item. The size of this expense will depend on the value and location of the property and, of course, the local tax rate. The tax rate, in turn, generally will be a function of the level of demand in the community for public services such as schools, roads, and utilities. In a fast-growing community, the tax rate usually is also fast growing.

Property insurance will ordinarily cover fire and casualty losses, and at times policies can be obtained to provide some special type of protection, such as flood insurance. Also liability insurance is usually obtained that provides protection against claims for damages suffered by individuals using the subject property. *Utilities expenses* including electricity, water, gas, and heating fuel, are another inevitable form of expense, but these are often at least in part the responsibility of the tenant. *Administrative expenses* will include outlays for general management expenses and for accounting and legal services unless the latter are broken out as separate expense items.

Maintenance and repairs, the last of the listed basic operating expenses, is one of the major expense items for most real estate properties. In this category are included interior and exterior repairs of various kinds, such as are often required for plumbing, wiring, and heating systems, and repairs to appliances, and roofs. Also included are exterior painting and other upkeep requirements. The important distinction between *repairs* and *improvements* is not always clear cut, as is discussed in Chapter 6. The Other Types of Operating Expenses section of the above list is suggestive of the wide range of possible property expenses.

Forecasting Future Operating Expenses

The nature and level of the operating expenses that can be expected to be incurred for a particular real estate investment will depend partly upon the general type of property that is involved, and upon the nature of the services provided by the owner–investor. Office building leases, for example, often call for the owner to provide janitorial and cleaning services, and often the office building owner is called upon to make alterations in interior layouts to fit the needs of prospective tenants. Apartment owners are usually faced with recurring interior painting and decorating expenses. Motel owners generally incur significant expenses for maid services, and for a wide range of other services.

In addition to the type of property involved, many other factors will influence the nature and level of operating expenses, such as the *age and design features of the structure,* the *location of the property,* and the *nature and efficiency of the maintenance and operating practices.* The portion of the total future operating expenses that will have to be borne by the owner–investor of an investment property will depend upon the lease contract terms. In the case of a *net lease* arrangement, the lessee is responsible for all operating expenses, as we have defined them above. In other cases, the lessor will have to bear at least some of the operating expenses.

The starting point for estimating future operating expenses is to review past and present expense figures in as much detail as is available for the subject property. The next step is to estimate future changes; some expenses may be expected to go higher because of inflation or for other reasons, and some may be reducible by more efficient operation. The analysis of expense levels will be aided by comparing the present expense patterns for the property being analyzed with the average figures for other similar properties. One widely used comparative expense measure is the percentage that *Total operating expenses* represents of *Gross possible income,* (that is, gross income at full occupancy); the measure is referred to as the *Expense ratio,* and may be computed with the use of Equation 3–1.

$$\textit{Expense ratio} = \frac{\textit{Total operating expenses}}{\textit{Gross possible income}} \times 100 \qquad [3\text{–}1]$$

The expense ratio will tend to vary with the basic type of property involved; for example, shopping centers typically have lower ratios than do apartments. The expense ratio also tends to vary with the age of the property, as will be discussed in more detail below.

The various individual operating expense items, such as, say, real estate taxes, should also be measured as a percentage of gross possible income in making a comparative analysis, to determine if any individual operating expense is out of line with the average for similar properties. Data on average expense percentages for most properties of a given type, age, and geographical location are available from various real estate trade sources. As an example, data analyzed by age group are presented in Table 3–2 for some 433 unfurnished elevator apartment buildings surveyed in 1974 by the Institute of Real Estate Management. The dates at the head of the columns in the table refer to the dates that the apartment buildings were constructed. Additional examples of industry data are presented in Part IV.

As indicated in Table 3–2, the average expense ratio for the sample apartment buildings increased steadily with the rise in the age of the building, from 48.5 to 61.0 per cent. While the exact pattern will naturally vary with the particular samples chosen for study, the general pattern usually observed is that the older the building, the higher the percentage of income that will be claimed by operating expenses. It appears that new buildings tend to have a honeymoon period in terms of operating expenses, which is followed by rising expense levels.[3]

The sample data in Table 3–2 also point to some specific types of operating expenses that appear to be a function of the age of the apartment building. The first item to be noted is *maintenance and repairs,* which clearly would be expected to increase as buildings become older. Other individual increasing expense items indicated for the sample are *heating fuel, total payroll expenses, interior painting and decorating, insurance,* and *real estate taxes.*

There are many other factors to consider in projecting operating expenses for a particular property in addition to the general type and age factors. Also to be considered, for example, would be the geographical location, in terms of the availability and cost of goods and services; the outlook for future local property tax levels; the construction quality, design features, and quality of appliances in the apartment building for which the estimates are being undertaken. Among other factors to be considered in the estimating process would be expected general economic conditions in the country and in the local trade area—including the outlook for the general rate of inflation and expected price rises for certain individual expense items such as heating fuel. An analysis of the many factors described above and perhaps others, together with a review of past operating performance records, and a comparative analysis of the property with other similar properties, should put the analyst in a position

[3] *Case Studies in Apartment House Valuation* (2nd ed.; Chicago: American Institute of Real Estate Appraisers, 1969), p. 32.

TABLE 3-2. Average Income and Operating Costs for Unfurnished Elevator Buildings, by Age Group

(a) $/room/annum (b) %-of-gross-possible-total-income/room/annum (c) $/sq.-ft-gross/annum
(d) $/sq.-ft.-rentable (figures in parenthesis = total No. buildings reporting)

	1920 & Prior	1921 to 1930	1931 to 1945
NUMBER OF BUILDINGS	27	76	28
NUMBER OF APARTMENTS	2,485	5,151	2,709
NUMBER OF RENTABLE ROOMS	7,795	16,699	7,116
NUMBER OF BUILDINGS	22	39	16
NUMBER OF APARTMENTS	2,063	2,439	1,611
NUMBER OF RENTABLE ROOMS	6,531	7,618	4,284
GROSS SQUARE FEET	2,084,490	2,741,288	1,527,865
RENTABLE SQUARE FEET	1,696,763	1,551,555	1,097,951

	1920 & Prior	(A)	(B)	(C)	(D)	1921 to 1930	(A)	(B)	(C)	(D)	1931 to 1945	(A)	(B)	(C)	(D)
INCOME															
RENTS-APARTMENTS	(27)	729.57	96.3%	2.29	2.84	(76)	687.66	96.6%	1.83	2.29	(28)	758.07	96.0%	2.09	2.91
RENTS-GARAGES-PARKING	(8)	----	2.6	.05	.07	(20)	----	2.5	.07	.10	(12)	----	2.1	.05	.06
RENTS-STORES	(7)	----	4.2	.09	.12	(8)	----	9.8	.13	.15	(2)	----	1.3	.03	.04
RENTS-OFFICES	(1)	----	2.0	.05	.07	(4)	----	2.9	.02	.02	(2)	----	5.2	.13	.18
GROSS POSSIBLE RENTAL INCOME	(27)	746.97	98.8%	2.35	2.93	(76)	703.46	98.8%	1.87	2.65	(28)	776.22	98.3%	2.17	3.02
MISCELLANEOUS OTHER INCOME	(19)	10.46	1.4	.02	.03	(53)	11.93	1.6	.03	.04	(26)	14.55	1.8	.05	.06
GROSS POSSIBLE TOTAL INCOME	(27)	757.85	100.0%	2.37	2.96	(76)	711.97	100.0%	1.89	2.67	(28)	790.08	100.0%	2.21	3.08
LESS: VACANCIES-DEL RENTS	(27)	24.08	3.2	.08	.10	(76)	12.23	1.7	.04	.06	(28)	16.90	2.1	.06	.08
TOTAL ACTUAL COLLECTIONS	(27)	733.77	96.8%	2.31	2.88	(76)	699.74	98.3%	1.85	2.62	(28)	773.18	97.9%	2.17	3.02
EXPENSES															
TOTAL PAYROLL EXPENSES	(27)	80.21	10.6	.27	.34	(76)	98.15	13.8	.26	.28	(27)	96.37	12.2	.27	.38
SUPPLIES	(26)	10.34	1.4	.04	.04	(75)	7.13	1.0	.02	.02	(28)	10.43	1.3	.03	.04
PAINTING-DECORATING (INT ONLY)	(25)	20.52	2.7	.06	.08	(75)	23.16	3.3	.07	.10	(28)	24.64	3.1	.06	.08
MAINTENANCE REPAIRS (INT & EXT)	(27)	47.11	6.2	.15	.19	(76)	43.37	6.1	.12	.18	(28)	52.51	6.7	.15	.21
SERVICES	(19)	9.42	1.2	.03	.03	(71)	11.84	1.7	.04	.04	(27)	12.45	1.6	.03	.04
MISCELLANEOUS OPERATING EXPENSE	(19)	5.12	.7	.02	.02	(33)	6.27	.9	.03	.04	(10)	2.97	.5	.01	.02
SUBTOTAL-MAINT AND OPERATING	(27)	172.72	22.8%	.57	.70	(76)	189.92	26.8%	.54	.66	(28)	199.37	25.4%	.55	.77
ELECTRICITY	(27)	38.72	5.1	.12	.15	(75)	25.75	3.6	.09	.10	(28)	53.82	6.8	.14	.20
WATER	(27)	10.95	1.5	.04	.04	(76)	10.19	1.4	.03	.04	(28)	18.32	2.3	.05	.07
GAS (EXCLUDING HEATING FUEL)	(18)	12.16	1.7	.04	.05	(59)	4.46	.7	.02	.03	(23)	5.76	.7	.02	.05
HEATING FUEL	(24)	46.74	5.7	.15	.18	(74)	52.55	7.3	.15	.20	(26)	57.88	7.3	.15	.21
SUBTOTAL-UTILITIES	(27)	108.57	14.0%	.34	.42	(76)	92.86	13.0%	.29	.37	(28)	135.78	17.1%	.36	.51
MANAGEMENT FEES	(26)	42.94	5.6	.12	.15	(73)	31.51	4.7	.10	.14	(26)	33.20	4.2	.10	.13
OTHER ADMINISTRATIVE EXPENSE	(23)	11.52	1.5	.04	.05	(67)	10.49	1.5	.04	.06	(19)	18.88	2.3	.07	.09
SUBTOTAL-ADMINISTRATIVE	(27)	54.46	7.1%	.16	.20	(76)	42.00	6.2%	.14	.20	(28)	52.08	6.5%	.17	.22
INSURANCE	(27)	14.33	1.9	.05	.06	(76)	11.56	1.6	.03	.05	(26)	8.97	1.1	.02	.03
REAL ESTATE TAXES	(27)	133.67	17.6	.43	.54	(76)	129.01	18.1	.31	.48	(28)	85.74	10.7	.24	.34
OTHER TAXES	(21)	3.22	.4	.01	.01	(55)	2.89	.4	.01	.02	(23)	6.47	.8	.02	.03
SUBTOTAL-TAXES AND INSURANCE	(27)	151.22	19.9%	.49	.61	(76)	143.46	20.1%	.35	.55	(28)	101.18	12.6%	.28	.40
TOTAL ALL EXPENSES	(27)	462.55	61.0%	1.48	1.84	(76)	458.09	64.3%	1.26	1.72	(28)	470.71	59.6%	1.31	1.82
NET OPERATING INCOME	(27)	262.45	34.6%	.80	1.01	(76)	241.47	33.9%	.59	.89	(28)	302.47	38.3%	.86	1.20

	1946 to 1960	1961 to 1967	1968 to Date
NUMBER OF BUILDINGS	63	148	91
NUMBER OF APARTMENTS	10,223	26,001	17,113
NUMBER OF RENTABLE ROOMS	35,839	100,469	66,830
GROSS SQUARE FEET	6,602,239	22,634,618	14,317,562
RENTABLE SQUARE FEET	5,000,318	20,345,322	12,991,482

	1946 to 1960 (A)	(B)	(C)	(D)	1961 to 1967 (A)	(B)	(C)	(D)	1968 to Date (A)	(B)	(C)	(D)
INCOME												
RENTS-APARTMENTS	(63) 778.38	94.9%	2.58	3.41	(148) 845.36	92.1%	2.66	3.38	(91) 804.72	93.5%	2.67	3.32
RENTS-GARAGES-PARKING	(41) -----	3.8	.10	.14	(101) -----	4.4	.14	.17	(67) -----	4.1	.16	.16
RENTS-STORES	(6) -----	1.1	.03	.04	(19) -----	2.9	.07	.10	(11) -----	5.4	.16	.20
RENTS-OFFICES	(3) -----	4.3	.16	.17	(18) -----	7.7	.25	.29	(11) -----	5.5	.14	.21
GROSS POSSIBLE RENTAL INCOME	(63) 805.71	98.2%	2.69	3.54	(148) 900.33	98.0%	2.65	3.63	(91) 846.58	98.0%	2.82	3.51
MISCELLANEOUS OTHER INCOME	(55) 15.93	2.0	.07	.09	(131) 19.17	2.1	.07	.09	(88) 12.36	1.5	.03	.05
GROSS POSSIBLE TOTAL INCOME	(63) 820.43	100.0%	2.76	3.63	(148) 918.36	100.0%	2.91	3.71	(91) 860.84	100.0%	2.85	3.56
LESS: VACANCIES-DEL RENTS	(63) 16.62	2.0	.06	.09	(148) 32.87	3.6	.11	.13	(91) 51.99	6.0	.16	.24
TOTAL ACTUAL COLLECTIONS	(63) 803.81	98.0%	2.70	3.55	(148) 885.49	96.4%	2.80	3.58	(91) 808.86	94.0%	2.69	3.32
EXPENSES												
TOTAL PAYROLL EXPENSES	(63) 98.40	12.0	.32	.42	(146) 83.05	9.0	.27	.34	(89) 62.64	7.3	.21	.27
SUPPLIES	(62) 7.95	1.0	.03	.03	(143) 8.11	.9	.03	.03	(89) 6.81	.8	.02	.03
PAINTING-DECORATING (INT ONLY)	(61) 20.22	2.5	.07	.09	(144) 19.42	2.1	.06	.08	(88) 16.31	1.9	.06	.07
MAINTENANCE REPAIRS (INT & EXT)	(63) 41.39	5.0	.13	.17	(148) 48.11	5.2	.15	.19	(91) 34.40	4.0	.12	.15
SERVICES	(62) 7.77	1.0	.02	.02	(144) 12.97	1.4	.04	.05	(87) 10.76	1.3	.04	.05
MISCELLANEOUS OPERATING EXPENSE	(40) 7.05	.9	.03	.04	(106) 14.34	1.6	.05	.06	(56) 8.80	1.0	.03	.04
SUBTOTAL-MAINT AND OPERATING	(63) 182.78	22.4%	.60	.77	(148) 186.00	20.2%	.60	.75	(91) 139.72	16.3%	.48	.61
ELECTRICITY	(63) 47.59	5.8	.14	.19	(146) 51.85	5.6	.16	.20	(89) 40.82	4.8	.14	.17
WATER	(62) 10.52	1.3	.03	.04	(147) 12.92	1.4	.04	.04	(89) 12.48	1.5	.04	.05
GAS (EXCLUDING HEATING FUEL)	(53) 3.99	.5	.01	.02	(90) 5.18	.6	.02	.02	(56) 7.67	.9	.02	.03
HEATING FUEL	(63) 37.10	4.5	.12	.16	(138) 40.47	4.4	.12	.17	(79) 39.34	4.6	.15	.18
SUBTOTAL-UTILITIES	(63) 99.20	12.1%	.30	.41	(148) 110.42	12.0%	.34	.44	(91) 100.31	11.8%	.35	.43
MANAGEMENT FEES	(61) 38.02	4.6	.13	.17	(146) 38.28	4.2	.12	.16	(90) 36.07	4.2	.12	.15
OTHER ADMINISTRATIVE EXPENSE	(52) 10.43	1.3	.03	.04	(135) 17.32	1.9	.05	.07	(86) 19.48	2.3	.06	.09
SUBTOTAL-ADMINISTRATIVE	(63) 48.45	5.9%	.16	.21	(148) 55.60	6.1%	.17	.23	(91) 55.55	6.5%	.18	.24
INSURANCE	(61) 8.46	1.0	.03	.04	(142) 9.37	1.0	.03	.04	(91) 8.49	1.0	.03	.03
REAL ESTATE TAXES	(63) 132.94	16.2	.45	.60	(147) 129.05	14.1	.42	.53	(90) 125.22	14.5	.41	.51
OTHER TAXES	(53) 3.75	.5	.01	.01	(106) 3.81	.4	.01	.02	(62) 2.44	.3	.01	.01
SUBTOTAL-TAXES AND INSURANCE	(63) 145.15	17.7%	.49	.65	(148) 142.23	15.5%	.46	.59	(91) 136.15	15.8%	.45	.55
TOTAL ALL EXPENSES	(63) 470.34	57.3%	1.54	2.03	(148) 484.52	52.8%	1.54	1.95	(91) 417.16	48.5%	1.41	1.74
NET OPERATING INCOME	(63) 333.47	40.7%	1.16	1.53	(148) 400.97	43.7%	1.26	1.63	(91) 391.26	45.5%	1.28	1.58

Footnote: Subtotals represent the sum of all figures within a given subtotal section. Therefore, a summation of all subtotals may not necessarily add up to the figure under Total All Expenses. The above calculations are based upon the number of rooms reporting the particular item. Averages and percents, therefore, may not total 100%. The right-hand column directly under each date heading, refers to the maximum sample size used for the data in columns (C) and (D).

Source: Income/Expense Analysis: Apartments, Condominiums, and Cooperatives (1975 ed.; Chicago: Institute of Real Estate Management, 1975), pp. 44-45. Used with permission.

to make a schedule of expected annual operating expenses for the planned holding period of the property.

FUTURE SELLING PRICE

Despite the difficulties involved in forecasting periodic future rental income and operating expense levels, the future selling price of the property being analyzed is generally the most difficult figure to estimate. The longer the planned holding period for the property, the more difficult the forecasting task. Of course, security analysts face a similar task when attempting to predict the future selling price of a stock as well as the company's future earnings and dividends. Notwithstanding the estimating problems, the future selling price of the property being considered for acquisition must be estimated as part of most real estate investment analyses. The particular attributes of the individual property, including its use potentials will usually play a key role in the forecast.

Prior to considering some specific forecasting techniques, it should be noted that in general it is land itself, more than buildings, that will be subject to major price changes over the years. Because of the limited-supply characteristic of land, that is, limited quantity available in a given area, the value of land is often subject to dramatic changes as demand for property in the particular area changes. One dramatic instance of this situation was in the area of the new Dallas–Fort Worth airport. A prime site there sold for some $5,000 an acre in 1969, and was appraised three years later at more than $50,000 an acre.[4] Because a building structure can be replaced unless the building has historic or other unique intrinsic value, its price appreciation potential is less than that for land. Even buildings, however, have at times (especially during periods of high inflation) experienced significant increases in dollar value, as costs increase for new, substitute construction.

In the following sections are presented two types of forecasting techniques that in the right circumstances can be helpful

---

[4] "The Land Boom at a Texas Airport," *Business Week,* March 11, 1972, p. 116.

in making estimates of future selling prices. The first technique involves the use of the *gross income multiplier,* and the second is the *annual-growth forecasting model.*

Gross Income Multiplier

The gross income multiplier (GIM) is a number, which when multiplied by the annual gross income of a particular piece of property, yields the value or price of that property. As described more fully in the following chapter, the GIM technique is used widely by appraisers as one way to find the present value of a piece of real estate. The GIM that is selected for application in a particular appraisal assignment would be based primarily upon a review of multipliers that are observed for recent sales of similar properties. To make an estimate of the future selling price of a property being considered for acquisition by this technique, one simply estimates the annual gross income in the year of anticipated sale and multiplies that figure by the GIM that is estimated will be applicable at that time. For example, if it is anticipated an apartment project will have gross income of $120,000 in the future year of sale, and a GIM of 6, the resulting estimated selling price would be $720,000.

While there is no doubt that there will be some relationship between the income-producing power of an asset and that asset's market value in the year of sale; and while this technique has the advantage of ease of application, it is also clear that a high level of subjective judgment is required in selecting the appropriate GIM figure to use, especially for a time well in the future.

Annual-Growth Forecasting Model

One approach that is sometimes appropriate for use in forecasting future selling price is to assume a certain uniform rate of annual growth in the value of the property.[5] The growth

---

[5] This general scheme of annual value appreciation or depreciation is incorporated in the Ellwood Tables that are discussed in Chapter 7. As students of finance will recognize, an annual growth rate assumption is incorporated in the common stock rate-of-return model, $k = D/P + g$.

rate that is used, which could be positive or negative, would be determined by considering such things as: (1) the recent growth rate in the value of like or similar properties in the same geographical area, (2) expected future inflation rates, and (3) the unique environmental and other factors that are expected to influence the future value of the individual property being analyzed.

The arithmetic for implementing this annual-growth forecasting model for the property in question involves finding the *compound future sum* of the amount of the original purchase value—as of the end of the planned holding period; as in Equation 3–2, where *cost* is the original purchase price, *g* is the

$$\textit{Estimated future selling price } = \textit{ Cost } (1 + g)^n \qquad [3\text{–}2]$$

expected annual growth rate, and *n* is the number of years in the planned holding period.

For an example, assume that a mobile-home park is available for purchase at a price of $100,000. Assume further that the investor considering purchase would plan to resell the park at the end of five years. If it is estimated that the market value of the park will grow at the uniform rate of 3 per cent a year during the 5-year holding period, then the estimated future selling price of $115,900 can be found with Equation 3–2 by solving for the value of $100,000 (1.03).[5] The same future value can be conveniently calculated with the use of a compound sum table; in the Appendix at the back of the book, in *Column 1,* headed *Amount of 1 at Compound Interest,* we determine that the appropriate *interest factor* for 5-years and 3 per cent is 1.159. This is the value of $1 only, so to find the future value of the mobile-home park we must multiply $100,000 by 1.159 to obtain the estimated selling price of $115,900. If the projected annual growth rate had been 5 per cent instead of 3 per cent, the estimated selling price would be $127,600, as the reader can verify with the help of the tables.

Super-growth-rate model.   One variation of the annual-growth forecasting model is the super-growth-rate model. At times this variation would be appropriate in real estate investment analysis; namely, when the property value is expected to experience a limited period of rapid, or *super* growth, followed by a slower or more normal growth period. The super-growth-rate model would take the mathematical form of Equation 3–3, where *Cost,* and n

$$\text{Estimated future selling price} = [\text{Cost} (1 + g_1)^m] (1 + g_2)^{n-m} \quad [3\text{--}3]$$

are as previously defined; and g_1 is the super-growth rate, g_2 is the normal-growth rate, and m is the number of years during which super growth is expected.

If, for example, the above-cited mobile-home park is expected to grow in value at 20 per cent a year for 2 years, and then to grow at only 3 per cent annually for the remaining 3 years of the holding period, the *Estimated future selling price* can be found by the use of Equation 3–3, formulated as follows:

$$\text{Estimated future selling price} = [\$100{,}000 (1.20)^2] (1.03)^{5-2}$$

Making use of the compound sum factors, we find that the estimated selling price of the property at the end of 2 years, the first part of the Equation 3–3, to be $\$100{,}000 (1.20)^2 = \$144{,}000$; and the estimated selling price at the end of 5 years to be $(\$144{,}000)$ $(1.03)^3$, or $\$157{,}392$. Figure 3–1 shows the pattern of estimated future selling prices over the five years of the holding period for the mobile-home park, under both the normal-, and the super-growth-rate assumptions discussed above.

Other growth-pattern assumptions could, of course, be accommodated with other specially designed equations. Where future price changes are not expected to follow at least approximately some regular pattern, then a different estimating approach is required. For some projects; especially those involving a short holding period, a detailed, year-by-year economic analysis may be called for. In cases where a relatively high degree of uncertainty exists, the analyst may wish to employ risk-adjustment techniques such as sensitivity analysis or probability theory as described in Chapter 7.

SUMMARY

The basic economic data required for real estate investment analysis includes data relating to future rental income, future oper-

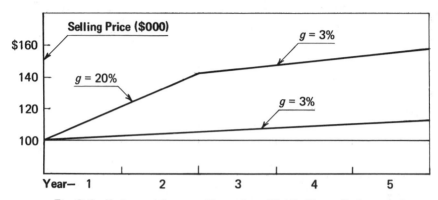

Fig. 3–1. Estimated future selling prices, Mobile Home Park example.

ating expenses, and future selling price. *Future rental income* estimates represent the cornerstone of the investment analysis. In addition to reviewing the past and present rental levels for the property being considered for purchase, a market study should be undertaken that will include an analysis of factors that can be expected to influence the supply and demand for the rental space provided by the property. National economic and financial factors should be considered as well as expected conditions in the *trade area* served by the subject property.

The nature and level of *future operating expenses* will have to be estimated as well as rental income for the years of the planned holding period for the property. The level of future operating expenses will be a function of many variables such as the type, age, design, and location of the property, and maintenance practices. The analysis of operating expenses will be strengthened by comparing the subject property's expense levels with average figures for similar properties. The *expense ratio* is useful for that purpose.

The *future selling price* is often extremely difficult to forecast. Because the future selling price for an income-producing property will be related to the income earning power of the property, one technique that can be used to forecast selling price is to multiply future expected gross income by an appropriate *gross income multiplier* (GIM). The annual-growth forecasting model (Equation 3–2) can be used as a selling price forecasting technique when the analyst expects the value of the property to increase (or decrease) at least approximately at a uniform rate. Where other regular patterns of value changes can be anticipated, other forecasting models can be applied, such as the super-growth-rate model described in the chapter (Equation 3–3).

II

Real Estate Investment Analysis

4

Real Estate
Investment
Income

Here in Part II the assumption is made that the data necessary for analyzing a proposed real estate investment are on hand. Ways of organizing and structuring the data are discussed, along with the federal income tax provisions related to real estate investment analysis. Techniques are also developed that can be used in measuring a project's prospective returns and risks, so that investment conclusions can be drawn in accordance with the goals of maximizing income or cash flow, tax-shelter benefits, and price appreciation.

In the present chapter we focus on measuring the *periodic income returns* of a proposed real estate investment project, both in absolute terms and in relative terms, that is, estimated periodic income in relation to the amount invested in the project. While the amount invested is usually defined as either total capital investment or as owners' investment, there are various alternative ways of defining periodic income, as will be discussed next.

LEVELS OF INCOME

The basic levels of income that can be used to measure periodic or recurring real estate investment returns, and their interrelationships, are shown in Table 4–1. Additional levels are used where required by the nature of a particular project. For example, if *other income* is a significant figure, then the gross possible income level can be subdivided into such categories as *gross possible rentals* and *other income*.

Gross Income

In Table 4–1 *gross possible income* refers to what the total revenue would be if the property were fully rented or occupied, and all rental payments collected in full. Expected losses of revenue because of vacancies and bad debts are deducted from the first income level to obtain actual or effective gross income. The nature and dimension of these losses, which are often calculated as some assumed percentage of full-occupancy rentals, are to some extent a function of the particular type of property involved. Henceforth the expression *gross income* will be used to refer to actual gross income, unless otherwise indicated.

The principal source of periodic gross income or revenue for most real estate investment is, of course, rental payments received by the lessor in return for his providing space and facilities. *Other income* becomes a significant source of income when the investor provides such services as room cleaning, laundry, and food services; and other income is received from a variety of sources, such as from vending machines. The general flow of rental income is most often determined by the lease terms. Under a lease contract the lessor transfers the right to use the property to the lessee for a specified time period in return for specified periodic rental payments. Some of the more common and basic types of real estate leases in use today are now briefly described.

Gross lease. The lessor agrees to provide maintenance, and to assume the burden for other operating expenses.

Net lease. The lessee contracts to pay for all operating expenses including maintenance, insurance, and property taxes. At times the expression *net net lease* is used to emphasize that *all* of the operating expenses are for account of the lessee. For our pur-

---

TABLE 4–1. Levels of Income

Gross Possible Income	$ XXXX
less: Vacancies and bad debts	XX
Gross Income, Actual	$ XXX
less: Operating expenses	XX
Net Operating Income	$ XXX
less: Depreciation expense	XX
less: Interest expense	XX
Taxable Income	$ XXX
less: Income taxes	XX
Earnings After Tax	$ XX

---

poses, however, we shall not make a distinction between the net lease and the net net lease.

Ground lease. The use of vacant land is leased. Usually the lessee is given the right to construct one or more buildings on the leased land, and accordingly these leases are usually long-term contracts.

Percentage lease. The payments under this form of lease are based upon a percentage of the tenant's gross income from the leased property, with some minimum rent amount usually specified. These leases are commonly used in shopping center leasing and other commercial-property leasing.

Index lease. With this type of lease the amounts of the rental payments will vary with changes in some stipulated index, such as the consumer price index.

Sale–leaseback (or *purchase–leaseback* from the purchaser's viewpoint). The property owner sells his property to a buyer who, in turn, leases the same property back for a long term to the seller. The seller is often the owner–user of a large industrial or commercial property, and the purchaser is often an insurance company.

Projecting gross income. The projection of gross income is greatly simplified for some real estate investment proposals; namely, those involving a long-term lease, a lessee with top credit standing (triple-A tenant), and fixed-amount rental payments rather than variable rentals such as attend the index or percentage leases. Where such ideal forecasting conditions as just described do not exist, the future yearly gross income figures become an uncertain variable, and an analysis of future market and environmental conditions must be undertaken, as was described in the last chapter. One practical approach that is sometimes appropriate is to assume some uniform future pattern for gross income, such as a steady decline as the property ages. Often a constant, annual gross income figure is projected or assumed, in which case certain rule-of-thumb, return-on-investment measures can be used, as will be described later in this chapter. The constant future gross income assumption might be used where inflation or other conditions are expected to offset rent declines associated with an aging property.

To help illustrate the calculations and uses of the gross income and other income levels, the data for a hypothetical real estate investment proposal, the *Park Project,* are presented below.

The park project.   A fifty-space mobile-home park can be purchased for $100,000. The land is valued at $60,000 and the improvements including such things as recreation facilities and utilities installations are valued at $40,000. The improvements have a remaining useful life of 5 years, and an estimated *residual,* or salvage value of zero. Straight-line depreciation will be used. A local financial institution will provide the purchaser with a 5-year, first mortgage loan of $40,000, at 7 per cent interest, with the principal to be fully amortized with level-loan payments to be made at the end of each of the 5 years of the loan.

The investor would plan to hold the property for five years without making any significant improvements to the property, and then sell it for an estimated $115,900. It is anticipated that the annual gross possible income, the vacancies and bad debts allowance, and the operating expenses will amount to $24,000, $1,000, and $7,000, respectively. We assume that the investor–purchaser is now in the 30 per cent tax bracket, and expects to continue to pay taxes on ordinary income at that rate during the next five years. The relevant financial data are summarized below.

The *Park Project's* annual gross income (actual) is found to be $23,000 for each of the 5 years of the planned holding period

THE PARK PROJECT

Price	$100,000
Loan	$ 40,000, 5 years, 7% level-annual payments
Down-payment	$ 60,000
Holding period	5 years
Estimated selling price	$115,900
Gross possible income	$ 24,000
Vacancies allowance	$ 1,000
Operating expenses	$ 7,000
Depreciable value	$ 40,000, 5 years, St.-Line, zero estimated residual value
Income tax rate	30%

by deducting the $1,000 vacancies allowance from the given annual gross possible income figure of $24,000.

Net Operating Income

Net operating income, sometimes referred to as *net income,* or *broker's net income,* is found by subtracting estimated operating expenses from estimated actual gross income, as shown in Table 4–1. As discussed in the last chapter, the proportion of gross income that is absorbed by the various operating expenses will vary from project to project, depending upon operating efficiency, and upon such things as the type, age, and location of the property.

The *Park Project's* 29.2 per cent *Expense ratio* can be found by using Equation 3–1 presented in the last chapter, as follows:

$$Expense\ ratio = \frac{Total\ operating\ expenses}{Gross\ possible\ income} \times 100$$

$$= \frac{\$7,000}{\$24,000} \times 100$$

$$= 0.292 \times 100$$

$$= 29.2\%$$

In this case the ratio remains constant over the five years of the planned holding period.

Where the operating expenses are expected to represent a high proportion of gross income, and the equity investor is responsible for covering such expenses, forecasting procedures become very important, and the use of probability theory or other techniques discussed in Chapter 7 may be appropriate. An analysis of the nature of operating expenses for various individual types of properties is presented in Part III. Net operating income for our *Park Project* is a uniform amount of $16,000 in each of the 5 years of the project, calculated by subtracting each year's operating expenses of $7,000 from annual gross income of $23,000.

Taxable Income

To arrive at the figure for taxable income, also referred to as *earnings before tax,* the investor must estimate future depreciation and interest expenses. The deduction of these expenses from net operating income gives the amount of earnings available to the equity investor prior to the adjustment for income taxes. Because real estate investments often generate depreciation and interest expenses that substantially reduce the amount of net operating income subject to taxation, it is important to consider in some detail the tax provisions relating to these two deductions.

Depreciation Expense

In many real estate investments substantial depreciation expense deductions are permitted by the tax provisions. This is especially true where the value of buildings and other depreciable improvements represents a high proportion of the total cost of the investment property, and extra-heavy depreciation deductions in the early years of the investment are generated by the use of *accelerated depreciation.* The accelerated-depreciation methods as well as the straight-line method will be discussed and illustrated with the *Park Project* example, following a description of just what property qualifies for depreciation expense treatment, and the determination of useful lives.

Depreciable property. Only property that is subject to physical decay or obsolescence, and has a definitely limited life, is permitted to be depreciated for tax purposes. Therefore, land itself is not depreciable. Additionally, for real property to be depreciable for tax purposes it must be either (1) property held for income production, hence a house used solely as a personal residence is excluded—or (2) property used in the taxpayer's trade or business, such as a manufacturing plant.[1]

Because depreciation is not permitted on land value, the investor would usually prefer to have as little as possible of the purchase price for a piece of property allocated to the land itself, while the federal tax authorities would have the opposite preference. The purchaser can have the dollar portion of the purchase price allocated to the land and to the buildings specified in the contract of sale, but this procedure has been held to be insufficient evidence of appropriate allocation. The taxpayer–investor should be prepared to support his allocation with additional evidence such as the local property tax assessor's allocation, and data on the land value of nearby properties. Additions to the property or other improvements made to the property subsequent to the original acquisition are added to the depreciable value of the property. The distinction between *improvements* and *repairs* is an important issue that arises in this connection, but we postpone our discussion of it until Chapter 6.

Useful life. As noted above, depreciable property has, by definition, a definitely limited useful life, and the depreciable value is depreciated by one of the allowed methods over the appropriate specified useful life of the property. The taxpayer–investor would ordinarily prefer to use as short an estimated useful life as possible in order to boost the period depreciation deductions. The investor is allowed to specify the estimated useful life for his property but he must do so with reference to the Treasury Department "Depreciation Guidelines" unless evidence of unique factors would support a shorter useful life estimate. Some sample guideline lives are: apartments and hotels, 40 years; office buildings, 45 years; stores, 50 years; and warehouses, 60 years.

Depreciation methods in general. The portion of the property value that can be allocated to each year of the useful life as a

[1] When a leasehold interest is purchased for a stated sum and sub-leasing is permitted, then a reasonable allowance for exhaustion is permitted.

deduction for tax purposes will depend upon the particular depreciation method employed. In this section we shall discuss and illustrate the basic depreciation methods, and in the following section we shall review the depreciation methods allowed under current income tax provisions for different categories of real estate investment properties.

Straight-line depreciation method. The amount of depreciation taken each year under the straight-line method is of uniform amount, and is found by dividing the *depreciable value* by the number of years of estimated useful life. The depreciable value is found by subtracting the estimated *residual value,* or *salvage value* from the original cost of the property.[2] In the *Park Project,* we have depreciable property costing $40,000, an estimated residual value of zero, and therefore a depreciable value of $40,000, which when divided by the 5 years' useful life gives an annual straight-line depreciation deduction of $8,000. The annual straight-line *depreciation rate* in this case is 20 per cent, found by dividing 100 per cent by 5 years.

Declining-balance depreciation methods. With these methods the undepreciated value of the property is multiplied by a percentage of the annual straight-line depreciation rate. The residual value (estimated selling price less the estimated costs of selling the depreciable property), is *not* deducted from the original cost in the periodic depreciation calculation, as contrasted to the straight-line method. The most common forms of the declining-balance method are the double-declining-balance method (200%) and the 150%- and 125%-declining-balance methods.

To illustrate the application of the double-declining-balance method we shall again use the *Park Project,* with its depreciable property cost of $40,000. It is to be emphasized that under *current* tax provisions, this five-year project could *not* take advantage of accelerated depreciation methods, such as the declining-balance methods, for tax purposes, as will be shown in the next section of this chapter. The *Park Project* is used as a short-term example for simplicity. Of course, the rules on the depreciation methods usage continue to be subject to change.

---

[2] It should be noted that if the investor anticipates making depreciable improvements during the planned holding period, an adjustment would be required in estimated future depreciation amounts.

If the double-declining-balance method (DDB) could be used for the *Park Project,* the depreciation deduction in the first year would be $16,000, as against the $8,000 by the straight-line method. The $16,000 figure is found by applying double the straight-line depreciation rate to the first year's undepreciated balance of $40,000. As the straight-line depreciation rate in the *Park Project* is equal to 20 per cent as previously calculated, the DDB is 2 × 20 per cent, or 40 per cent, which, times $40,000, gives first-year depreciation of $16,000.

The second year's DDB depreciation expense amounts to $9,600, computed by multiplying 40 per cent times the undepreciated balance of $24,000 [$40,000 − $16,000 first-year depreciation]. The other three years' DDB depreciation amounts are shown in Table 4–2. The same table also shows the annual depreciation amounts under the straight-line, the 150%-declining-balance, and the sum-of-the-years'-digits methods. The application of the 150%-declining-balance method gives a $12,000 depreciation deduction in the first year, by applying 150% of the 20% straight-line rate to the undepreciated balance, as follows: 150% × 20% × $40,000 = $12,000. The 125%-declining-balance method would give a first-year deduction of $10,000 [125% × 20% × $40,000 = $10,000].

Sum-of-the-years'-digits depreciation method. To find the periodic depreciation amounts under this method one must first find the total digits of all of the years of the useful life; in the *Park Project:* [3] 1 + 2 + 3 + 4 + 5 = 15. To determine the first year's depreciation expense, one multiplies 5/15 times the depreciable value; so in this example we have first-year depreciation of $13,333 [(5/15) × ($40,000 − $0)]. To determine second-year depreciation for the *Park Project,* the depreciable value of $40,000 is multiplied by 4/15, resulting in a $10,667 depreciation deduction. In the other three years the multipliers are 3/15, 2/15, and 1/15, respectively. Depreciation figures under the sum-of-the-years'-digits method are also included in Table 4–2. It will be noted that the

---

[3] The following equation can be used as a short-cut to determine the *Total digits* figure, with N equal to the number of years in the useful life:

$$\text{Total digits} = N\left(\frac{N+1}{2}\right)$$

TABLE 4–2. Four Depreciation Methods—Park Project

Year	Straight-Line	DDB	150%–DB	SOY-Digits
1	$8,000	$16,000	$12,000	$13,333
2	8,000	9,600	8,400	10,667
3	8,000	5,760	6,533[a]	8,000
4	8,000	4,320[a]	6,533	5,333
5	8,000	4,320	6,534	2,667

[a]Switch to straight-line method.

estimated residual value is deducted from original cost before multiplying by the appropriate factor, as contrasted with the declining-balance methods.

Depreciation switch. The Internal Revenue Code currently permits tax-payers to switch at anytime *from* a declining-balance method *to* straight-line depreciation. Accordingly, the procedure to maximize early depreciation tax deductions would be to compare for each year in the future useful life, the deduction arising from the accelerated depreciation method actually employed with the straight-line depreciation amount based on the number of years of remaining useful life, and to plan a switch to straight-line in the first year that that method generates a larger deduction. The switch to straight-line is illustrated in Table 4–2.

As the data in Table 4–2 indicate, the declining balance and the sum-of-the-years'-digits methods (the accelerated depreciation methods) give significantly higher depreciation deductions in the early years of the useful life, but lower deductions in the later years of the investment. It will be noted that even where the total depreciation deductions would be equivalent, such as if a property is held for its entire useful life, the accelerated depreciation methods are advantageous to the investor in the early years because *the immediate tax savings can be reinvested in other projects.* Of course, the investor's expected future tax bracket would have an influence on this situation, as would also the preference tax discussed in the next section.[4] A sale of the property prior to the end of the useful life involves the depreciation-recapture tax provisions, but we postpone our discussion of that subject until Chapter 6.

Impact of the 1969 and 1976 TRA's. The traditional benefits of accelerated depreciation of real property were cut back in three principal ways by the 1969 Tax Reform Act (TRA): (1) the depreciation-recapture provisions were made more severe, (2) a 10 per cent preference tax was applied to "excess depreciation," and (3) the extent to which accelerated depreciation can be used was sharply restricted. The first item, the recapture provisions, will be discussed in Chapter 6, and the other two items will be discussed below.

Ten per cent tax on preferences. The 1969 TRA imposed a separate 10 per cent tax (for corporations and individuals) on items considered to represent preferential tax treatment. One of these items, which relates directly to real estate investment, is accelerated depreciation.[5] The amount of a particular year's accelerated depreciation deduction that is subject to the special 10 per cent tax is *the excess of the accelerated depreciation deduction over what the straight-line depreciation deduction would have been, had that method been used.* Before the 10 per cent tax is applied to the excess depreciation, however, the amount of such excess over straight-line is added to other tax preference amounts and an exemption is applied, which is equal to $30,000 (or $15,000 for a married person filing a separate return) *plus* the amount of federal income taxes for the same year.

The 1976 Tax Reform Act increased the minimum tax on preferences from 10 per cent to 15 per cent, starting in 1976. The 1976 TRA also sharply reduced the exemption amount starting in 1976 for individuals to $10,000, or to one-half the regular income tax for the year—whichever is greater. For corporations, the 1976 TRA reduced the exemption amount to $10,000, or to the

[4] If the investor expects low tax rates in the early years, and higher tax rates in more distant years, this would make the later years' deductions with straight-line depreciation relatively more attractive.

[5] Another tax preference item relating to real estate investment is capital gains, as will be discussed in Chapter 6.

TABLE 4–3.   Real Estate Depreciation Methods Allowed by the Tax Reform Act of 1969

Type of Property	Allowable Methods
New residential rental property	S-L, DDB, 150%-DB, SOY-Digits
Other new property	S-L, 150%-DB
Used residential rental property (with a remaining useful life of at least 20 years)	S-L, 125%-DB
Other used property	S-L
Rehabilitation cost of low-income housing	S-L, Use 5-yr life

full amount of the regular income tax for the year—whichever is greater; the new exemption rules for corporations, however, are not fully effective until 1977.

Depreciation methods under the 1969 and 1976 TRA's. Prior to the 1969 TRA, all *new* properties (or first-owner properties) could be depreciated with any of the accelerated depreciation methods discussed above, or by any other methods giving equivalent or lower deductions; and all *used* real properties could be depreciated with the 150%-declining-balance or equivalent method. The extent to which the 1969 TRA cut back on the usage of favorable depreciation methods is indicated in Table 4–3, which contains the tax provisions applicable to property acquired or constructed after July 24, 1969.

As will be observed in Table 4–3, residential rental property is allowed favored depreciation treatment. While the intention of this favored treatment was to stimulate low- and moderate-income housing, the accelerated depreciation tax benefits are applicable to all residential rental properties. At least 80 per cent of the gross rental income from a building must come from dwelling units for it to qualify as a residential rental property.

The rehabilitation cost item contained in Table 4–3 refers to a special 5-year write-off using straight-line depreciation that the 1969 Tax Reform Act permits for capital expenditures made after July 24, 1969 (and before 1975), for the rehabilitation of old

TABLE 4–4. Depreciation Schedule—Park Project		
Year	Depreciation Expense	Undepreciated Balance
1	$8,000	$32,000
2	8,000	24,000
3	8,000	16,000
4	8,000	8,000
5	8,000	0

properties having dwelling units rented to persons of low or moderate income. These special amortization rules for rehabilitation costs were extended through 1977, by the 1976 Tax Reform Act. The 1976 legislation also raised the amount of rehabilitation expenditures that can be written off under these rules—from $15,000 to $20,000 per dwelling unit.

The depreciation schedule. In preparing data for real estate analysis it is useful to prepare a depreciation schedule showing the annual depreciation expense and undepreciated balance for each future year of the investment proposal. Such a schedule is presented in Table 4–4 for the straight-line depreciation method originally specified for the *Park Project.*

Interest Expense

Because real estate has the attribute of immobility and other characteristics that make it attractive security for relatively large amounts of creditor financing, the related interest-expense deduction, sometimes referred to as the *leverage deduction,* is an important factor in many investments. Interest deductions are usually largest in the earliest years of the investment, when the interest component in level-mortgage-loan payments is at the highest levels. Tax reductions arising from interest expense deductions represent permanent tax savings rather than tax deferment as sometimes result with depreciation deductions.

Interest deduction limitation. Under the provisions of the 1969 Tax Reform Act, a limitation was placed for years beginning in 1972 on the amount of investment interest expense that is deductible in a given year by non-corporate taxpayers. The maximum deductible amount in any one year equals $25,000 (or $12,500 for the married person filing a separate return) *plus* the amount of the taxpayer's net investment income *plus* excess net long-term capital gains over net short-term capital losses *plus* one half of the excess of investment interest over the sum of the three previous items.[6] There is also a provision for carrying over a limited amount of unused (disallowed) investment interest to the following year.[7]

Some of the special rules and exceptions applying to the interest deduction limitation that are germane to the real estate investor are:

1. Property leased on a net lease basis is treated as property held for investment if (a) business expense deductions total less than 15 per cent of rental income, or (b) the lessor is guaranteed a specified return, or is guaranteed against loss.
2. Interest expense incurred in the construction of property to be used in the trade or business is not investment interest.

In summary, we can say that the 1969 interest deduction limitation provisions favor the small investor because of the $25,000 minimum limitation; the provisions favor investment in income-producing properties, because periodic income is added to the maximum amount of allowable interest deductions; and the provisions favor investors who take capital gains (excess capital gains also expand the allowable interest expense deduction) rather than defer capital gains by using installment sales or property exchanges, as described in Chapter 11.

The amount of investment interest deduction allowed by the 1969 TRA was sharply cut back by the Tax Reform Act of 1976. Under the new law the deductible amount of investment interest expense relating to indebtedness incurred after September 10, 1975, is limited to only $10,000 (or $5,000 for married taxpayers filing separate returns) *plus* the amount of the taxpayer's net investment income.

[6] Capital gains and losses are discussed in detail in Chapter 6.

[7] The amount allowed to be carried over in the following year is limited to $\frac{1}{2}$ of the excess of net investment income for the carry-over year plus $25,000 *over* the greater of investment interest paid in the carry-over year or $25,000. If in the carry-over year, part of the disallowed investment interest is nondeductible because of the above limitation, the amount that can be carried over to a third year is reduced by the amount of the 50 per cent capital gains deduction.

The mortgage-loan schedule. The mortgage-loan schedule is a table showing periodic payments to be made on the mortgage loan, along with the periodic interest and amortization ("principal") components of the loan payments, and the amount of the loan outstanding after each period's loan payment. The first step in the preparation of the mortgage-loan schedule is to determine the periodic payments to be made on the loan, often referred to as *debt service.* The most common repayment schedule for investment-property mortgages, as well as for home mortgages, is the level-payment plan, with all periodic payments being of uniform amounts. To simplify the example, we assume that the *Park Project* mortgage calls for *annual* rather than for monthly or quarterly level payments.

The proportion of the original loan amount represented by the periodic loan payment is referred to as the *mortgage constant.* The original mortgage loan amount multiplied by the mortgage constant will give the amount of the periodic loan payment or debt service. For example, in the *Park Project,* the annual mortgage constant of 0.243891 times the $40,000 mortgage loan gives an annual debt service of $9,756. The appropriate mortgage constant can be found in a mortgage-constant table, such as found in *Column 6* of the Appendix.[8] The interest expense and amortization portions of each year's mortgage loan payment of $9,756 can now be determined, and a mortgage-loan schedule prepared, such as in Table 4–5.

The entries for the mortgage schedule may be computed as follows:

1. Debt service is a constant amount, calculated by using the annual mortgage constant discussed above.
2. Interest for the first year is 7 per cent of the amount of the mortgage outstanding during the first year; that is, $40,000 $\times$ 0.07 = $2,800.

[8] Comprehensive tables of mortgage constants are found in the *Ellwood Tables* compiled by L. W. Ellwood and published by the American Institute of Real Estate Appraisers, Chicago. The annual mortgage constant is equivalent to the reciprocal of the present value of an annuity factor. Such reciprocal values are found in engineering economy texts, under the heading of *capital recovery factors.* See, for example, Eugene L. Grant and W. Grant Ireson, *Principles of Engineering Economy,* (6th ed.; New York: The Ronald Press Company, 1976).

TABLE 4–5. Mortgage-Loan Schedule—Park Project
$40,000 Loan, 7%, 5 Years, Annual Payments

Year	Debt Service	Interest	Amortization	Unpaid Mortgage
1	$9,756	$2,800	$6,956	$33,044
2	9.756	2,313	7,443	25,601
3	9,756	1,792	7,964	17,637
4	9,756	1,235	8,521	9,116[a]
5	9,756	638	9,118[a]	0

[a]The $2 discrepancy is due to rounding.

3. The balance of the $9,756 mortgage loan payment represents the first year's amortization of $6,956, and the unpaid mortgage after the first year's amortization is $33,044.

4. The complete computations for the first two years of the Park Project's mortgage schedule are summarized below, with the last three years to follow a similar pattern.

Year 1: Debt service .... $ 9,756
         Interest = 0.07 × $40,000 2,800
         Amortization = $9,756 − $2,800 6,956
         Unpaid mortgage = $40,000 − $6,956 ... 33,044

Year 2: Debt service .... $ 9,756
         Interest = 0.07 × $33,044 2,313
         Amortization = $9,756 − $2,803 7,433
         Unpaid mortgage = $33,044 − $7,443 ... 25,601

The smoothed pattern of the changing interest and amortization components of the level annual mortgage payments are shown for the *Park Project* mortgage in Figure 4–1. It will be noted that interest expense decreases over the life of the mortgage as the amount of the loan outstanding decreases.

Computing taxable income. Having calculated the depreciation and interest expense deductions for all five years of the *Park Project,* the amount of periodic taxable income for each of the five years can be determined by deducting such expenses from net

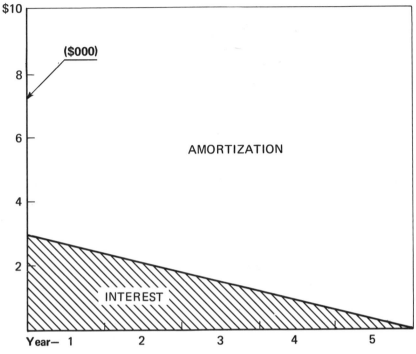

Fig. 4–1. Mortgage amortization, Park Project.

operating income, which was determined previously to be $16,000 annually. The first year's taxable income, for example, equals $5,200 [$16,000 − $8,000 − $2,800]. All of the five years' taxable income figures are in the investment profile in Table 4–6.

Earnings After Tax

The amount of earnings after tax for a particular year is found by subtracting income taxes from taxable income. While state and local income taxes would have to be included in the tax figure, we shall focus here on federal income taxes. Because taxable periodic income is treated as ordinary income for tax purposes, the amount of federal income taxes payable is found by multiplying taxable income by the investor's marginal tax rate on ordinary income. As used here, the term *marginal tax rate* refers to the rate to be applied to the investment project's income after taking into account the investor's other income expected to

TABLE 4–6. Investment Profile—Park Project

	Year—1	2	3	4	5
		Periodic Returns			
Gross Possible Income	$24,000	$24,000	$24,000	$24,000	$24,000
less: Vacancies and bad debts	1,000	1,000	1,000	1,000	1,000
Gross Income, Actual	$23,000	$23,000	$23,000	$23,000	$23,000
less: Operating expenses	7,000	7,000	7,000	7,000	7,000
Net Operating Income	$16,000	$16,000	$16,000	$16,000	$16,000
less: Depreciation expense	8,000	8,000	8,000	8,000	8,000
Interest expense	2,800	2,313	1.792	1,235	638
Taxable Income	$ 5,200	$ 5,687	$ 6,208	$ 6,765	$ 7,362
less: Income taxes (30%)	1,560	1,706	1,862	2,029	2,209
Earnings After Tax	$ 3,640	$ 3,981	$ 4,346	$ 4,736	$ 5,153

Financial Analysis

GIM	4.3				
Expense Ratio	29.2%				
Income Yield	16.0%				
Return on Equity		6.1%	5.9%	5.8%	5.8%	5.7%

be received in the same year. The investor's marginal tax rate for the *Park Project* was given as 30 per cent, and therefore, the federal income tax amounts to $1,560 for the first year of the project [$5,200 × .30]. This results in first-year after-tax earnings of $3,640. All of the five years' after-tax earnings figures are shown in Table 4–6.

Tax treatment of ordinary income. The marginal tax rate for a particular investor will depend on the amount of his other income, and upon his family status if he is a non-corporate investor. The marginal tax rates on ordinary income can be summarized as:

1. *For corporations,* 20 per cent on the first $25,000 of taxable income, 22 per cent on the next $25,000 of taxable income, and 48 per cent on taxable income over $50,000.[9]
2. *For individuals,* and partners taxed as individuals, marginal tax rates range from 14 to 70 per cent. Since 1971, the maximum rate has been only 50 per cent on income received in the form of salary or income from personal services, but the 70 per cent rate still applies to the individual's other income.

Tax provisions relating to operating losses are discussed in the next chapter, and the capital gains tax provisions relating to gains received at the time of property disposition are discussed in Chapter 6.

REAL ESTATE INVESTMENT PROFILE

While many of the rate-of-return measures used by real estate investors call only for the first year's income figures, it is nonetheless desirable to make projections of future income and expenses in the form of *pro-forma,* or hypothetical, *income statements* for all years of the planned holding period. This will give a much more complete picture of the attributes of the prospective investment and will serve as a useful tool for many forms of analysis to be discussed in this book. As all of the necessary data or techniques for obtaining the data have been accumulated, we can now prepare pro-forma income statements for the five individual years of the *Park Project,* as shown in the investment profile in Table 4–6, which also includes some financial analysis measures that are defined and discussed later in the present chapter. The profile will be expanded in future chapters with the development of additional analytical techniques.

[9] The tax rates shown were originally scheduled by the Tax Reduction Act of 1975, and were extended through 1976 and 1977 by the Tax Reform Act of 1976. The pre-1975 rates were: 22 per cent on the first $25,000, and 48 per cent on taxable income exceeding $25,000.

Additional tax provisions applicable to corporations and other ownership forms, including the real estate investment trust, are discussed in Chapter 8.

ANALYZING PERIODIC INCOME RETURNS

A return measure is useful because it assists the decision maker in comparing the relative attractiveness of various alternative outlets for investment funds. In evaluating real estate investment proposals that offer prospective periodic or recurring income benefits, one could use any of the income levels discussed in the last section. However, the most commonly used levels are gross income, net operating income, and earnings after tax. The relative-return measures employing those three levels are described next.

Gross Income Multiplier

The gross income multiplier (GIM) that was introduced in the last chapter relates the current gross income of the property to the purchase price of the same property in the manner indicated by Equation 4–1.

$$\text{GIM} = \frac{\textit{Purchase price}}{\textit{Current gross income}} \qquad [4-1]$$

The gross income multiplier is a technique used by real estate appraisers as one way to appraise, or price, an income-producing property. The procedure used is to multiply the *Current gross income* of the property by an appropriate multiplier (the *GIM*) to determine one estimate of the market value for the property being appraised. In this application the equation would be: *Market price = GIM × Current gross income.*

For most properties, *annual* gross income is used in the GIM calculation, but *monthly* gross income is used for certain residential properties including single-family residential rental units. For example, suppose the monthly GIM is 150 for rental houses in a certain community or neighborhood; if the monthly rent for a particular residence is $200, then the application of the GIM would give one estimate for the property's market value of $30,000. Because of its wider application, we assume *annual* gross income is involved in our future references to the multiplier, unless otherwise specified.

The GIM is called a *direct conversion ratio* because it directly converts rental value into present property value. This technique is a rule-of-thumb technique not unlike the *price/earnings ratio* (P/E ratio) used in securities analysis, where one measure of the value of a common stock is found by multiplying an appropriate P/E ratio times the current earnings per share. Both the GIM and the P/E ratio do not assume necessarily a constant, perpetual future income stream because, for example, if the gross income or earnings per share are expected to grow in the future, then a higher multiplier can be used to reflect that fact. Hence, a growth stock would generally have a relatively high P/E ratio.

The real estate investor can use the GIM technique in the same manner as the appraiser by applying a multiplier to gross income and comparing the resulting value with the asking price—or the investor can use Equation 4–1 directly to find the GIM for an available investment property and compare that figure with the prevailing GIM's for similar properties. In the *Park Project* example, the GIM of 4.3 is found by dividing the purchase price of $100,000 by the project's annual gross income of $23,000, which we shall assume is the current as well as the future gross income figure.

Although it is widely used, the GIM technique has also been widely criticized, mainly on two counts; (1) it is difficult to meaningfully interpret or use a particular multiplier because even properties of the same basic type, for example, motels, will have differing expense ratios and other expense features; and (2) the equity investor should be more concerned, it is argued, with income returns *after* taking account of the unique operating expenses, financing arrangements, and tax aspects of each project.

However, the technique is so widely used by appraisers and brokers that market prices are actually influenced by its application, and therefore real estate investors should be aware of this technique and use it cautiously as a rough guide to investment property values.[10] Real estate industry sources make available

[10] A comprehensive survey conducted in the mid-60's found that 77 per cent of the surveyed real property appraisals included the use of either the GIM technique or other direct-conversion ratios such as the net income multiplier. See Richard U. Ratcliff, "Capitalized Income is not Market Value," *The Appraisal Journal,* January 1968, p. 37.

average gross income multipliers for various types of properties, often classified by age, geographical area, and so forth.[11]

Income Yield

To find this popular rate-of-return measure, sometimes referred to as *investment yield,* net operating income is related to total investment, as reflected in Equation 4–2.

$$\text{Income yield} = \frac{\textit{Net operating income (first year)}}{\textit{Total investment}} \qquad [4\text{--}2]$$

In the *Park Project* we have an income yield of 16.0 per cent [$16,000/$100,000]. This rate-of-return measure is useful to the investor because comparable data are available on other properties. This, in turn, is because the measure is widely used by appraisers who work with it as a *capitalization rate.*[12] In making comparisons with other properties, however, the income-yield measure should be considered only as a rough rule-of-thumb because of inconsistencies in the way net operating income is calculated and reported.

It should be noted that the income-yield measure is a *perpetuity formulation.* With this measure no time limit is specified for the duration of the net operating income benefits, and there is an implied assumption that the net operating income amount will be received annually in perpetuity. This is, however, a commonly used formulation in financial analysis, which in practice means that annual benefits of approximately the same amount will be received indefinitely, or for the foreseeable future. It would not be appropriate to use the income yield measure when the future net operating income level is expected to change significantly over the years. Another rate-of-return technique employing the net operating income level is the Inwood method described in Chapter 7.

---

[11] See, for example, *Case Studies in Apartment House Valuation* (2nd ed.; Chicago: American Institute of Real Estate Appraisers, 1969).
[12] Real estate appraisers use an assumed capitalization rate to find value for an income-producing property: *Value = Net operating income/Capitalization rate.*

Return on Equity

Real estate equity investors are naturally interested in measuring the return on *owners' investment,* as well as return on total investment. While most investors are perhaps primarily interested in *cash returns* to their investment, as described in the next chapter, some investors are also interested in accounting income returns. The return-on-equity (ROE) measure can be used for this purpose, as reflected in Equation 4–3, where t represents the particular time period, or year, for which the ROE calculation is made.

$$ROE_t = \frac{\text{Earnings after tax}_t}{\text{Owners' investment}_t} \qquad [4\text{--}3]$$

The ROE calculations for the first 2 years of the *Park Project* are shown below. The denominator in the ROE_2 formulation represents the owners' initial investment of $60,000 plus the $6,956 mortgage amortization payment made at the end of the first year.[13]

$$ROE_1 = \frac{\$3,640}{\$60,000} = 6.1\%$$

$$ROE_2 = \frac{\$3,981}{\$66,956} = 5.9\%$$

The ROE figures for the last three years of the *Park Project* can be calculated to be 5.8, 5.8, and 5.7 per cent.

It will be observed that the ROE formulation described here gives a separate return figure for each year rather than a single, overall project-return figure, as does the income-yield measure. The use of a single ROE return measure, such as $ROE = Earnings$ *after tax (first year)/Owners' initial investment,* is usually inappropriate, because the perpetuity assumption would be invali-

---

[13] One variation of this formulation would be to reduce the denominator each year by the amount of annual depreciation because the numerator is so reduced. The theory would be that the value of the property is declining each year. However, because accounting depreciation often does not correspond to economic depreciation for real estate, we have not made that adjustment.

dated, in that both the numerator and denominator amounts will change from year to year for investments involving mortgage financing.

As previously mentioned, perhaps most real estate investors are primarily interested in cash return on investment. However, investors having publicly held common stock outstanding are often primarily interested in after-tax earnings, often called *bottom-line earnings*, because of shareholder demands for favorable earnings per share performance.[14] The ROE formulation is also a convenient measure to use in illustrating *leverage* concepts as will be done in the next, and final, section of this chapter.

LEVERAGE

Leverage, or more precisely *financial leverage,* may be defined as *the extent to which the owner–investor employs borrowed funds to finance his investment.*[15] Perhaps the most commonly employed measure of leverage is: the amount of debt divided by total capital; or in real estate terms, the *loan-to-value-ratio.* By this measure, the first year's leverage in the *Park Project* is 40 per cent [$40,000/$100,000]. Because, as described previously, real estate lends itself to relatively high amounts of mortgage debt financing, many real estate investments are highly leveraged. Because leverage magnifies the returns to the equity investor one often hears the comment that leverage is one of the most important benefits of real estate investing, as contrasted to other investment forms.

Using the first year of the *Park Project* as an example, let us suppose that the investor had borrowed no funds and his own investment accordingly amounts to $100,000. There being no interest expense under this assumption, the first year's taxable income would be $8,000, and earnings after the 30 per cent tax

[14] It has been observed that the quick payoff in the form of earnings per share has led many corporations to the land sales and single-home construction areas of real estate investment; Charles Biderman, "No Green Pastures," *Barrons,* April 3, 1972, p. 5.
[15] Besides *financial leverage,* which is the concept we shall refer to as *leverage,* there is the financial management concept of *operating leverage,* which refers to the extent to which fixed costs are incurred in operations.

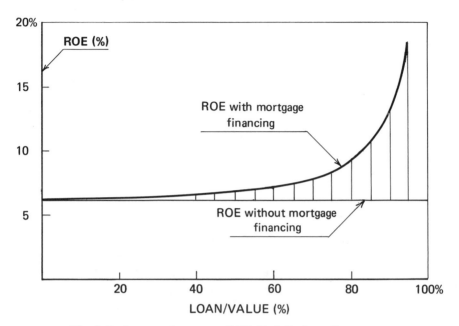

Fig. 4–2. Leverage impact on ROE, Park Project—first year.

would be $5,600. This would represent a 5.6 per cent ROE, based on owners' equity investment of $100,000. As calculated in the last section, however, the actual ROE for the *Park Project's* first period was 6.1 per cent, using 40 per cent leverage, as compared with 5.6 per cent with no leverage. If we suppose that the investor had borrowed $95,000 instead of $40,000, at the same 7 per cent interest cost, then the first year's ROE would amount to 18.9 per cent. Figure 4–2 indicates the rising pattern for ROE as the degree of leverage is increased.

The magnification of owners' return with the use of borrowed funds as illustrated in Figure 4–2 is said to be a result of *favorable leverage,* which exists whenever the investment generates earnings at a higher rate than the cost of the borrowed funds.[16] On the other hand, when the mortgage interest rate exceeds the return on total investment, *unfavorable leverage* is

---

[16] In the *Park Project* example, the first year's return on total investment, i.e., earnings before interest and taxes, amount to 8 per cent, which was slightly higher than the 7 per cent interest cost of the mortgage loan.

said to exist and the ROE will decline as additional funds are borrowed. It should also be noted that the magnification or demagnification of ROE because of leverage can be much more extreme than shown in the *Park Project* because many projects have a larger spread between the return on total investment and the mortgage interest rate.

Thus far we have ignored the matter of project risk which will increase as leverage is increased, all else being the same; the nature of this so-called *financial risk,* or *leverage risk* will be discussed in Chapter 7, along with other forms of real estate investment risks.

SUMMARY

Many real estate investments are looked to by equity investors to generate periodic or recurring income returns. There are various levels of income that can be used to measure income returns, including *gross possible income, actual gross income, net operating income, taxable income,* and finally, the bottom-line income level of *earnings after tax.* In the determination of the various levels, the federal income tax provisions become important, especially those relating to the interest and depreciation deductions.

In analyzing the income–return patterns during the expected life of a project, it is helpful to prepare a *mortgage-loan schedule* and a *depreciation schedule,* which, in turn, are useful in developing *pro-forma income statements.* The pro-forma statements show all levels of income expected to be received during each year of the investment project. The pro-forma income statement data can be included in an *investment profile* like the one developed in this chapter for the hypothetical *Park Project,* which also contained financial analysis measures for the project, including the *expense ratio,* a popular measure of operating efficiency; the *gross income multiplier* (GIM), an appraisal technique widely used as a rough guide to property value; and *income yield,* a rule-of-thumb return measure based on net operating income returns on total investment.

An additional return measure, *return on equity,* is most useful to investors concerned with satisfactory earnings per share performance. The term *leverage* refers to the use of debt financing, and is important because leverage tends to magnify investment risks and returns to the equity investor. The impact of leverage is often very pronounced in real estate equity investing because a high proportion of debt is usually used when financing real property acquisitions.

5

Cash Flow and
Tax Shelter

As a measure of periodic real estate investment returns, many investors focus on periodic cash flow rather than, or in addition to, accounting income measures. The prospective cash generation of a project is of great importance because of the investor's typical need for cash to sustain and develop other projects. The annual income figures are often quite different from the amount of cash generated annually by the same project. One reason is that the interest portion of the mortgage debt service reduces accounting income, but *not* the mortgage amortization portion of the mortgage-loan payment. Thus, cash flow will be less than accounting income to the extent of the mortgage amortization payments, which are often substantial amounts. Another major factor resulting in differing accounting income and cash flow amounts is depreciation expense, which is a non-cash charge against accounting income. Thus, where relatively substantial depreciation charges are involved, accounting income correspondingly understates cash inflows to a substantial extent.

The first part of this chapter describes techniques that can be used to find periodic cash flow, both before tax and after tax. Cash flow will be measured in *absolute terms,* that is, in terms of dollars; and in *relative terms,* that is, in relation to the amount of cash invested in the project. To complete the discussion of periodic returns to real estate investment, we describe in the latter part of this chapter some techniques that can be used for measuring tax-shelter benefits. For many investors in very high tax brackets, the immediate investment goal is to maximize such shelter benefits as part of an overall attempt to maximize after-tax cash flow.

PERIODIC CASH FLOW

Before-tax as well as after-tax return measures are widely used in the investment community. One reason is that some investing entities, such as qualifying real estate investment trusts, pay little or no income taxes.[1] Pre-tax and after-tax cash flow measures are discussed in the present section.

Pre-Tax Cash Flow

Before-tax cash flow, often called *cash spendable income before income taxes,* is employed as one measure of a project's cash-flow production. As reflected in Equation 5–1,[2] cash flow before tax, *CFBT,* can be ascertained for a particular year by simply subtracting the mortgage loan payment, or *Debt service,* from *Net operating income* for that year. Both the interest and amortization components of the loan payment are payable in cash and so must be deducted from net operating income.

$$CFBT = Net\ operating\ income - Debt\ service \qquad [5\text{–}1]$$

In the not uncommon situation where net operating income is estimated to be a uniform amount during the planned holding period of the proposal, *and* a level-payment mortgage is involved, then the periodic CFBT will be a constant amount.[3] This situation prevails in our previously introduced *Park Project*

[1] Real estate investment trusts are discussed in Chapter 8.
[2] An alternative but more circuitous method for finding pre-tax cash flow would be to add depreciation expense to taxable income, and then subtract the mortgage amortization amount for the year.
[3] The cash flow arising at the time the property is sold is discussed separately in the next chapter.

example. In that project, subtracting the level debt service payment of $9,756 from the uniform net operating income of $16,000 results in a periodic CFBT amount of $6,244, for each of the five years of the project, as shown in the investment profile in Table 5–1. It will be observed in the table that the pre-tax cash flow for the first year of $6,244 exceeds the taxable income of $5,200 for the same year. The reader should understand the reasons for the $1,044 difference between the two figures.

Pre-tax cash yield. A widely used relative-return measure relates cash flow before tax to the owners' cash down-payment, in the manner expressed by Equation 5–2, where *Pre-tax cash yield* symbolizes cash flow return on owners' initial equity investment.

$$\text{Pre-tax cash yield} = \frac{\text{CFBT (first year)}}{\text{Owners' initial investment}} \qquad [5\text{--}2]$$

In the *Park Project,* pre-tax cash yield amounts to 10.4 per cent [$6,244/$60,000]. Pre-tax cash yield is a rule-of-thumb measure that is appropriate where the first year's CFBT will be at least approximately representative of (a proxy for) the remaining years of the project, or better yet, when the periodic CFBT is expected to be a uniform or constant figure, as in the *Park Project.*

After-Tax Cash Flow

While the pre-tax cash flow measures are sufficient for investors paying no taxes, or very low taxes, most investing individuals and organizations face high tax rates and seek to measure cash flow returns on an after-tax basis. The cash flow after tax (CFAT) amount can be found by adding back the depreciation, to the after-tax earnings figure, and then subtracting mortgage amortization for the period involved. In the event the project generates a tax loss (negative taxable income) in a given period, then the offset of the loss against other income produces tax savings. The amount of the savings is found by multiplying the tax loss by the investor's tax rate. Any such tax-loss savings generated by the project should be included in calculating the

TABLE 5-1. Investment Profile—Park Project

	Year—1	2	3	4	5
			Periodic Returns		
Gross Possible Income	$24,000	$24,000	$24,000	$24,000	$24,000
less: Vacancies and					
bad debts	1,000	1,000	1,000	1,000	1,000
Gross Income, Actual	$23,000	$23,000	$23,000	$23,000	$23,000
less: Operating expenses	7,000	7,000	7,000	7,000	7,000
Net Operating Income	$16,000	$16,000	$16,000	$16,000	$16,000
less: Depreciation					
expense	8,000	8,000	8,000	8,000	8,000
Interest expense	2,800	2,313	1,792	1,235	638
Taxable Income	$ 5,200	$ 5,687	$ 6,208	$ 6,765	$ 7,362
less: Income taxes (30%)	1,560	1,706	1,862	2,029	2,209
Earnings After Tax	$ 3,640	$ 3,981	$ 4,346	$ 4,736	$ 5,153
plus: Depreciation					
expense	8,000	8,000	8,000	8,000	8,000
less: Mortgage amorti-					
zation	6,956	7,443	7,964	8,521	9,118
plus: Tax-loss savings	0	0	0	0	0
Cash Flow After Tax	$ 4,684	$ 4,538	$ 4,382	$ 4,215	$ 4,035
Cash Flow Before Tax	$ 6,244	$ 6,244	$ 6,244	$ 6,244	$ 6,244
			Tax Shelter		
Cash-Flow Shelter	$ 1,044	$ 557	$ 36	$ 0	$ 0
Tax-Loss Shelter	0	0	0	0	0
Total Tax Shelter	$ 1,044	$ 557	$ 36	$ 0	$ 0
Total Tax-Shelter Savings	$ 313	$ 167	$ 11	$ 0	$ 0

Financial Analysis

GIM	4.3					
Expense Ratio	29.2%					
Income Yield	16.0%					
Pre-Tax Cash						
Yield	10.4%					
Cash Payback						
Period	5 years					
Return on Equity		6.1%	5.9%	5.8%	5.8%	5.7%
After-Tax Cash Return		7.8%	7.6%	7.3%	7.0%	6.7%

project's after-tax cash flow. The amount of the tax loss generated by an investment project is considered a form of tax shelter, as discussed later in this chapter. In Equation 5–3 we have all the elements for finding *CFAT* for an individual project year.

$$
\begin{aligned}
\text{CFAT} = \text{Earnings after tax} &+ \text{Depreciation} \\
&- \text{Amortization} \qquad\qquad [5\text{–}3] \\
&+ \text{Tax loss savings}
\end{aligned}
$$

For the *first year* of the *Park Project,* for example, we find that cash flow after tax amounts to $4,684 [by Equation 5–3: CFAT = $3,640 + $8,000 − $6,956 + $0 = $4,684]. An alternative way of finding CFAT would be to deduct federal income taxes from CFBT for the year; or in the event of a taxable loss, to add the tax-loss savings to CFBT [CFAT = $6,244 − $1,560 = $4,684].

Over the next 4 years of the *Park Project* the CFAT amount steadily declines until it reaches $4,035 in the fifth year, as indicated in the investment profile in Table 5–1.[4] The reader will recognize that the reason for the decreasing after-tax cash flow for the *Park Project* is that the interest component of the annual debt service declines each year (even though the total annual debt service amount remains unchanged); therefore, a smaller interest-expense deduction results, with a corresponding increase in federal income taxes, and reduction in after-cash flow.

Because the amount of cash flow after tax will usually change each year, a rate-of-return measure that relates the first year's cash flow after tax to the owners' investment is usually an inappropriate overall project-return measure. The most appropriate overall rate-of-return measure using annual CFAT figures is found by the discounted cash flow techniques, discussed in detail in Chapter 7. As a practical matter, however, many investors are interested less in a carefully measured, overall rate-of-return estimate for a project than in the expected *spendable* after-tax cash expected to be generated in its first few years. The concern relates to a desire for cash *throw-off* that can be

---

[4] Again, we exclude the cash proceeds of sale at the end of the five-year holding period of the project.

employed in starting other new projects, or in continuing and expanding existing projects. Also, in many projects the near-term cash benefits are of special interest because they can often be estimated more accurately than the returns of more distant periods. Hence there is often more emphasis placed on the periodic after-tax cash flow figures (especially for early years), than in an overall rate-of-return figure that would take into account distant returns.

After-tax cash return. After-tax cash return is a relative-return measure of the expected after-tax cash throw-off from a project, found by expressing the CFAT figure as a percentage of the owners' initial cash investment, for each year of the holding period. In mathematical terms, we have Equation 5–4, where t is the year in which the $CFAT$ is received.

$$\text{After-tax cash return}_t = \frac{CFAT_t}{\text{Owners' initial investment}} \qquad [5\text{--}4]$$

In the *Park Project,* we have a first-year, after-tax cash return of $\$4,684/\$60,000 = 7.8$ per cent. All five years' figures are included in the investment profile in Table 5–1. It should be noted, however, that this technique of employing the annual CFAT as a percentage of owners' initial investment would qualify only as a rough rule-of-thumb measurement because it fails to take account of. the time value of money, as discussed in Chapter 7, and it ignores the often very large CFAT amount expected to arise at the time of sale.

Cash payback period. As a measure of the early cash throw-off from a project one can determine the time period (number of years) that it will take for accumulated after-cash inflows to be equal to, that is, to pay back, the initial cash investment by the owners. The technique involved would be to simply add up the CFAT amounts expected for each succeeding year in the planned holding period until the owners' total initial cash investment amount is reached. The number of years that it takes to reach the investment amount would represent the cash payback period. The advantage of this technique is that it focuses on early cash inflows. The drawbacks are the same as those found with the payback period technique used in corporate financial management, namely: (1) the measure ignores the cash returns after the payback period, which would be substantial in many real estate investments; and (2) the time value of money is ignored, as discussed further in Chapter 7.

In the *Park Project,* the *cash payback period* is five years. The *periodic* CFAT amounts for the 5 years total only $21,854, and therefore it is not until the cash flow at the time of sale is received in the amount of $107,515 (computed in the next chapter), that the original cash investment of $60,000 is fully paid back. The CFAT and CFBT amounts for each of the 5 years of the *Park Project* are shown in the investment profile in Table 5–1. Also included in the profile are: *pre-tax cash yield,* calculated previously in this chapter; *after-tax cash return; cash payback period,* just discussed; and *tax-shelter data,* to be explained shortly.

TAX SHELTER

Because of the very high federal income tax rates that have prevailed during the past several years, which currently reach up to 70 per cent of ordinary business income for an individual and to 48 per cent for corporations, high-income individuals and organizations have sought out investments offering significant tax savings. In very recent years many investment programs have been offered under the label *tax-shelter investment,* ranging from vineyards in California to pure-bred cattle and oil wells in Texas. In 1972, some 20 per cent of all filings with the Securities Exchange Commission for public offerings were tax-shelter offerings. Some real estate investments have attractive tax features and are looked to by many high-tax-bracket investors for tax-shelter benefits. In fact, tax shelter is often cited as a major benefit, or goal, in real estate investing—as contrasted to common-stock investing.

Despite the widespread use of the term *tax shelter,* it is used in a wide variety of different ways. In the present section of this chapter we shall define, analyze, and establish quantitative measurements for the amount of tax shelter and tax-shelter benefits generated by real estate investments. The particular types of properties and particular forms of legal ownership best suited to tax-shelter investing are discussed in later chapters of this book.

Tax shelter defined. At times the expression *tax shelter* is used broadly to mean any tax-savings features of an investment. For example, the favorable capital gains treatment often enjoyed in real estate investment is sometimes referred to as a source of tax-shelter savings. This concept could even be applied to tax savings resulting from the use of one particular ownership form (corporation, limited partnership, etc.) rather than some other forms giving higher immediate tax burdens.

However, we shall reduce this general concept of tax shelter to a more narrow and more workable definition that is also widely used, and relates to *periodic returns:* tax shelter is *the amount of periodic cash income that is sheltered from immediate federal income taxes.* In turn, *tax-shelter benefits* can be defined as: *the amount of taxes saved because of tax shelter.* With these definitions we are continuing our focus on periodic returns, and ignoring sale proceeds.

In the broader concept as well as in the more specific definition relating to periodic returns that was just introduced, the emphasis is on *immediate* tax savings. In many cases the immediate savings represent a postponement of tax burden rather than a permanent savings. However, even where the immediate tax savings are expected to be exactly offset by extra tax payments in later years, the return obtained on the interim use of the deferred tax funds usually makes tax shelter advantageous to the investor.

A further distinction can be made as to the *source* of the periodic income being sheltered from immediate taxes; the two sources are: *project-related income,* and *investors' other income.* These two separate types of sheltered income will be discussed below under the headings, *cash-flow shelter,* and *tax-loss shelter;* and we shall later combine the two to determine total or combined periodic tax shelter.

Cash-Flow Shelter

The dollar amount of periodic, project-related cash flow sheltered from taxes is what we shall call *cash-flow shelter.* That the sheltering of project-related cash from taxes is important to high-tax-rate investors is illustrated by the fact that to an investor in the 70 per cent tax bracket, $5,000 of tax-free cash is equivalent to taxable or "non-sheltered cash" of $16,667.[5] The amount of cash-flow shelter can be found by Equation 5–5, where *CFBT* represents cash flow before tax. It will be recalled that CFBT is equal to net operating income less debt service.

$$\text{Cash flow shelter} = \text{CFBT} - \text{Taxable income} \qquad [5\text{--}5]$$

where: If CFBT $\leq$ 0, then Cash flow shelter = 0
If taxable income $\leq$ 0, then Cash flow shelter = CFBT

Because cash-flow shelter has been defined as the amount of cash income (CFBT) sheltered from taxation, there is no cash-flow shelter if there is no CFBT, as reflected in the first constraint to Equation 5–5. The second constraint stating that—if *Taxable income* $\leq$ 0, then *Cash flow shelter* = *CFBT*—means that if an operating loss (i.e., negative taxable income) is involved, then the amount of the loss will not result in increased cash-flow shelter. In other words, we are measuring only the amount of *project-related cash flows* that are shielded from taxes.

Previously in this chapter it was determined that, for the first year of the *Park Project*, cash flow before tax is $6,244, and taxable income is $5,200. Therefore, by Equation 5–5, cash-flow shelter amounts to $1,044, which means that $1,044 or 16.7 per cent of the project's cash flow escapes taxation. To measure the amount of taxes saved as a result of this sheltered cash flow, we simply multiply the investor's marginal tax rate times the amount of shelter. In the *Park Project*, where the investor's tax rate is 30 per cent, the cash flow shelter benefits, or savings, are $313.20 [$1,044 × 0.30].

What is the reason for the generation of cash-flow shelter savings? The principal factor is, of course, depreciation charges that reduce taxable income but do not reduce cash flow before tax, as discussed earlier in this chapter. As long as non-cash-reducing depreciation charges exceed cash-reducing mortgage amortization

---

[5] To convert after-tax cash flow to before-tax cash flow, one need only divide the after-tax cash by $(1 - t)$, where t = the investor's marginal tax rate.

payments in a particular period, then some of that period's cash flow will escape taxation.

The amount of cash-flow shelter and related tax savings are ordinarily greatest in the early years of a real estate investment project because: (1) where accelerated depreciation methods are used, extra-large depreciation charges are made against taxable income in the early years; and (2) the tax-deductible interest portion of level mortgage payments is highest in the early years. Because straight-line depreciation was used in the *Park Project* example, the declining tax shelter, shown in Table 5–2, is a consequence of the second factor listed, the declining interest expense.

In this example cash-flow shelter amounts are somewhat modest and they decline steadily as the interest-expense deduction drops over the years of the investment. In the last two years none of the pre-tax cash flow escapes taxation, and therefore by our definition the cash-flow shelter is zero in those years. While the data in Table 5–2 indicate that for the *Park Project* some cash-flow shelter is generated with the use of straight-line depreciation, the use of accelerated depreciation methods would bring much greater shelter in the early years of the project, as shown later in this chapter.

Tax-Loss Shelter

In the previous section we discussed the sheltering from immediate taxes of cash flows that are expected to be generated by the real estate investment itself. Where the investment is expected to generate losses for tax purposes, that is, negative taxable income, then additional tax shelter will be generated because *income from other sources* will be sheltered in whole or in part by the investor's deduction of his real estate project's losses. This component of total tax shelter we label *tax-loss shelter*.[6] The amount of tax-loss shelter is equal to the amount of the period's tax loss. Multiplying the tax-loss shelter amount by the investor's marginal tax rate will give the amount of tax-loss-shelter benefits, that is, the amount of taxes saved because other income is shel-

---

[6] This form of tax shelter is sometimes referred to as *depreciation overflow*, because when a particular period's depreciation deduction is very large it may result in a loss for tax purposes.

TABLE 5-2. Cash-Flow Shelter—Park Project

Year	Cash Flow Before Tax	Taxable Income	Cash Flow Shelter	Cash Flow Shelter as a Percentage of CFBT
1	$6,244	$5,200	$1,044	16.7%
2	6,244	5,687	557	8.9
3	6,244	6,208	36	0.6
4	6,244	6,765	0	0
5	6,244	7,362	0	0

tered. This procedure assumes that the individual or corporate investor will have sufficient income from other sources against which to offset the particular real estate project's losses.

Under current federal income tax provisions, the investment losses of individuals and of individual members of partnerships can be deducted from the individual's other income.[7] The corporation can offset the operating losses from an investment against other corporate income. If the corporation as a whole suffers an operating loss, however, the loss cannot be offset against the income of the individual shareholders; but the loss can be carried back three years and forward seven years.

Deductible losses are naturally especially attractive to high-tax-bracket investors. The professional entertainer or lawyer in a high bracket, for example, will usually seek to shelter or shield as much as possible of his professional earnings from immediate federal income taxes. In many cases the investment plan would be to seek an investment offering tax-deductible losses in the early years when the investor is at his peak earnings level, and then generate profits and cash flow in later years when it is expected that the investor's professional earnings will slack off and place him in a relatively low tax bracket. The particular types of real estate projects that lend themselves to this kind of tax-shelter investment goal are those with heavy tax deductions, and projects that involve heavy construction or other early expenses. Part IV

[7] There exist limitations on the amount of partnership losses that can be deducted by general and limited partners, as discussed in Chapter 8.

of this book analyzes the individual types of properties best suited for this and for other investment goals.

Impact of the Tax Reform Act of 1976

Tax-loss shelter benefits were a primary target in 1976. The sharpest restrictions are not imposed on real estate investments, but rather on investments in farming, oil and gas exploration, motion picture films, equipment leasing, and sports franchises.

There are, however, some 1976 tax rules that do limit the deductibility of certain real estate investment expenses. When such deduction constraints are reached by an investor in a particular year, the result will be restricted tax-loss shelter benefits. The new limits are applied to the important *investment interest expense deduction* that was discussed in the last chapter, and the deductions allowed for *construction period interest and taxes,* as described in Chapter 17. Further, the 1976 TRA, in effect, disallows immediate deductions for *prepaid interest,* which were previously permitted to a limited extent.

The benefits of the tax-loss form of tax shelter are illustrated by the following intentionally extreme example involving investor *Jones,* who receives enough taxable income from his own retail business to put him in the 70 per cent marginal tax bracket. *Jones* is offered the opportunity to invest the same amount in two alternative real estate investments that are equivalent in every way except that, in the first year of operations, investment *B* generates $10,000 less in net operating income, and $10,000 more in depreciation deductions than investment *A*. As a result, investment *B* generates a loss of $10,000, while investment *A* yields taxable income of $10,000, as shown in Table 5–3.

That the unprofitable investment *B* is a more attractive investment, in terms of after-tax cash received by the investor, than the profitable investment *A* is indicated by the CFAT figures shown in Table 5–3. The reason for this curious result is that the $10,000 loss of investment *B* will shelter from taxes $10,000 of income received by Jones from his retail business, thereby resulting in a tax-loss shelter of $10,000, which generates tax savings of $7,000 [$10,000 × 0.70]. If *Jones'* marginal tax rate were 25 per cent in lieu of 70 per cent, then investment *A* would be found to generate $5,000 more after-tax cash than investment *B*, indi-

TABLE 5-3.   Tax-Loss Shelter Example—Investor Jones

	Investment A	Investment B
Net Operating Income	$15,600	$ 5,600
less: Depreciation expense	1,600	11,600
less: Interest expense	4,000	4,000
Taxable Income (loss)	$10,000	($10,000)
less: Income taxes (70%)	7,000	0
Earnings After Tax	$ 3,000	($10,000)
plus: Depreciation expense	1,600	11,600
less : Mortgage amortization	1,600	1,600
plus: Tax-loss savings	0	7,000[a]
Cash Flow After Tax	$ 3,000	$ 7,000

[a]The offset of the $10,000 loss against Jones' other income results in a tax savings of $7,000.

cating the greater value of tax-shelter benefits to investors enjoying higher marginal tax rates.

It should be emphasized that we have assumed in the *Jones* example that everything else is equivalent between the two investments. When investing for expected losses the investor should not lose sight of the capital invested in the project, which could quickly dwindle if the operating losses giving the tax shelter benefits are other than temporary tax-accounting losses.[8]   Also, it should be noted that we have examined only the first year of the two investments and that the results would ordinarily be expected to change over the years the investments are held.

Total Tax Shelter

Thus far we have separately considered two forms of tax shelter and tax-shelter benefits: cash-flow shelter, and tax-loss

[8] A non-real-estate tax-shelter example is the Black Watch Farms, Inc., tax shelter, which resulted in substantial financial losses to investors when real losses in the value of the capital (black angus cattle) were sustained; *The Wall Street Journal,* April 6, 1971, and June 1, 1973.

[9] We can do this by dropping the second constraint in the equation for finding cash-flow shelter (Equation 5-5). The amount of total tax shelter can also be found by subtracting the period's mortgage amortization from the same period's depreciation deduction.

TABLE 5–4. Total Tax Shelter—Park Project—DDB Depreciation

Year	DDB Depreciation	Taxable Income	Cash-Flow Shelter	Tax-Loss Shelter	Total Shelter
1	$16,000	($ 2,800)	$6,244	$2,800	$9,044
2	9,600	4,087	2,157	0	2,157
3	5,760	8,448	0	0	0
4	4,320	10,445	0	0	0
5	4,320	11,042	0	0	0

shelter. These two types of shelter can be combined to give total periodic tax shelter and tax-shelter benefits.[9] For an illustration we shall assume the use of the double-declining-balance depreciation method (DDB) for the *Park Project*. Before proceeding, the cautionary note contained in the last chapter is repeated: that for tax purposes DDB depreciation would not currently be permitted for such a project, and it is used as an example here only for simplicity of illustration.[10]

The annual depreciation expense amounts for the 5 years of the *Park Project*, using the DDB depreciation method, were presented in Table 4–2, and are shown again in Table 5–4, together with the annual taxable income that would result with the DDB depreciation method, and the corresponding tax-shelter amounts.

As indicated in Table 5–4, with the use of DDB depreciation, a loss of $2,800 is experienced in the first year of the *Park Project*. This loss gives tax-loss shelter of that amount, which when added to the cash-flow shelter of $6,244 yields total tax shelter of $9,044 for the period. It will be recalled that with straight-line depreciation the first year's total tax shelter amounted to only $1,044 (all in the form of cash-flow shelter). The $8,000 difference between the two tax shelter figures is the amount of additional depreciation expense generated by the use of accelerated depreciation.

Figure 5–1 illustrates the pattern over the 5 years of the *Park Project* of total tax shelter generated with straight-line depreciation, contrasted with the double-declining balance method of depreciation.

[10] Another application of accelerated depreciation is contained in the *Garden Apartment Project* example in Chapter 7.

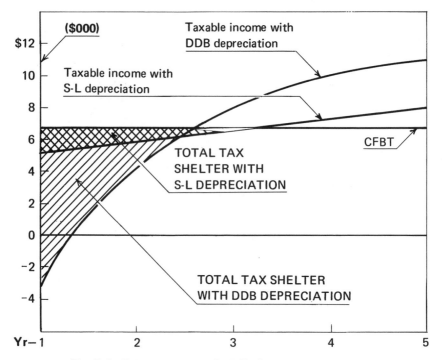

Fig. 5–1. Total tax shelter, Park Project.

The total tax-shelter amounts for the original *Park Project* data, using straight-line depreciation, are included in the investment profile in Table 5–1, earlier in the chapter.

Analyzing Tax-Shelter Benefits

Thus far we have discussed techniques for measuring the amount of periodic tax shelter expected to be generated by an investment proposal. Further, we stated that the dollar value of the immediate taxes saved as a result of such tax-shelter amounts can be found by multiplying the estimated tax-shelter amount for each year by the investor's estimated marginal tax rate for the same years.

We have not, however, developed any rate-of-return or other techniques that can be used for measuring the *relative worth* of estimated tax-shelter savings, that is, relative to owners' investment, or to alternative projects. A technique for finding an overall rate-of-return for real estate projects is discussed in Chapter 7. Because that technique uses after-tax cash flow data, the tax-shelter benefits, if any, would be taken into account, along with other cash benefits. To approach the problem of developing a separate relative-return measure for tax-shelter benefits, we must look into the general pattern of tax-shelter benefits over the useful life of the property. For the reasons previously cited, tax-shelter benefits are usually highest in the early years of an investment, and thereafter steadily decline and disappear. In many cases the benefits disappear approximately mid-way through the useful life of the property. As a consequence of this pattern the early years' tax savings are offset to some extent by extra taxes in the later years of the project.

For the professional investor described earlier in this section, who anticipates that lowered income from his practice will move him into a much lower tax bracket at a time roughly coinciding with the expected disappearance of tax-shelter savings, the higher taxable income received from real estate investment in the later years would be taxed at lower rates. One possible approach for estimating his overall tax-shelter benefits would be to multiply the amount of the immediate tax shelter by the difference between the tax rates expected to apply in the early years and in the later years. One would then add the amount that it is estimated could be earned on the use of the tax dollars saved and the taxes merely deferred until the future payment date. This could then provide the basis for a rate-of-return analysis.

For real estate investors, on the other hand, who expect no significant change in their tax bracket during the useful life of a project, the practice has often been to hold property for the early years only, that is, to sell the property when tax-shelter benefits disappear, or are substantially reduced. A rough, overall tax-shelter measure for this situation would be to add up the total tax-shelter savings that it is estimated will be achieved during the limited holding period, and relate the total savings to the amount invested. A more complete rate-of-return analysis, however, would involve *depreciation recapture* and other factors that will be considered in later chapters of this book.

In sum, it is convenient to calculate and include in an investment profile, the amount of future periodic tax shelter expected to be generated by the real estate project being analyzed, as in Table 5–1 for the *Park Project*. These data will be useful in identifying the tax-shelter features of the investment and the degree of dependence of project returns on the continuance of favorable tax-shelter legislation. Such data are useful also in helping to determine holding-period strategy, as described in Chapter 10. Some possible approaches were suggested for measuring overall project return from tax-shelter benefits for two different types of investors; however, the most comprehensive rate-of-return approach would be the discounted cash flow analysis, which takes tax-shelter benefits into account along with other features of the investment proposal, as discussed in Chapter 7.[11]

SUMMARY

In addition to the various levels of accounting income available for use in measuring the anticipated periodic benefits associated with investments in real estate, taxpaying investors often find it advantageous to measure prospective cash flow and tax-shelter benefits. These last two forms of periodic investment benefits were analzed in some detail in the present chapter.

Periodic cash flow. Because a real estate project's income figures that are based on traditional accounting concepts will often differ sharply from the same project's cash-flow figures, and many investors are concerned about a project's cash-generation potential, the cash-flow return measures have been widely used, either alone, or in conjunction with income measures. The pre-tax and after-tax flows for a particular year can be calculated with the use of Equations 5–1 and 5–3.

Some useful techniques for measuring the size of the estimated future cash flow in relation to the amount of cash invested in the project are represented by Equations 5–2 and 5–4. *Pre-tax cash yield* is the prospective overall before-tax cash return for the project, based on the assumption that yearly project cash flows are of at least approximately equal amounts. *After-tax*

---

[11] Another way of computing a rate-of-return contribution for tax-shelter benefits is to calculate the rate of return on the tax savings expected to be generated because of the project's future interest and depreciation deductions. See, for example, Paul F. Wendt and Sui N. Wong, "Investment Performance: Common Stocks versus Apartment Houses," *The Journal of Finance,* December, 1965, pp. 633–46.

cash return, on the other hand, measures after-tax cash return on investment for each individual year of the planned holding period. The *cash payback period* measures the time it is expected will be required for incoming cash flows to pay back the equity investor's original cash outlay.

Tax shelter. Real estate is looked to by many investors as a source of tax-shelter benefits. In this chapter tax shelter was defined to be the amount of periodic cash income that is sheltered from *immediate* federal income taxes. The two components of total tax shelter for a particular year are as follows: (1) *cash-flow shelter,* being the shelter of project-related cash flows; and (2) *tax-loss shelter,* being the shelter, equal in amount to the project's operating loss during the period, of the investor's other income. Equation 5–5 can be used to measure the amount of cash-flow shelter.

The amount of immediate tax savings for each year of the project that will result from total estimated tax shelter can be found by multiplying each year's projected tax shelter amount by the investor's estimated marginal tax rates for the corresponding years. Tax-shelter benefits are often found to be highest in the early years of a project and then to disappear about mid-way through the useful life of the property. While some rough measures can be made of the shelter returns in relation to the amount invested in the project, the most comprehensive rate-of-return approach would be the discounted cash-flow analysis, discussed in detail in Chapter 7.

6

Price Appreciation

Even when an investor is seeking primarily periodic investment benefits he cannot be indifferent to the changing market value of the producing real-estate asset—any more than the investor in long-term corporate bonds or mortgages can ignore the price fluctuations of his bonds or mortgages if he plans to sell them short of maturity. Other real estate investors look to price appreciation as the exclusive, or at least as the essential investment goal, with any periodic returns considered as extra or peripheral benefits. Many, if not most, of the fortunes in real estate investment have, in fact, been generated by extremely favorable value changes in investment property.

In analyzing price appreciation benefits it is necessary to define and measure the cash proceeds expected to be received at the time of property disposition, which will be the source of funds from which price appreciation gains will be realized. Of course real estate may be disposed of in many ways, but in the present chapter the focus is on the *cash* sale of property. Other disposition forms such as installment-basis sales and property exchanges are discussed in Part III. It is also assumed for most of this chapter that the investor has a predetermined holding period for each project being analyzed, and we reserve for a later chapter the discussion of holding-period strategies.

PRE-TAX SALE PROCEEDS

Because of the prevailing high level of federal income taxes we must give consideration to the tax provisions relating to the cash sale of real property, especially the capital gains and depreciation recapture provisions. We first, however, discuss the measurement of pre-tax sale proceeds.

Measuring Pre-Tax Proceeds

For unmortgaged properties the selling price or residual value represents the pre-tax cash proceeds of sale. The two expressions *selling price* and *residual value* will be used here to refer to the amount of cash received, net of any selling expenses. When a mortgage loan is outstanding at the time of sale, the amount of the loan would have to be subtracted from the selling price to obtain the amount of before-tax cash proceeds of sale. The generalized equation can, therefore, be expressed as Equation 6–1, where *CFBT(sale)* represents before-tax cash flow from the sale of the property.

$$CFBT(sale) = Selling\ price\ -\ Unpaid\ mortage \qquad [6\text{–}1]$$

Because the amount of the mortgage outstanding at the end of the planned holding period is known in advance, the real task in applying Equation 6–1 is in forecasting the future selling price. In the *Park Project* example (discussed in the past two chapters), with the selling price estimated at $115,900, and the unpaid mortgage equal to zero at the time of sale at the end of the fifth year, the CFBT(sale) equals $115,900.

Forecasting price changes. As with returns from any sort of investment, the only true measurement can take place after the investment is terminated. Only when the investment is liquidated can one be certain of the actual income and outgo figures. Nonetheless, the investor must work with projections when considering the purchase of property. The existence of long-term leases, especially net leases with top-quality tenants, helps make more certain the present estimates of future periodic benefits, and if the lease rentals are tied to an appropriate inflation-rate index, the benefits can even be forecasted in "real terms." Even in this latter case, however, future tax impacts and other governmental impacts on cash flows cannot be known with certainty in advance.

Despite the difficulties of forecasting periodic returns, the future selling price is generally the more difficult future benefit to forecast. In Chapter 3, some forecasting techniques were considered that sometimes are appropriate for use in forecasting selling prices, including the use of the *gross income multiplier* (GIM), the *annual-growth forecasting model,* and the *super-growth-rate model.*

Measuring Price Appreciation and Equity Build-up

As previously indicated with Equation 6–1, the pre-tax cash proceeds of sale can be found by subtracting the outstanding mortgage debt at the time of sale from the estimated selling price. Presented in Equation 6–2 is an alternative formulation for determining the same *CFBT(sale)* figure.

$$CFBT(sale) = Cash\ down\ payment + Equity\ build\text{-}up \qquad [6\text{-}2]$$
$$+\ Price\ appreciation$$

The formulation of Equation 6–2 suggests that the amount of cash proceeds (before tax) to be received at the time of sale is equal to the total cash invested in the project by the owner (his cash down-payment and his equity build-up) plus any price appreciation (or less any price depreciation) expected to be experienced at the time of sale. The alternative Equation 6–2, while giving the same result as Equation 6–1, is presented principally to introduce the price appreciation and equity build-up concepts, which will be used as we proceed with additional real estate investment analyses. These two concepts will be defined and discussed in the following sections.

Price appreciation. The term price appreciation (or price depreciation) is used here in the usual sense of its being the difference between the selling price and the cost of the property, with *cost* here defined to include the original purchase price plus the cost of any additional capital improvements made to the property prior to sale. The concept of price appreciation, or price gain, is to be distinguished from *capital gain*, which is a term used for federal income tax purposes, as discussed later in this chapter. For the *Park Project*, with an estimated selling price at the end of the fifth year of $115,900, and a cost of $100,000, the price appreciation amounts to $15,900.

Equity build-up. In the typical real estate investment financed with a mortgage loan calling for periodic amortization payments that reduce the outstanding mortgage debt, the investor is adding to his cash investment in the project, that is, building up his equity position during the course of the holding period. Hence, the development of the commonly used expression *equity build-up*, which we shall define as *the cumulative total of mortgage loan amortization payments*. Mathematically, this definition can be expressed as Equation 6–3, where t is the individual year in which the amortization payment is made, n is the number of years in the holding period, and *Amortization* is the amount of the mortgage amortization payment in period t. The summation sign (Σ) with its notation, indicates the addition of all the years' payments, from year 1 through year n.

$$\text{Equity build-up} = \sum_{t=1}^{n} \text{Amortization}_t \qquad [6\text{--}3]$$

Applying Equation 6–3 to the *Park Project* data, we find that equity build-up during the planned five-year holding period is as shown below.[1] It will be noted that the $40,000 equity build-up reflects the fact that in this project the original mortgage debt of $40,000 will be completely liquidated at the end of the fifth year.

$$\text{Equity build-up} = \$6,956 + \$7,443 + \$7,964 + \$8,521 + \$9,116$$
$$= \$40,000$$

As we have computed the amount of price appreciation and equity build-up for the *Park Project*, we can now calculate the

[1] The *Park Project* amortization amounts are shown in the mortgage-loan schedule in Table 4-5.

estimated pre-tax proceeds of sale using the alternative methods of Equations 6–1 and 6–2.

1. *Using Equation 6–1:*

$$\textbf{CFBT (sale)} = \textbf{\textit{Selling price}} - \textbf{\textit{Unpaid mortgage}}$$
$$= \$115,900 \quad - \quad \$0$$
$$= \$115,900$$

2. *Using Equation 6–2:*

$$\textbf{CFBT (sale)} = \textbf{\textit{Cash down-payment}} + \textbf{\textit{Equity build-up}} + \textbf{\textit{Price appreciation}}$$
$$= \$60,000 \qquad + \$40,000 \qquad + \$15,900$$
$$= \$115,900$$

The changing pattern of the pre-tax cash flow and its component elements are diagramed in Figure 6–1, for the 5-year life of the *Park Project.* The annual equity build-up figures and the CFBT(sale) figure are included in the complete *Park Project* investment profile in Table 6–1, appearing later in the chapter.

Price Appreciation Analysis

By subtracting the amount of any federal income tax obligation relating to the sale of property from the before-tax cash flow arising from sale, we obtain the after-tax proceeds of sale, which together with periodic after-tax cash flows represent the complete cash inflows for the project. These cash flows can then be used in an overall rate-of-return analysis for the project. Before considering the federal income tax provisions relating to the sale of real property and the overall rate-of-return analysis, some techniques will be described below that can be used to measure pre-tax price appreciation benefits.

For some investment projects the investor considers price appreciation the only important goal, and he wishes to measure the return just from this source—especially if income and outgo during the planned holding period are expected to approximately offset each other, that is, if the net outgo is expected to be a relatively unimportant amount. Land is commonly the kind of property involved in this kind of investment, often with a short-term holding period planned at the time of purchase.[2] The investor

[2] Land as an investment medium is considered in detail in Chapter 12.

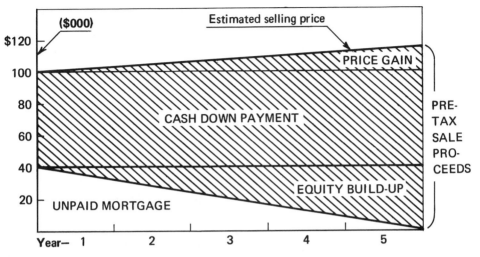

Fig. 6–1. Pre-tax sale proceeds, Park Project.

wishes a measure that focuses on price-gain returns, ignoring periodic cash flows, income taxes, and financing arrangement. For an example, let us assume that 100 feet of lake-front land can be purchased for $10,000. The investor estimates that the land can be sold in 3 years for $20,000. Assume also that the investor would not borrow funds for the investment, that carrying costs such as property taxes and insurance are nominal and to be ignored in the analysis, and that federal income taxes are also to be ignored. The question now is how to measure the prospective annual rate of return on this investment, assuming the investor would plan to sell the property at the end of three years.

Crude rate-of-return measure. The total estimated price appreciation in the lake-front property mentioned just above amounts to $10,000—the difference between the estimated selling price of $20,000 and the cost of $10,000. The gain represents 100 per cent of the original $10,000 investment. As a rough, or crude, *annual rate-of-return* measure for the planned 3-year holding period, one could assume that one-third of the price gain ($3,333) would be earned each year, and then find the annual rate of return to be equal to 33 per cent [$3,333/$10,000].

Compound rate-of-return measure.   A more precise rate-of-return measure would be to assume compound annual growth in the value of the property, and therefore a rate of return based on the increasingly larger price appreciation earned in each of the three years of the planned holding period. One can find the rate-of-return figure by solving for *g* in the *annual growth forecasting model* presented as follows:

$$\text{Estimated future selling price} = \text{Cost } (1 + g)^n$$

It will perhaps be recalled that in the example in Chapter 3 using Equation 3–2, it was found that given a *Cost* of $100,000, and an annual growth in value (*g*) of 3 per cent, the property value grew to $115,900 in 5 years. In our present lake-front land example, we are given all values for the equation, except for *g*, as follows:

$$\$20,000 = \$10,000 \, (1 + g)^3$$

To solve for *g*, which we now take to represent the annual rate of return, or *internal rate of return,* we use the *trial and error method.*   That is, a possible rate is selected and plugged into the equation. If both sides of the equation are not equal, a second rate is attempted; then a third, and so forth, until both sides are finally made equal. As in our previous use of Equation 3–2, the compound sum factors in the Appendix (*Column 1*) can be used to expedite this process. Detailed illustrations of finding the internal rate of return with the trial and error method are given in Chapter 7. In the lake-front land example we find that *g* equals 26 per cent.

Target multiple.   Some investors seeking price gains make use of what might be called a target multiple. This is best described by examples: "the property is expected to triple in four years," or to "double in three years." The latter case is what we have for the lake-front land investment just discussed. This is obviously a rough form of measuring a proposed investment's return, especially as many investors focus primarily on the target multiple itself; for example, double in value, with only secondary emphasis on the time expected to achieve that target. However, for the investor practiced in investing in projects featuring substantial possible gains and at the same time involving a high degree of uncertainty as to the size and timing of the gains, the target multiple approach can be useful.

It should be noted that if the investor wishes to convert the target multiple to the rate-of-return measure, it can be done by the technique described above for the lake-front land example. That is, the target multiple of "double in three years" is equivalent to a crude rate of return of 33 per cent, and an internal rate of return of 26 per cent.

Leverage. Just as the periodic returns on owners' investment can be magnified by employing leverage, that is, the use of borrowed funds, so too with returns received at the time of sale. As high as the expected returns are in the lake-front land example above, the prospective returns to the owner would be much higher if a significant part of the $10,000 initial cost had been borrowed at a reasonable and fixed interest cost.

AFTER-TAX SALE PROCEEDS

The amount of taxes payable on a gain at the time of sale will depend on the tax provisions expected to prevail at the planned time of sale. We shall discuss in this section the current federal income tax provisions, but note that while the basic tax structure has and probably will continue to remain unchanged, the tax provisions relating to capital gains and depreciation recapture were made more restrictive by the Tax Reform Acts of 1969 and 1976, and that some foresee the possibility of future additional changes unfavorable to the realty investor. The amount of taxes payable at the planned time of sale therefore should be treated as an uncertain variable, as with the estimated selling price.

Capital Gains Taxes

One of the attractive features of real estate investing has been that lower tax rates have been applied to *qualifying* capital gains received at the time of sale. This advantage is not unique to real estate investing and applies to qualifying gains received on the sale of many other assets, such as corporate securities. Because, however, many real estate properties are heavily depreciated prior to sale, the amount of gains are often magnified. Depreciation recapture provisions come into play here, as described later in this section.

Before discussing details of the tax treatment of capital gains and losses, and the various statutory requirements to be met to qualify for favorable tax treatment, we must first define capital gains and losses, as the terms are used for federal income tax purposes.

Capital gains and losses defined. The amount of capital gain (or loss) experienced at the time of sale is computed by subtracting the *Adjusted basis* of the property (at the time of sale) from the selling price. The *Adjusted basis* is calculated by subtracting the amount of *Accumulated depreciation* expense taken on the property prior to sale *from* the cost of the property, with *Cost* defined to include the costs of any capital improvements. In mathematical shorthand we have Equations 6–4 and 6–4a.[3]

$$\text{Adjusted basis} = \text{Cost} - \text{Accumulated depreciation} \qquad [6\text{–}4]$$

$$\text{Capital gain (loss)} = \text{Selling price} - \text{Adjusted basis} \qquad [6\text{–}4a]$$

Applying Equations 6–4 and 6–4a and to the *Park Project* example, we have: *Adjusted basis* = \$100,000 − \$40,000 = \$60,000; and *Capital gain* = \$115,900 − \$60,000 = \$55,900. For bookkeeping purposes separate data would be kept on the costs, depreciation amounts, and so forth for each of the property components of land and improvements; and if the situation required, separate records for individual facilities or structures included in the project's improvements. To simplify the *Park Project* illustration we have lumped all property components together in computing the capital gain, with the assumption that *all* com-

[3] Equations 6–4 and 6–4a could, of course, be combined as follows:

$$\text{Capital gain (loss)} = \text{Selling price} - \text{Cost} + \text{Accumulated depreciation}$$

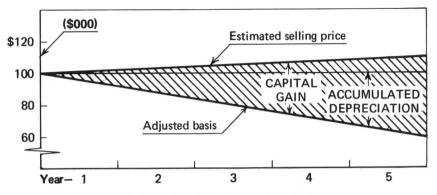

Fig. 6–2. Estimated capital gains, Park Project.

ponent values grow at 3 per cent a year, with the total value of the property increasing from $100,000 to $115,900 in 5 years. Figure 6–2 illustrates the *Park Project* capital gain growth pattern over the 5-year holding period.

As stated above, capital improvements are treated for tax purposes as additions to cost, and thereby serve to increase the adjusted basis, and to reduce the taxable capital gain. This raises the issue whether cash expended on investment property is to be considered a *repair expense* that is chargeable against periodic income taxed at ordinary rates, or is to be treated as a *capital improvement*. In the latter treatment the cost incurred is added to the capital investment in the property and cannot be written off as an expense in the year in which the cost is incurred. Rather, the cost will be gradually written off in future years through depreciation expenses.

In general, when one is adding to the permanent use of the property, then an *improvement* is involved. If one is merely retaining the present value of the property, then a *repair* is involved. For example, adding a room would be consider an improvement, whereas painting a room is generally considered a repair expense. Legal advice may be required in interpreting a particular expenditure. When the taxpayer is undertaking *a general plan of reconditioning*, then the painting and other expenditures that would otherwise be considered repair expenses must be capitalized, that is, considered as improvements.

Requirements for favorable capital gains tax treatment. Whether a particular gain or loss, such as the $55,900 gain just computed for the Park Project, will qualify for favorable capital gains treatment, that is, capital gains tax rates to be applicable, or will be taxable as ordinary income, that is, as periodic taxable income, will depend on whether the particular gain or loss on the sale meets the various statutory requirements described below.

Property qualifications. Two basic categories of real estate properties (aside from personal residences) are specified in the Internal Revenue Code as qualifying for capital gains treatment; (1) *capital assets,* which are assets held as investment property rather than assets purchased for resale in the ordinary course of a firm's business; and (2) *Section 1231 assets,* which are assets used in a trade or business (not as inventory), and are granted capital gains treatment as to net long-term gains. These 1231 assets receive a unique treatment in the case of net long-term losses, as discussed later in this chapter. Such assets are named for the pertinent section of the Internal Revenue Code. As long as rented real estate is not held primarily for sale to customers in the ordinary course of business, then for tax purposes it is generally considered to be a Section 1231 asset, although there are instances when it will be treated as a capital asset.

Investor qualifications. To qualify for the favorable capital gains rates, the sale must be made by an *investor* rather than by a *dealer, as relates to the particular property sold.* The distinction is generally expressed in terms of the dealer's being one who held the particular piece of real property primarily for sale to customers in the ordinary course of business; that is, as an inventory item analagous to a car held for sale by an automobile dealer. The investor, on the other hand, is one who held the property as an investment. Whether the seller will be found to be a dealer or an investor for a particular property sale will depend on a combination of factors. The courts have applied several tests, such as the following: [4]

—The purpose or reason for the taxpayer's acquisition of the property and disposing of it

—The continuity of sales or sales-related activity over a period of time

[4] *Standard Federal Tax Reporter,* 72 Vol. 5A (Chicago: Commerce Clearing House, Inc., 1971), p. 55,053. There are special tax provisions relating to the sale of subdivision lots, as described in Chapter 16.

—The number and frequency of sales
—The extent to which the taxpayer or his agents engaged in sales activities by developing or improving the property, soliciting customers, or advertising
—The substantiality of sales when compared to other sources of the taxpayer's income
—The desire to liquidate unexpectedly obtained land holdings (such as by inheritance)
—Over-all reluctance to sell the property
—The length of time that the property was held
—(and, more recently) The substantiality of the gain obtained on the sale

Holding period. The favorable capital gains tax treatment is available only for long-term capital gains, which means that the property must be held for *more than six months.* Gains on property held for less than or just six months are taxed as ordinary income. However, for 1977, the required holding period is increased to *more than nine months;* for years after 1977, the holding period increases to *more than one year.*

Assuming that the investor in the *Park Project* example does not hold an inventory of mobile-home parks, it appears that the $55,900 gain would qualify for favorable capital gains tax treatment because the property itself would be considered a capital asset, and the holding period exceeds six months, and accordingly qualifies as a long-term capital gain. The currently applicable tax treatment of qualifying capital gains and losses will now be described.

Tax-treatment of qualifying capital gains. Before applying the special capital gains tax rates one must first offset the year's long-term capital losses against the year's long-term capital gains, to obtain net long-term gains (or losses). Short-term capital losses are offset against short-term capital gains to obtain net short-term capital gains (or losses). If a net short-term gain results, then this is taxed at ordinary income tax rates. If a short-term loss is obtained this is subtracted from *net* long-term gains, if any. If there is an excess of net long-term capital gains over net short-term losses, then this excess is subject to the favorable capital gains treatment.

For the individual investor receiving qualifying net long-term capital gains in excess of short-term capital losses, *one-half of the net long-term gain* is included with the investor's other income to be taxed at ordinary income tax rates. The traditional maximum capital gains tax rate of 25 per cent applies currently to only the first $50,000 of gains, but not on gains in excess of $50,000. The effective maximum rate for gains over $50,000 is 35 per cent, because of the 70 per cent ceiling on the ordinary tax rate.

The tax rate on net long-term capital gains for *corporations* is 30 per cent, compared with the 48 per cent marginal ordinary income tax rate for corporate taxable income exceeding $50,000. If capital gains and other corporate income together total $25,000 or less, the 20 per cent ordinary tax rate would be applied (and 22 per cent on the next $25,000), rather than the 30 per cent capital gains rate.

The current rates outlined above were programmed by the 1969 Tax Reform Act to be more stringent than the previous rates, which for many years featured a 25 per cent maximum rate on all individual and corporate net long-term gains. The investor in forecasting future cash flows should consider the possibilities of future changes in the capital gains rates.

There are three special situations where capital gains that otherwise would be taxed at capital gains rates are not so taxed:

1. The depreciation recapture portion of capital gains is taxed at ordinary income tax rates (described later in this chapter).
2. The fifteen per cent tax on preferences applies to capital gains.
3. The investment interest deduction limitation affects capital gains tax treatment, for investment interest obligations created or paid before September 11, 1975.

The last two "special situations" are described below.

Fifteen per cent tax on preferences. The capital gains tax is an area touched by the special 15 per cent tax on preferences. Another preference item relating to real estate investment is accelerated depreciation (discussed in Chapter 4). *For individuals,* 50 per cent of the excess of net long-term capital gain over net short-term capital loss is considered the amount of tax preference subject to the 15 per cent tax. *For corporations,* the amount of tax preference is equal to: the excess long-term capital gain, multiplied by the difference between the corporation's regular tax rate and its capital gains rate, divided by the corporation's regular tax rate. For example, if a corporation's excess net long-term capital gain amounts to $50,000, and the company's regular tax rate and capital gains tax rate are 48 per cent and 30 per cent, respectively, then the amount of tax preference would equal:

$$(\$50,000) \; \frac{0.48 - 0.30}{0.48} = \$50,000 \times 0.375 = \$18,750$$

For both individuals and corporations, the amount of the capital gain preference would be added to other preference amounts and taxed at 15 per cent, after deduction of the allowable exemption, as described in Chapter 4.

Limitation on investment interest. As discussed in Chapter 4, the amount of the deduction allowed for investment interest in a particular year is increased by the amount of any excess of net long-term capital gain over short-term capital loss. To the extent that interest is actually made deductible because of such excess gain, then such gain is taxed at ordinary income tax rates, and such gain is also exempt from the tax on preferences.

The Tax Reform Act of 1976, however, eliminated excess capital gains from the calculation of the allowable investment interest deduction—for interest obligations created after September 10, 1975. As noted in Chapter 4, the interest deduction limitation provisions apply to *non-corporate* taxpayers.

Tax treatment of qualifying capital losses. If the taxpayer's offset of long-term capital losses against long-term capital gains results in a net long-term capital loss, or the taxpayer ends the year with a net short-term loss, then special tax rules apply. The tax treatment of capital losses again depends upon the individual-vs.-corporation distinction. *For individuals,* 100 per cent of the short-term losses, and 50 per cent of the long-term losses, up to a combined maximum amount of $1,000 can be offset against *ordinary income* in the year of loss. Any excess over $1,000 can be carried forward indefinitely to offset up to $1,000 of ordinary income in individual future years. By the 1976 Tax Reform Act, the maximum deductible amount rises from $1,000 to $2,000 in 1977, and to $3,000 per year starting in 1978.

For *corporations,* net short-term losses and net long-term losses cannot be offset against ordinary income, with the exception noted below, but net capital losses can be carried back three years and forward five years, to be applied against net capital gains received in those years. The exception referred to, by which corporate losses can be offset against *ordinary income,* applies in the case of net long-term losses suffered on the sale of Section 1231 assets, as were previously described. Net losses on sales of such assets can be carried back against ordinary income for three years and forward five years.

Measuring After-Tax Proceeds

Once the federal income tax obligation relating to the cash sale is computed by applying the capital gains tax provisions described above, and the depreciation recapture provisions described in the next section, the after-tax proceeds of sale can be found by simply subtracting the tax figure from the CFBT(sale) figure. An alternative procedure would be to subtract the amount of the mortgage outstanding at the time of sale, and the tax amount from the estimated selling price, as symbolized in Equation 6–5, where *CFAT(sale)* represents cash flow after tax from the sale, and *Taxes* are federal income taxes.

$$CFAT\ (sale) = Selling\ price - Unpaid\ mortgage - Taxes \quad [6\text{–}5]$$

Park property sale. In the *Park Project* we have assumed a 30 per cent marginal tax rate for all 5 years of the project, and therefore, we assume, that the investor retains the 30 per cent rate in the fifth year despite the large capital gain received in that year. This would be the case if other ordinary or capital losses offset the amount of this particular gain. Therefore, to find the amount of federal income tax payable on the sale, we multiply one-half the amount of the capital gain ($55,900/2), $27,950, by the investor's marginal tax rate of 30 per cent. The resulting tax amounts to $8,385. This tax obligation is not altered by the depreciation recapture provisions, because straight-line depreciation was used for the project (as discussed in the next section of this chapter).[5]

---

[5] An adjustment should be made for the 15 per cent tax on preferences' impact on the *Park Project* capital gain, if it is anticipated that the investor would have net preference amounts exceeding the authorized exemptions.

The after-tax cash flow arising from the sale of the *Park Project* property amounts to $107,515, computed by deducting the tax of $8,385 from the CFBT(sale) figure of $115,900. The CFAT(sale) figure can also be found by using Equation 6–5, as follows: $CFAT(sale) = \$115{,}900 - \$0 - \$8{,}385 = \$107{,}515$. This figure is included in the investment profile for the *Park Project* in Table 6–1, and completes the cash flow data collection for that investment proposal. The *Inwood ROR* and the *DCF ROR* measures contained in the financial analysis section of the profile are calculated in the next chapter.

Depreciation Recapture

In the *Park Project* example, the tax related to the sale of the property was paid not just on the $15,900 *price gain,* but rather on the larger amount of capital gain of $55,900. The $40,000 additional taxable gain resulted because $40,000 depreciation expense was taken on the property, while in actual fact the property did not depreciate in value at all. Therefore, it could be said that too much depreciation expense was taken, in the amount of $40,000. At the time of sale, therefore, the investor, through a decrease in his adjusted basis, must pay tax on the excess depreciation amount of $40,000.

It is important to note that the investor paid tax at the rate of only 15 percent on this $40,000 excess depreciation,[6] while he saved taxes at the rate of 30 per cent of the $40,000 depreciation expenses by charging that amount against ordinary income taxable at 30 per cent during the course of the five-year-holding period. Hence, the investor actually saved taxes rather than merely deferred taxes by means of his periodic depreciation write-offs.[7] This process has been referred to as *converting ordinary income into capital gains.* It will also be observed that while the investor ultimately paid some tax on the excess depreciation, the investor had the use of the deferred tax funds up until the time the tax was paid on the sale.

[6] Because the taxpayer was taxed on only one-half of the amount of the gain, in effect he paid tax at one-half his ordinary income tax rate, which in this case was 30 per cent.

[7] The amount of the tax savings would be measured by multiplying the *excess depreciation* amount by the capital gains tax rate, less the investor's ordinary tax rate.

TABLE 6–1. Investment Profile—Park Project

	Year—1	2	3	4	5
		Periodic Returns			
Gross Possible Income	$24,000	$24,000	$24,000	$24,000	$24,000
less: Vacancies and bad debts	1,000	1,000	1,000	1,000	1,000
Gross Income, Actual	$23,000	$23,000	$23,000	$23,000	$23,000
less: Operating expenses	7,000	7,000	7,000	7,000	7,000
Net Operating Income	$16,000	$16,000	$16,000	$16,000	$16,000
less: Depreciation expense	8,000	8,000	8,000	8,000	8,000
Interest expense	2,800	2,313	1,792	1,235	638
Taxable Income	$ 5,200	$ 5,687	$ 6,208	$ 6,765	$ 7,362
less: Income taxes (30%)	1,560	1,706	1,862	2,029	2,209
Earnings After Tax	$ 3,640	$ 3,981	$ 4,346	$ 4,736	$ 5,153
plus: Depreciation expense	8,000	8,000	8,000	8,000	8,000
less: Mortgage amortization	6,956	7,443	7,964	8,521	9,118
plus: Tax-loss savings	0	0	0	0	0
Cash Flow After Tax	$ 4,684	$ 4,538	$ 4,382	$ 4,215	$ 4,035
Cash Flow Before Tax	$ 6,244	$ 6,244	$ 6,244	$ 6,244	$ 6,244
		Tax Shelter			
Cash-Flow Shelter	$ 1,044	$ 557	$ 36	$ 0	$ 0
Tax-Loss Shelter	0	0	0	0	0
Total Tax Shelter	$ 1,044	$ 557	$ 36	$ 0	$ 0
Total Tax-Shelter Savings	$ 313	$ 167	$ 11	$ 0	$ 0

	Sale Proceeds	
Selling Price		$115,900
less: Unpaid mortgage		0
Cash Flow Before Tax from Sale		$115,900
less: Income taxes		8,385
Cash Flow After Tax from Sale		$107,515

TABLE 6-1. Continued

	Year—1	2	3	4	5
		Mortgage Loan			
Mortgage Loan	$40,000	$40,000	$40,000	$40,000	$40,000
Equity Build-up	$ 6,956	$14,399	$22,363	$30,884	$40,000
Unpaid Mortgage	$33,044	$25,601	$17,637	$ 9,116	$ 0

		Financial Analysis			
GIM	4.3				
Expense Ratio	29.2%				
Income Yield	16.0%				
Pre-Tax Cash Yield	10.4%				
Inwood ROR	18.2%				
DCF ROR	18.4%				
Cash Payback Period	5 years				
Return on Equity	6.1%	5.9%	5.8%	5.8%	5.7%
After-Tax Cash Return	7.8%	7.6%	7.3%	7.0%	6.7%

Because the tax savings arising from the situation just described can be substantial in the early years of an investment when accelerated depreciation methods are used, many investors were led to sell properties after a relatively short holding period. The federal government, in turn, developed increasingly strict limitations on such real estate tax savings by *recapturing* some part of the excess depreciation; that is, applied ordinary income tax rates rather than capital gains rates to a part of the excess depreciation.

The basic recapture rules, set by the 1969 Tax Reform Act, call for complete, or 100 per cent, recapture of depreciation on the following part of the excess depreciation for real estate properties acquired after 1969: that part of the excess depreciation that represents the excess of accelerated depreciation actually deducted by the investor *over* what the straight-line depreciation amount *would have been,* had that method been used. Therefore, for real estate properties, depreciation recapture applies only where an accelerated depreciation has been used.

There were, however, *two exceptions* to the recapture rules of the 1969 TRA, for properties acquired since 1969: (1) property held for twelve months or less, *all* depreciation is subject to recapture; and (2) for residential rental housing and rehabilitation improvements, less than 100 per cent recapture applies—if the property is held for more than 8 years, 4 months; or for more than 20 months on government-subsidized projects.[8] For properties acquired prior to 1969, less than 100 per cent recapture is made of the excess of accelerated depreciation over straight-line depreciation under tax provisions that will not be detailed here.

The 1976 TRA modified the second recapture exception described in the last paragraph to the extent that post-1975 excess depreciation on residential rental property will be subject to 100 per cent recapture. The 1976 TRA also made more restrictive the recapture provisions relating to government-subsidized housing.

For an example of depreciation recapture, we return once again to the *Park Project*. Let us assume for now that *Park* depreciated its property with double-declining-balance depreciation, and sold it at the end of only 2 years. We assume that the selling price of the property increased 3 per cent a year during the first 2 years, rising from $100,000 to $106,100. The total declining-balance depreciation for the first 2 years would total $25,600 [$16,000 + $9,600], compared with what the straight-line depreciation would have been during the first 2 years, $16,000 [$8,000 + $8,000]. The $9,600 excess of accelerated depreciation over straight-line represents the amount of depreciation subject to recapture at the time of sale, and therefore taxable at ordinary tax rates rather than at capital gains rates.

The total federal income tax obligation arising from the property sale would be $6,195, as can be calculated in two steps:

1. *Compute Capital Gain*

$$
\begin{aligned}
\textit{Adjusted basis} &= \textit{Cost} - \textit{Accumulated depreciation} \\
&= \$100,000 - \$25,600 \\
&= \$74,400 \\
\textit{Capital gain} &= \textit{Selling price} - \textit{Adjusted basis} \\
&= \$106,100 - \$74,400 \\
&= \$31,700
\end{aligned}
$$

---

[8] For each full month after the stated holding periods, the percentage of the excess over straight-line that is recaptured drops by 1 per cent.

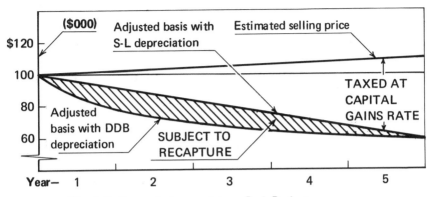

Fig. 6–3. Depreciation recapture, Park Project.

2. *Apply Tax Rates*

	Amount	Rate	Tax
Recaptured depreciation	$ 9,600 ×	0.30 =	$2,880
Balance of taxable gain	22,100 ×	0.15 =	3,315
Total tax obligation			$6,195

In Figure 6–3 is presented a diagram showing the excess over straight-line depreciation that would be subject to recapture if the *Park* property were sold before the end of the 5-year holding period, assuming the use of the double-declining-balance depreciation method.

With this discussion of depreciation recapture, we have completed our description of the federal income tax provisions related to the cash sale of real estate. We, therefore, have completed the developments necessary to determine complete after-tax cash flow projections for a real estate investment proposal, including periodic returns and sale proceeds. In the next chapter techniques are presented that can be used to find a rate of return encompassing all such cash flows. We repeat, however, that a *cash sale* has been assumed thus far. In Part III of this book we consider other forms of property disposition that can be used to reduce the income tax burdens that may apply to a cash sale of property.

SUMMARY

For most real estate equity investments, the cash proceeds of sale represent a significant part of the expected returns; and in some cases, property value increases represent the principal investment goal. The pre-tax proceeds of sale can be calculated with Equation 6–1: *CFBT(sale) = Selling price − Unpaid mortgage.* Forecasting the future selling price of a property can be a most difficult task. A forecasting technique that is sometimes suitable is to assume a certain uniform annual growth (or decline) in market value, or to assume a variant pattern such as super-growth rate for a few years, followed by years of more normal growth in market value.

An alternative method for determining the pre-tax cash proceeds of sale is symbolized by Equation 6–2: *CFBT(sale) = cash down-payment + Equity build-up + Price appreciation.* This formulation suggests that sales proceeds will be equal to the amount invested in the project by the owner, that is, his cash down payment and equity build-up (accumulated mortgage amortization payments), plus any price appreciation (or less any price depreciation).

Where an expected price gain is the dominant consideration, some rough, relative-return measures can be used for a quick analysis of proposed property acquisitions. Three such techniques were discussed in this chapter, including the *crude rate-of-return measure,* the *compound rate-of-return measure,* and the *target multiple.* For a comprehensive return analysis, however, of the cash flow expected to be received at the time of sale, such cash flow should be adjusted to an after-tax basis. This, in turn, calls for consideration of the capital gains and depreciation recapture provisions. These important provisions were reviewed in the last part of the chapter.

7

Risk/Return Analysis

In the present chapter techniques are discussed that can be used to measure the overall rate of return for a project. These techniques take account of both periodic returns and sale proceeds, and they also take account of the time value of money. Rate-of-return measures by themselves, however, are incomplete measures of the attractiveness of a proposed real estate investment. Among other factors to consider would be the degree of riskiness of the proposed investment. We complete this chapter, and Part II, with some definitions and techniques that can be employed in dealing with investment risks.

With the increasing availability of and familiarity with the computer, along with the widening application of quantitative analysis in corporate finance and in securities analysis, there has recently been an increase in the use of quantitative analysis (often computer-aided) in real estate investment analysis, especially by large institutional investors. Such sophisticated techniques are especially useful in analyzing projects where the investment cash flows are at least partially predetermined by contract, such as with sale-leaseback arrangements; and consequently, where relatively hard data are available.

Before presenting the comprehensive return techniques of this chapter, we note our continuing use of two important assumptions. *First,* it is assumed that the investor plans to hold the property for a given number of years, and seeks to find the prospective return for that given holding period, rather than to determine through analysis the appropriate length of the holding period. It will be recalled that with the *income yield* and *pre-tax-cash yield* return measures previously discussed, perpetual income and cash flow streams were assumed, and therefore it was unnecessary to specify a holding period. *Secondly,* we assume that the investor plans to sell the investment property for cash at the end of the specified holding period, rather than to dispose of the property in some other manner.

TIME-ADJUSTED RETURN ANALYSIS

The general approach used for comprehensive rate-of-return analysis takes account of *the time value of money.* The general idea is that a dollar to be received at a future date, say in one year, is considered to be worth less to the investor than a dollar received today. This would be the case even if we assumed that the future payment will be made without fail (assuming away uncertainty), and assumed that the value of the dollar, in *real terms,* will not decline within the next year (assuming away inflation). The reason that the dollar received now is worth more than the dollar to be received in one year is that the present dollar can be invested to earn a return so as to be worth more than one dollar in one year's time.

The future value of a present amount that will grow at a given rate, g, can be found by multiplying the present value amount by $(1 + g)^n$.[1] To find the present value of an amount to be received at some future date we divide by the same factor $(1 + g)^n$. This latter process is called *discounting* and is used in real estate and other investment rate-of-return analyses. As will be illustrated below, present value tables will expedite the discounting calculations, as will also, of course, the computer.

While the use of discount, or present-value, techniques for analyzing corporation capital investment projects is of relatively

---

[1] This basic formulation was previously introduced in Chapter 3 by means of Equation 3–2: *Estimated future selling price = Cost* $(1 + g)^n$.

recent origin, there is a long tradition in real estate analysis for using these techniques, most notably through the use by real estate appraisers of the so-called Inwood tables described below.[2]

Inwood Method

The Inwood method goes back to the early nineteenth century, when William Inwood developed the famed Inwood tables, which have been used by real estate appraisers as one technique for determining the present value, that is appraisal value, of an income-producing property. In particular, the tables are used by appraisers in cases where the period of future benefits does not extend into perpetuity but rather is a predetermined number of years, as is the case with leasehold operations. The Inwood tables are also used by insititutional investors for analyzing sale-leaseback investments.

The factors in the Inwood tables are based on the time-value-of money concepts described above, and the appraiser uses the tables to find present value, given certain estimated future benefits, and given an overall rate of return on the investment which is referred to by appraisers as the capitalization rate.[3] The real estate investor is generally interested in determining the capitalization rate, which we shall refer to as the *rate of return,* with a given specified asking price (present value), and specified expected future benefits. Presented in Equation 7–1 is the rate-of-return formulation using Inwood concepts. The return rate would be found by solving for r.

$$\text{Purchase price} = \sum_{t=1}^{n} \frac{\text{Net operating income}}{(1+r)^t} + \frac{\text{Selling price}}{(1+r)^n} \qquad [7\text{--}1]$$

where: t = Time period (year)
         n = Number of years in the holding period
         r = Internal rate of return (capitalization rate)

---

[2] The basic discounted cash flow techniques as used in corporate finance were developed by Joel Dean, and popularized through his book *Managerial Economics* (Englewood Cliffs, N.J.: Prentice-Hall, Inc., 1951).

[3] The student of finance will note the similarity between the appraisers' technique of finding appraisal value, and the *present value method* used in corporate capital budgeting analysis.

The preceding equation may be translated into words as follows: the cost of the property equals the present value of the future annual income returns and the future sale proceeds, when those future benefits are discounted at the rate of return, r.

The following important points will be observed regarding the rate of return obtained with the Inwood formulation:

1. The net operating income level is used as the measure of periodic benefits, or returns, and estimated selling price is used as the sale-proceeds measure; hence, depreciation and financing impacts on the project are ignored in this rate-of-return measure.
2. Federal income taxes are ignored in the analysis.
3. The rate of return obtained with this method represents the return on total investment (total purchase price) rather than the return on owners' investment. Of course, where no mortgage financing is employed, owners' investment equals total investment.

As previously mentioned, for appraisal purposes a given r, or *required rate of return,* would be imputed to find the present value of the property. For investment analysis, however, we seek the rate-of-return, r, at a given purchase price. In the familiar *Park Project,* for example, we are given the price or cost of \$100,000 for the mobile-home property; expected net operating income of \$16,000 a year for 5 years; and an estimated selling price in five years of \$115,900. Therefore, the formulation with the Inwood method would be:

$$\$100{,}000 = \sum_{t=1}^{5} \frac{\$16{,}000}{(1+r)^t} + \frac{\$115{,}900}{(1+r)^5}$$

The task at hand is to solve the equation for r. The so-called *trial and error method* is used; that is, a certain r value is assumed and plugged into the right-hand side of the equation. If the resulting value of the right-hand side of the equation is larger than the left-hand value (\$100,000 in this example), then a higher r value is assumed and the new value on the right-hand side determined. The process is continued until the right-hand side just equals the left-hand side. Tables giving present value *interest factors* for both annuities and for single-payment amounts are available to speed the calculations.

Because an annuity is defined as a uniform series of periodic payments, the *Park Project's* estimated periodic net operating income of a uniform $16,000 during each of the next five years qualifies as a five-year annuity. By using the interest factors included in annuity tables, the analyst saves the task of using a separate interest factor for each individual year's income figure. A separate interest factor is required, however, to find the present value of the estimated selling price.

Presented in Figure 7–1 are the calculations for finding the Inwood rate of return (Inwood ROR), for the *Park Project* example. The trial and error process for finding r is begun by trying 20 per cent. The interest factors used below are found in the Appendix at the end of the book. The 2.991 interest factor, for example, is from *Column 5, Present Value Ordinary Annuity 1 per Period*, for 5 years, 20 per cent; and the 0.402 factor is from *Column 4, Present Value Reversion of 1*.

Using 20 per cent, the resulting value of the right-hand side of $94,448 is smaller than the $100,000 left-hand side cost figure, so a lower rate must be tried. Using 18 per cent next, the resulting value of the right-hand side of $100,680 is very close to the left-hand side of $100,000; thus the r value (Inwood ROR) is very close to 18 per cent. If a more precise return figure is desired, interpolation between 18 and 20 per cent is required, as shown in Figure 7–1.

By the above trial and error technique, we find the Inwood rate of return amounts to 18.2 per cent. That is, the 5 years' benefits as measured in the Inwood formulation represent a return of the original $100,000 invested in the project, plus an 18.2 per cent annual return on the $100,000 investment. The fact that taxes, depreciation, and financing are ignored with the Inwood method, and because the return is based on total investment rather than on owners' equity investment, many contemporary authorities favor the discounted-cash-flow method described later in this chapter. However, the Inwood method still finds wide use.

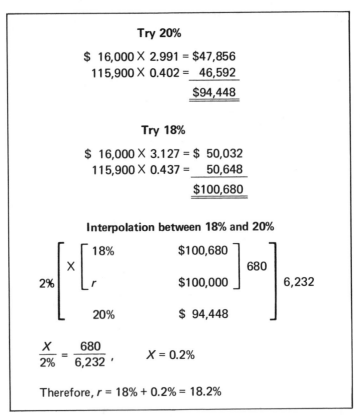

Try 20%

$$\$\ 16{,}000 \times 2.991 = \$47{,}856$$
$$115{,}900 \times 0.402 = \underline{\ \ 46{,}592}$$
$$\$94{,}448$$

Try 18%

$$\$\ 16{,}000 \times 3.127 = \$\ 50{,}032$$
$$115{,}900 \times 0.437 = \underline{\ \ 50{,}648}$$
$$\$100{,}680$$

Interpolation between 18% and 20%

$$\frac{X}{2\%} = \frac{680}{6{,}232}, \qquad X = 0.2\%$$

Therefore, $r = 18\% + 0.2\% = 18.2\%$

Fig. 7–1. Trial and error calculations, Inwood method.

Ellwood Method

The Ellwood tables were first published in 1959, and have since become widely used by real estate appraisers and mortgage lenders.[4] An experienced user of the tables can quickly find the overall capitalization rate (the discount rate) that can be divided into the project's expected annual income to find the present value of a given property. The Ellwood method differs from Inwood in that more input data are accommodated, including: the prospective mortgage terms and interest rate; the required rate-of-return figure for the owners' equity investment in the project;

[4] The *Ellwood Tables* were developed by Leon W. Ellwood and are published by the American Institute of Real Estate Appraisers, Chicago.

and an estimate of the expected appreciation or depreciation in the property's market value during the holding period.

By specifying, therefore, a given required rate of return on owners' investment and the other required input data, the equity investor can determine the price he can afford to pay for a given investment property and just earn his required rate of return. The investor should, however, be familiar with the limitations of the Ellwood method. In order to keep the tables to a reasonable size, there is a limited number of input data categories covered by the tables; for such things as the mortgage years, which are specified in five-year increments only. Therefore, an 18-year mortgage is not covered. More importantly, however, the tables ignore the impact of federal income taxes on the project's returns, and therefore accelerated depreciation usage and other tax aspects are ignored. Both of the indicated limitations of the Ellwood tables are overcome by using the discounted-cash-flow model discussed next.

Discounted-Cash-Flow Model

The discounted-cash-flow model is really a variation of the real estate appraiser's Inwood method—a variation that emphasizes *cash flows* rather than accounting income, and emphasizes return on *owners'* investment, rather than return on total investment, which are two considerations of great interest to most real estate equity investors. The discounted cash flow model may be expressed mathematically as in Equation 7–2, which makes use of symbols previously defined.

$$\text{Owners' initial investment} = \sum_{t=1}^{n} \frac{CFAT_t}{(1+r)^t} + \frac{CFAT\ (sale)}{(1+r)^n} \qquad [7\text{--}2]$$

By solving for r, we find the cash flow return on owners' investment. In previous chapters we developed the data necessary to find the discounted-cash-flow rate of return (DCF ROR) for the *Park Project*. Plugging those data, which are summarized in the investment profile in Table 6–1, into Equation 7–2, we have the following formulation: ·

$$\$60,000 =$$
$$\frac{\$4,684}{(1+r)} + \frac{\$4,538}{(1+r)^2} + \frac{\$4,382}{(1+r)^3} + \frac{\$4,215}{(1+r)^4} + \frac{\$4,035}{(1+r)^5} + \frac{\$107,515}{(1+r)^5}$$

By combining the last two terms, to obtain total cash flow after tax to be received in the fifth year, we have:

$$\$60,000 = \frac{\$4,684}{(1+r)} + \frac{\$4,538}{(1+r)^2} + \frac{\$4,382}{(1+r)^3} + \frac{\$4,215}{(1+r)^4} + \frac{\$111,550}{(1+r)^5}$$

The only remaining task is to solve for the value of r; that is, we seek to answer this question: If the investor receives the periodic after-tax cash flow specified for each of the five years, and $107,515 after-tax cash when he sells the property at the end of five years, then what after-tax, annual rate of return is received during the life of the investment on the owners' original investment in the project of $60,000? The method for finding r is the same trial-and-error technique used for finding the Inwood ROR, as described in the last section. It will be noted, however, that with the discounted-cash-flow model, the annual cash flows are not uniform amounts, and therefore the annuity interest factors cannot be employed. The necessity of using a different interest factor for each future year's cash flow increases the computations significantly when several years are involved. However, the computer is ideally suited to handle this type of problem. For the relatively short, 5-year holding period of the *Park Project,* the calculations can be done manually as indicated in Figure 7–2.

By applying the trial-and-error method it is found that the rate of 18.4 per cent makes the right-hand side of the equation equal to $60,000; therefore, 18.4 per cent represents the after-tax return on the owners' investment (DCF ROR). The return figure, it is to be emphasized, is the overall return expected to be realized from the project, including returns from periodic cash receipts, and from the price appreciation gains, if any, received at the time of sale. *Because all calculations are adjusted for federal income taxes, the tax-shelter benefits of the investment are included in the DCF ROR figure.*

As a means of reviewing the concepts and techniques of invest-

	Try 20%				Try 18%		
Year	Cash Flow	IF	PV	Year	Cash Flow	IF	PV
1	$ 4,684	0.833	$ 3,902	1	$ 4,684	0.847	$ 3,967
2	4,538	0.694	3,149	2	4,538	0.718	3,258
3	4,382	0.579	2,537	3	4,382	0.609	2,669
4	4,215	0.482	2,032	4	4,215	0.516	2,175
5	111,550	0.402	44,843	5	111,550	0.437	48,747
			$56,463				$60,816

Interpolation between 18% and 20%

$$2\% \left[X \left[\begin{array}{ll} 18\% & \$60,816 \\ r & \$60,000 \end{array} \right] 816 \right] 4,353$$

$$20\% \qquad \$56,463$$

$$\frac{X}{2\%} = \frac{816}{4,353}, \qquad X = 0.4\%$$

Therefore, r = 18% + 0.4% = 18.4%

Fig. 7–2. Trial and error calculations, discounted-cash-flow model.

ment analysis presented thus far in Part II of this book, a complete financial analysis will now be undertaken, including the preparation of an investment profile for a comprehensive example—the *Garden Apartment Project.*

Garden apartment project. The *Garden Apartment Project,* with 26 apartments, has been placed on the market at a price of $560,000. The building itself is valued at $420,000, and has a remaining useful life of 20 years, thereby just qualifying for the use of 125%-declining-balance depreciation. The estimated selling price at the end of the 20-year holding period of $1,011,360 is based upon an assumed 3 per cent annual growth rate in the property's market value. The remaining details of relevance are as follows.

GARDEN APARTMENT PROJECT

Price	. . . .	$ 560,000
Loan	. . . .	$ 420,000, 20 years, 8%, level annual payments
Down-payment	. . . .	$ 140,000 (25%)
Holding period	. . . .	20 years
Estimated selling price	. .	$1,011,360
Gross possible income	. .	$ 84,000
Vacancy allowance	. . . . .	$ 4,000
Operating expenses	. . . .	$ 28,000
Depreciable value	. . . . . .	$ 420,000, 20 years, 125% DB, zero estimated residual value
Income tax rate	. . . .	70%

The first step in organizing or structuring the data is to prepare pro-forma statements showing all periodic income and cash flow levels for the 20 years of the project. Statements for every other year are shown in the first part of the investment profile in Table 7–1.[5] In preparing such statements the analyst may wish to first develop depreciation and mortgage-loan schedules as illustrated in Chapter 4; however, that step is omitted here because the same data will be shown in the project's investment profile. The heavy depreciation and interest expense charges in the early years result in tax losses (negative taxable income) in the first four years of the project; however, periodic after-tax cash flows are positive in the first thirteen years. The periodic tax-shelter amounts can be calculated by using the equations presented in Chapter 5. The first four years' tax losses give equivalent amounts of *tax-loss shelter* in those years; and *cash-flow shelter* is generated for the first eleven years of the project, or for about one-half of the planned holding period. The eighth year's cash-flow shelter would be computed, for example, by Equation 5–5, as shown below. Cash flows and tax shelter amounts for every other year are shown in the investment profile in Table 7–1.

[5] While we have recommended that full-scale pro-forma statements be prepared as a first step toward computation of financial analysis measures, it will be recognized that an appropriate set of equations could be used to directly compute the same measures. For example, the $CFAT_t$ variable in Equation 7–2 could be presented as: Net operating income$_t$ — Interest$_t$ — Amortization$_t$ — Taxes$_t$ + Tax loss savings$_t$.

$$\text{Cash-flow shelter} = \text{CFBT} - \text{Taxable income}$$
$$= \$9,222 - \$4,674$$
$$= \$4,548$$

Using the given estimate of \$1,011,360 for the selling price of the property, and the other available data, we can compute the estimated cash flow after tax expected to be received at the time of sale, by using Equation 6–5:

$$\text{CFAT (sale)} = \text{Selling price} - \text{Unpaid mortgage} - \text{Taxes}$$
$$= \$1,011,360 - \$4 - \$299,976$$
$$= \$711,380$$

The twenty-year mortgage will be almost completely paid off by the time of sale, so this factor will not significantly reduce cash sale proceeds. However, federal income taxes will amount to \$299,976, using the assumed investor's rate of 70 per cent. The total tax obligation can be determined as follows:

1. *Compute capital gain:*

$$\text{Adjusted basis} = \text{Cost} - \text{Accumulated depreciation}$$
$$= \$560,000 - \$420,000$$
$$= \$140,000$$
$$\text{Capital gain} = \text{Selling price} - \text{Adjusted basis}$$
$$= \$1,011,360 - \$140,000$$
$$= \$871,360$$

2. *Apply tax rates:*

	Amount	Rate	Tax
Recaptured depreciation	$ 0 ×	—	$ 0
Balance of gain (1st $50,000)	50,000 ×	0.25	12,500
Balance of gain	821,360 ×	0.35	287,476
Total tax obligation			$299,976

The 15 per cent minimum tax on preferences called for by the 1976 Tax Reform Act has been ignored in the above example. If the investor's other transactions in the year of sale do not add to his preference exemptions in that year, then a preference tax obligation would be created by the large capital gain generated by the

TABLE 7–1. Investment Profile—Garden Apartment Project

	Year–1	2	4	6	8	10	12	14	16	18	20
					Periodic Returns						
Gross Possible Income	$84,000	$84,000	$84,000	$84,000	$84,000	$84,000	$84,000	$84,000	$84,000	$84,000	$84,000
less: Vacancies and bad debts	4,000	4,000	4,000	4,000	4,000	4,000	4,000	4,000	4,000	4,000	4,000
Gross Income, Actual	$80,000	$80,000	$80,000	$80,000	$80,000	$80,000	$80,000	$80,000	$80,000	$80,000	$80,000
less: Operating expense	28,000	28,000	28,000	28,000	28,000	28,000	28,000	28,000	28,000	28,000	28,000
Net Operating Income	$52,000	$52,000	$52,000	$52,000	$52,000	$52,000	$52,000	$52,000	$52,000	$52,000	$52,000
less: Depreciation expense	26,250	24,609	21,629	20,277	20,277	20,278	20,278	20,278	20,278	20,277	20,278
Interest expense	33,600	32,866	31,216	29,293	27,049	24,431	21,378	17,818	13,664	8,820	3,169
Taxable Income	($ 7,850)	($ 5,475)	($ 845)	$ 2,430	$ 4,674	$ 7,291	$10,344	$13,904	$18,058	$22,903	$28,553
less: Income taxes (70%)	0	0	0	1,701	3,272	5,104	7,241	9,733	12,641	16,032	19,987
Earnings After Tax	($ 7,850)	($ 5,475)	($ 845)	$ 729	$ 1,402	$ 2,187	$ 3,103	$ 4,171	$ 5,417	$ 6,871	$ 8,566
plus: Depreciation expense	26,250	24,609	21,629	20,277	20,277	20,278	20,278	20,278	20,278	20,277	20,278
less: Mortgage amortization	9,178	9,912	11,561	13,485	15,729	18,347	21,399	24,960	29,114	33,958	39,609
plus: Tax-loss savings	5,495	3,833	592	0	0	0	0	0	0	0	0
Cash Flow After Tax	$14,717	$13,055	$ 9,815	$ 7,521	$ 5,950	$ 4,118	$ 1,982	($ 511)	($ 3,419)	($ 6,810)	($10,765)
Cash Flow Before Tax	$ 9,222	$ 9,222	$ 9,222	$ 9,222	$ 9,222	$ 9,222	$ 9,222	$ 9,222	$ 9,222	$ 9,222	$ 9,222
					Tax Shelter						
Cash-Flow Shelter	$ 9,222	$ 9,222	$ 9,222	$ 6,792	$ 4,548	$ 1,931	$ 0	$ 0	$ 0	$ 0	$ 0
Tax-Loss Shelter	7,850	5,475	845	0	0	0	0	0	0	0	0
Total Tax Shelter	$17,072	$14,697	$10,067	$ 6,792	$ 4,548	$ 1,931	$ 0	$ 0	$ 0	$ 0	$ 0
Total Tax-Shelter Savings	$11,950	$10,288	$ 7,047	$ 4,754	$ 3,184	$ 1,352	$ 0	$ 0	$ 0	$ 0	$ 0

126

Sale Proceeds

Selling Price	$1,011,360
less: Unpaid mortgage	4
Cash Flow Before Tax from Sale	$1,011,356
less: Income taxes	299,976
Cash Flow After Tax from Sale	$ 711,380
	4

Mortgage Loan

Mortgage Loan	$420,000	$420,000	$420,000	$420,000	$420,000	$420,000	$420,000	$420,000	$420,000	$420,000
Equity Build-up	9,178	19,090	41,356	67,328	97,621	132,955	174,169	222,241	278,311	343,712	419,996
Unpaid Mortgage	410,822	400,910	378,644	352,672	322,279	287,045	245,831	197,759	141,689	76,288	4

Financial Analysis

GIM	7.0
Expense Ratio	33.3%
Income Yield	9.3%
Pre-Tax Cash Yield	6.6%
Inwood ROR	10.6%
DCF ROR	11.1%
Cash Payback Period	20 years

Return on Equity	(neg.)	(neg.)	0.4%	0.6%	0.8%	1.0%	1.2%	1.3%	1.4%	1.6%
After-Tax Cash Return	10.5%	9.3%	7.0%	5.4%	4.3%	2.9%	1.4%	neg.	neg.	neg.	neg.

sale of the *Garden Apartment* property.[6]

In the early years of the *Garden Apartment Project,* there are some relatively modest amounts of excess depreciation (excess over straight-line amounts) that would represent tax preference items. Such amounts are less than the $10,000 minimum annual exemptions permitted under the 1976 Tax Reform Act, but would have to be added to any other preference amounts that the investor would have in the relevant years.   Note also that if the investor does not anticipate significant income from other investments during the planned holding period for the *Garden Apartment Project,* the 1976 TRA limits on investment interest deductions will prevent the full deduction of interest expenses as assumed above. The interest deduction limitations are discussed in Chapter 4.

Computer analysis. The computer can be programmed to perform the trial-and-error calculations and to print out the resultant DCF ROR value.   This is, of course, a great time-saver where the cash flows are scheduled for several years, as in the *Garden Apartment Project.*   In addition to computing the rate of return, with given annual after-tax cash flows as inputs, the computer can be programmed to actually compute all future cash flows.   This again is most helpful on long-term projects, both in terms of time reduction and in the elimination of computational errors.   This operation simply calls for the provision of basic input data such as mortgage terms, tax rates, depreciation details, and so forth. The program can also be written to compute mortgage-loan and depreciation schedules; other supplementary data; and to make extensive sensitivity analysis as described in the Risk Analysis section of this chapter.

Applying the discounted-cash-flow model.   We have described and illustrated the mechanics necessary for finding the DCF ROR, with little discussion of the merits and limitations of the discounted-cash-flow model as an investment-return measure.   Among its advantages would be:

1. It takes into account the specific tax impacts on the cash returns.
2. It takes account of the project's financing arrangements.

---

[6] The amount of preference relating to the sale would be one-half of the $871,360 gain, or $435,680. The preference exemption would be 50 per cent of the income taxes paid in the year of sale, or $159,981. [50% × ($19,987 + $299,976)]. The preference tax would therefore amount to $41,355. [15% × ($435,680 − $159,981)].

3. It takes account of the time value of money.
4. The DCF ROR figures, such as the 11.1 per cent figure for the *Garden Apartment Project,* serves as a convenient measure for comparing various alternative projects.
5. It measures return on the *owners'* investment, rather than on the total investment in the project.

In short, the DCF model is growing in favor with many analysts because it is so all-inclusive, reflecting the quantity and timing of all after-tax cash flow benefits returned to the dollar investment of the owner.

Regarding point (5) in the above list of advantages, it should be pointed out that it can be argued that a return on total investment measure is preferable to return on owners' investment, because the latter return will depend on the amount of mortgage financing used by the investor; that is, the investor by his decision on how large a mortgage to take in effect controls his own rate of return. It will be recalled that a large mortgage loan magnifies the owner's rate of return when there is favorable leverage. In this connection, it should be noted that in corporate capital budgeting use of the discounted cash flow model, the particular project-related debt financing is ignored and an ROR is found on the total investment in the project. The resultant ROR figure is compared with an *average cost of capital* figure based on the assumption that the corporation's overall capital structure (debt/equity) should be the assumed financing base for all investment proposals.

While the corporation's average-cost-of-capital concept may be valid for real estate investment for large industrial corporations and for large financial institutions having large numbers of investments, the more common situation in real estate would be for the project under consideration to be large enough, and have unique-enough financing and other aspects, that the particular debt financing features for the proposed investment should be accounted for in the periodic cash flows. In fact, in many if not most real estate investments the owner would take as large a mortgage as the lenders will provide; therefore, he does not really completely control his own leverage and rate of return.

It is important to note, however, that the rate of return on owners' equity investment is not a legitimate method to use where there is an extremely high *loan/value ratio,* and the owners' investment (cash down payment) is a very small or nominal amount.

In fact, the return on owners' investment approaches infinity as the owners' equity investment approaches zero. At times, mortgage financing has even exceeded 100 per cent of the project cost, resulting in a negative owners' investment.

Some drawbacks to the DCF ROR measure, aside from the special situation just described, would include:

1. The difficulty in making the year-by-year cash flow estimates, especially for the distant future; that is, the *input demands* are heavy.
2. The calculations can be time-consuming, and expensive to undertake, with the computer a practical necessity for long-term project analysis.
3. The seeming precision of the final rate-of-return figure, and the elaborateness of the calculations, could lead to a false sense of security in the return figure; while it may be that the underlying data assumptions are way off the mark.
4. The overall rate-of-return measure itself (DCF ROR) does not reflect the attractiveness of the project in terms of short-term cash throw-off, which is of primary importance to some investors.
5. Because of the mathematics of the compounding process, there is an implied assumption that the periodic cash inflows on the investment will be *reinvested at the rate found as the DCF ROR.* Accordingly, the method may not be the most appropriate where the assumed reinvestment rate cannot be expected to be at least approximately achieved.[7]

Having reviewed some of the advantages and disadvantages of the discounted cash flow approach we can say, in general, that the use of the DCF ROR measure is more appropriate in some situations than others. It is most appropriately applied where there is sufficient information on hand to make the necessary projections; for example, projects involving long-term-lease contracts covering major income and expense items. On the other hand, for projects involving short-term leases, or other factors resulting in cash-flow forecasting problems, or for properties purchased mainly for price appreciation, then the rule-of-thumb measures

---

[7] A technique related to the discounted cash flow model is the *present-value,* or *net-present-value* technique used in corporate capital budgeting. With this technique, the future cash flows are discounted at the required rate of return, and the present value thereof compared with the initial investment. Here the reinvestment rate is assumed to be the required rate of return.

are, at least in some cases, more appropriate. For investors interested primarily in early-years' cash flows, the cash throw-off data indicated by the pro-forma statements are useful, as well as the cash-flow return measures, such as the cash payback period described in Chapter 5. For corporate investors interested in earnings-per-share performance, the return on equity measure (ROE) would be useful.

However, the DCF ROR measure should be used in conjunction with other return measures, to obtain a complete analysis, whenever the investor has the facilities for working up the analysis. The discounted cash flow model described above does not take account of risk directly, but it can be modified to take account of risk as discussed in the next section.

RISK ANALYSIS

The rate-of-return measures discussed thus far represent data for use in decision making rather than decision making itself. For example, in the *Garden Apartment Project,* the DCF ROR was found to be 11.1 per cent, but we are still left with the judgment as to whether 11.1 per cent is high enough to justify making the investment.

The answer to this depends on the expected returns from alternative investments that are available to the investor. For alternative investment proposals having approximately the same risks and other similar features, the DCF ROR's computed for the various proposals can be compared directly, along with other return measures. However, *alternative investments often have differing degrees of risk and of liquidity, and have other distinct characteristics.* In other words, the rate of return is only one factor entering the investment decision, albeit an important factor. For example, triple-A rated corporate bonds, which are heavily invested in by life insurance companies and others, were returning on a discounted cash flow basis over 9 per cent (before-tax) in late 1974. These bonds are of relatively low risk, are highly liquid, and require few management responsibilities for the holder. With such an alternative use for investment funds available, most real estate equity investments would be expected to earn considerably more than the return from such bonds.

Assuming that the rate-of-return model can be adjusted to accommodate such things as management time spent on the project, and that other techniques can be used to reveal the liquidity features of the investment, we are still left with the task of adjusting our analysis for risk or uncertainty. The terms *risk* and *uncertainty* will be used interchangeably in this book.

The general nature of investment risks can be examined by distinguishing between financial risk and business risk. *Financial risk,* or *leverage risk,* is the risk of project failure or project losses because of the burden of meeting heavy mortgage payments. In this context, the higher the leverage (the relative amount of debt), the higher the financial risk, all else being the same. The reader will recall from Chapter 4 that leverage usage magnifies owners' returns—losses as well as gains. Chapter 9 has a further discussion of the risks associated with the use of leverage, including the calculation of *debt-service-coverage ratios,* and *break-even occupancy rates.*

Business risk, on the other hand, relates to the degree of uncertainty as to the amount of project benefits to be received in future years. The degree of business risk varies in real estate investment from low-risk investments involving high-quality, long-term leases, to high-risk land investments. The specific risks attending various types of investments are discussed in Part IV.

In the present section the focus will be on risk/return relationships, without proceeding further with the specific risks related to different individual property investments. In general, one can say that the investor should require (demand) a higher return from a riskier investment than from a less risky one, but can we be more specific? Is there some way of adjusting the return figures calculated for the project, for the amount of project risk? Several quantitative techniques have been developed for this purpose, some of which are beyond the scope of this book.[8] Presented below are five techniques that are among the least complex, and among the most practical, for use in actual investment problems.

---

[8] Some other risk-adjustment approaches include: complete probability distributions, full-scale simulation, decision trees, and portfolio selection. A good review of these and other techniques is found in James C. Van Horne, *Financial Management and Policy* (3rd ed.; Englewood Cliffs, N.J.: Prentice-Hall, Inc., 1974).

Risk Avoidance

The first technique is simply one of investing exclusively in low-risk projects, and is often used by large institutional investors. When this technique or policy is followed, all projects accepted for rate-of-return analysis have, in effect, been adjusted for risk, and the rate-of-return criterion can be applied directly in selecting among various real estate proposals available for investment. Of course, those selected would generally be expected to offer rates of return higher than lower-risk investments such as government securities.

Sensitivity Analysis

A very useful technique or tool that can be used as an indirect approach to appraising the risk of a particular project is to determine just how sensitive the DCF ROR or other return measure is to changes in the assumptions underlying the data on which the return measure was based. This procedure, called *sensitivity analysis,* involves recalculating the rate of return based on the new assumptions.

For example, suppose the analyst suspects that operating expenses may amount to as much as twice his initial estimates. The rate-of-return analysis could then be redone with the expense figures doubled to determine the size of the decline in the project's rate of return, that is, to determine the sensitivity of the rate of return to changes in operating expenses. For another example, suppose that in the *Garden Apartment Project,* discussed earlier in this chapter, the analyst foresees the possibility of no price gain in the value of the property during the twenty-year holding period. By recalculating the rate of return with the discounted cash flow model, the new DCF ROR is found to be 8.4 per cent, compared with the 11.1 per cent found under the original assumption of a 3 per cent annual gain in property value. Two other possible applications of sensitivity analysis would be to assume certain tax law changes (such as tax-shelter tax provisions), and to assume a different mortgage loan amount for the project.

For the rule-of-thumb return measures, such as income yield, the sensitivity analysis can conveniently be done manually; but a computer would be required for extensive sensitivity analysis of a project such as the *Garden Apartment* investment.

Summation Rate

An approach developed by the real estate appraisal profession for use in determining capitalization rates for use in property valuations can be adapted by the equity investor in determining a required rate of return for a particular project. This approach calls for finding a summation rate (or *build-up rate*), by starting with a *safe-rate*, that is, the rate of return on a "riskless" investment, such as in U.S. Government securities, and then adding a premium for the amount of risk attending the real estate project, and other premiums for any other factors attending the real estate project as opposed to the riskless investment, as illustrated in the example below, using before-tax figures.

Safe rate	8%
Rate for risk	8%
Rate for non-liquidity	2%
Rate for burden of management	2%
Required rate of return	20%

After adjusting the 20 per cent required rate of return found above for federal income taxes, it then can serve as a standard against which to measure the expected DCF ROR calculated for the project.

Certainty-Equivalent Approach

An alternative to adjusting the required rate of return upwards for risk as with the summation rate approach, would be to adjust downwards the real estate project's estimated returns. This latter approach is often done in a rough way when the analyst makes so-called conservative estimates. A more formal quantitative approach to adjusting future project flows for uncertainty is found in corporate financial management theory, and is called the certainty-equivalent approach.

Under this approach, the analyst applies an alpha factor (a) to each future year's cash flow, and thereby marks down each year's cash flow figure to make it equivalent in amount to what would be considered a certain cash flow. The a factors range from 0 to 1.0. If the analyst is relatively highly certain that, for example, the first year's cash flow will be received in the amount estimated for that year, then he might apply an a value of, say, 0.9. The values assigned to the a factors by the investor will reflect the investor's attitude towards risk, that is, the extent to which he will penalize uncertain future returns. The DCF model as adjusted with certainty-equivalent factors is shown in Equation 7–3, followed by a number example.

$$\text{Owners' initial investment} = \sum_{t=1}^{n} \frac{a_t CFAT_t}{(1+r)^t} + \frac{a_n CFAT\ (sale)}{(1+r)^n} \quad [7\text{–}3]$$

For a simple illustration of this equation let us assume that the owners' initial investment (cash down-payment) is $9,500, and the owners expect cash flow after tax of $5,000 to be received at the end of each of the 3 years of the holding period, and they expect zero sale proceeds. Because the investors believe each succeeding year's cash flow to be increasingly uncertain as to the amount to be received, they assign a factors of 0.9, 0.8, and 0.7 to the cash flow after tax amounts in years 1, 2, and 3, respectively. We now have the data necessary to use Equation 7–3, as follows:

$$\$9,500 = \frac{(0.9)(\$5,000)}{(1+r)} + \frac{(0.8)(\$5,000)}{(1+r)^2} + \frac{(0.7)(\$5,000)}{(1+r)^3}$$

$$\$9,500 = \frac{\$4,500}{(1+r)} + \frac{\$4,000}{(1+r)^2} + \frac{\$3,500}{(1+r)^3}$$

Solving for r, we find the DCF ROR equals 13.3 per cent. This rate can then be compared with the risk-adjusted returns on other available projects in making the investment decision.

The difficulty in applying the certainty-equivalent approach is, of course, how to determine the a values. This problem is similar to that of determining the risk and other rate premiums required as inputs in the summation rate method. About all that can be said is that subjective judgment is called for.

Probability Theory

Another approach that can be used in adjusting the analysis for uncertain cash flow returns, is the use of probability theory. We present here only the most simple, but perhaps the most practical, version of this approach. The approach calls for making three estimates for *each year's cash flow*. The three forecasts are often labeled the *pessimistic*, the *most-probable*, and the *optimistic* estimates. The next step is to assign a subjective probability factor to each cash flow estimate; with each factor being a number between 0 and 1.0, and with all three factors totaling 1.0. Each year's *expected value*, that is, *weighted average*, is then found. The process is best explained by means of an example.

Let us assume again a $9,500 initial investment, and a most probable cash flow for each of the next 3 years of $5,000. However, there is only a 50 per cent chance or probability that the amount received will actually be $5,000, and therefore, the $5,000 figure is multiplied by the probability factor of 0.5. There is a 25 per cent chance that the cash flow in each year will be a negative $1,000 (pessimistic estimate), and a 25 per cent chance of an $8,000 positive cash flow (optimistic estimate). These last two estimates are multiplied by a 0.25 probability factor. The three probability factors add up to 1.0, meaning that there is a 100 per cent chance that the actual cash flow figure will be one of the three estimated amounts. Each year's expected value of cash flows is computed to be $4,250, as follows:

	Estimated cash flow		Subjective probability factor		
Pessimistic estimate	−$1,000	×	0.25	=	−$ 250
Most probable estimate ..	5,000	×	0.50	=	2,500
Optimistic estimate	8,000	×	0.25	=	2,000
Expected value of cash flow after tax					$4,250

With the figure in hand of $4,250 for the expected value for each of the 3 year's cash flow, we can now find the project's rate of return using the risk-adjusted, expected-value cash flow of $4,250, instead of the most probable $5,000 cash flow figure, by using Equation 7–4, where $CFAT$ symbolizes the *expected* value of the after-tax cash flow.

$$\text{Owners' initial investment} = \sum_{t=1}^{n} \frac{\overline{CFAT_t}}{(1+r)^t} + \frac{\overline{CFAT}\ (sale)}{(1+r)^n}$$

$$\$9{,}500 = \frac{\$4{,}250}{(1+r)} + \frac{\$4{,}250}{(1+r)^2} + \frac{\$4{,}250}{(1+r)^3}$$

$$r = 16.3\%$$

The rate-of-return figure of 16.3 per cent is then compared with the risk-adjusted return expected from other available projects in making the investment decision.

SUMMARY

A theoretically correct overall rate-of-return measure for a real estate or other investment proposal should take account of the *time value of money,* by which distant returns are given less weight than near-term returns estimates. Three methods were discussed that make the time-value adjustment. The *Ellwood tables* can be used to find the present value of a piece of real property, based on various inputs, including an owners' required return rate. With the *Inwood method,* and the *discounted cash flow model,* the internal rate of return of an investment proposal can be determined. Both techniques require the use of the *trial-and-error method* for finding the return rate. The equations for the two methods are the following:

$$\text{Purchase price} = \sum_{t=1}^{n} \frac{\text{Net operating income}}{(1+r)^t} + \frac{\text{Selling price}}{(1+r)^n} \quad [7\text{–}1]$$

$$\text{Owner's initial investment} = \sum_{t=1}^{n} \frac{CFAT_t}{(1+r)^t} + \frac{CFAT\ (sale)}{(1+r)^n} \quad [7\text{–}2]$$

The discounted cash flow model has many advantages in addition to the fact that it takes account of the time value of money, but it also has some limitations as discussed in the chapter. It is most appropriately used when relatively hard data are available to satisfy the demanding input requirements.

Risk analysis. The relative attractiveness of a proposed investment depends on its risk features as well as its return features. Many techniques have been developed to adjust project analysis for expected risks. Five such techniques were discussed in the chapter that can be applied in practical investment decision making, as follows: *risk avoidance, sensitivity analysis, summation rate, certainty-equivalent approach,* and a *probability-theory approach* requiring three subjective probability estimates for each future year's cash flows.

III

Real Estate Investment Strategy

8

Ownership
Strategy

Thus far we have been concerned with defining the economic goals of real estate investing, and with techniques for measuring the goal satisfaction potential of particular investment proposals. To maximize economic returns from a real estate investment the investor also will have to make appropriate decisions on: (1) the form of legal organization, (2) the manner of financing the project, (3) the length of the holding period, and (4) the manner of disposing of the property. These four strategy decision areas are discussed in the present Part III.

In this chapter we consider alternative forms of legal organization that can be used for investing in real estate. The fact that in 1970 there were almost 40 million owner-occupied, year-round homes in this country suggests that the most common form of real estate ownership is individual ownership (or co-ownership by married couples). However, other forms of ownership (in addition to individual ownership) such as the partnership or the corporation are widely used for holding title to properties that are held primarily as investment properties.

The various ownership forms will be considered as falling into one of these three categories: (1) individual, (2) private-group, and (3) public-group ownership. Most forms are not unique to real estate investing but some are, as will be discussed. The focus of the discussion will be from the viewpoint of the equity investor controling the organizational-form decision, rather than from the viewpoint of the individual having a passive interest in a real estate investing unit; such as the holder of a few shares of a large, publicly held real-estate corporation. In terms previously defined, we are primarily interested in the *direct* equity investor rather than the *indirect* equity investor.

Because there are many technical points relating to the various legal forms of doing business, the investor will often have need to seek legal counsel. However, the investor should have an awareness of the principal economic, legal, tax, and other consequences of using the various ownership forms. As will be discussed in some detail in the following sections of this chapter, the principal consequences of the different ownership forms relate to: (1) the extent of personal liability for the investor, (2) the facilitation of raising capital, (3) the minimization of the investor's tax burdens, and (4) other features, such as ease of formation, and management control.

The investor's strategy in selecting a particular form of ownership with its own distinctive consequences will depend on the investor's personal financial position, for example, the extent of his personal assets and his tax bracket, and will depend on his investment goals, and on his personal resources of time, investment funds, and skills. The form that is most appropriate will also depend upon the nature of the particular investment project involved. There are also times when a change in organizational form is appropriate once a particular investment project has reached a certain stage of developmnt.

INDIVIDUAL OWNERSHIP

There are many advantages to individual ownership (also called the *proprietorship*); management can be said to be relatively efficient, with the owner having absolute control in the sense that he need not consult other owners on daily decisions relating to management of the investment project.[1] Ease of formation also favors this form, with a relative lack of the red tape and delays sometimes attending other forms discussed in this chapter.

---

[1] With the individual ownership form, as with the other forms, substantial latent—if not exercised—control often resides with creditors. The *control* referred to in this chapter, however, is ownership control.

One disadvantage often cited for the proprietorship form is the existence of the owner's personal liability, that is, *unlimited liability,* for any debts or obligations incurred in relation to the investment. Essentially this means that the owner's liability does not stop with the amount that he has invested in the real estate project, but extends beyond to his other investment and personal assets. While this can be a serious consideration it should be recognized that for many real estate investment risks, insurance protection is available, such as the risk of injuries to individuals using the property.

Where the real estate investor defaults on financial obligations relating to a property—say, because of high vacancy rates and low rental income—his personal assets, as well as the real estate itself, may be exposed to creditors' legal actions. In many instances, however, the value of the mortgaged property will be high enough to more than cover the mortgage loan obligation outstanding at the time of the investor's default.

Another restrictive feature of the individual ownership form is that most investors have limited personal resources to invest in a project. The resources referred to include not only time and money, but also skills and experience.

Tax features. The taxable periodic income and capital gains from real estate investments will be included with the individual investor's other income and taxed at the investor's personal tax rates, in the year in which the income and gains are recognized for tax purposes. In the case of periodic income received by the investor with a marginal income tax rate of 70 per cent, the investor will keep only $300 of every $1,000 of such investment income. With the individual ownership form there is no tax deduction allowed for withdrawals by the investor in the form of salary related to his management time devoted to the investment, whereas a reasonable salary to the shareholder–manager of a corporation would be deductible from periodic investment income.

Because of the factors mentioned above, individual ownership is generally not an attractive alternative for the investor in a very high tax bracket who is investing in a project expected to generate significant taxable income. On the other hand, the individual ownership form is attractive to the high-tax-bracket owner when he is investing in a project expected to produce *operating losses*. Such losses can be used by the investor to offset his taxable income received from other sources in the same years. Such tax-shelter benefits were described in Chapter 5.

PRIVATE GROUPS

The individual new to real estate investment often uses the individual ownership form, because, as noted previously, it is relatively simple to organize and account for and is a favorable ownership form for projects generating taxable periodic income as long as the investor is not in a relatively high tax bracket. As the investor moves to a higher tax bracket, however, or as he becomes more concerned with the unlimited liability feature of the individual ownership form, he often looks to one of the small, private-group forms of organization. Also, because of the resource constraints on the individual investor (together with the fact that most real estate investments are of relatively large scale), one often finds relatively small local groups formed to invest in real estate. Such groups often are composed of some combination of the following: real estate promoter, lawyer, contractor, banker, politician, or local investor. Group investing makes possible the pooling of equity funds and professional skills and experience, a sharing of risks, and perhaps the facilitation of debt-financing arrangements.

General Partnership

The general partnership is a legally recognized association of two or more persons that carry on, as co-owners, a business for profit. While the technical details of formation and the detailed attributes of the partnership form depend on individual state laws, the generally applicable features can be described as in the following paragraphs.[2]

The general partnership is relatively simple to form. While no written formalities are legally required, it is best to have a lawyer draw up articles of partnership; that is, a written contract

[2] Most states have adopted the *Uniform Partnership Act,* which has brought about increased uniformity in this branch of the law.

between the partners. There usually are no delays or significant expenses in the formation process and no state or other governmental approval is required. The general partnership form does not provide for a centralized management arrangement, as do the corporation and the individual ownership forms. Each partner can make decisions that bind the partnership, which can result in inefficient decision making where partners disagree.

All partners in the general partnership have unlimited personal liability for the acts and obligations of the partnership. Hence the liability feature is the same as for the individual form, except that, as noted, each partner will be personally liable for obligations incurred by other partners on behalf of the partnership business.

The general partnership form is clearly superior to the individual ownership form from the standpoint of raising capital funds. Equity (ownership) funds are bolstered by the addition of partners to the partnership, and the higher equity base of the organization will in turn support higher debt financing levels. Of course, the raising of additional equity capital by taking on partners means offering decision-making interests to the other investors.

The partnership articles can provide for the individual partner's disposition of his interest, often with first rights given to the other partners to acquire the interest. However, the problem of the method of valuation to be used, and the usual lack of an active market for such interests mean that transferring such interests is often not as convenient as, say, transferring shares of public corporations—but this is generally true for other private group forms of organization as well. The lack of continuity often cited with regard to the termination of a partnership because of the death of a partner can be offset by provisions in the articles of partnership calling for the surviving partners to acquire the deceased partner's interest. This can be facilitated by having life insurance policies on all partners with policy benefits going to the surviving partners.

Tax features. At the time income is earned by the partnership it is considered to be earned personally by the individual partners. Accordingly, the partner's distributive share of ordinary partnership profits and losses (and capital gains and losses) are treated for tax purposes as if they were received by him as an individual owner. Of special interest here is the ability of the general partner to offset his share of partnership operating losses against his income received from other sources in the same year. A partner's deduction relating to partnership operating losses is limited, however, to the amount of the adjusted basis of the partner's interest in the partnership at the end of the partnership year in which the loss occurred. Generally, the initial basis of a partner's interest is equal to the amount of cash and the basis of any property contributed by the partner to the partnership.[3]

Use of the general partnership. The partnership is a strategically appropriate ownership form for a small group of two or more individuals wishing to pool their financial and other resources to undertake some larger, more complex investment than they could take on separately, hopefully with *synergistic* benefits—"the whole is greater than the sum of its parts." The formation is relatively simple and inexpensive. From a tax standpoint, the partnership is a sensible choice if the investment is looked to for operating losses; that is, it is ideal for tax-shelter investments. If, on the other hand, the partnership's real estate investments are expected to generate substantial taxable profits, then the form is less attractive for the high-tax-bracket investor because ordinary partnership income will be subject to marginal tax rates as high as 70 per cent.

The potential problems of the partnership relating to management decision making, unlimited liability for partners, continuity, and transferring of interests can be protected against, at least to some extent, by the careful selection of partners, by carefully drawn partnership agreements, and with insurance protection against the untimely death of a partner and against possible personal-injury claims related to the investment property.

Limited Partnership

The limited partnership is a legally recognized modification of the general partnership form. While the general partnership

---

[3] The partner's adjusted basis will be increased by the amount of his share of partnership liabilities.

can be formed without a written agreement, the limited partnership can only be created by a written agreement (certificate) duly executed and recorded in the public records.

The limited partnership must have one or more general partners and one or more limited partners. While state laws differ, the usual characteristics of the two types of partners are as follows: the *general partner* has management control; that is, day-to-day decision-making power. The general partner has unlimited personal liability for partnership acts and obligations, and his interest is not assignable. The *limited partner* has no management control and has limited liability, that is, limited to the amount of his capital contribution to the partnership; and his interest is assignable, usually with the contract providing first refusal rights for the remaining partners.[4]

The features described above point to some advantages of this form over the general partnership form. In partnerships where there is only *one* general partner, centralized decision-making is provided for. The features of the limited partnership interest, that is, limited liability and assignability, are often attractive to investors wishing a passive investment interest. Accordingly, the equity financing possibilities are enhanced. As for debt financing, however, because creditors can rely only on the personal unlimited liability of the general partners, the limited partners' personal resources cannot be used as direct support for partnership borrowings.

Tax features.   While the limited partnership form involves the same limited liability feature (for limited partners) as corporations, the tax treatment of the limited partnership is similar to that of the general partnership, rather than the corporation. The fact that the limited partners as well as general partners can immediately offset partnership losses against their other income makes this investment interest attractive to the seeker of operating-loss tax-shelter benefits. This, in turn, facilitates raising equity capital for the organization. The amount of partnership losses that a limited partner can use in a given year is restricted, how-

---

[4] Most states have adopted the *Uniform Limited Partnership Act.* In certain states, such as California, the limited partner may vote on the purchase and sale of partnership property, if this is provided for in the partnership agreement.

ever, to the basis of the limited partner's interest in the partnership.[5]

The limited partnership agreement must be carefully drawn to avoid having the organization taxed as a corporation. Even though the organization is legally recognized as a limited partnership in the state where it was organized, the Internal Revenue Service will tax the unit as a corporation if too many features of the corporate form are present.

Use of the limited partnership. For the individual investor seeking group investment benefits in the form of additional ivnestment capital, the limited partnership has many attractive features. If the organizing investor is the sole general partner he enjoys extensive management control, although he also has unlimited personal liability. In addition he can offer an appealing interest to other investors wishing an assignable, passive, investment interest with limited liability. As noted, the form is especially well suited to investors seeking operating-loss tax-shelter benefits, as were described in Chapter 5.

The limited partnership form has also been used by large financial institutions that establish subsidiaries to invest in real estate on a joint-venture basis with a developer. The parent company of the financial institution will at times hold a limited partnership interest, in order to restrict its own liability for the partnershp obligations, and the subsidiary of the financial institution will hold a general partnership interest so as to have a management voice in the real estate partnership.[6]

Closely Held Corporation

The terms *closely held corporation,* and *private corporation,* are used to refer to the corporation whose stock is owned by an individual or by a relatively small group of individuals who tend to regard themselves as partners. The corporation is generally somewhat more expensive and somewhat more complex to form and to operate than the partnership. However, in most instances the incorporation steps for small, private corporations are routinized, and no major expenses are incurred.

[5] The tax rules relating to limited partnership losses are considered in more detail in Chapter 17.

[6] This arrangement and variations thereof are described in Sanford Rose, "The Future Largest Landlords in America." *Fortune,* July–August, 1970.

As corporations are separate legal entities, or *persons,* created by state statutes and regulated by state laws, the technical points on the organization and functioning of corporations will vary from state to state. Again, however, as with partnerships, we can describe characteristics that are generally applicable.

The corporate investors (shareholders) have limited liability, that is, limited to the amount of capital that they have pledged to invest. Shareholders also have a share in the control of the corporation in accordance with the proportion of total shares that they own; however, management is centralized as regards day-to-day decision making, with power concentrated in the corporation's officers appointed (usually annually) by the company's board of directors.

Because investors are offered limited liability and a voice in the selection of the board of directors the corporation form is attractive from the standpoint of raising capital. Further, the equity investor's shares are assignable, and generally more marketable than limited-partnership interests. This is partly because corporation equity interests are divisible; that is, the investor can sell a discerte number of shares representing a total dollar amount suitable to the needs of the purchaser.

Capital raising is also facilitated by the wide variety of investment interests that can be issued by a corporation to the investment group members—ranging from many types of bonds and preferred stock (including issues convertible into common stock), to various forms of common stock itself. *Continuity* is often cited as an advantage of the corporate form because the corporate business will continue in the event of the death, insanity or retirement of an owner, director, or officer of the corporation.

Tax features. Because the corporation is a separate person under the law, it is taxed as a separate entity, apart from its owners, with a separate scale of tax rates, and special tax provisions. The basic corporate rates are summarized below.[7]

Ordinary Income Tax Rates: First $25,000 of taxable income, 20%
Next $25,000 of taxable income, 22%
Over $50,000 of taxable income, 48%
Capital Gains Tax Rate: 30%

[7] These rates are scheduled by the Tax Reform Act of 1976 to extend through 1977.

TABLE 8-1. Selected Corporation Marginal, and Average Tax Rates on Ordinary Income

Taxable Income	Marginal Tax Rate	Average Tax Rate
$ 10,000	20%	20.0%
30,000	22	20.3
50,000	48	21.0
100,000	48	34.5
500,000	48	45.3
1,000,000	48	46.6

The ordinary income rates cited above represent marginal rates as contrasted to the average tax rate that will apply to total taxable income earned in a particular year. The distinction is made clear in Table 8-1.

In addition to the taxes on ordinary income and on capital gains paid by the corporation itself, the owner–shareholder pays tax at his own personal tax rate on the earnings of the corporation that are paid out to the owner in the form of cash dividends. Therefore, the corporation's earnings are subject to double taxation.

Suppose, for example, that a corporation has taxable ordinary income of $50,000, which, less the $10,500 corporation tax, is completely distributed to its only two shareholders, each in the 70 per cent tax bracket. The total taxes paid ($37,870) on the $50,000 of corporate income would be calculated as shown below. The calculations are based on the assumption that each of the two shareholders files a joint tax return and claims a $200 dividend exclusion.

Corporate tax	$10,500	[$25,000 × 0.20 + $25,000 × 0.22]
Shareholders' tax on dividends	27,370	[($50,000 − $10,500 − $400) × 0.7]
Total tax	$37,870	[75.7% of the original $50,000 of taxable income]

Had the same two investors used the partnership form, their tax on $50,000 taxable income would have been the lower $35,000 [$50,000 × 0.70]. However, there are two important points to be noted here. *First,* if we assume that the two investors were actively managing the business they would have been able to deduct reasonable salary amounts from corporate taxable income, whereas they could not do so with the partnership form. If we modify the above, to give the two investor–managers $15,000 each in tax-deductible salary, this would reduce the total tax bill to $35,920; bringing it more in line with the partnership tax figure. *Secondly,* if the corporation had paid a smaller dividend (or none at all) the investors' tax bills for that particular year would have been considerably less than under the partnership alternative. The retention of corporate earnings, however, raises some other tax considerations to be discussed later in this chapter.

It will be noted that while a corporation receives favored treatment on its qualifying capital gains (favorable compared to ordinary income treatment), when any dividends corresponding to those gains are paid to shareholders, the shareholders will pay tax at ordinary income tax rates. This contrasts with partnership capital gains that will be taxed to the partners at favorable capital gains tax rates.

Operating and capital losses. When operating losses are suffered by the corporation, such losses *cannot* be used in the year of loss by the shareholders as a direct offset against their other income. Rather, as stated in an earlier chapter, corporate operating losses can be carried backwards three years and forward for seven years. A newly formed corporation having operating losses in the first few years of operations, therefore, can not apply the losses until the corporation starts generating taxable profits sometime in the future, against which the present losses can be applied. Similarly, net capital losses cannot be directly passed on to shareholders in the year incurred as they can be with the partnership form. Rather, net capital losses must be carried back three years and forward five years by the corporation.

Special corporate tax provisions. Several attempts have been made to reduce the impact of corporate income taxes in general, and the double-taxation feature in particular. In response to such attempts several special tax provisions have been developed over the years, including those provisions included in the 1969 Tax Reform Act. Some of the major special corporate tax provisions germane to real estate investing are summarized below.

Multiple corporations. Many real estate investors have made a practice of forming several separate corporations to hold their various individual investment properties. This practice is sometimes convenient for administrative purposes, especially where there are different co-investors involved in each project. This practice was also convenient from a tax standpoint. If the taxable income of each corporation could be kept low enough, the marginal corporate tax rate would be kept at less than half the 48 per cent level. Further, the accumulated earnings tax, to be discussed below, could be minimized or even avoided by the use of multiple corporations. However, the 1969 Tax Reform Act provided for the elimination by 1975 of the just-described tax advantages of the multiple corporations, by treating a *controled group of corporations* as a single unit.

Accumulated earnings tax. Penalty taxes are applied to any portion of a particular year's earnings retained by a corporation that are considered unnecessary for the reasonable needs of the business. The purpose is to offset the taxes lost to the government, by way of shareholders' leaving corporate earnings in the company in lieu of receiving earnings as dividends that would be taxed at ordinary income tax rates to the shareholders.

The first $150,000 of accumulated retained earnings is legally presumed to be a reasonable and proper accumulation, which, of course, is a provision favoring small corporations. Above the first $150,000, any accumulated earnings shown to be unnecessary to meet the reasonable needs of the business, called *improperly accumulated earnings,* are taxed at the rates of: 27.5 per cent on the first $100,000 thereof, and 38.5 per cent on improper amounts above $100,000.

Personal holding company tax. A corporation having more than 50 per cent of the value of its stock owned by five or fewer individuals, and at least 60 per cent of its *adjusted ordinary gross income* in the form of *personal holding company income* (i.e., passive-source income, such as interest and rental income) may be classified as a *personal holding company.* As such, a flat tax of 70 per cent will be imposed on *all of* its undistributed earnings for a particular year. The rules pertaining to the personal holding company tax are contained in the Internal Revenue Code, Sections 541–547.

Collapsible corporations. One procedure that has been used to distribute corporate earnings to shareholders on a capital gains basis rather than on an ordinary income basis (the latter relates to paying corporate dividends) involves liquidating the corporation, with the shareholders receiving corporate assets as liquidating dividends. The result may be capital gains treatment for the amount of gain in value obtained by the shareholders. If, however, the corporation is found to be a *collapsible corporation,* ordinary income tax rates may be applicable rather than capital gains rates. The pertinent rules are contained in Section 341 of the Internal Revenue Code.

Subchapter S corporations. The Internal Revenue Code makes provision for a corporation, that so elects, to be taxed as if the corporation were a partnership. If a corporation can qualify as a so-called *Subchapter S corporation,* its shareholders can enjoy the limited liability and other benefits of a corporation, but avoid the double-taxation to which regular corporate income is subjected. The Subchapter S treatment would also allow the owners to take deductions for corporate operating losses, and allow shareholders to receive preferential tax treatment for corporate capital gains distributed to them as dividends. Most corporations primarily engaged in real estate investing, however, would have difficulty qualifying, because corporations receiving more than 20 per cent of their gross income from passive investments in income-producing properties do not have the Subchapter S option. The use of this device, therefore, would be restricted to those real estate corporations having projects generating substantial income from construction or service activities.

If the corporation can retain its earnings and thereby avoid paying dividends to the owners, the immediate total taxes payable on investment income can be substantially lower than with the partnership or individual form of organization, because the corporation's marginal tax rates are 20, 22, and 48 per cent, while personal marginal tax rates range up to 70 per cent. The immediate taxes saved can be put to work to expand investment activities. The practical problem with the procedure of leaving retained earnings in the corporation is that a major tax burden may face the investor when he ultimately wishes to withdraw funds from the corporation. It will be recognized that the withdrawal of corporate earnings may be encouraged by the possible application of the accumulated earnings tax or the personal holding company tax. Some possible strategies for reducing corporate income taxes, or for withdrawing funds *trapped* in the corporation would include:

1. The payment of substantial salaries and fees to owners who are also providing services to the corporation. While the payments received will be taxable to the recipients, they also will provide a deduction against corporate taxable income, as long as the amounts paid can be considered *reasonable*.

2. The owner–shareholder can *lend* significant funds to the corporation as an alternative to providing more equity capital, and thereafter take out interest payments in lieu of dividends. As with salary payments, the interest payments would be taxable income to the recipient but a tax deduction for the corporation—as long as the interest rate is set at a *reasonable* level and the loan does not have too many incidents of an equity capital contribution.

3. When the corporation has built up a substantial amount of retained earnings, and the value of the shares has risen, the investor can sell some of his shares, paying tax on the gain at the favorable capital gains tax rates. However, the various special corporate tax provisions described previously would have to be considered.

4. The investor can wait to withdraw dividends until he falls into a much lower income level, for example, in retirement years; or not withdraw funds during his own lifetime, but have the corporate shares pass to his heirs and devisees *on a stepped-up basis.*[8] However, the accumulated-earnings tax and the personal-holding-company tax, and the new *basis* rules of the Tax Reform Act of 1976 would have to be considered.

Use of the corporation.   At first appearance, perhaps, the corporate form seems to offer many advantages. On balance, however, for the individual investor or for small groups investing in real estate, this form is usually not the most attractive organizational form. Some reasons are:

1. While the limited liability feature is important, it is often the case with new or small-scale corporations that lenders require

---

[8] The tax aspects of disposing of property to heirs and devisees is discussed in more detail in Chapter 11.

the principal owners to personally sign for corporate obligations. Further, in many investments the exposure to liability is not high because property values often are substantially in excess of the amount of mortgage debt outstanding on the property.

2. From the tax standpoint, the combination of corporate tax provisions referred to previously often leads to the principal owner–shareholder's having funds *trapped* in the corporation, which become increasingly difficult to withdraw without a substantial tax burden.

3. If the investor is anticipating losses in at least the first few years of the investment, as would be sought by the tax-shelter investor, the corporation is an inappropriate form because operating losses and capital losses cannot be used directly by the shareholder.

4. If substantial capital gains are obtained by the corporation they will be taxed first in the corporation at favorable corporate capital gains tax rates, but when they are distributed as dividends, the shareholders will pay tax at ordinary rates on the amounts received. With the partnership or proprietorship organizational forms the capital gains would be taxed only once, and then at the investor's favorable capital gains rates.

Despite the points just raised, there are still situations where the corporate form would be the most appropriate strategy for a small group; such as where limited liability is especially important to investors, or the corporate tax rates of 20 and 22 per cent will apply, and when dividend withdrawals can be postponed for a significant time period without undue tax obligations arising. The corporation is a generally very useful form, indeed, when the real estate investor seeks very large amounts of capital, as will be discussed later in this chapter.

Other Private Groups

Before leaving this discussion of private groups we briefly describe in the present section some other forms of nonpublic forms of co-ownership used in real estate investment.

The *joint venture* is a combination of two or more persons who join in a partnership of limited duration. The co-venturers typically join together to undertake a single transaction or series of transactions. Generally, the same legal rules of partnership apply to the joint venture. In the real estate investment area, joint ventures range from small local ventures to large real estate development projects. Such large-scale projects as housing developments and large office building projects are often undertaken with a real estate developer joining with either a large financial institution, such as an insurance company, or with an industrial corporation. The developer in such joint ventures typically handles the overall supervision of land development, construction, and leasing activities, while the financial institution or industrial corporation provides the capital funds.

The condominium is a fast-growing, relatively new form of co-ownership of real estate (though it reflects a concept dating back to ancient Rome). The purchaser of a *condominium* buys ownership in a single unit in a multiunit structure (such as an individual apartment) and also an undivided interest in common with other owners in the land and other parts of the structure (such as hallways). While the first condominiums involved apartments and townhouses, the form also has been used for co-ownership of office buildings.

In purchasing a *cooperative apartment* within a multiunit structure, the apartment dweller obtains shares in the overall cooperative, and typically one owner cannot sell his interest without the consent of the other owners. Because the property title, mortgage, and insurance, are in the name of the overall cooperative, default in payment by one sharing owner may affect the title of the entire property. In contrast, the individual condominium is separately mortgaged and insured in the name of its individual owner.

The distinction between joint tenancy and tenancy in common should also be noted. When two or more persons hold title to real property as *joint tenants,* there exists a right of survivorship, whereby if one of the tenants dies the surviving joint tenants automatically take title to the deceased's interest. All joint tenants have personal liability for all expenses incurred on the property.

Tenancy in common is a form of common ownership whereby each of the tenants in common retains an undivided interest in the property, and each has the right to force a sale of the property to claim his part of the property value. Because there is no right of survivorship with this form, the interest held by a tenant in common passes to his heirs upon his death, or to whomever is designated in his will.

PUBLIC GROUPS

When the individual investor or small group of investors wishes to move to a larger scale of operations, an alternative to forming a joint venture with a large industrial corporation or financial institution is to sell equity shares to the general public. The organization can then use the new equity capital as a base upon which to obtain additional debt financing. By taking this route some previously relatively small investors have rather quickly come to assume day-to-day control over several million dollars worth of real estate investment properties. While historically the public corporation has been the traditional vehicle for going public, two other organizational forms have increasingly been used for this purpose, namely, *public syndication* (in limited partnership form), and the *real estate investment trust* (REIT). The particulars of each form will be discussed shortly; however, there are some general characteristics of these three forms that are useful to discuss by way of introduction.

Along with rising levels of discretionary, or spendable, funds in the hands of the general public since World War II, there has been growing interest on the part of *non-professional* investors in real estate equity investment. Since these part-time investors are often persons that have traditionally invested in the stock market, the interest in real estate investment has increased most markedly during periods of stock market declines. This was evidenced in the early 1970's when securities prices were declining and real estate values were continuing to rise.

The public corporations, syndicates, and REIT's all issue securities having common characteristics that generally appeal to the investing public. For example, their shares all feature limited liability for the investor; that is, liability is limited to the amount of capital invested or subscribed. There is usually a relatively small minimum investment amount required for the purchase of shares in the three different organizational forms, and such shares generally have some degree of liquidity or marketability. Further, all three public-group forms are regulated in varying degrees by state and federal governments.

As stated previously, equity investors can use the three public-group forms to raise large amounts of capital and thereby expand their investment activities. There exist other benefits of going public that are sometimes looked to by their organizers, including the opportunities for substantial salaries, management fees, advisory fees, brokerage commissions, and other payments for services. As with non-real-estate organizations that go public, substantial profits have been realized by promoter–organizers in the form of capital gains on their holdings of the organization's ownership shares after the organization goes public. At times shares are held in a private corporation that later sells shares to the public with a dramatic increase in share value. In the case of the formation of *new* public, real-estate investment organizations, the organizers at times take shares at reduced prices, or they take options to purchase shares in the future at favorable prices.

Because some abuses have been experienced in relation to the above described activities there has been growing public regulation of these organizations' activities. The nature and extent of such government regulation varies from one organizational form to another, as do the tax features of the various forms.

Public Corporation

The most carefully regulated organizational form is the public corporation. The full range of corporate financial disclosure requirements apply, including the required registration with the Securities and Exchange Commission (SEC) of a prospectus for all interstate public securities issues of at least $500,000 in amount. The prospectus preparation and approval generally mean delays and expenses for the corporation. If the corporation's shares are traded on a securities exchange, the relevant disclosure rules of the Securities Exchange Act of 1934, and the rules of the exchanges themselves, must be observed. Such rules relate to such things as the filing of interim financial statements, and information on insider transactions.

One of the most attractive aspects of the public corporation form of organization is the opportunity to tailor securities to the particular investment requirements of a wide variety of investors. The corporation can issue various types of debt securities as well as preferred- and common-stock issues. When an active secondary market for the corporation's shares exists, that is, when the shares are traded on one of the principal securities exchanges or in the over-the-counter market, then the additional liquidity so provided will help attract investment capital as new issues are offered in the future. Control can, of course, be kept by the organizing individual or group by selling less than 50 per cent of the ownership shares to the public; but also, with the use of the proxy mechanism, effective control can often be retained by the organizers even when they personally hold less than a majority of the shares.

The various other attributes of the private corporation described earlier in this chapter apply to the public corporation as well, such as centralized management, and continuity. The basic tax features likewise apply, except those relating to the personal holding company. The double-taxation feature, and the inability of the shareholders to directly make use of the organization's losses and capital gains can make the corporate form less appropriate than the two other public-group forms for many real estate investments. The corporate form should be considered for use, however, whenever the organizers wish: to raise large amounts of capital; to retain limited liability for themselves (as contrasted to the general partner in the public syndication); to retain a majority or controlling position; and when, also, the investments are expected to generate profits (rather than losses).

Public Syndication

The term *syndicate* is broadly used to refer to a pooling of funds for investment purposes. However, in recent years the term has been associated with the limited partnership legal form used for investing in real estate. Accordingly, for purposes of this discussion, public syndication is considered to be a limited partnership, with the organizers being the general partners and with the limited partnership interests held by the public. The equity is publicly syndicated by obtaining the participation of a substantial number of individual or institutional investors (say 50 or more) who seek a passive, limited-liability equity interest in real estate. Public syndications have a relatively recent history, going back to about the early 1950's. The first very large syndication was used in 1961 as a vehicle to acquire the Empire State Building, at a cost of $85,000,000, with some 3,000 limited partners participating.[9]

The general partners have day-to-day control of the organization, even though they may have as little as 5 per cent or less of the total equity investment of the organization. The general partners also have unlimited liability. The general partners usually receive management fees and other forms of compensation related to the syndicate's operations. For example, public syndications are often formed by real-estate brokerage firms that look for brokerage fees to be generated by the syndicate's future transactions.

Tax features. As noted previously, the income, losses, capital gains, and capital losses are not taxed separately as they are received by the partnership organization, as contrasted with the corporation; rather they *flow through* directly to the partners and are treated as if personally received by them. This is advantageous in the event of capital gains, because these will be taxed to the partners at the favorable capital gains rates. More significant in recent years, however, has been the ability of the limited partners to use the operating losses generated by many syndicates.

Because of the strong investor demand for tax-shelter investments, and because there are opportunities for such benefits in real estate investing, as discussed in a previous chapter, the number of real estate syndicates has grown rapidly in recent years, with many large-scale syndicates formed not only by local real estate brokers and other local groups, but also by the large, traditional Wall Street investment banking houses. Because some instances of abuses have occurred with public syndications involving overreaching by general partners, the syndications have become increasingly subject to government regulation.

Real Estate Investment Trust

The real estate investment trust (REIT) is a form of investment organization having special standing under the tax laws. It

[9] *Forbes,* November 1, 1970, p. 42.

was created in 1961 by Sections 856–858 of the U.S. Internal Revenue Code, and was designed as a vehicle by which small investors can invest in real estate. The REIT's features are similar to those of the regulated closed-end investment companies, commonly known as mutual funds, which were established some 20 years previously as tax-favored units for small investors wishing to participate in securities investments.

The trusts that are engaged principally in acquiring real estate equity interests are known as *equity trusts*. Another large number of REIT's called *mortgage trusts* invest most of their funds in mortgages, as described more fully in the next chapter. A third group called *hybrid trusts* have significant holdings of both types of real estate investments.

Investors in REIT's receive shares called *certificates of beneficial interest,* and they receive some of the advantages of both the corporate and partnership forms, as here summarized:

1. Limited liability.
2. Centralized and professional management.
3. Transferable shares that are often readily marketable because many REIT's have shares traded on the over-the-counter market, or on the major stock exchanges.
4. Diversification benefits because the REIT usually invests in a large number of projects.
5. Avoidance of double taxation, as long as earnings are distributed in accordance with the terms of the statute.

Qualifications for REIT status. There are extensive requirements for the establishment and maintenance of REIT status. Some of the principal requirements are summarized below.

Ownership. There must be at least 100 shareholders; corporations and other organizations as well as individuals can own shares. No five individual shareholders combined can own directly or indirectly more than 50 per cent in value of the organization's outstanding shares (during the last six months of the organization's tax year).

Sources of income. The Internal Revenue Code specifies a series of gross income and investment requirements designed to assure that the principal activity of the organization is investment in real estate properties, and that investing is done on a generally passive, longer-term basis, rather than engaging in short-term trading of properties or primarily engaging in brokerage or other real estate service activities. For example, at least 75 per cent of the organization's gross income must be derived from interests in real property or from mortgages.

Distribution requirements. To qualify for tax benefits, at least 90 per cent of the organization's earnings must be distributed to the owners, either in the year in which earned or in the following year. If less than 90 per cent is distributed, then all of the organization's income for that year is taxable as if it were corporation income; however, if at least 90 per cent is distributed, only the undistributed portion of earnings is subject to tax. For example, if 94 per cent of a year's earnings is distributed, only 6 per cent is subject to tax.

Tax features. As just noted, as long as the organization distributes at least 90 per cent of its earnings, the earnings that are distributed to shareholders *pass through* the organization free of taxes; that is, double taxation is avoided. The capital gains of the organization, distributed as *capital gains dividends,* also pass through to the shareholders to be taxed to them at favorable capital gains rates. In this way the real estate investment trust investors' tax benefits are similar to the limited partners' benefits: as contrasted with the limited partnership, however, the operating losses of the REIT cannot be passed on to the investors by the REIT.

Under the provisions of the 1976 TRA, the minimum earnings distribution requirement will increase from 90 to 95 per cent, for years starting in 1980. Also starting in 1980, a special excise tax will be imposed if the REIT delays to the following year the distribution of over 25 per cent of a year's earnings.

Other of the 1976 Tax Code amendments affecting REIT's recognize the earnings difficulties experienced by many trusts in the 1970's—under the 1976 TRA, definitions of the acceptable types of gross income sources are less restrictive, operating losses can offset undistributed net capital gains, and corporations voluntarily giving up their REIT status can carry forward their previous REIT net operating losses for eight years.

Use of the REIT. The organizers of real estate investment trusts (who must number at least six to have voting control) can, as with the other public forms of organization, raise substantial amounts of capital with the REIT. The Virginia Real Estate

Investment Trust, for example, was organized in August, 1970, with eleven trustees and officers. The organizing group contributed capital totalling $100,100, and a few months later the REIT sold an issue of beneficial shares to the public to raise $15 million. As the public issue was sold interstate and was above the minimum amount, a prospectus was registered with the Securities and Exchange Commission.

The fact, however, that to qualify for tax benefits the REIT's must distribute at least 90 per cent of each year's earnings means that the trusts cannot look to retained earnings as a major source of funds for new investments. Rather, the trusts must continually seek new external capital to finance expansion.

SUMMARY

One strategic decision for the real estate investor is the selection of the form of organization that is most appropriate for a particular real estate investment project. The decision will be based on the nature and scale of the project, and upon the financial and tax position of the investor.

The *individual ownership* form gives the investor exclusive control over the project, but the owner has unlimited personal liability for the financial obligations relating to the property investment. The taxable returns from the investment are added to the owner's income from other sources and taxed at the owner's personal tax rates.

Should the owner wish to seek limited liability, he can form a closely held corporation; and if he wishes to form a small private group to invest in a project, he can use the closely held corporation or the general or limited partnership form. The tax and other features of these organizations were discussed in the chapter. Other small group forms were briefly described, including the *joint venture, condominum, cooperative apartment, joint tenancy,* and *tenancy in common.*

If the real estate investor wishes to take on large-scale projects by raising capital funds from the public, there are three principal vehicles that can be used: the *public corporation, public syndication,* and the *real estate investment trust.* The tax and other features of these three forms were described in this chapter.

9

Financing Strategy

As indicated in the previous chapter, there are a number of ways to raise *equity* (ownership) funds for real estate investments, ranging from the taking on of a co-venturer, to the selling of trust shares to the general public. In the present chapter we consider the use of *debt* funds in financing real estate investments. The principal debt-financing instruments and sources are reviewed, as well as strategies relating to repayment schedules, and the impact of debt financing on the equity investor's risks and returns.

In this, as in previous chapters, we are concerned primarily with investments in land and in developed properties; hence only *permanent,* long-term financing is discussed. The shorter-term *interim* financing used for the development and construction of real estate will be discussed in Part V, and the *refinancing* of existing loans on developed properties is considered in the next chapter.

BASIC FINANCING PATTERNS

The basic debt financing technique for acquiring developed real property is, of course, for the purchaser to pay only part of the purchase price in cash, and to borrow the remainder of the funds, the lender to be given a security interest in the property being acquired. The general pattern would be to offer a first-priority security claim on the property (a *first-lien*) to the first lender; if additional debt funds are required, one or more junior-lien security interests are offered to other lenders. While there are countless ways of arranging financing for the acquisition of real estate, it is useful to consider some of the more common patterns. Accordingly, six basic financing patterns are described below.

For the six cases, we assume *A* wishes to purchase *B's* property, which has a price of $100,000; and *A* has $25,000 in cash to apply toward the purchase price, and will require $75,000 in debt financing. It is further assumed that at the time the property is offered for sale, *D* holds a $75,000 first mortgage on *B's* property.

CASE I. *A* pays $100,000 cash to *B,* using $25,000 of his own cash (equity funds) and $75,000 borrowed from a third party, *C;* lender *C* (the *mortgagee*) takes a first mortgage on *A's* property. *A* is the *mortgagor. B* will *pre-pay* to *D* his outstanding mortgage loan with part of the proceeds of sale.

CASE II. *A* pays $25,000 cash to *B,* and *A* assumes *B's* first mortgage obligation in the amount of $75,000. *A* would generally prefer to assume *B's* mortgage rather than arrange a new mortgage loan when *B's* mortgage carries a lower interest rate or has other desirable features. The mortgage assumption would also be sought by *A* when new mortgage money is in short supply.

CASE III. *A* pays $25,000 cash to *B,* and *A* takes the property *subject* to *B's* first mortgage, in favor of *D,* in the amount of $75,000. This is similar to CASE II, except that *A* will not be held personally liable for any deficiency in the event that the property is foreclosed because of default in loan payments. For example, if the proceeds of the foreclosure sale amount to $30,000, and the amount of the mortgage loan outstanding at the time of sale is $34,000, then *B* will be liable for the $4,000 deficiency, but not *A.* However, *A* will, of course, lose the property in the event of such a sale.

CASE IV. *A* pays $25,000 cash to *B,* and *A* gives a note for $75,000 to *B* secured by a first mortgage (*purchase-money mortgage*) on the property in favor of *B.* No third party is involved.

CASE V. *B* splits the property into the land and building components for financing purposes. *B* leases the land, worth $30,000 to *A* under a long-term ground lease, and *B* sells the building to *A* for $70,000. *B* *takes back* a $52,500 first mortgage on the building (75 per cent of $70,000). In this case, *A's* cash down payment is reduced from $25,000 to $7,500.

CASE VI. *A* can obtain first-lien financing for only $60,000, but is able to find a lender who will provide the balance of the financing needed ($15,000), with *A* giving to the lender (often the seller) a second mortgage on the property.

BASIC FINANCING INSTRUMENTS

While the *mortgage* is the most familiar of the legal instruments used in financing the acquisition of real estate, the *deed of trust* and *land contract* are also widely used. Some basic features of these three instruments are described in this section.

Mortgage

There are two basic parts to the mortgage financing arrangement: (1) the *note* (or *bond*), which is a promise by the borrower (*mortgagor*) to repay the amount of the loan to the lender (*mortgagee*) with interest at a specified rate; and (2) the mortgage itself, which pledges a specific property as security for the obligation represented by the note related thereto. The note and the mortgage may be separate instruments, or may be combined in one instrument.[1] The expression *first mortgage* refers to a mortgage having a primary security interest in the property; that is, if the mortgaged property is sold because of the borrower's failure to make payments, then the proceeds of the sale will be used to satisfy the obligation to the first mortgagee—before the remaining proceeds, if any, are made available to satisfy the obligations to those holding *junior* or secondary mortgages on the same property.

Types of Mortgages. Some of the types of mortgages commonly used in financing developed properties are described below. Some other specialized mortgage forms used primarily in financing property development and construction are described in Part V.

Conventional mortgage. This label is used for a mortgage that does *not* have U.S. Government backing; that is, the mortgage is not backed by Federal Housing Administration insurance, nor by a Veterans Administration guarantee.

Junior mortgage. This type of mortgage involves a security interest in the real property that comes after that of the first mortgage on the same property. The *second mortgage,* and other

---

[1] In *title theory* states, the mortgagee holds the property title while the loan is outstanding; as contrasted to *lien theory* states, where the mortgagor (borrower) retains title, and the mortgagee holds a lien on the property.

more junior mortgages, generally involve higher interest rates and shorter terms than do first mortgages.

Purchase-money mortgage. This mortgage is one that is used when the seller provides financing for the buyer of his property. It can be a first mortgage or a junior mortgage.

Package mortgage. This refers to a mortgage that covers equipment and fixtures that are attached to the property, as well as the land and building covered by the same mortgage.

Blanket mortgage. This mortgage is often used to finance the acquisition of land that will be subsequently subdivided for resale. The financing would generally be so arranged that individual lots will be released from the mortgage as they are sold, and as corresponding repayments are made on the outstanding mortgage loan.

Wrap-around mortgage. This mortgage is used in refinancing and is described in more detail in the next chapter; it is given by an owner who at the time already has an existing mortgage on his property. He does not wish to pay off the existing mortgage, because of prepayment penalties, or because of an attractive interest rate, or for other reasons, and hence offers a wrap-around mortgage to a lender who agrees to meet the payments on the existing mortgage and also to loan him additional funds. He will make payments on the wrap-around mortgage of sufficient size to service both the previously existing mortgage and the loan advanced to him under the new wrap-around mortgage.

Mortgage clauses. Some of the typical mortgage clauses that are usually of special interest to the investor in developed properties are now briefly described.

Acceleration clause. By this typical mortgage clause, the due dates of all of the future loan payments are *accelerated* in the event of *default*, that is failure to make loan payments as due or to pay property taxes or to meet other specified requirements. In other words, the entire outstanding obligation becomes due and payable immediately, with the mortgagee having the right to force sale of the property, or *foreclose*, in the event the loan is not repaid in full. The technical requirements relating to such matters as the grace periods allowed, and the equity of redemption right of the mortgagor will depend on the terms of the contract and upon the laws of the state where the mortgaged property is located. The *equity of redemption* refers to the right of the mortgagor who has defaulted on his mortgage loan to redeem his property (upon payment of the full amount due on the mortgage note plus certain penalties) prior to the sale of the property, and in some states even after the property is sold.

Late-payment penalties. If mortgage payments are late but still timely enough to avoid a default, the mortgage terms usually call for penalty payments calculated as some percentage of the late payment amounts.

Prepayment penalties. Many mortgages contain a clause allowing the mortgagor to repay the mortgage loan, that is, to repay part or all of the loan ahead of schedule. When this right is given, it is generally attended by a provision for penalty payments, with the amount of the penalty being highest in the early years of the mortgage. This can be an important clause for the investor, of course, if an early future sale of the property is anticipated. The prepayment penalty serves to reimburse the lender for his loan-origination expenses. Borrowers will not only wish to prepay the mortgage loan when they sell the property, but also when they wish to take advantage of a decline in interest rates by replacing the existing mortgage with a new one (refinancing) at lower rates. If interest rates rise significantly after the mortgage loan is granted, the lender will usually be willing to accept prepayment with a waiver or reduction of the prepayment penalties.

Deed of Trust

In many states the deed of trust is widely used in lieu of the mortgage instrument. Title to the property is conveyed to a third party who holds it in trust as security for the payment of the borrower's obligation. The lender is generally referred to as the *beneficiary,* and the party holding the title is called the *trustee.* The trustee reconveys the property to the borrower when the debt is paid, or alternatively sells the property in the event of non-payment. The trust deed is often preferred by lenders to the mortgage instrument because trustees are usually permitted by state laws to sell the property in the event of default, without the usual delays and expenses of court proceedings accompanying mortgage foreclosure.

Land Contract

The land contract is an instrument used when the buyer receives financing from the seller of the property. Under this arrangement the seller retains title until all loan repayments have been made by the buyer. The land contract is often used by developers who sell subdivision lots on installment terms.

Corporate Financing Instruments

A wide range of short-term and long-term instruments are used in obtaining debt financing by corporations and financial institutions. Where the organization seeks to sell a bond issue, it may be necessary or advantageous to have the bond issue backed by a mortgage or deed of trust on the organization's real property.

SOURCES OF FUNDS

There are various sources that the investor can look to for mortgage loan funds to be used for the acquisition of developed real estate. A brief review of the principal sources is undertaken in the present section.

The Seller

The seller of real estate will often be found willing to finance the buyer by taking a note as partial payment, and a purchase-money mortgage for security; or he may be willing to sell the property on a land-contract basis. Seller financing would be motivated by such situations as described below.

1. When buyers are scarce and seller financing is required to make a desired sale go through, the seller may be willing to take the buyer's note. Even where the seller wishes to obtain cash from the sale of his property it is sometimes to his advantage to accept a buyer's note and later sell it (*discount it*). By doing so he may obtain higher net cash proceeds than by selling the property to any

other available buyer who is willing to pay the whole purchase price in cash.

2. When the seller achieves a substantial capital gain on the sale he may desire to sell the property on the installment basis in order to reduce the immediate impact of federal income taxes on the gain. The tax aspects of installment-basis sales and other deferred-payment sales are described in Chapter 11.

3. The buyer's note may represent an attractive investment for the seller. This would tend to be the case when the interest rate on the note is relatively high, and when the seller is willing to hold a passive investment interest (the note).

The seller would become an especially important source of funds when financial institutions hesitate to do the financing because of their lack of funds, or because of the nature of the particular property involved, or for some other reason. For example, seller financing is widely relied upon for the acquisition of raw land because of the general reluctance of financial institutions to finance non-income-producing property.

In addition to being a source of first-mortgage financing, the seller is often looked to as a supplier of junior-mortgage funds—where a financial institution has agreed to provide the buyer with a first mortgage loan that is insufficient to cover all the buyer's needs.

Financial Institutions

The *life insurance companies* as a group are the single most important supplier of long-term mortgage funds for the financing of income-producing property. The larger life insurance companies are not restricted to local lending as are some other financial institutions, and they have the necessary experience and expertise to handle the intricate facets of financing large real estate investment projects. The *mutual savings banks*, most of which are located in New York and in the New England states, provide substantial amounts of mortgage money for residential properties including apartment projects. They also provide lesser amounts for financing non-residential properties.

The *real estate investment trusts* principally investing in mortgages (the mortgage trusts) that were mentioned in the last chapter have become another source of permanent real estate debt funds, although many of the trusts have placed a high proportion of their funds into the higher-yielding and shorter-term development and construction loans.[2] The *pension funds,* while traditionally geared toward investments in common stocks and bonds, have in recent years become suppliers of real estate mortgage money.

The major role of *commercial banks* in mortgage lending is that of supplying interim financing for commercial and industrial real estate projects, and permanent financing for home residences. The commercial banks also provide some permanent mortgage funds, however, for financing industrial and commercial properties. In recent years the commercial bank holding companies have acquired some of the *mortgage banks* as subsidiaries. These latter banks serve primarily as originators and servicers of mortgages for other financial institutions. The *savings and loan associations* as a group supply the largest amount of mortgage funds of the various financial institutions. However, most of their funds are invested in mortgages on single-family residences. Some of the larger S&L's, however, have supplied permanent loan funds for financing real estate investment properties.

Because the financial institutions are entrusted with deposits or other funds supplied by the public, the investment policies of the institutions are subjected to state and national regulations. Such regulations affect the mortgage lending flexibility of the institutions relating to such things as the proportion of their funds that can be invested in mortgages, and the types and terms of the mortgages that they do invest in. Some commercial banks and savings and loan associations are prohibited, for example, from directly making junior mortgage loans.[3]

One of the most significant developments in recent years in the area of real estate lending is the growing demand by financial institutions for *equity participation* in the projects for which they are asked to provide mortgage loan funds. The equity participa-

---

[2] Many of the trusts having large portfolios of development and construction loans experienced severe financial difficulties in the mid-1970's as construction projects faltered, for a variety of reasons.

[3] For a detailed review of real estate lending by financial institutions, see William Atteberry, *Modern Real Estate Finance* (Columbus, Ohio: Grid, Inc., 1972).

tion would be in the form of a specified percentage of project income or cash flows. The objective is to give the lending institution an opportunity for higher returns than are generated by their more traditional, fixed-return mortgage investments.

The growing pressure by financial institutions to apply a *variable interest rate* to their long-term mortgage loans is another important development in real estate financing. The objective is to have the interest rate on the loan change as the general level of interest rates changes. Such an arrangement, of course, adds another element of uncertainty to the equity investor's forecast of future returns from real estate investments.

Other Sources of Funds

Included among the other sources of mortgage loan funds would be *individual investors*. Such investors often seek to place their funds in relatively high-yield, junior-mortgage loans. Some of the many other sources of real estate mortgage funds include industrial corporations, universities, trust funds, small business investment companies, and state and local development authorities.

While the *U.S. Government,* through its many agencies, is a major factor in the mortgage markets, it is principally involved in: (1) the secondary markets, by purchasing mortgages originated by financial institutions; (2) mortgages on residential properties; and (3) the insuring and guaranteeing of FHA and VA loans originated by financial institutions. Some direct mortgage loans are made available for farm properties by the Federal Land Banks and by the Farmers Home Administration, and some direct mortgage loans for acquiring and building residential properties are provided by the Veterans Administration.

REPAYMENT STRATEGY

There is an endless variety of repayment schedules for real estate loans because such loans can be *customized* to meet the requirements of a particular lender or group of lenders. That is, the equity investor who is *selling a mortgage* to raise cash will tailor the mortgage loan terms to meet the needs of particular buyers (mortgagees), so as to maximize the amount of cash to be raised. The equity investor will also attempt to arrange repayments so that they will not unfavorably affect the project's cash flows, and the project's rate of return.

Zeckendorf describes, for example, a *dormant mortgage* as a mortgage calling for *no* payments of amortization (principal) or interest until after the first mortgage on the same property has been paid in full—say, in 25 years; at which time, the holder of the dormant mortgage would take a first-lien claim on the property, and periodic payments would commence. The buyer of such a mortgage would possibly be an individual who wishes to arrange for future income for his children.[4]

A more common variation of the extreme repayment situation just described is where a second mortgage is sold that calls for interest payments only, until the first mortgage on the same property is repaid in full; at which time principal reduction would begin on the second mortgage. Despite the many repayment scheduling possibilities, most real estate mortgage loans fall into one of the three basic categories described below: *straight-term mortgage, partially amortized mortgage,* and *fully amortized mortgage.*

Repayment Schedules

Straight-term mortgage. Under this loan arrangement, periodic interest payments *only* are made during the term of the mortgage, with the full principal amount of the loan payable at the end of the mortgage term.

Partially amortized mortgage. This type of mortgage loan calls for some periodic interest payments and some periodic principal payments during the term of the mortgage, with part of the principal still outstanding at the end of the term, to be paid in one lump sum with a so-called *balloon payment*. This is very widely used in second-mortgage financing. The fluctuations in interest rates in recent years has prompted a variation of the partially amortized mortgage whereby repayments are scheduled

[4] William Zeckendorf, *Zeckendorf* (New York: Holt, Rinehart and Winston, 1970), p. 147.

over a long-term period of, say, twenty-five years, but with the loan technically maturing at the end of a shorter term, say five years; at which time a new interest rate for a continuation of the loan would be negotiated.

Fully amortized mortgage. The most familiar repayment schedule, and probably the most widely used is the fully amortized mortgage, whereby periodic payments of interest and principal combined are scheduled so as to fully liquidate the mortgage loan by the end of the mortgage term. Two commonly used types of repayment schedules for fully amortized mortgage loans are described in the following section.

Level- and Variable-Payment Plans. The level-payment plan, characterized by periodic uniform *total* payment amounts (including interest and amortization payments combined) is the most widely used repayment arrangement. In Chapter 4 the computational steps necessary to complete a mortgage-loan schedule with level payments were described. Another often-used repayment arrangement is the variable-payment plan, which calls for periodic uniform *amortization* payments together with periodic interest on the loan balance outstanding at the time the payments are made. For example, assume a $100,000, fully amortized mortgage with a 10-year term, and a 9 per cent interest rate, calling for annual mortgage payments. The mortgage-loan payments under the two just-described repayment plans are shown in Table 9–1. The annual debt service payment of $15,582 for the level-payment plan is found by multiplying the annual mortgage constant of 0.155820 by the loan amount of $100,000. The appropriate annual constand for the mortgage in the example is found in *Column 6* of the Appendix.

The two mortgage schedules in Table 9–1 can serve to illustrate some distinctions between the two commonly used mortgage repayment schedules involved. For example, the level-payment plan (LPP) will provide for lower total annual debt service payments in the early years of the project (and higher in the later years) than with the other plan. In the first three years of the above example the LPP calls for total cash payments for debt service of $46,746, as against $54,300 for the variable-payment plan (VPP); and while in the first three years of the project the

TABLE 9–1. Two Mortgage Repayment Schedules
$100,000 Loan, 9%, 10 Years, Annual Payments

End of Year—	Level-Payment Plan			Variable-Payment Plan		
	Amortization	Interest	Debt Service	Amortization	Interest	Debt Service
1	$ 6,582	$ 9,000	$ 15,582	$ 10,000	$ 9,000	$ 19,000
2	7,174	8,408	15,582	10,000	8,100	18,100
3	7,820	7,762	15,582	10,000	7,200	17,200
4	8,524	7,058	15,582	10,000	6,300	16,300
5	9,291	6,291	15,582	10,000	5,400	15,400
6	10,127	5,455	15,582	10,000	4,500	14,500
7	11,039	4,543	15,582	10,000	3,600	13,600
8	12,032	3,550	15,582	10,000	2,700	12,700
9	13,115	2,467	15,582	10,000	1,800	11,800
10	14,296	1,287	15,582	10,000	900	10,900
Totals	$100,000	$55,821	$155,821	$100,000	$49,500	$149,500

total debt service payments are *lower* with the LPP than with the VPP, the total tax-deductible interest expense amounts are *higher*. Accordingly this plan is favored by those seeking to maximize project cash flows in the early years of the investment.

The variable-payment plan will give greater *equity build-up,* that is, accumulated amortization payments, in the early years, and would therefore be favored by those wishing this form of *forced savings.* In the above example, the VPP provides for $30,000 equity build-up in the first three years, as against $21,576 with the LPP. The general year-to-year patterns for the two mortgage payment schedules just described are diagramed in Figure 9–1.

Minimizing Debt Service

The real estate equity investor seeking to minimize the impact on near-term cash flows of the mortgage debt service payments can consider many approaches, such as the following:

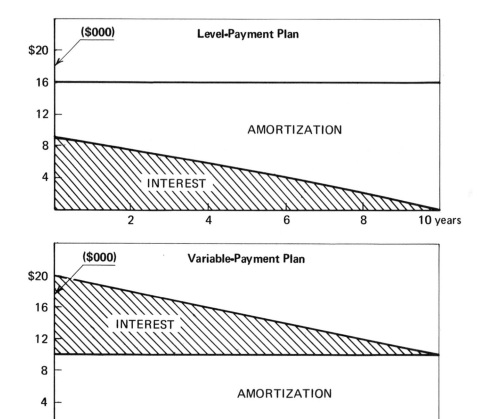

Fig. 9–1. Two mortgage repayment plans, $100,000 loan, 9%, 10 years.

1. The use of the straight-term mortgage, the partially amortized mortgage, or any other mortgage-loan arrangement under which the amortization payments are deferred, will of course reduce near-term cash outflows for debt service.

2. When the fully amortized mortgage is used, the level-payment plan will result in lower debt-service payments in the early years of the project than will the variable payment plan, as noted in the last section.

3. The impact of debt service payments on project cash flows can be made more favorable than otherwise by the careful scheduling of debt-service payments in relation to expected future cash inflows, and other cash outflows, during each year of the planned

holding period. By the use of cash forecasting, an appropriate day of the month for monthly payments can be determined. Generally, a quarterly, semi-annual, or annual payment schedule will provide more flexibility for the borrower than the monthly schedule.

4. The total debt service amount in each year of the mortgage loan will be reduced, of course, if the investor can obtain a reduced interest rate. Suppose, for example, that by extra effort in seeking a lower interest rate or because of the fortunate timing of financing arrangements, a 15-year, level-payment mortgage loan of $200,000 with annual payments is acquired at 9 per cent, instead of at 10 per cent. The 1 per cent interest-rate differential will reduce the mortgage constant from 0.131474 to 0.124059. The annual debt-service amount is correspondingly reduced by $1,483, as calculated below. Because the higher interest expense associated with the 10 per cent loan would be deductible, however, the after-tax savings would be less than $1,483; the precise after-tax amount would be tied to the particular investor's marginal tax rate.

	Annual Mortgage Constant	Loan Amount	Annual Debt Service
15-yr mortgage (10%)	0.131474	$200,000	$26,294.80
15-yr mortgage (9%)	0.124059	200,000	24,811.80
Reduction in debt service			$ 1,483.00

5. The annual debt service amount will also be reduced by taking a longer-term mortgage than otherwise. For example, a 25-year, $200,000 mortgage loan with a 9 per cent interest rate, and annual payments will have a yearly debt service of $4,450.60 less than an otherwise similar mortgage having a term of only 15 years; calculated as shown below. To the extent that taxes are saved, however, by deducting the extra interest, the advantage of the 25-year mortgage would be reduced.

	Annual Mortgage Constant	Loan Amount	Annual Debt Service
15-yr mortgage (9%)	0.124059	$200,000	$24,811.80
25-yr mortgage (9%)	0.101806	200,000	20,361.20
Reduction in debt service			$ 4,450.60

The examples just cited suggest that there may well be occasions where the investor who is primarily interested in minimizing the size of annual debt-service payments may be quite willing to pay a higher interest rate in order to receive a longer-term mortgage loan. For example, a 25-year, 10 per cent mortgage loan will require a significantly lower annual debt service amount than a 15-year, 9 per cent loan, as shown below (on a before-tax basis) for a $200,000 loan.

	Annual Mortgage Constant	Loan Amount	Annual Debt Service
15-yr mortgage (9%)	0.124059	$200,000	$24,811.80
25-yr mortgage (10%)	0.110168	200,000	22,033.60
Reduction in debt service			$ 2,778.20

LEVERAGE STRATEGY

In the present section we consider the question of just what proportion of the property's cost should be financed with debt (mortgage) funds. In other words, what is an appropriate loan-to-value ratio, or *debt-equity mix,* for a particular investment property being considered for acquisition. As discussed in a previous chapter, the term *financial leverage* is used to refer to the relative amount of debt used to finance an investment project. The decision on the appropriate debt-equity mix will depend on the risks and returns that can be expected to be associated with alternative amounts of leverage. Of course, the investor will not have many alternative leverage strategies to consider if only very limited amounts of mortgage loan funds are available to him.

Availability of Funds

Because of its physical attributes, such as immobility and long life, real estate is a desirable form of security for long-term lending. This is especially true for income-producing properties that not only have solid underlying capital value but also have good prospects for generating favorable cash flows over the life of a mortgage. It will be noted further that as payments are made on a fully amortized mortgage, the outstanding mortgage debt amount declines each year, often as the property value itself is increasing and thereby reducing the lender's risk.

The amount of permanent, long-term financing that is available, therefore, for real estate investment projects is often substantial. In some states, life insurance companies, for example, can lend up to 75 per cent of the property's value, and REIT's at times will lend an even higher percentage. When financing of this general magnitude is combined with a second-mortgage loan from the seller (or other source) or a sale-leaseback of the land, the equity investor can at times achieve close to 100 per cent financing.

The real constraint on the amount that will be available for financing a particular real estate property acquisition, aside from the underlying value of the property itself and the credit standing of the borrower, is in *capital market conditions,* that is, the supply and demand situation for long-term money. When market conditions result in a shortage of funds, relatively high loan-to-value ratios may be difficult to achieve, without at least major concessions to the lender with regard to the interest rate level, or in providing the lender with some form of equity participation in the project.

Within the constraints described above relating to the availability of funds, the equity investor must decide on the appropriate amount to borrow for a particular real estate project. One possible strategy that is sometimes observed in practice is for the investor to borrow as much as possible so as to minimize the investor's cash outflow for the property acquisition. This policy results, however, in relinquishing the debt-equity mix decision to the lender, and can lead to risky debt levels for the investor, especially when the lender is actively seeking outlets for otherwise idle funds and he is at the same time convinced that a sale of the property will generate sufficient funds to cover the loan amount outstanding in case of the borrower's default.

In short, a sound financing strategy should be developed by the equity investor before approaching creditors for long-term financing. The strategy as to the appropriate amount of debt financing will depend upon an analyis of the impact of alternative quantities of debt upon the project's prospective risks and returns.

Leverage Impact on Returns

By borrowing funds to help finance a real estate investment project, the equity investor not only reduces the amount of his own cash investment in the project but he also has the opportunity to achieve a higher return on the amount of equity capital that he does invest in the project, than otherwise. The extent to which the equity investor's return will be increased with the use of borrowed funds will depend upon the extent of *favorable leverage* that exists, as was illustrated in Chapter 4.

By the use of *sensitivity analysis* one can determine the impact of different degrees of leverage on the discounted cash flow rate of return for a particular investment project. Following are the basic input data for a hypothetical investment in a *Commercial Property*.

COMMERCIAL PROPERTY

Price	$100,000
Loan	(See below)
Down-payment	(See below)
Holding period	10 years
Estimated selling price ..	$ 75,000
Gross income, actual ...	$ 20,000
Operating expenses ...	$ 6,000
Depreciable value	$ 85,000, 10 years straight-line, zero estimated residual value
Income tax rate	50%
Capital gains tax rate .	25%

For the *Commercial Property* costing $100,000, we shall assume three alternative financing strategies, as follows:

> Case 1: 40% mortgage loan, $40,000, 10 years, 9%
> Case 2: 66⅔% mortgage loan, $66,667, 10 years, 9%
> Case 3: 80% mortgage loan, $80,000, 10 years, 9%

All three loans would be fully amortized over ten years, with level-annual payments. Summary income and cash flow figures

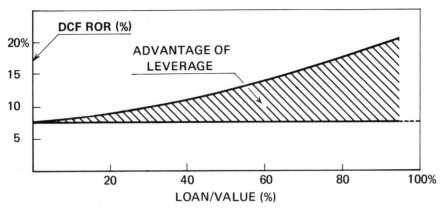

Fig. 9-2. Impact of leverage on equity returns—Commercial Property example.

resulting from the three different financing alternatives are shown in Table 9–2, along with the corresponding discounted cash flow rates of return (DCF ROR) that can be calculated manually, or much more quickly with a computer, as was discussed in Chapter 7.

The impact of the use of leverage in the *Commercial Property* example is shown to be favorable by the data in Table 9–2, because the after-tax return on equity rises from 10.5 per cent, with the use of the $40,000 mortgage loan, to 16.3 per cent, with the $80,000 loan. In this *example,* the after-tax interest cost is 4.5 per cent [9% × 50%], which is considerably lower than the after-tax return rate on total investment of 7.3 per cent. Hence, in this *example,* the higher the proportion of investment funds that is borrowed, the higher will be the return on owner's equity. The advantage of using leverage in the form of increased DCF ROR is shown for the *Commercial Property* example in Figure 9–2.

Leverage Impact on Risk

The risk attending the use of debt funds—that is, the risk of the property's being sold in the event of default on the loan—is related to the acceleration clause contained in the mortgage, as described previously in this chapter. A forced sale of property under distress conditions can mean the loss of the investor's

TABLE 9–2. Sensitivity Analysis for Three Financing

	Year–1	2	3	4
	Case 1.	Property Cost, $100,000		

	Year–1	2	3	4
Net Operating Income	$14,000	$14,000	$14,000	$14,000
less: Interest expense	3,600	3,363	3,105	2,823
Depreciation expense	8,500	8,500	8,500	8,500
Taxable Income	$ 1,900	$ 2,137	$ 2,395	$ 2,677
less: Income taxes	950	1,068	1.198	1,338
Earnings After Tax	$ 950	$ 1,069	$ 1,197	$ 1,339
Cash Flow After Tax	$ 6,817	$ 6,699	$ 6,570	$ 6,429

Discounted Cash Flow Rate of Return, 10.45%

	Case 2.	Property Cost, $100,000		

	Year–1	2	3	4
Net Operating Income	$14,000	$14,000	$14,000	$14,000
less: Interest expense	6,000	5,605	5,175	4,705
Depreciation expense	8,500	8,500	8,500	8,500
Table Income	($ 500)	($ 105)	$ 325	$ 795
less: Income taxes	0	0	163	397
Earnings After Tax	($ 500)	($ 105)	$ 162	$ 398
Cash Flow After Tax	$ 3,862[a]	$ 3,665[a]	$ 3,449	$ 3,215

Discounted Cash Flow Rate of Return, 13.29%

	Case 3.	Property Cost, $100,000		

	Year–1	2	3	4
Net Operating Income	$14,000	$14,000	$14,000	$14,000
less: Interest expense	7,200	6,726	6,210	5,646
Depreciation expense	8,500	8,500	8,500	8,500
Taxable Income	($ 1,700)	($ 1,226)	($ 710)	($ 146)
less: Income taxes	0	0	0	0
Earnings After Tax	($ 1,700)	($ 1,226)	($ 710)	($ 146)
Cash Flow After Tax	$ 2,384[a]	$ 2,147[a]	$ 1,889[a]	$ 1,608[a]

Discounted Cash Flow Rate of Return, 16.32%

[a] Includes tax-loss savings.

Strategies—Commercial Property Example

5	6	7	8	9	10
Mortgage Loan, $40,000					

5	6	7	8	9	10
$14,000	$14,000	$14,000	$14,000	$14,000	$14,000
2,516	2,182	1,817	1,420	987	515
8,500	8,500	8,500	8,500	8,500	8,500
$ 2,984	$ 3,318	$ 3,683	$ 4,080	$ 4,513	$ 4,985
1,492	1,659	1.841	2,040	2,257	2,493
$ 1,492	$ 1,659	$ 1,842	$ 2,040	$ 2,256	$ 2,492
$ 6,275	$ 6,108	$ 5,926	$ 5,727	$ 5,511	$ 5,275

Mortgage Loan, $66,667

5	6	7	8	9	10
$14,000	$14,000	$14,000	$14,000	$14,000	$14,000
4,194	3,637	3,029	2,367	1,645	858
8,500	8,500	8,500	8,500	8,500	8,500
$ 1,306	$ 1,863	$ 2,471	$ 3,133	$ 3,855	$ 4,642
653	932	1,236	1,567	1,928	2,321
$ 653	$ 931	$ 1,235	$ 1,566	$ 1,927	$ 2,321
$ 2,959	$ 2,680	$ 2,376	$ 2,045	$ 1,684	$ 1,291

Mortgage Loan, $80,000

5	6	7	8	9	10
$14,000	$14,000	$14,000	$14,000	$14,000	$14,000
5,033	4,364	3,635	2,840	1,974	1,029
8,500	8,500	8,500	8,500	8,500	8,500
$ 467	$ 1,136	$ 1,865	$ 2,660	$ 3,526	$ 4,471
234	568	933	1,330	1,763	2,235
$ 233	$ 568	$ 932	$ 1,330	$ 1,763	$ 2,236
$ 1,301	$ 966	$ 602	$ 204	($ 229)	($ 701)

equity; and if he is personally liable for any deficiency on the loan after applying the loan proceeds, it could lead to bankruptcy. Where the property has been heavily depreciated, a forced sale can lead to a substantial tax bill arising from the sale, if the selling price is significantly higher than the property's book value. The ultimate risk of excessive debt financing, therefore, is extreme financial loss, and possibly bankruptcy.

Generally, speaking, the greater the proportional amount of debt employed, the greater the financial risk. The safest policy toward financial risk, therefore, is to use no debt financing—a policy observed by some conservative investors. The opportunity cost of this policy can be high, however, because of the loss of the benefits of favorable leverage on owners' equity returns, as illustrated in the last section. At the other extreme are the investors seeking to mortgage out with 100 per cent or more debt financing.

As the investor's rate of return increases with an increase in the loan-to-value ratio when favorable leverage exists, so also does the risk of being unable to meet the debt-service payments. As one measure of the relative amount of project risk one can measure the relationship between net operating income (NOI), and the amount of debt service. The spread between these two amounts represents a *margin of safety,* because NOI represents the amount of the project's cash flow that will be available to cover the debt service cash requirements. It was pointed out in Chapter 5 that the difference between the NOI and the debt service for a particular year represents the amount of net cash flow (before tax) generated by a real estate investment.

To measure the relative amount of risk associated with using different amounts of leverage for a project, one can calculate the *debt-service-coverage ratio* (NOI/debt service) for various alternative loan-to-value ratios being considered for the project.[5] This technique can be illustrated by using the *Commercial Property* example above, involving a $100,000 property, with 40, 66⅔, and 80 per cent mortgage loans being available for financing the acquisition. The loans would all be for 10 years, have level-annual payments, and have a 9 per cent interest rate. The debt-service-coverage ratios are presented below.

[5] It will be noted that this ratio is a variation of the *times-interest-earned ratio* used in corporate financial management.

	Loan Amount	Property Value	Loan/ Value Ratio	NOI	Debt Service	Debt- Service- Coverage Ratio
Case 1	$40,000	$100,000	40%	$14,000	$ 6,233	2.3
Case 2	66,667	100,000	66⅔	14,000	10,388	1.4
Case 3	80,000	100,000	80	14,000	12,466	1.1

As would be expected, the highest loan-to-value ratio represents the highest risk as measured by the debt-service-coverage ratio, which is only 1.1 in the above example for the $80,000 financing alternative of *Case 3*. The very low 1.1 figure means that if the net operating income for the project drops a relatively small amount, then the project cash flows will be insufficient to cover the annual debt-service amount.

Break-even occupancy.   Another approach to measuring a project's risk associated with the use of leverage, is to measure the relationship between the debt-service amount and the amount of net operating income expected to be generated *at different rates of occupancy* for the property in question.

To illustrate, we shall continue with the *Commercial Property* project considered in the last section. We assume for this illustration that the $100,000 property will be financed with a $40,000 mortgage loan having an annual debt service requirement of $6,233. In Table 9–3, the impact on the project's debt-service-coverage ratio at various selected occupancy rates is shown.

The data contained in Table 9–3 can be plotted as shown in Figure 9–3, and the *break-even occupancy rate* will be found at the intersection of the NOI and debt-service curves. As indicated in Figure 9–3, the break-even point is just over 61 per cent. Below that point, insufficient cash flows will be available to cover the mortgage payment of $6,233. Above the break-even point, there will be excess cash flows generated by operations. The surplus cash flows (before taxes) is indicated by the shaded area in Figure 9–3.

The occupancy break-even figure can also be found with the use of a mathematical equation such as Equation 9–1.

$$\text{Break-even occupancy rate} = \frac{\text{Operating expenses} + \text{Debt service}}{\text{Gross income}} \quad [9\text{--}1]$$

TABLE 9-3. Occupancy-Rate Impact on Debt-Service-Coverage
Ratio—Commercial Property Example

Occupancy Rate	Gross Income	Vacancies	Operating Expenses	NOI	Debt Service	Debt-Service Coverage Ratio
20%	$20,000	$16,000	$6,000	($ 2,000)	$6,233	(neg.)
40	20,000	12,000	6,000	2,000	6,233	0.3
60	20,000	8,000	6,000	6,000	6,233	1.0
80	20,000	4,000	6,000	10,000	6,233	1.6
100	20,000	—	6,000	14,000	6,233	2.3

For the *Commercial Property* project involving a $40,000 mortgage loan (*Case 1* above) with Equation 9–1 we can find the break-even point to be 61.2 per cent:

$$\text{Break-even occupancy rate} = \frac{\$6,000 + \$6,233}{\$20,000}$$
$$= \frac{\$12,233}{\$20,000}$$
$$= 61.2\%$$

If we wished to find the break-even occupancy rates that would apply if the $100,000 property were financed with 66⅔ and 80 per cent mortgage loans, we can plug the corresponding debt-service amounts of $10,388 and $12,466 into Equation 9–1, and calculate the break-even points to be 81.9 and 92.3 per cent, respectively.

Where debt-service payments are required to be made more than once a year, the investor should attempt to forecast any seasonal variations in net operating income during the course of each year of the future holding period. For the mortgage loan calling for level-monthly payments, for example, the *margin of safety* (NOI − debt service) could be reduced sharply during certain months if rental income or operating expenses, such as property taxes, are characterized by sharp seasonal fluctuations.

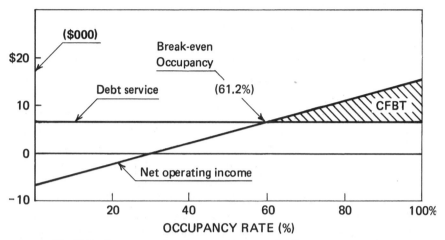

Fig. 9–3. Occupancy break-even. Commercial Property example.

Once an analysis has been made of the impact of different amounts of leverage on the project's returns and risks, a decision can be made as to the appropriate amount of debt financing to employ for a particular investment project. Such a decision will depend on the investor's personal degree of *risk aversion,* that is, the way the investor views the trade-off between added returns and added risks. For most investors the degree of risk aversion for a particular investment proposal will depend in part on the size of the particular project, in relation to the investor's total investment portfolio.

SUMMARY

The basic instruments used in obtaining long-term debt financing, for the acquisition of developed real estate, include the mortgage, the deed of trust, and the land contract. Some of the principal types of mortgages and mortgage clauses were reviewed in this chapter. The principal sources of funds for such financing include the property seller and various financial institutions. Life insurance companies are the most important of the institutions in terms of mortgage lending on income-producing real estate.

When arranging permanent financing, the equity investor

should consider the various alternative repayment schedules in the light of the impact of future debt-service payments on project cash flows. The type of repayment schedule, the applicable interest rate, and the length of the term of the mortgage will all influence the periodic debt-service demands for a mortgage loan of a given size.

Sensitivity analysis is a technique that can be used to help make a determination of the appropriate amount of leverage (debt–equity mix) that the equity investor should seek to use for a particular real estate investment project. By the use of sensitivity analysis, the impact of alternative financing arrangements upon project returns and project risks can be studied. The use of favorable leverage will increase returns to the equity investor but will usually also increase the risk. Two measures of project risk were described in the chapter: the *debt-service-coverage ratio,* and the *break-even occupancy rate.*

10

Holding Period Strategy

The specification of an explicit holding period is required for many of the rate-of-return measures used in this book. It is necessary, for example, to specify a holding period with the discounted cash flow model that was discussed in Chapter 7. Even when a formalized rate-of-return analysis is not undertaken, it is still convenient to consider a proposed real estate investment in terms of a probable future holding period—or as it is also called, a *planning horizon*. Various factors that would enter into a determination of the planned holding period for a particular real estate investment are considered in this chapter.

The use of a specified holding period for the purpose of analyzing a proposed investment does not by itself, of course, prevent the investor from disposing of the property before or after the planned period. After a property is acquired, there will usually be environmental changes affecting the value of the property, and opportunities for alternative investments that were unknown at the time of acquisition. Also, as is discussed later in the chapter, it may be advantageous for the investor to *refinance* the investment rather than to dispose of the property at the end of what would otherwise appear to be a logical holding period.

INVESTMENT GOALS

An important factor in determining the planned holding period for a particular investment project is the *investment goal* that the investor has in mind for the project. For the investor seeking an entrepreneurial profit from the construction of a new building or from the rehabilitation of an old building, the planned holding period would be the time necessary to complete the construction work and to sell the property at an appropriate price. For those investing in existing new or used properties (land or developed properties), the determination of an appropriate planned holding period can usually be related to the three investment goals of: (1) price appreciation; (2) long-term income; and (3) periodic cash flows. A particular investor may, of course, acquire a variety of real estate projects (a portfolio) for which he has various planning horizons.

It will be noted in the following discussion that certain types of properties tend to be used for particular investment goals. Raw land, for example, purchased for subsequent resale, is usually acquired with the price appreciation goal in mind. Part IV explores the investment features of individual types of properties in more depth than will be found in the present chapter.

Investing for Price Appreciation

Property purchased for resale at a higher price in the future is usually acquired under one of three basic plans: (1) the purchase of property as an inflation hedge; (2) the purchase of under-valued property for quick resale; and (3) the purchase of property in anticipation of a significant future change in the use of the property.

Inflation hedge. Over the past several years, real estate has been shown to be one of the best inflation hedges available to investors. In the past ten years, for example, real estate investments have, on the average, proved to be a much better hedge against inflation than have common stocks. Undeveloped land in particular has steadily risen in value in many parts of the country—over periods of several years. The value of developed property has also generally increased in value during periods of high inflation because the rising costs of new construction at such times tend to make existing buildings more valuable.

Where property is purchased by an individual investor primarily as an inflation hedge, the specification of a holding period is not really necessary to the investment analysis. One simply plans to hold the property indefinitely; or until the cash proceeds are expected to be needed for some future purpose, such as for college expenses, or for retirement income. Six months, however, would be a minimum practical holding period in order not to preclude capital gains tax treatment of the sale.

Quick Turnover. Some real estate investors focus their activities on the seeking of properties that can be purchased and resold shortly thereafter at a profit. The *purchase option* is one technique sometimes used for this purpose. The procedure would be for the investor to pay a certain amount in order to receive the exclusive right (option) to purchase the property at a specified price, within a given time period. Generally, the option money will be lost if the investor does not exercise the option by purchasing the property. On the other hand, the option money is usually applied against the purchase price if the option is exercised. After taking an option on the property, some investors will immediately set out to find a buyer for the same property. If a suitable buyer is found, the investor will buy the property himself by exercising the option, and resell the property to the new-found buyer.

Whether the option technique is used or not, the planned holding period in the quick-turnover situation would be tied to the time period expected to be required to consummate the purchase and resale. Again, the six-months holding period requirement for capital gains treatment would have to be considered.

Expected Change in Property Use. Another opportunity for price gains exists when a property's value rises because a new and *higher* use becomes available for the property. Some new future uses are not really predictable at the time of acquisition, such as the unexpected future discovery of minerals, unexpected changes in road patterns, or other sudden changes in the area surrounding a particular property.

Property—especially land—is often purchased, however, because a new use for the property *is* anticipated. While there exist situations when it is reasonably certain that special area changes will take place, such as the placement of new roads, airports, and schools, probably the most common instance of an expected change in land use is agricultural land or woodland that becomes desirable for residential or recreational usage. A study of urban and suburban growth patterns, and of local changes in land value, may, for example, indicate that land for residential use is valued at $4,000 an acre, while agricultural land in the environs is valued at only $1,500.

The planning horizon for an investment made in anticipation of a changed use of the property would logically be set as the time that is estimated will pass before the property will be desired for the new use. An estimate of the time period involved for land to become useful for residential purposes would require an analysis of the pace and direction of past and expected future population changes, as well as of the time expected for the installation of new roads, and sewer and water systems.

Assuming, for example, that it is expected to take 5 years for a particular 20-acre piece of farm land priced at $1,500 per acre to take on a residential land value of $4,000 per acre, then five years would be the logical planning horizon for analyzing a proposed investment in the land. Assuming further that cattle-grazing rentals or other income to be received during the holding period will just cover the carrying costs of the property including taxes, insurance, and fence repairs; and also that the investor finances the investment without debt funds, and he pays capital gains taxes at the rate of 25 per cent—then the discounted, after-tax rate of return can be found to be 17.6 per cent, as calculated below.

Find after-tax cash flow from sale in five years:

$$CFAT\ (sale) = Selling\ price - Unpaid\ mortgage - Taxes$$
$$= \$80,000 - 0 - \$12,500$$
$$= \$67,500$$

To find Taxes:

$$
\begin{aligned}
\text{Taxes} &= \text{Amount of gain} \times \text{Tax rate} \\
&= (\$80{,}000 - \$30{,}000) \times 0.25 \\
&= \$50{,}000 \times .25 \\
&= \$12{,}500
\end{aligned}
$$

$$
\text{Owners' initial investment} = \sum_{t=1}^{n} \frac{\text{CFAT}}{(1+r)^t} + \frac{\text{CFAT (sale)}}{(1+r)^n}
$$

$$
\$30{,}000 = 0 + \frac{\$67{,}500}{(1+r)^5}
$$

Solve for r, *by trial and error method;* [1] r $= 17.6\%$.

Investing for Long-term Income

Real estate investments are at times made with the goal of obtaining a long-term future stream of income benefits. Such investments are often characterized by having relatively low risk. Life insurance companies commonly make long-term income investments because they have long-term liabilities, as contrasted to the commercial banks and thrift institutions that have large amounts of demand deposits or other short-term liabilities. The properties involved in long-term income-producing investments often include industrial properties, such as manufacturing plants and warehouses, or office buildings. One common form of the long-term investment is the *purchase–leaseback,* where the investor, such as an insurance company, purchases real estate and immediately leases it back to the seller for a long-term period.

The appropriate planning horizon for long-term income-producing investments would logically be some long-term period —perhaps tied to the expected useful life of the property as used for depreciation purposes; or to the term of years of the related mortgage loan, if one is used to finance the property acquisition. In the case of a purchase–leaseback, the term of the lease would sometimes represent the most appropriate planning horizon.

---

[1] The use of the trial and error method is illustrated in Chapter 6.

Investing for Periodic Cash Flows

Many real estate investments can be expected to generate relatively high after-tax cash flow returns to the investor in the short and intermediate term—with the after-tax cash flows becoming significantly lower and even turning negative after the property is held for a certain number of years. Here the investor would often plan to dispose of the investment property and seek a new property at the time future cash flows are expected to decline to a low point.

When properties are financed with level-payment mortgage loans or are depreciated with an accelerated depreciation method, then the annual cash flows will be highest in the early years of the investment—even where rental income, property expenses, and tax rates are all constant amounts during the years the property is held as an investment.

The declining cash flow pattern just described will be exaggerated when the investor is in a very high tax bracket, because the higher early-years' cash flows are generated by tax deductions relating to depreciation and interest expenses. Such deductions will, of course, be most valuable to the taxpayer with relatively high marginal tax rates.

For an example, we return to the *Garden Apartment Project* example used in Chapter 7. At the time of acquisition the apartment property has a remaining useful life of 20 years. The cost of the property is $560,000, and it is to be financed with a 20-year, 8 per cent, first mortgage loan of $420,000, calling for level-annual payments. The 125 per cent declining balance method of depreciation is to be used on the $420,000 depreciable value. The investor has a 70 per cent marginal tax rate. The investment profile in Table 7–1, pages 126–127, contains the projected annual income and cash flows for the project.

As shown in Table 7–1, the projected after-tax cash flow for the *Garden Apartment Project* amounts to $14,717 in the first year, and declines steadily to the level of $4,118 in the tenth year of the project. After 13 years, the annual after-tax cash flow is projected to be a negative amount. The projected cash flow pattern over the first 13 years is shown in Figure 10–1. Also included in the Figure are the patterns for interest and depreciation expense deductions for all 20 years of the project.

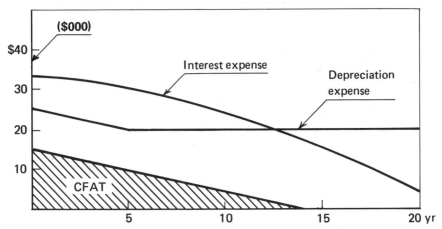

Fig. 10-1. Cash flow, interest, depreciation patterns, Garden Apartment Project (data from Table 7-1).

For the *Garden Apartment Project,* the interest expense deduction is the principal factor responsible for the higher level of early-years after-tax cash flow. In the first year of the project, the deductible interest expense of $33,600 accounts for over 78 per cent of the total debt-service payment on the mortgage of $42,778. In the 20th year of the project, the interest expense of $3,169 represents only 7.4 per cent of the annual debt service. As noted in Chapter 7, however, there would be strict limits placed by the 1976 TRA on the deductibility of large investment interest expenses associated with a project—unless there was adequate offsetting income from other investments.

The use of 125% declining-balance depreciation also helps to increase the early-years' cash flows in this example, because the accelerated method generates slightly higher depreciation deductions in the first 4 years than would be provided by the straight-line method. The extra depreciation deductions, however, are relatively small in this case as compared with the interest expense deductions.

Ten-year holding period. It is often found that, for real estate investments having characteristics similar to those of the *Garden Apartment Project,* ten years is a convenient planning horizon to use in the investment analysis. For many such projects the bulk of the *periodic* after-tax cash flows will be received within the first 10 years that the property is held. This is indicated for the *Garden Apartment Project* by the CFAT pattern in Figure 10–1. During the first 10 years of the *Garden Apartment Project,* almost 68 per cent of the 20 years' total interest expense deductions have been taken, and almost 52 per cent of the 20 year's depreciation deductions have been used.

New properties. The ten-year planning horizon is often appropriate for the newly constructed property (first-user property) as well as for the used property. Even though a very long useful life is used for depreciation purposes, such as 40 years for an apartment property, it is still often the case that the bulk of the after-tax cash flows are received in the first ten years. This is so because the term of the mortgage will usually be in the range of 20 or 25 years, and hence the bulk of the interest expense deductions will be received in the first ten years.

It will also be recalled that for first-user properties, more liberal accelerated depreciation methods are permitted than for used properties; for residential rental properties the double-declining-balance method can be used for tax purposes. Hence, during the first ten years of a project a substantial amount of depreciation expense is taken. For example, if the double-declining-balance method is used with a 40-year useful life, approximately 40 per cent of the project's depreciation will be taken in the first ten years.

While ten years is recommended as a planning horizon for general use in analyzing projects that are looked to for future cash flows, an alternative approach would be to make the planning horizon equal to the number of years in which *positive* cash flows are expected to be received (13 years for the *Garden Apartment Project*). Another possible choice would be the number of years during which tax-shelter benefits are expected to be received, which is 11 years for the *Garden Apartment Project,* as shown in Table 7–1.

Other Holding-Period Considerations

While the above paragraphs have described some general approaches that can be used in setting planned holding periods in relation to different basic investment goals, there will be individual cases where special planning horizons are required, such as when the investor plans to dispose of the property in a given number of years in order to use the proceeds for some personal or family requirement.

The *depreciation recapture* provisions should also be considered in the planning-horizon decision. As discussed in Chapter 6, whenever an investment property that is being depreciated with an accelerated depreciation method is sold at a price high enough above book value, the tax benefits that can be attributed to accelerated depreciation (excess over straight-line amount) will be recaptured. After residential rental property is held for 8 years and 4 months (100 months), the amount of excess depreciation that is recaptured declines by 1 per cent a month. Hence, if the property is held for 10 years, the amount of excess depreciation that is recaptured would be 80 per cent [100% − (1% × 20 months)]; after 16 years and 8 months (200 months), there would be no recapture.

As noted, however, in Chapter 6, post-1975 excess depreciation for residential property is subject to 100 per cent recapture under the 1976 Tax Reform Act.

In the investment situations described above, where a planned holding period in the general area of ten years is appropriate, a possible alternative to a sale or other disposition would be to refinance the property, as described below.

REFINANCING

To refinance a real estate investment is to replace existing financing arrangements with new ones. The basic means of refinancing is to take a new mortgage loan and use part or all of the proceeds of that loan to repay (liquidate) the existing mortgage loan on the same property. The benefits of refinancing can take two basic forms: (1) the improvement of periodic cash flows; and (2) the receipt of tax-free cash at the time of the refinancing.

Improving Periodic Cash Flows

It is clear that taking a new loan at a significantly lower interest rate than the rate on the existing loan will improve the after-tax cash flows of a real estate investment. This would be true for refinancing at any point after property acquisition, as long as the costs of refinancing, including any loan-origination fees on the new loan and any prepayment penalties on the existing loan, do not outweigh the interest savings associated with the new loan.

It is also true that a refinancing of an existing loan at an appropriate time, even with a new loan at the *same* interest rate as on the old loan, can improve the *periodic* cash flows generated by a particular real estate project. As has been discussed previously, the interest portion of the debt-service payments on a level-payment mortgage loan *declines* each year that the loan is outstanding. This means that a smaller portion of the cash used each year for servicing the loan is tax deductible. This, in turn, will mean higher taxes and lower after-tax cash flows than otherwise. Because improvement in periodic cash flows is possible through refinancing, even with an unchanged interest rate, the investor may plan to undertake to refinance an investment property rather than dispose of the property at a point when the project's cash flows decline to very low levels.

To illustrate the possible improvement in cash flows by refinancing we return to the *Garden Apartment Project* referred to in the last section and described in detail in Chapter 7. The original mortgage loan is in the amount of $420,000 (8%, 20 years, level-annual payments), and by the end of the first 10 years the loan amount outstanding will be reduced to $287,045.

During the first 10 years of the *Garden Apartment* investment a total of $86,654 is projected to be received in the form of periodic after-tax cash flows. However, because of the declining tax-deductible interest expense portion of the annual debt-service payments, the annual after-tax cash flows are projected to be relatively small in the years *11* through *13,* and negative amounts of increasing size in the years *14* through *20,* as shown in Table 10–1.

The annual after-tax cash flows will be substantial positive amounts in all of the last 10 years of the project, however, if the original mortgage loan with $287,045 still outstanding at the end of 10 years is refinanced at that time with a new mortgage

TABLE 10-1. **Refinancing Impact on Cash Flows—Garden Apartment Project,[a] New Loan Amount is $287,045**

| | Cash Flow | | |
Year—	Without Refinancing	With Refinancing	Difference
1-10 (total)	$ 86,654	$ 86,654	—
11	3,091	16,632	$ + 13,541
12	1,981	16,282	+ 14,301
13	783	15,903	+ 15,120
14	(511)	15,492	+ 16,003
15	(1,909)	15,050	+ 16,959
16	(3,419)	14,573	+ 17,992
17	(5,049)	14,056	+ 19,105
18	(6,810)	13,499	+ 20,309
19	(8,711)	12,897	+ 21,608
20	(10,765)	12,247	+ 23,012
	$ 55,335	$233,285	$ +177,950
20 (sale proceeds)	$711,380	$515,206	$ - 196,174

[a]Complete financial data for the Garden Apartment Project are contained in Table 7-1.

loan in the amount of $287,045—with the new loan having the same interest rate as the old loan (8%), and calling for level-annual payments over a new 20-year term. Table 10-1 shows for the *Garden Apartment Project* both the expected future after-tax cash flows that are associated with the original 20-year financing plan, and the cash-flow patterns attending the refinancing plan just described.

The reason for the improved periodic cash flows generated by the refinancing arrangement over the second 10-year period is that the annual debt-service for the new loan is only $29,236 per year, as contrasted with the $42,778 loan payments required

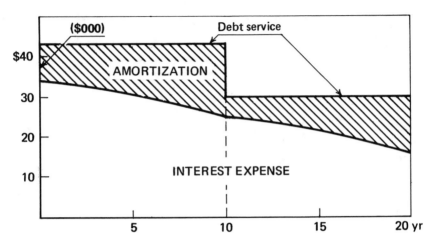

Fig. 10–2. Refinancing impact on debt service, Garden Apartment Project; new loan amount is $287,045.

by the old (existing) loan. Also, during the period the cumulative tax-deductible interest payments are greater with the new loan than with the old. It will be observed in Table 10–1 that the cash *sale* proceeds projected to be received after holding the property for 20 years amounts to only $515,206 under the refinancing alternative, as compared with the $711,380 expected to be received under the original financing plan. The difference of $196,174 represents the amount of the new mortgage loan that will be outstanding at the end of its first ten years at which time it is forecasted that the property will be sold for $1,011,360.

Figure 10–2 indicates the pattern of debt-service payments that would prevail if the refinancing arrangement described above is undertaken. Because the cash proceeds expected to be received at the time of sale, with the refinancing alternative, are expected to be almost $200,000 less, as noted above, the overall discounted rate of return for the project is not significantly improved by refinancing with the new loan at the same 8 per cent interest rate as the old loan. However, the improved annual cash flows in the second 10-year period, prior to the disposal of the property, would lead many investors to choose the refinancing alternative.

Tax-Free Cash

It is sometimes possible to replace an existing loan with a new one for an amount greater than the amount outstanding on the old loan at the time of the refinancing. This opportunity arises when the property has increased in value, or at least has not significantly decreased in value, since the time that the original mortgage loan was taken on the property.

At the time that a new loan is taken for an amount greater than the amount outstanding on the old loan, the investor, of course, receives cash in excess of the amount necessary to use in liquidating the old loan. Such excess is often referred to as *tax-free cash,* because no tax is paid on the cash received, as contrasted with the cash proceeds received from the *sale* of property involving a taxable gain.

To return to the *Garden Apartment Project* example, if the property is refinanced at the end of the first 10 years, any new loan cash proceeds received in excess of $287,045 would be received tax free. Assuming that a new loan equal to the original amount of the old loan, that is, $420,000, is used to refinance the property at the end of 10 years, then $132,955 in tax-free cash will be received by the investor after he repays the $287,045 amount still outstanding on the original loan. The comparative cash flows associated with the original financing arrangement for the *Garden Apartment Project,* and with the $420,000 refinancing arrangement, are shown in Table 10–2.

It will be observed in Table 10–2 that not only will $132,955 in after-tax proceeds be received at the end of the tenth year, but also that in each year of the second ten-year period the periodic after-tax cash flows are greater with the $420,000 refinancing plan. While the annual debt-service payments with and without the refinancing will be identical ($42,778: both mortgages for $420,000, at 8 per cent, for 20 years), the interest portion of the debt-service payments is greater under the refinancing plan, as is shown in Figure 10–3. Offsetting these cash-flow advantages of the refinancing plan is, of course, the smaller net cash proceeds (associated with refinancing) to be received when the property is disposed of

TABLE 10–2. Refinancing Impact on Cash Flows—Garden Apartment Project,[a] New Loan Amount is $420,000

	Cash Flow		
Year—	Without Refinancing	With Refinancing	Difference
1–10 (total)	$ 86,654	$ 86,654	0
10 (end-of-year)	0	132,955	$ +132,955
11	3,091	10,537	+ 7,446
12	1,981	10,023	+ 8,042
13	783	9,468	+ 8,685
14	(511)	8,868	+ 9,379
15	(1,909)	8,221	+ 10,130
16	(3,419)	7,552	+ 10,971
17	(5,049)	6,766	+ 11,815
18	(6,810)	5,951	+ 12,761
19	(8,711)	5,070	+ 13,781
20	(10,765)	4,118	+ 14,883
	$ 55,335	$296,183	$ +240,848
20 (sale proceeds)	$711,380	$424,335	$ – 287,045

[a]Complete financial data for the Garden Apartment Project are contained in Table 7–1.

in twenty years. The $287,045 reduction in cash-flow proceeds related to the refinancing plan, shown in Table 10–2, represents the amount of the new loan that will be outstanding when the property is expected to be disposed of.

Wrap-Around Mortgage

The refinancing procedure described above called for prepayment of an existing mortgage loan. When, however, the property holder does not wish to prepay the existing mortgage loan because of a favorable interest rate, or because of prepayment penalty requirements, the wrap-around mortgage may be an ap-

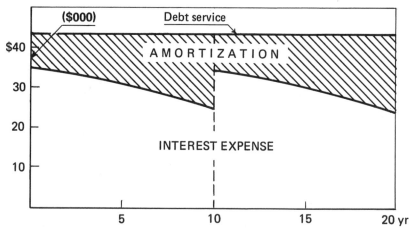

Fig. 10-3. Refinancing impact on debt service, Garden Apartment Project; new loan amount is $420,000.

propriate technique for acquiring additional financing. The procedure would be for a new lender to provide an "all-inclusive loan" in the amount desired by the property holder; and for the lender to take a mortgage that will "wrap around" the existing mortgage and the additional amount loaned to the investor. The new lender will then use part of each of the payments on the wrap-around mortgage to service the continuing existing mortgage.

Suppose, for example, that after holding the property for 10 years, the value of the *Garden Apartment Project* will support a total mortgage loan of $565,000, with, say, annual debt-service payments of $57,546. Suppose further that the original *Garden Apartment* investor wishes to retain the existing mortgage loan, which has $287,045 still outstanding. If a lender is found who will provide the wrap-around mortgage loan of a nominal $565,000, then of each $57,546 payment made to the lender on the new, all-inclusive loan, $42,778 will be used by the new lender to service the previous, continuing mortgage; the balance of each payment will be retained by the lender. At the outset, the holder of the *Garden Apartment Project* would receive $277,955 [$565,000 − $287,045] in tax-free cash from the arrangement. (See also the application of the wrap-around technique in the discussion of deferred-payment sales in Chapter 11.)

SUMMARY

For analyzing the attractiveness of a proposed real estate investment, it is useful to have an explicit planning horizon in mind
for the investment; and for some rate-of-return analyses, a planned
holding period of a specified number of years is part of the required input data. The length of the planned holding period
for a particular property will usually depend on the investment
goals for the planned investment in that property. Some planning
horizons were discussed in this chapter that might be expected to
be associated with investing for *price appreciation,* for *long-term
income,* and for *periodic cash flows.*

For many real estate investments involving relatively large
mortgage loans, or accelerated depreciation methods, the after-
tax cash flows are generally highest in the early years of the investment. For those investing in such projects primarily to obtain
cash flows, ten years is often a convenient planned holding period,
because the bulk of the positive cash flows will usually be received
in the first ten years or so of the project.

In the situation just described, the investor may plan to
refinance the investment, rather than to dispose of the property at
a time when it appears that the after-tax cash flows will drop to a
relatively low level. By taking an appropriate new mortgage loan,
the annual cash flows will be improved because of the large interest
deductions associated with the early years of new mortgage loans.
Where new-loan proceeds exceed the amount outstanding on the
old loan at the time of refinancing, the investor will receive tax-
free funds that can be used for investing elsewhere.

11

Property
Disposition
Strategy

When mentioning the disposition of real estate in previous chapters we made reference almost exclusively to the *cash sale* of property. There are of course a variety of other means of disposing of properties, including, among others *deferred-payment sales* (including *installment-basis sales*), *property exchanges, involuntary conversions,* and *donations.* The various alternative disposition strategies will be considered in the present chapter, along with the factors involved in making disposition decisions. As in most of the other areas of investment decision making, federal income taxes are found to be a major consideration; however, other factors are often involved, such as the cash needs of the person disposing of the property, the nature of the real estate market, and the specific requirements of the person receiving the property.

PROPERTY SALES

The most common way of disposing of real estate investment properties is to sell them by means of either a *straight sale* for cash (or for cash plus mortgage assumption), *or* by a *deferred-payment* sale, whereby the seller accepts a promissory note as partial payment for the property. The tax and other aspects of these two basic sale forms will be discussed in the present section along with the sale–leaseback arrangement.

Straight Sale

The straight sale for cash (or for cash plus mortgage assumption) has been discussed in previous chapters, including the tax aspects thereof. The principal consequences of a straight sale are that the seller receives his equity interest in the property in the form of cash at the time of sale, and any taxable gain on the sale is recognized in the year of sale. If a loss is involved, it likewise is recognized for tax purposes in the year of sale.

As a means of reviewing the computations for finding the after-tax cash proceeds of a sale [CFAT (sale)], we introduce the following fact situation: *Mr. Bengy* purchased a used commercial piece of real property on January 1, 1969, for $50,000. The purchase was financed with a $10,000 cash down payment and a 20-year, 9 per cent mortgage loan in the amount of $40,000. The depreciable part of the property was valued at $45,000, and was to be depreciated at the rate of 5 per cent a year (20-year life, straight-line method), or $2,250 per year.

On December 31, 1973, *Bengy* sold the property for $75,321 cash (net of selling expenses), of which $35,321 was used to pay off the outstanding mortgage loan in that amount. During the 5-year holding period, a total of $11,250 had been taken in depreciation, leaving a book value of $38,750. The after-tax proceeds of sale [CFAT (sale)] amounted to $30,857, calculated as shown below, assuming a 25 per cent capital gains tax rate:

$$
\begin{aligned}
CFAT \ (sale) &= Selling \ price - Unpaid \ mortgage - Taxes \\
&= \$75,321 - \$35,321 - \$9,143 \\
&= \$30,857
\end{aligned}
$$

To find Taxes:

$$
\begin{aligned}
Adjusted \ basis &= Cost - Accumulated \ depreciation \\
&= \$50,000 - \$11,250 \\
&= \$38,750
\end{aligned}
$$

$$Capital\ gain = Selling\ price - Adjusted\ basis$$
$$= \$75,321 - \$38,750$$
$$= \$36,571$$
$$Taxes = Capital\ gain \times Tax\ rate$$
$$= \$36,571 \times 0.25$$
$$= \$9,143$$

If the buyer had *assumed Bengy's* mortgage outstanding in the amount of $35,321, and *Bengy* is released from his obligation by the mortgagee, then for *Bengy* the final result would be the same as if the sale were for all cash. He would still receive $30,857 in after-tax cash proceeds from the sale. In the case of a mortgage assumption, *Bengy* would receive $40,000 [$75,321 − $35,321] directly from the buyer, and the tax on *Bengy's* gain ($9,143) would be the same as with the all-cash sale.

Consequences of the straight sale. The obvious benefit of the straight-sale form of property disposition is that the seller receives cash equal to his equity interest in the property immediately upon the consummation of the sale, less any selling expenses and taxes payable on the gain, if any. The net proceeds ($30,857) in the above example can, therefore, be immediately reinvested in other real estate projects, or used for other purposes.

As noted above, when there is a taxable gain involved in the disposition of the property by means of a straight sale, then the gain will be fully recognized and taxed in the year of the sale. If the gain qualifies as a capital gain, then the maximum rate for an *individual* is 25 per cent for gains totaling up to $50,000; and up to 35 per cent on gains over $50,000. If the gain is taxed as ordinary income, for example, because the seller is considered a *dealer* rather than an *investor,* then the individual's ordinary tax rate of up to 70 per cent would be applied to the gain, leaving the taxpayer relatively little of the cash proceeds of sale, after the mortgage outstanding is repaid and the selling expenses are paid.[1]

The harsh tax treatment just described of gains relating to the cash sale of property is often experienced by farmers and others wishing to sell acreage that has risen in value to a high multiple of its original cost. The subdivision and sale of the land in the

[1] The tax rules and rates relating to corporations were described in Chapter 8.

form of lots could lead to the application of the ordinary income tax rates, and hence to a very heavy tax burden in the year of sale. Even if the land is sold in one piece and a capital gains situation exists, the tax burden will be heavy, with the rate between 25 and 35 per cent.[2] If a loss, rather than a gain, is realized on the sale of property, then quite a different tax situation arises when the straight-sale form of disposition is used. The straight sale in this case could be advantageous from a tax standpoint because the loss in its entirety would be recognized in the year of sale. This is especially attractive when the loss qualifies as an ordinary loss for an investor in a high tax bracket who has other income against which the loss can be offset.

Deferred-Payment Sale

When property is sold on a deferred-payment basis, the seller helps to finance the buyer by accepting the buyer's note along with partial cash and any other immediate compensation. The instruments used would be a purchase-money mortgage, deed of trust, or land contract. The seller's motivations would include such things as:

1. The seller may be forced to sell the property on a deferred-payment basis in order to accommodate a particular buyer—or lose an otherwise advantageous sale. That is, the seller's credit extension is used as a sales tool.

2. The seller may wish to become a passive investor (note holder) to obtain a steady annual income for his retirement, or for other purposes. This motivation would be reinforced if the seller views current interest rates as being extraordinarily high.

3. In practice, some successful investors tend to think of the installment note received in a real estate transaction as "gravy." The seller may have paid, say, $25,000 for property that he later sells for $100,000; with $25,000 received as a cash down-payment, along with a note for $75,000. The seller may view the cash down-payment as a return of his original investment, and the $75,000 note the gravy. His aim would often be to hold such notes as long-term investments.

4. The seller may wish to obtain the tax advantages attending a qualified installment-basis sale.

[2] The tax rules relating to land subdivisions are discussed in Chapter 16.

The qualified installment-basis sale and its tax consequences will be discussed next, followed by a brief discussion of other forms of deferred-payment sales.

Installment-basis sale. When the seller of real estate provides financing for the buyer in a way that satisfies certain defined statutory requirements contained in the Internal Revenue Code, the sale may (at the seller's option) be reported for tax purposes as an installment-basis sale. This form of sale could have favorable tax consequences for the seller, as any gain on the sale will not be recognized for tax purposes until the periods in which the cash proceeds of the sale are received. The principal requirements for a qualifying installment-basis sale are summarized in the following list.

1. The payments received in the year of sale (including any cash down-payment, plus any installment) must not exceed 30 per cent of the selling price.
2. Sales for a loss do not qualify—only sales yielding a gain.
3. Sales of personal assets for a price of over $1,000 may qualify.
4. The taxpayer must report his election to use the installment-basis method of reporting for a particular sale in his tax return in the year of sale. The election is binding in future years.

Installment-basis computations. The amount of gain on the installment-basis sale of the property would be calculated the same way as the gain on a straight sale. The amount of gain under qualified installment-basis reporting, however, would be recognized for tax purposes partially in the year of sale, and the remainder during the future years in which the installment payments are received. The portion of each year's cash received from the buyer that is taxable in the year received is labeled, in the terminology of the Internal Revenue Code, the *gross profits percentage.* This percentage figure, in turn, is defined as being equal to the *realized gain* divided by *the contract price.* The realized gain is calculated the same way as the gain on a straight sale, and the contract price is the selling price less the amount of any mortgages assumed by the buyer.[3]

---

[3] If the amount of the assumed mortgage is greater than the seller's basis, the excess is included in the contract price.

TABLE 11-1. Instalment-Basis Sale—Bengy Property Example

End of Year—	Cash Received (1)	Capital Gains Recognized 91.4% × (1) (2)	Capital Gains Tax (25%) (3)	Interest Payments (9%) (4)	Tax on Interest (50%) (5)	Total Tax (3) + (5) (6)	Net Cash Flow (1) + (4) − (6) (7)
1973	$20,000	$18,280	$4,570	—	—	$ 4,570	$15,430
1974	2,000	1,828	457	$1,800	$ 900	1,357	2,443
1975	2,000	1,828	457	1,620	810	1,267	2,353
1976	2,000	1,828	457	1,440	720	1,177	2,263
1977	2,000	1,828	457	1,260	630	1,087	2,173
1978	2,000	1,828	457	1,080	540	997	2,083
1979	2,000	1,828	457	900	450	907	1,993
1980	2,000	1,828	457	720	360	817	1.903
1981	2,000	1.828	457	540	270	727	1,813
1982	2,000	1,828	457	360	180	637	1,723
1983	2,000	1,839	460	180	90	550	1,630
Totals	$40,000	$36,571	$9,143	$9,900	$4,950	$14,093	$35,807

As an illustration we return to the *Bengy* property example used in the preceding section. The following data relate to the straight sale of the *Bengy* property:

Selling price	$75,321
Mortgage outstanding at time of sale	35,321
Capital gain	36,571
Capital gains tax (25%)	9,143
After-tax proceeds of straight sale	30,857

And it is now to be supposed that the *Bengy* property is sold and reported on a qualified installment basis, rather than as a straight sale for cash. It is assumed that of the selling price of $75,321, *Bengy* receives only $20,000 in cash from the buyer (less than 30 per cent of the $75,321). The buyer assumes *Bengy's* mortgage outstanding in the amount of $35,321, and gives *Bengy* a purchase-money mortgage (and note) for the balance of the price. The purchase-money mortgage in the amount of $20,000 is a *variable-payment mortgage,* for 10 years, at 9 per cent interest, and calls for annual payments.

Summarized below are the component parts of the selling price received by *Bengy,* and a listing of the realized gain, contract price, and gross profits percentage figures.

Cash	$20,000	(26.6% of $75,321)
Mortgage assumption	35,312	
Purchase-money mortgage	20,000	(10 years, 9%, variable payment)
Selling price	$75,321	
Realized gain	$36,571	[same as for cash sale]
Contract price	$40,000	[$75,321 − $35,321]
Gross profits percentage	91.4%	[$36,571/$40,000]

The gross profits percentage figure of 91.4 per cent means that the $36,571 taxable gain on the sale represents 91.4 per cent of the $40,000 in cash to be received by the seller. As the cash is received, a capital gains tax will be applied to 91.4 per cent of the amounts received, in the years in which they are received. Hence, in the year that the property is sold (1973, in this example), when the $20,000 cash down-payment is received, the capital gains tax will amount to $4,570, assuming a 25 per cent tax rate [$20,000 × 91.4% × 25% = $4,570]. Because the $20,000 mortgage loan features a variable repayment plan, $2,000 a year for 10 years will be received as amortization payments (interest payments on the amount outstanding each year will also be received). Hence, in the year following sale *Bengy* will pay capital gains tax of $457 on the first $2,000 amortization payment received [$2,000 × 91.4% × 25%].

Table 11–1 contains the full schedule of amortization and interest payments to be received by the seller, before and after taxes. The capital gains tax rate of 25 per cent is assumed to hold for all 10 years, and a 50 per cent ordinary tax rate is assumed for all 10 years. The ordinary rate is applied to the interest payments received by the seller.

Economic consequences of the installment sale. It will be noted in the *Bengy* property example that the seller receives only $15,430 in cash (after taxes) in the year of sale [$20,000 − $4,570], as compared with the $30,857 after-tax cash proceeds of a straight sale, computed previously. The $15,427 difference in the amount of cash received in the year of sale is offset by the 9 per cent note received in the amount of $20,000. Whether or not the $20,000 note is an attractive alternative to the $15,427 extra after-tax cash that would be received if a cash sale had been used, would depend on the seller's opportunity cost of the cash involved, that is, the amount he could earn from the best alternative use of the $15,427 cash funds given up for the note. In many instances the investor would prefer the immediate cash funds, for initiating or expanding other real estate equity investments.

It should be noted also that the cash situation arising from the installment sale that was just described can be even more severe where the buyer does *not* assume the seller's outstanding mortgage. With reference to the *Bengy* property example, if the $35,321 mortgage had not been assumed, but rather added to the amount of the note, then the $20,000 cash received from the buyer at the time of the sale would be insufficient to liquidate the outstanding mortgage (and to cover the amount of capital gains taxes payable in the year of sale). The net result in that situation would be a *negative* cash flow in the year of sale of $17,751, calculated as follows:

Cash received at time of sale	$20,000
Mortage outstanding	− 35,321
Capital gains tax	− 2,430
Net cash flow, after tax	($17,751) (negative)

To find the capital gains tax:

Gross profit percentage = Realized gain/Contract price
                        = $36,571/$75,321
                        = 48.6%

Capital gains tax   = $20,000 × 48.6% × 25%
(in year of sale)   = $2,430

In this example, the installment sale represents a net cash flow of $48,608 less than with the all-cash sale [$30,857 − ($17,751)]. While this cash flow differential in the year of sale would be offset by a large note signed by the buyer (in this example a note for $55,321 would be received), the immediate cash flow shortfall with the installment sale would often make the installment sale impractical, despite the tax advantages this type of sale may offer.

Of course, when the seller's property is unmortgaged, or has a relatively small mortgage, the severe cash problem described above does not usually arise. Even where there is a relatively large mortgage that will not be assumed by the buyer, there are some possibilities for alleviating the cash problem, such as: (1) the buyer's taking the property subject to the mortgage; or (2) the use of a wrap-around mortgage, as described below.

If the buyer is willing to take the property *subject to the outstanding mortgage,* the seller will remain responsible for the mortgage but will not have to repay it at the time of sale. This arrangement is often unacceptable to the buyer, however as the property remains exposed to claim by the mortgagee in the event of default.

Wrap-around mortgage. This technique has already been discussed in Chapter 10 as a means of refinancing. For a proposed sale, if the holder of an existing mortgage (the mortgagee) blocks its transfer to (assumption by) a buyer of the mortgaged property, or the buyer himself considers it desirable not to prepay an existing mortgage at the time of sale (because of a favorable interest rate, or for other reasons) then the buyer may offer a wrap-around mortgage to the seller as part payment.

For example, assume a property has a selling price of $100,-000, and an existing mortgage (with favorable terms) with an unpaid balance of $40,000; the buyer has only $25,000 for a cash down-payment. If the seller accepts the $25,000 cash and a $75,-000 wrap-around mortgage from the buyer, the existing mortgage can be kept intact. The seller, of course, will use part of the installment debt-service payments on the $75,000 loan to service the $40,000 balance of the original mortgage loan.

Tax consequences of the installment sale. When the sale of the property involves *capital gains* rather than ordinary income, the total amount of capital gains taxes paid will be the same with the sale reported on the installment basis as with the cash sale ($9,143 in the above *Bengy* property example)—assuming that the capital gains tax rate of the seller remains unchanged during the years in which the installments are received. The tax benefit in this case would be the *deferral* of the payment of part of the taxes. There can also be a *reduction* in total capital gains taxes paid if the seller's marginal capital gains tax rate is lower in the year of sale because of less gain recognized at the time of the sale. In some cases, for example, installment sale reporting could keep the total gains under $50,000 in any one year, and thereby keep the individual's marginal capital gains tax rate at a maximum of 25 per cent. Similarly, the installment-basis sale reporting could in some cases keep the corporation's income below $50,000 a year, and thereby keep its tax rate down to 20 and 22 per cent; rather than having the 30 per cent capital gains tax rate applied.

For the installment sale of property on which *ordinary* income tax rates will be applied—for example, when heavy depreciation recapture is involved, or where the seller is considered to be a dealer rather than an investor—then the tax benefits can be substantial with the profitable sale reported on the installment basis.

As in the case of capital gains, the amount of the taxable ordinary profit on qualified installment-basis sales of property will be spread out over the years in which the cash payments are received by the seller of the property. Because the marginal tax rate goes up to 70 per cent of an individual's investment income, the spreading out over the years of taxable income will mean for most taxpayers the application of a lower average tax rate than would apply if the entire profit from the sale were taxed in the year of sale. It should be noted, however, that the tax burden in the latter case would be eased by the income averaging tax provisions.

Installment-sale interest income. The interest received by the seller relating to the buyer's note is, as noted above, taxed as ordinary income in the years in which it is received, whether the gain on the sale is taxable as a capital gain or as ordinary income. Where the sale brings a gain taxable as a capital gain, there usually would be a preference on the seller's part for a higher selling price as a trade-off for a lower interest rate on the note, in order to shift funds from ordinary tax liability to capital gains tax liability. If, however, the investor seeks to achieve the result just described by having the note bear no interest or an "unrealistically" low interest charge (less than 4 per cent per year, simple interest), the government may impute additional interest to the note, to bring it to a more realistic level, and, of course, thereby subject more income to taxation at ordinary rates.

The amount of additional interest imputed to the note would be deducted from the selling price figure, which in some cases could in turn make the first year's cash payments exceed 30 per cent of the selling price, and thereby disqualify the sale for installment-basis-reporting benefits.

Other deferred-payment sales. Where the seller provides part of the financing for the buyer, but the sale does not qualify for installment-basis reporting because, say, more than 30 per cent is received as a cash down-payment, or because the sale involves a taxable loss—or if the seller elects not to report the sale on the installment basis—then the seller reports the entire gain or loss on the transaction in the *year of sale.*

In the situation just described, the calculation of the amount of the gain on the sale must take into account the fair market value of the note received from the buyer, as well as the cash received. That is, the stated selling price will not by itself determine the amount of the gain. Suppose, for example, an individual sells his $150,000 property for $50,000 cash, plus a note for $100,000 that calls for five annual payments of $20,000 each and interest at the rate of 4 per cent. The cash payments relating to the note that are to be received by the seller are scheduled as follows:

End of Year	Amortization	Interest (4%)	Total Payment
1	$ 20,000	$4,000	$24,000
2	20,000	3,200	23,200
3	20,000	2,400	22,400
4	20,000	1,600	21,600
5	20,000	800	20,800
	$100,000		

Suppose, however, that the fair market rate of interest for such a note at the time it is accepted by the seller is 9 per cent. In that case, the fair market value of the note received would be less than $100,000, because the note's interest payments at 4 per cent are below the market rate. Discounting the total payments indicated in the above schedule by 9 per cent gives a *present value* (fair market value) of the note of only $87,648. The present value calculations are as follows (the interest factors are found in *Column 4* of the Appendix):

Year	Total Payment	×	Interest Factor (9%)	=	Present Value
1	$24,000		0.917		$22,008
2	23,200		0.842		19,534
3	22,400		0.772		17,293
4	21,600		0.708		15,293
5	20,800		0.650		13,520
			Total present value		$87,648

The fair market value of the note of $87,648 combined with the $50,000 cash down-payment, gives a total fair market value for the proceeds of the sale of $137,648. It is this amount rather than the stated selling price of $150,000 that will be used in determining the amount of gain on the sale that will be taxed in the year of sale.

Land-contract sale. As was discussed in Chapter 9, when property is sold on a land contract basis, the seller keeps title to the property until all scheduled payments are made by the buyer. Because the buyer is not personally liable on the note, the title is simply retained by the seller in the event of default; the buyer loses his past payments but he is not liable for any future payments.

Sale–leaseback. At times there are benefits accruing to the property owner who sells his property and then leases it back from the buyer. The buyer in such cases is often a life insurance company. While the seller continues to use the property, his equity interest is converted by the sale–leaseback into a leasehold interest, and the seller loses the residual interest in the property. The primary motive for the sale–leaseback from the seller's standpoint is to obtain immediate cash from the sale, and if the property is used for business or investment purposes, the future lease payments may represent significant tax deduction amounts.

A not uncommon case would be a property developer who holds title to unmortgaged land, and is seeking to finance his planned construction on the site. As part of his financing arrangements he may sell the land to an insurance company for, say, $5 million, and lease the land back for, say, 99 years at $400,-000 a year. The $5 million cash received from the sale will then be used to help finance construction. The $400,000 lease payments will be tax deductible. In effect, the seller has received 100 per cent financing for the land portion of the project but has lost his equity interest in the land.

The financing package for a major urban property often includes a wide assortment of leases, including ground leases for the land portion of the property, and *sandwich leases* and other leases on the building itself. An example of one such finance package is the complex *fractionalized sale* of an office building in New York (One Park Avenue) arranged by William Zeckendorf, that is described in an appendix to this chapter.

PROPERTY EXCHANGES

In lieu of selling property, the owner may exchange it for another's property. If the exchange satisfies the statutory requirements, the newly acquired property will be considered as an extension of the old investment and any gain on the old property will not be taxed at the time that it is disposed of, except to the extent that *boot* is involved, as is discussed below.[4] While the gain escapes immediate taxation, the result is tax deferment, or postponement, rather than tax forgiveness; nonetheless, tax deferment helps immediate cash flows, and thereby helps the investor to build up his real estate holdings. The process of trading (tax free) a series of increasingly valuable properties is known as *pyramiding,* or *pyramiding equity.*

The business reasons for the exchange strategy, as distinct from the tax reasons, are really the same as when the owner sells property X so that he can buy property Y. Such motives include, for example, a change in investment goals, or a changed outlook for property X.

Requirements for a Tax-Free Exchange

For property disposed of by *exchange* to qualify for at least partial relief from taxes that would otherwise attend the property disposition, the following rules would be observed:

1. There must be an exchange of *like property*—for example, real estate business or investment property exchanged for other real estate business or investment property; and equipment for equipment. Real property that is transferred in exchange for stock in a corporation controlled by the transferror is considered a like exchange.
2. The exchanged property must be business or investment property, not a personal asset such as a personal car.
3. Real estate held by dealers for sale to customers does not qualify.

[4] *Internal Revenue Code,* Section 1031.

In addition to the requirements just listed for a tax-free exchange, the properties being exchanged must both have the same fair market value, for the exchange to be *completely* tax free. Suppose, for example, that *A's* property with a book value of $70,000, and a fair market value (FMV) of $120,000, is exchanged for *B's* property, also having a FMV of $120,000. In this case, *A* pays no tax at the time of the exchange. If, instead of exchanging his property, *A* sold the property for $120,000 cash, then his $50,000 gain would be subject to tax.

While *A's* property will be disposed of completely free of taxation by means of the exchange described in the above example, *A's* new property will take on *A's* original property's book value of $70,000 (for tax purposes) and the holding period of the original property will be taken by the new property. In other words, the new property is treated as a continuation of the old property investment. This means: (1) the $50,000 difference between the book value and FMV at the time that the old property is disposed of will eventually be subjected to tax, if the new property is later sold for at least $120,000; and (2) *A* will have to use $70,000 as the depreciable value of the new property, rather than $120,000, thereby reducing future tax deductions for depreciation expense compared to the amount of depreciation he could take if he had sold his property and purchased new property having a depreciable value of $120,000.

If the fair market value of *A's* property were below the book value of his property, then a loss would be recognized for tax purposes if *A* sold the property, rather than exchanged it for *B's* property having the same fair market value. No loss would be recognized for tax purposes if the property is exchanged rather than sold.

Partially Taxed Exchange

When the person exchanging property receives cash or other *unlike* property in order to balance the trade, then this cash or other property, called *boot,* is taxable up to the amount of the realized gain on the old property. Suppose, for example, that *A* exchanges his property having a book value of $70,000, and a fair market value of $120,000, for *B's* property having a FMV of $110,-000 plus $10,000 cash. The full amount of the boot (the $10,000 cash) is taxable because it is less than the $50,000 of realized gain on the original property.

When boot is received as part of an exchange transaction, the basis of the new property can be calculated with Equation 11-1 shown below.

$$\textit{Basis of new property} = \textit{Basis of old property} - \textit{Boot received} \quad [11\text{-}1]$$
$$+ \textit{Taxable gain}$$

In the example, the basis of *A's* new property would be $70,000 [$70,000 − $10,000 + $10,000]. The same formulation would be used to determine the depreciable value of the new property; in this example, also $70,000.

Mortgage Assumption in an Exchange

When the property being exchanged has an outstanding mortgage to be assumed by the other party to the exchange, the amount of the mortgage is treated for tax purposes as *boot.*

For example, *A* exchanges his property, having as before a FMV of $120,000 and a book value of $70,000, but now with a mortgage outstanding of $30,000, for *B's* property, having a FMV of $80,000, plus *B's* cash of $10,000 and *B's* assumption of *A's* $30,000 outstanding mortgage. In this case, the total boot to *A* is $40,000 [$10,000 + $30,000], which is fully taxable to *A,* again because the total boot is less than the $50,000 realized gain. Using Equation 11-1, the basis of *A's* new property (and here its depreciable value also) is found to be $70,000 [$70,000 − $40,000 + $40,000].

If, in addition to the assumption of *A's* mortgage by *B, B's* property had a mortgage outstanding that was assumed by *A,* then the net difference between the two outstanding mortgage amounts represents boot to the person assuming the smaller outstanding mortgage. Modifying slightly the previous example, we now suppose that *A* assumes *B's* $20,000 mortgage, and that *A* receives *B's* $100,000-FMV property, plus *B's* $10,000 in cash and *B's* assumption of *A's* $30,000 mortgage. The amount of taxable gain (here again the same as the total boot) received by A amounts to $20,000, as follows:

Cash received by A	$10,000
Plus: B's assumption of A's mortgage	+30,000
Less: A's assumption of B's mortgage	−20,000
A's taxable gain	$20,000

The basis for A's new property becomes: $70,000 − $20,000 + $20,000 = $70,000.

Multiple Exchange

Suppose A wishes to exchange his unmortgaged property with a basis of $70,000 and FMV of $120,000, for B's property having a FMV of $120,000; however, B wishes to sell his property for cash, rather than exchange it for A's property. A three-way exchange would be a possible solution. By this arrangement, a third party, C, would be sought who wishes to acquire A's property for $120,000 cash. It would then be arranged for C to buy B's property for cash, and then for C to exchange that property for A's. All three parties would then have accomplished their individual investment goals. The contrast between the two-way exchange and the three-way exchange (also called a three-cornered deal) just described is illustrated in Figure 11–1. In some cases it may be necessary to involve more than three parties in order to satisfactorily achieve the investment objectives.

As may readily be seen, a multiple exchange arrangement can become extremely complex when various properties are involved, and where multiple mortgages and other boot complications are involved. In this regard it should be noted that we have thus far ignored consideration of any depreciation recapture involved at the time of the exchange. Where recapture is involved because of the use of accelerated depreciation prior to the exchange, then the calculation of the tax on any recognized gain (because of boot) will have to take the recapture tax provisions into account. Experienced tax counsel may well be required by the investor to sort out the full tax consequences of complex exchange transactions.

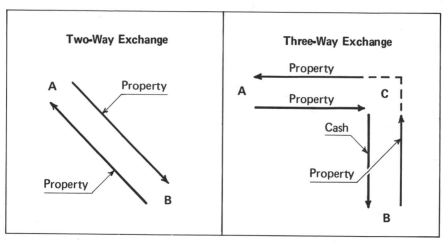

Fig. 11–1. Two-property exchange patterns.

OTHER PROPERTY DISPOSITION FORMS

The sale and the exchange are not the only means by which an investor can dispose of his real property. We conclude this chapter with a discussion of some alternatives, including involuntary conversion, long-term lease, gift, and devise.

Involuntary Conversion

The technical expression for the involuntary disposition of property is *involuntary conversion.* It refers to: (1) the taking of property by the government's exercise of eminent domain powers, through *condemnation proceedings,* and (2) the loss of real property in whole or in part by fire or other *casualty.*

The amount of realized gain (or loss) on involuntary conversions is measured by the difference between the amount of the condemnation award or insurance proceeds received by the investor, and the adjusted basis of the property at the time the property is seized or destroyed. If the property is held for more than the required number of months prior to the involuntary conversion, the taxpayer can have the gain, if any, treated as a long-term capital gain (if he is not categorized as a dealer with regard to the property); if a loss is involved, it can be treated as an ordinary income loss. The depreciation recapture rules apply, as on a sale of real estate. Instead of waiting for a condemnation award, the owner may report as involuntary conversion proceeds, the amount received from selling the property before condemnation—as long as the taxpayer can demonstrate that the sale was made under *the threat or imminence of condemnation.*

Tax-deferment provisions. As with qualifying property exchanges discussed in the last section, the taxpayer can postpone paying any tax on the gain realized upon involuntary property conversion if the Internal Revenue Service rules are followed. The principal requirements for tax deferment are:

1. *For condemned property,* the taxpayer must replace the condemned property with *like property* within required time limits.
2. *For casualty property,* the taxpayer must replace the destroyed property, with other property that is *similar or related in use to* the old property, within required time limits; that is, the new property must serve the same function as the old property.

For both the condemned property and the destroyed property the taxpayer may still take advantage of the tax-deferment benefits if, instead of purchasing replacement property directly, he purchases a controlling interest (at least 80 per cent of the shares) in a corporation that purchases the replacement property. Again, as it is with tax postponement relating to qualifying property exchanges, the newly purchased property replacing involuntarily converted property will take on the basis of the old property and the depreciable value of the old property.

Long-Term Lease

When the investor wishes to dispose of property that has appreciated greatly in value, and he also desires to receive a series of future income payments, an alternative to selling the property on a deferred-payment basis would be for the owner to lease the property for a long term, say, for 99 years. A genuine lease arrangement, as contrasted with what the Internal Revenue Service could label an installment sale, will help to avoid capital gains tax at the time the property is disposed of; however, the lease payments will be taxed as ordinary income in the years in which they are received.

Gift of Real Property

Within certain limits, real property given to qualifying non-profit institutions, such as churches and universities, affords the donor a tax deduction equal to the fair market value (FMV) of the property at the time of the gift. For the high-tax-bracket investor holding property that has increased greatly in value, the tax-deductible gift may actually yield greater after-tax benefits to the donor than the sale of property for cash.

Suppose an investor sells unmortgaged property with an adjusted basis of $15,000, and a FMV of $150,000. If the owner is in the 70 per cent tax bracket and has other capital gains, then he will pay a capital gains tax rate of 35 per cent on the entire $135,000 gain, or $47,250. The net after-tax proceeds of the sale would be $102,750 [$150,000 − $47,250]. If, on the other hand the owner gives the property to a qualifying charitable institution, and deducts the $150,000 FMV from his income that is otherwise taxable at a rate of 70 per cent; the amount of cash tax savings from the gift deduction will amount to $105,000 [.70 × $150,000]—some $2,250 *more* than if the owner had sold the property. There are, however, limitations on the proportion of the donor's gross income in the year of the gift that such deductions can be allowed to offset. Of course, as the material in this chapter makes clear, the straight sale for cash would not be the owner's only alternative to the gift disposition.

For gifts to individuals and non-qualifying institutions there is no tax deduction allowed. Rather, the donor will be obliged to pay tax on the FMV of the property that is donated. However, the donor may annually give up to $3,000 free of tax to any number of donees, and he may give an additional amount of up to $30,000 free of tax during his lifetime. For gifts above the exempted amounts just stated, the gift tax that is applied will range from 1/4 to 57 3/4 per cent, depending on the value of the property involved and on the timing of the donations. Some of these gift tax rules were modified by the 1976 TRA, as discussed below.

The donee's basis for the property will be equal to the

donor's basis at the time of the gift, plus the amount of any gift tax paid on the gift, excepting that such basis will not be higher than the FMV of the property at the time of the gift. As a consequence of these rules, no gain or loss is recognized at the time of the disposition of property by way of a gift. Any gain or loss will of course be recognized, if realized, at the time the donee sells the property.

Devise of Real Property, Pre-1976 TRA

Real property that is passed to others upon the owner's death *by devise* (by will), or *by inheritance* (where there is no will) is subject to federal (and state) estate taxes. The federal estate tax rates range from 3 to 77 per cent; however, there is a flat exemption amount of $60,000, and a marital deduction that allows one-half of the property to pass free of estate taxes to the surviving spouse.

Real estate passes to heirs and devisees on a stepped-up basis; that is, such recipients *generally* will take, as a basis for the property received, the FMV of the property at the time of the decedent's death, rather than the decedent's own basis for the property. Hence, any increase in property value prior to the decedent's death will escape income taxes; but the higher property value will be subject to the inheritance tax burden.

These estate tax rules, however, were changed by the 1976 TRA, as described next.

1976 Tax Reform Act Changes

A major restructuring of the tax rules for gifts and estates was made part of the TRA of 1976. Some of the highlights of the new structure are now briefly described. New tax rates ranging from 18 to 70 per cent are applied uniformly to the cumulative amount of taxable gifts and estates. In lieu of the previous lifetime gift exemption of $30,000, and the estate tax exemption of $60,000, a new *unified credit* is applied against cumulative gift and estate taxes that would otherwise be payable. The unified credit amounts to $30,000 in 1977, and gradually increases to a new total of $47,000 in 1981. Donors of gifts, however, will remain entitled to the annual gift tax exclusion of $3,000 per donee.

The size of the marital deduction is liberalized for estates of less than $500,000, and there are special estate tax benefits for family farms and businesses.

A significant change was made in the rules regarding the basis to be used by the recipient of a decedent's property, as follows: For property acquired by a decendent *after* 1976, the recipient takes the decedent's basis; i.e., the basis is not *stepped-up,* as under previous law. For property acquired by the decedent *before* 1977, the recipient takes the decedent's property with the basis stepped-up to the fair market value of the property as of December 31, 1976.

SUMMARY

There exist a number of ways for the real estate investor to dispose of property, in addition to the commonly used straight sale. The property disposition strategy chosen would often be determined by a consideration of the key tax aspects of each available alternative, particularly when a significant gain or loss is involved. However, other considerations can be important, such as the cash requirements of the seller, and market conditions.

The straight sale of property that has increased significantly in value since it was acquired can result in a heavy tax burden in the year of sale. On the other hand, a sale of the property on a qualified installment basis will spread out (defer) the tax burden on the gain, and in some cases will reduce the overall tax burden. The exchange of investment real property for other investment real property will also defer, at least in part, the imposition of taxes at the time the property is disposed of.

Other disposition forms that were reviewed in the present chapter included other deferred-payment sales, involuntary conversions, long-term leases, gifts, and the passing of real property to heirs and devisees.

APPENDIX: FRACTIONALIZED SALE

In many urban property transactions, a property is purchased with an immediate or short-term sale of the same property already prearranged at the time of purchase. William Zeckendorf, an innovator in arranging such transactions describes an arrangement whereby an office building ("1 Park Avenue") in New York City earning $1,000,000 in annual rentals, was purchased for $10,000,000, and shortly thereafter was sold in fractional interests for a total of $15.1 million. The basic steps in the elaborate property disposition in the Zeckendorf example, along with the amounts of cash received, are summarized below.* It will be observed that the first split of interests is between the land and the building thereon, as is common in financing urban properties.

The net result of the above transactions is that the seller has disposed of his entire interest in the property for cash totalling $15.1 million. The cost of the property was only $10 million. The underlying idea of the fractionalized sale is to create a variety of interests in the property, with each interest carefully tailored to meet the risk, return, and tax requirements of a particular financial institution, investing individual, or group. In this respect the fractioned interests are similar to the variety of specially tailored interests offered by corporations to their investors and creditors.

* William Zeckendorf, *Zeckendorf* (New York: Holt, Rinehart and Winston, 1970), pp. 145–48.

Land. The land fee is mortgaged to a life insurance company; $3 million is borrowed at 4% interest. Interest payments are $120,-000/yr, and there are no amortization payments. .... $ 3,000,000

The land is sold, subject to the $3 million mortgage, for $2 million cash, and leased back for 99 yr: $130,000/yr lease payments. 2,000,000

Total ground lease payments now = $250,000/yr.

Building. Note: at this point the net rentals to the building owner are $1,000,000 less $250,-000 ground lease payments: net $750,000.

An operating (outer) lease is sold for $3.6 million. The buyer would receive $ 1 million rentals/yr and pay $750,000/yr rent to the holder of the inner (sandwich) lease, leaving $250,000/yr for the outer lease holder (7% return on $3.6 million investment). 3,600,000

Inner lease (and building fee) interest is mortgaged for $4,000,000 with $350,000/yr mortgage payments. The inner lease holder receives $750,000/yr rent, of which $250,000 goes to ground rent. 4,000,000

The inner lease (and building fee) is sold for $2.5 million with the buyer assuming the $4 million mortgage. The buyer receives $750,000 rent, and pays $250,000 ground rent and $350,000 on the mortgage, leaving $150,000 net income (6% on $2.5 million investment). 2,500,000

Total Proceeds $15,100,000

IV

Property Selection

12

Investing in Land

Before selecting an individual real estate property to analyze for possible acquisition, the investor should determine the general *type of property* best suited to his investment goals, and best suited to his experience and investment resources. The general approach just described is somewhat analagous to that of the securities investor who selects the general type of security most appropriate to his investment objectives (for example, common or preferred stock, or bonds), and then proceeds with an analysis of individual securities within the chosen category.

The purpose of the present Part IV is to review some of the important investment considerations that apply to selected types of properties; starting in the present chapter with undeveloped land, and then proceeding on to residential rental properties, shopping centers, and motels. The discussion will focus on the general risk/return features of investments in the different types of property, and on such other factors as financing, property management, and property disposition.

When one invests in developed property he is usually investing in some combination of land and buildings. That is, most real estate investments involve some investment in land; although the seller of a building will at times only lease the land portion of the property. In the present chapter, attention is focused on the investment of funds in raw land, or in land having buildings or other improvements of only incidental value. We discuss here the purchase of such land for resale in its existing state, and reserve the dicsussion of land subdivision and development for Part V.

NATURE OF LAND

Land is defined in economics as one of the three factors of production. It is the *natural,* or nature-contributed factor; as contrasted to the other factors of labor and capital. We are concerned here with *surface land* rather than with mineral rights or air-space rights that generally accompany title to land, which are severable and sometimes valuable rights.

Some important general characteristics of land are that its supply is limited; it does not decrease in value with age, (time depreciation); it does not become obsolete; and it does not require repairs. These are generalizations, of course; grazing land, for example, does need to be renourished periodically to sustain successful grass production, and unchecked erosion will decrease the usefulness of land. Also, land can perhaps be said to suffer from *location obsolescence,* in the sense that its location can become less desirable for certain uses because of changed traffic patterns, adverse environmental conditions in the area, or for other reasons.

Types of Land

Most of the land area in the United States (approximately 1.9 billion acres) is in the form of farm and forest land, with less than ten per cent in urban and suburban residental land, and recreational land. It is the urban, suburban, and recreational land (and nearby farmland and woodland) that is generally the most suitable for investment purposes, because this land represents the areas in which the population is concentarted (for purposes of employment or for pleasure seeking). The U.S. Census data indicate the dramatic shift of the population to urban areas over the past several years. The general pattern is shown in Table 12–1.

As noted above, the type of land generally most suitable to acquire for investment purposes includes land in populous areas,

TABLE 12–1. U. S. Urban Population

Selected Years	Population Living in Places of—	
	2,500 or More	25,000 or More
1800	6.1%	2.4%
1850	15.3	8.9
1900	39.6	25.9
1950	59.6	42.2
1970	65.7	44.8

Source: U. S. Bureau of the Census, *Census of Population: 1970.*

including land in urban, suburban, and recreational centers, plus land that is within a reasonable driving time of such areas, or land that is expected to become a part of a populous area in the future. Existing and potential recreational areas are generally those located near water (oceans, rivers, and ponds) and in mountain areas. Another way of categorizing land is by the form in which it is transferred, that is, whether it is sold in the form of *lots,* or in the form of *acreage.* Most land in highly populous areas is, of course, transferred in the form of lots.

General Investment Characteristics

While land investments do require some degree of attention and maintenance responsibilities, especially those for which some interim income is obtained (such as farmland), most land investments can be considered to be relatively *passive* in nature. Land investments, therefore, can often be undertaken on a part-time basis. It can also be said that land is a relatively *illiquid* form of investment. While real estate investments in general are characterized as being illiquid, the market for raw land is often restricted to those planning to develop the land and to those investors seeking the rather specialized investment characteristics of land. Hence, it often takes several months for the conversion of land into cash. Of course, there are the exceptional situations when particular sites are highly sought after.

The primary investment goal for the purchaser of undeveloped land that is to be resold in its existing state is *price appreciation*. Land investments offer opportunities for extremely high returns; generally among the highest returns offered by the various forms of real estate investment. As will be discussed later in this chapter, the risks associated with land investments can also be substantial.

Valuation Changes

Because the profit, if any, from an investment in undeveloped land that is not producing significant periodic income will have to be generated in the form of price appreciation, successful investing in this type of property calls for appropriate judgments on the present and expected future value of particular pieces of land.

Land located in or near populous areas has tended to increase in value over the years because of the pressure of growing demand upon a limited quantity of land. In most areas, land values have probably risen, on the average, at least as fast as the general rate of inflation, and in many areas at a much higher rate. In areas of especially strong demand, increases in land prices have, in recent years, been on the order of 15 or 20 per cent per year, or more.

The growing, overall demand for land comes from two basic sources: (1) a general increase in population, and (2) a rising per capita demand for land. The population estimated for the year 2000 is 264 million, assuming that birth rates continue at about two children per family.[1] At the same time, each family, on the average, is demanding more land, often in the form of a second or even third homesite. Because of the increase in general demand, the investor in raw land in or near populous areas can, over the long run, usually expect the future value of his land to be higher than the acquisition price of the property. This assumes that the investor pays a reasonable price for the land.

Aside from the general long-run value pattern for land just

[1] "The New American Land Rush," *Time,* October 1, 1973, p. 87.

described, there are occasions when the value of a particular piece of land will increase sharply over a period of relatively few years. Such sharp increases are usually associated with land that becomes desirable for a new use. As was noted in Chapter 10, the classic example of a price rise being tied to a new use for land, is in agricultural property that becomes desirable for residential development use. There are, however, many other examples, including land that becomes desirable for some form of commercial or industrial development.

The present and potential use for a particular piece of land will depend in part upon its location, as discussed more fully below, and upon the physical attributes of the land. For agricultural use, for example, soil conditions and terrain are important; for residential use, water supplies and sewage disposal facilities (public services or percolation capacity for septic systems), as well as trees, terrain, views, and other factors are important.

Location analysis.   While the physical attributes of land will play some role in determining value, the most important factor in land valuation is usually the land's *location*. Most urban land, in particular, is almost wholly dependent upon location for its value determination. Because the location of a piece of land is fixed (immobile), future changes in the surrounding environment will bring changes in the value of the land.

The location factors to be analyzed in relation to the present and potential uses of the land would include such things as the applicable zoning regulations (for example, single-family residential, industrial, and commercial) and proximity to such things as public transportation, places of employment, tourist attractions, and shopping areas. The factors important for particular types of developed property are discussed in the following chapters of this Part IV.   Location analysis for rural land would require projections of the direction and timing of local population movements for residential, recreational, or other purposes.

Highest and best use study.   A study should be undertaken by the land investor to determine, in real estate appraisal terminology, the *highest and best use* for the particular piece of land being considered for acquisition. This is the particular use of the land that will maximize the property's income, and hence its value. The highest and best use study may determine, for example, that the most productive use for a particular piece of land (given its physical attributes and location) would be for a neighborhood shopping center. Such a study may determine, on the other hand, that the highest and best use of the land in question is for it to remain undeveloped for a given number of years, until the time is appropriate for implementing a future highest and best development use.

Land residual technique. A long-used real estate appraisers' technique that can be employed by the real estate investor in making an estimate of the future value for a piece of land is called the land residual technique. A simplified version of the technique would include the following steps: (1) a forecast is made of the annual income and expenses that would be expected from the highest and best use of the property; (2) the expected *net income* return is then capitalized to determine the total value of the developed property; and finally (3) the construction cost of the building is then deducted from the total value figure to find the *residual value* of the land.[2]

Suppose, for example, it is judged that the highest and best use for a particular piece of vacant land is to build an apartment house in five years' time. If the property under that use is expected to generate net operating income of $60,000 annually, and the capitalization rate (a weighted average of the rate of return required by the owner and the rate required by the lenders) is 12 per cent, and the cost of building the apartment units will be $350,000; then the *residual value* of the land will be $150,000:

$$\text{Residual value} = \frac{\textit{Estimated net operating income}}{\textit{Capitalization rate}} - \textit{Building cost}$$
$$= \$60,000/0.12 - \$350,000$$
$$= \$500,000 - \$350,000$$
$$= \$150,000$$

The $150,000 residual value would then be used as an estimate of the value of the land in five years, whether the land in-

[2] A detailed review of the land residual technique is contained in: Alfred A. Ring, *The Valuation of Real Estate* (2nd ed.; Englewood Cliffs, N.J.: Prentice-Hall, Inc., 1970), Chapter 19.

vestor plans to develop the property himself or to sell it to someone else for development.

LAND ACQUISITION

Because much of the value of a particular piece of undeveloped land will depend on the potential future uses of that property, an analysis of the attributes of the property that will affect present and future uses should be undertaken prior to making a purchase commitment. Some of the attributes to be considered would include such things as the applicable zoning regulations, the precise location of boundaries, water and sewage disposal facilities, and soil conditions. For an urban or suburban lot, such matters, can usually be determined quickly. For rural acreage, however, an extensive survey and extensive engineering and environmental-impact studies may be necessary. One means of obtaining the time necessary to accomplish these initial studies is to acquire an option on the property.

Financing Acquisition

Because of the benefits of leverage that will be illustrated later in this chapter, the investor in undeveloped land often seeks to finance a large portion of the acquisition price. Because, however, land in an undeveloped state will not be producing cash flows with which to cover debt-service payments, it is generally difficult to arrange for acquisition financing from a financial institution, unless the land is soon to be developed or subdivided by the investor, or the investor has other resources that could secure the loan.

Accordingly, in purchasing undeveloped land the investor will usually look to the seller for financing. As was discussed previously, there are many reasons for the seller to consider financing the sale. For example, if the seller seeks to obtain the benefits of a qualified installment-basis sale he will wish to finance at least 70 per cent of the selling price. For the acquisition of agricultural acreage, the investor may be able to obtain financing from one of the Federal Land Banks, or under the loan programs of the Farmers Home Administration.

Whatever source of financing is used, the land purchaser should seek to obtain the right from the mortgagee to sell portions of the land in the future, under specified conditions. The so-called *blanket mortgage* will provide for defined parts of the tract of land to be released from the mortgage upon their sale, and upon the payment of preset principal amounts.

HOLDING LAND

Holding undeveloped land for later resale, because of an expected general inflationary price rise or because of an anticipated new and higher use for the property, usually involves a periodic net cash drain for the investor, because of the often-substantial carrying costs.

Carrying Costs

For a land purchase that is financed with a loan calling for annual cash repayments of principal and interest, the major carrying costs of the land will include the *debt-service payments,* and *property taxes.* The annual debt-service payments will, of course, be higher with a relatively short-term mortgage, as is commonly found in land-acquisition financing. Often land sellers will provide financing over a 5-to-12-year period, as contrasted with developed-property financing that often extends to 25 years or more. The amount of annual property taxes to be paid will vary from a nominal level for some rural acreage, to as much as 3 per cent or more of the property's value for lots in urban and suburban areas. Often liability insurance coverage for property will be desired; however, this would usually involve a relatively minor annual cash outlay.

The level of *maintenance expenses* for land investments will depend on the nature of the property. The owner of an urban or suburban lot may incur costs for such things as sidewalk-snow removal, and landscape upkeep. For agricultural acreage, maintenance expenses would often be incurred for such things as the upkeep of grazing fields, and for repairs to barns and fences. Wooded acreage is a highly desirable form of land investment from the standpoint of maintenance expenses.

The holding expense factors described above can sometimes result in substantial cash outflows during the holding period; generally with little or no offsetting cash income. It is often observed, therefore, that despite probable annual increases in value for undeveloped land, the price gains may not be sufficient to cover the transaction and carrying costs of the investment.

Suppose, for example, that a 10-acre wooded tract of land located close to an urban center is acquired for $40,000; the seller provides 71 per cent financing, with a cash down-payment of 29 per cent, or $11,600. The purchase-money mortgage in the amount of $28,400 is for 10 years, at 9 per cent interest. The debt-service figure for the described loan ($4,425.29) can be found by multiplying the loan amount of $28,400 by the annual mortgage constant of 0.15582.[3] It is further assumed that annual property taxes amount to $450.00, and that the liability insurance premium is $20.00 per year. As the land is wooded, there are expected to be zero maintenance expenses. In this example, total annual cash outflows (before tax) amount to $4,895.29, or 12.2 per cent of the purchase price.

	Annual Cash Outflows	Percentage of Purchase Price of $40,000
Debt service	$4,425.29	11.0%
Real estate taxes	450.00	1.1
Liability insurance	20.00	0.1
Total (before tax)	$4,895.29	12.2%

The carrying costs, however, would be reduced by the tax-shelter benefits of the investment, if any. In the first year of the above example, the tax-deductible interest portion of the debt-service would amount to $2,556.00 [$28,400 × 0.09], which when added to the property tax and insurance expenses will give a total deduction of $3,026.00, to offset the investor's taxable income from other sources. Assuming a 30 per cent marginal tax rate, the tax-loss-shelter savings in the first year would amount to $907.80 [0.30 × $3,026.00]. The result is a net after-tax cash out-

[3] The mortgage constants are contained in *Column* 6 of the Appendix.

flow of $3,987.49 in the first year of the investment. The tax-shelter benefits will be lesser amounts in the following years because of the decreasing portion of debt-service payments represented by tax deductible interest expense.

For a land investment such as that described above, however, the investor's equity interest will be building up in each year of the holding period; and the investor will obtain a return of his mortgage amortization payments at the time of sale, if the property does not depreciate in value. Nonetheless, the loan amortization portion of the debt-service payments represents a non-deductible cash outflow in the years prior to the sale of the property. Because of the cash-flow requirements of a land investment such as the one described above, many investors seek to obtain *interest-only financing* for at least the first few years of the mortgage loan, and also seek to obtain whenever possible some income from the property during the holding period.

Interim Income

For the investor in rural acreage there are various possibilities for receiving interim income such as from the sale of timber, gravel, or sand; or from crop income under a sharecropping arrangement, or from animal-grazing rent. Rural land can sometimes be leased for such short-term activities as rodeos, horse shows, carnivals, and music festivals. Of course, the rural acreage may also have dwellings, or outbuildings that can be rented for machinery or hay storage.

If the land is to be held for some years, Christmas tree production may be a possible source of income, but cash income generally will not be forthcoming from this activity for at least four to six years after planting. The growing of turf for urban lawns has been a good income generator for some rural land-owners, as has catfish "farming," in some parts of the country. A mobile-home development may also be considered for interim income generation from rural acreage.

For land in more densely populated areas, it may be possible to produce interim income by using the property for such purposes as a parking lot, a miniature golf course, or a driving range. Another means of receiving interim cash flows is to periodically sell off parts of the property, within the constraints of the mortgage agreement.

In addition to seeking possible income from the property during the holding period, there are often other activities that the investor can undertake with a view toward increasing the property's resale value. Such activities, for example, would include working to change the zoning classification, and the location of future roads or sewer lines. The investor may also seek to acquire adjoining land to make a more attractive total piece of property, and if the land is being held for later sale to a residential developer, it may be desirable to partially develop the land by doing grading work or even installing a pond or lake.

Holding Period

With the exception of those investors holding land indefinitely as an inflation-hedged part of their investment portfolio, the holding period for the land investor will usually be tied in some way to the time necessary for the property to take on the new use that is expected for the property. If the investor anticipates that it will take four years for local residential subdivision activity to reach out to the investor's property, then four years would seem to be the logical planned holding period.

If the investor anticipates a very short-term or immediate new use for the property that the present offering price does not reflect, the investor may seek a buyer for the property as soon as he has made a cash down-payment or taken an option on the property. The investor purchasing the property will hold it for the required minimum number of months, however, if he seeks long-term capital gains treatment for the sale. Some investors who take a favorable option on a piece of land will seek to sell the option itself (at a profit) rather than exercise the option and then sell the land.

One difficulty in setting a planned holding period, and in determining the most appropriate time to sell land is that the market value of land will often rise in anticipation of some future use. For example, property that is widely expected to become used in about four years for residential subdivision purposes may enjoy the major value acceleration some years before the new use is implemented. One investment approach that is used to adjust to this phenomenon was discussed in Chapter 5 under the label of *target multiple*. The investor using that approach would plan to hold the property until the value rises to a pre-determined multiple of the purchase price; for example, he would plan to sell the land when the price doubles or triples in value because of an anticipated increased demand for the land. In this case, the planned holding period would become the time esti-mated for the target multiple to be reached.

LAND DISPOSITION

Where land has increased sharply in value, the landowner faces a major tax burden upon a straight sale of the property, although if capital gains treatment is received, the maximum rate of tax will be 35 per cent for the individual investor, and 30 per cent for the corporation. The installment-basis of reporting capital gains is widely used in sales where large gains are involved. As described in the last chapter, qualified installment-basis reporting will result in the spreading of the tax burden over the future years in which the installment payments are received from the buyer.

Among other means of softening the tax impact upon dis-position of land would be with a property-exchange arrangement, and possibly by leasing the land to a developer with whom a joint venture is formed to develop the land into an income-pro-ducing property.

RISK/RETURN ANALYSIS

As noted previously, the benefits from land investments are usually received by the investor in the form of price gains, a form of return that is favored by the tax laws over periodic in-come returns. The level of returns from land investment can be very high because, as with common stock investments, it is price appreciation rather than periodic income or cash flow that is the usual source of very large economic returns.

Land is not the most appropriate investment vehicle for those seeking periodic income, cash flows, or tax-shelter benefits.

As previously noted, the periodic taxable income and cash flows are usually negative amounts with land investments, and there will therefore be some tax-loss-shelter benefits. However, because *land itself cannot be depreciated for tax purposes,* the tax shelter benefits are not high in land investing in relation to investments in many income-producing properties.[4]

When sharp price increases in land values occur they are generally tied to the *new use* concept discussed in the previous section. Land used strictly for farmland, with no alternative foreseeable use, may be valued at anywhere from $50 per acre to, say, $1,000 per acre. However, similar land used for recreational or suburban lots may bring up to $10,000 per acre, or more, as would land that is developed for shopping centers or apartments.

Two other factors are involved with the high-profit potential for land. First is the often-cited fixed supply of land, in the face of increasing demand; the other factor is the relatively small portion of many real estate project costs that is represented by the land cost. The latter factor, of course, applies to land upon which major improvements will be made such as a major office building or industrial plant. When this situation exists, and there are few alternative land parcels available for the intended use, the land price is highly elastic; as with any input factor representing a relatively small portion of a product's total cost. For example, the director of purchasing for a major corporation has stated with regard to purchasing selected sites for his company's industrial plants: "We naturally negotiate the deal just as we would any other purchase. But whether you spend $15,000 or $17,000 an acre for a piece of property that will be providing income for at least 30 years, is relatively unimportant."[5]

The same principle noted above applies in an extreme form when a major developer is gathering acreage for a large real estate development project. The ultimate price paid can be extremely high for the seller of land that is needed to complete the required land package.

---

[4] Some limited amounts of depreciation expense will often be generated by producing farm properties—on fences, barns, and any other depreciable improvements on the property.

[5] "When Land is Just Another Commodity," *Purchasing Magazine,* December 19, 1972, p. 60.

It should be noted, however, that land prices in many areas have risen to the point where land is becoming a relatively high portion of the developed property's value. This is especially true for residential developments. Over the period 1950 to 1970, the land-cost portion of residential-dwelling properties is reported to have increased, on the average, from 11 to 24 per cent.[6] One result of this growth in the relative importance of land values has been the trend to higher-density developments, as described in the following chapter. With this higher level of development per acre of land, however, land tends to become again a relatively smaller portion of total project cost, and hence, relatively price elastic.

As a generalization, land investment is one form of real estate offering a very high profit potential. Unless buildings have historic value or other irreplaceable features, they will generally lose value in real terms, because they wear out, and become obsolete. During periods when new construction costs are rising rapidly, developed properties may well increase in value in terms of deflated dollars; however, in many cases of real price increases for used homes and other properties, the source of the increase is found to be the underlying land values, or the value of space, as with high-rise condominiums.

Use of Leverage

The equity investor's rate of return from an investment in land that appreciates significantly in value can, of course, be magnified by using borrowed funds to finance part of the acquisition cost, that is, by the use of *leverage*. As an example, we shall compare the results of a 3-year *Land Investment* that appreciates in value at the rate of 30 per cent per year; (1) using zero leverage, and (2) using 60 per cent leverage. The assumed facts are as detailed on the next page.

The comparative after-tax cash flows for the *Land Investment* example, and the discounted cash flow rates of return are shown in the investment profile in Table 12–2. With the use of 60 per cent leverage, the prospective rate of return is a relatively high

[6] Sara A. Frankel, "Rising Land Costs are Burying the Home Builders," *Real Estate Review*, Winter, 1972, p. 89.

LAND INVESTMENT

	Zero Leverage	60% Leverage	
Price	$ 50,000	$ 50,000	(50 acres @ $1,000)
Loan	0	$ 30,000	(10 yr, 10% level-
Down-payment	$ 50,000	$ 20,000	annual payments)
Holding peroid	3 yr	3 yr	
Estimated selling price	$109,850	$109,850	(value increase:
			30%/year)
Estimated selling expenses	$ 10,985	$ 10,985	(10% of selling price)
Gross possible income	0	0	
Operating expenses	$ 400	$ 400	
Depreciable value	0	0	
Income tax rate	50%	50%	
Capital gains tax rate	30%	30%	

31.6 per cent, as compared with the 18.7 per cent return for the same investment financed without borrowed funds. It should be noted, however, that high loan-to-value ratios are less likely to be achieved in land investing than for investments in income-producing properties; and when a high degree of leverage is achieved, the financial risk for the investor increases accordingly.

Land Investment Risks

As a general investment principle, the higher the expected return, the greater the risk. In bond investing for example, the higher the quality of a bond issue, the lower the investor's yield. Accordingly, as land investments can result in high capital-gain returns, the risks of land investments should be expected to be relatively high, as with investments in speculative common stocks.

The risks of land investing take essentially two different forms: (1) the inability to meet the cash flow requirements of carrying the property, and (2) the failure of the property to rise in value enough to offset the carrying and transaction (buying and selling) costs. The level of cash flow requirements for carrying land is raised when substantial funds are borrowed to help finance the property. Accordingly, the increased risk of not being able to meet cash flow needs is related to the higher returns that

TABLE 12–2. Investment Profile—Land Example

	Zero Leverage	60% Leverage		
	Years 1,2,3	Year—1	2	3
	Periodic Returns			
Gross Income	$ 0	$ 0	$ 0	$ 0
less: Operating expenses	400	400	400	400
Net Operating Income	($400)	($ 400)	($ 400)	($ 400)
less: Depreciation expense	0	0	0	0
less: Interest expense	0	3,000	2,812	2,605
Taxable Income	($400)	($3,400)	($3,212)	($3,005)
less: Income taxes (50%)	0	0	0	0
Earnings After Tax	($400)	($3,400)	($3,212)	($3,005)
plus: Depreciation expense	0	0	0	0
less: Mortgage amortization	0	1,882	2,070	2,277
plus: Tax-loss savings	200	1,700	1,606	1,502
Cash Flow After Tax	($200)	($3,582)	($3,676)	($3,780)
	Sale Proceeds			
Selling Price (net of expenses)	$98,865			$98,865
less: Unpaid mortgage	0			23,771
less: Income taxes (30%)	14,660			14,660
Sale Proceeds (after tax)	$84,205			$60,434
Discounted Cash Flow Rate of Return	18.7%	-------------- 31.6% ----------------		

are possible with the use of leverage. This risk is recognized by lenders who, in general, prefer that the proceeds of their loans be used for projects that will be expected to generate sufficient periodic cash flows to meet the scheduled debt-service payments. In the case of investments in undeveloped land, the funds for meeting debt service (and other carrying costs) will usually have to be generated by the investor's outside sources of income.

The land carrying costs can become increasingly difficult to meet when property taxes are rising rapidly, as often happens when land values are increasing sharply in the area. The failure of the investor to meet the carrying cost obligations can lead to a forced *distress sale,* which in turn adds to the second risk listed above, of the insufficiency of the sale proceeds to cover the investment outlays made prior to the sale.

A property's failure to achieve an expected price level increase is a risk attending most land investments, not only because of a possible hurried, distress sale by creditors, or because the investor may need to sell the property prematurely to raise funds for another immediate use; poor price achievement can be due to many other conditions. Such circumstances would include, for example, an adverse change in the environment surrounding the subject property, such as the deterioration of some inner-city residential and commercial neighborhoods, and changes in conditions that will prevent a higher use of the property, such as a change in zoning regulations, the imposition of strict environmental controls on land use, or an adverse change in highway and road patterns.

Another reason why land may fail to rise in value as expected is simply because the investor overpaid for the property at the time of acquisition. Also, national and local economic conditions relating to the general levels of income and employment will affect land values.

In sum, there are risks in land investing; and perhaps, in general, higher risks than with other forms of real estate investing; however, with a careful initial study of the land being considered for purchase, and with favorable market conditions, the returns can be extremely high. Table 12–3 presents a comparison of some of the major advantages of undeveloped land investments with the advantages generally attending investments in developed, income-producing property.

SUMMARY

Purchasing undeveloped or raw land for subsequent resale can generally be characterized as a relatively passive form of investment, and usually a relatively illiquid form of investment. Because undeveloped land usually produces little or no periodic

---

TABLE 12–3.   Investment Advantages, Land vs. Developed Property

---

Advantages of Land	Advantages of Developed Property

---

1. High price-appreciation potential.	1. Periodic income or cash flows, often sufficient to at least cover carrying costs.
2. Fixed supply, so value probably will increase with increases in population and in per capita demand.	2. Improvements can often be depreciated, to give significant tax-shelter benefits.
3. Built-in profit by buying large acreage (wholesale) and selling in smaller quantities (retail).	3. Often possible to finance with high loan/value ratio.

---

income or cash flow, investments in such land are made with the primary goal of achieving price appreciation benefits.

Rates of return on land investments can be among the highest in the field of real estate investing, and are usually taxed at favorable capital gains rates. One source of potential price appreciation arises from the long-term increase in demand for land resulting from population increases, and from rising demand per capita. Large price gains can occur in a relatively short time period when a particular piece of land becomes desirable for a new and higher use; such as when agricultural land becomes desirable for residential or recreational purposes. The owner's return on investment will be magnified by the use of favorable leverage.

The high potential returns from land investments tend to be accompanied by relatively high levels of risk associated with the burden of meeting the periodic costs of carrying land, often when the land is not generating positive cash flows, and the risks associated with a possible decline in the value of the property.

13

Residential Rental Property

In the present chapter and in the following two chapters we consider the investment characteristics of developed, income-producing properties. While there is usually a land factor to consider in such investments, there are also operating income and expense patterns to analyze, and the factor of property management to consider. The investment in income-producing properties generally involves more administrative responsibilities than the investment in undeveloped land; that is, the investment interest is an *active* interest, rather than a passive one.

The land use, of course, has been predetermined for the investor in a developed property, and hence a land-use study is not required; however, a market study will be a necessary first step in forecasting expected future revenues. The present chapter focuses on investments in land that has been developed as a *residential* rental property; the process of acquiring land and constructing residential or other income properties thereon is discussed in Part V.

TYPES OF RESIDENTIAL PROPERTY

Of the various forms of income-producing property, the most popular is residential property, that is, dwelling units. In 1970, there were over 23 million occupied *rental dwelling units* in the United States, representing some 37 per cent of all year-round occupied housing units. Because all of the various types of residential properties can be purchased as investment rental properties, we shall first review the different dwelling-unit types, and some overall trends. However, the focus in the rest of the chapter will be on apartment projects.

The first two major categories of dwelling units are *single-family residential units,* and *multiple-dwelling units.* The third category is *mobile homes.* Table 13–1 shows the relative importance of the three different housing categories, and the recent growth rate patterns for each type.

The faster growth shown in Table 13–1 for multiple-dwelling units (as compared with single-family units) is also reflected in the figures for new housing starts in recent years. In 1973, for example, the number of multiple-dwelling units that were started was 45 per cent of the number of single-family starts, as contrasted to only 26 per cent in 1960.

The reasons for the growing importance of multi-unit residential structures are numerous, including the rising cost of land available for residential development, and the economies of construction attending multi-unit structures. Demographic factors are also partially responsible for the trend, with an increasing proportion of the population being relatively young or relatively old. The people in those age categories have traditionally been most interested in the economies and low-maintenance responsibilities often associated with multiple-dwelling living arrangements. It also appears that a growing portion of the population in general is turning to multi-unit structures for the same basic reasons.

High-density residential construction has long been the traditional response to housing needs in high-priced land areas, as evidenced by the high-rise apartment buildings found in most cities, as well as by the ubiquitous *row houses,* or *brownstones* observed in such cities as New York, Baltimore, and Washington. What therefore is new about the recent acceleration in high-density residential construction is that: (1) multi-unit structures are built in suburban and recreational areas; and (2) there are new models of high-density development, such as the large *cluster,*

TABLE 13–1. Housing Units in the United States

Units in Structure	1960	1970	Change
One unit	43,759,000	46,901,000	+ 7.2%
Two or more units	13,790,000	18,860,000	+ 36.8
Mobile home or trailer	767,000	1,847,000	+140.8

Source: U. S. Bureau of The Census, U. S. Census of Housing: 1970.

or *open-space* developments, that combine various types of residential living arrangements in a single project. Many of the newer, large-scale residential projects offer a country-club type of atmosphere, with the provision of such amenities as clubrooms, tennis courts, swimming pools, and golf courses.

Illustrative of the trend towards higher-density land-use in residential dwellings is the *fourplex,* a design developed on the West Coast in the mid-1960's, which has since spread to other parts of the country. By joining four residential units in the one fourplex, builders have been able to place as many as sixteen units on one acre of land. Major economies are one result, because of the sharp drop in land per living unit, and because of the reduction in construction costs per unit through such means as centralized plumbing.[1]

That the number of multiple-dwelling units has been growing much faster in recent years than the number of single-family units would seem to suggest that the number of rental units has been growing faster than owner-occupied units, because multiple-dwellings have historically been predominantly rental units. However, this has not been the case. During the 1960's, the number of renter-occupied residential units increased by only 16.5 per cent, as compared with a 21.5 per cent increase in the number of owner-occupied units; and the trend toward increased owner-occupied housing continued into the early 1970's with the spread of the condominium concept.

[1] See "Housing Comes Cheaper by the Fourplex," *Business Week,* October 28, 1972, pp. 54–55.

Condominiums

The *condominum* project is usually an apartment project, or townhouse development, in which the occupants purchase rather than lease the dwelling units. The owner-occupants also have joint ownership of common areas, such as hallways, elevators, grounds, and any common recreational facilities in the project; such facilities range on up to swimming pools and yacht basins.

The "condo" boom first developed in this country in Florida, and by 1972 some 75 per cent of new residential construction in South Florida was in the form of condominiums, several of them very large apartment complexes having as many as 1,000 units.[2] The trend to condominiums has spread to other parts of the country, and in many large cities there has been widespread conversion of existing rental apartment complexes into condominiums. While this is a relatively new residential form in this country, the basic condominium apartment arrangement has long been used in other parts of the world, such as in Buenos Aires and Rio de Janeiro.

The condominiums have become a popular form of residence for a variety of reasons. They offer the buyer a number of advantages, as compared with apartment or townhouse renting, including the tax-shelter benefits attending home ownership (the deductibility of mortgage interest and property taxes), plus an equity interest in property that may well increase in value. Compared with the detached single-family residence, the condo projects offer relatively maintenance-free living and a club-like atmosphere that is especially appealing to those seeking a retirement dwelling or a second-home unit. Also, a lower cost per square foot of living space may be the result for the purchaser, which is generally an important consideration for young families.

The condominiums have some advantages for the investor, compared with rental units. With the condominium, for example, the investor avoids the tenant–landlord conflicts that have been on the rise in recent years. Mortgage lenders often favor the condominium development projects because the developer

[2] "Condominiums Capture the Florida Market," *Business Week,* November 4, 1972, p. 82.

often presells many or all of the units—as contrasted with new rental apartments that sometimes take three years or more after completion to reach full occupancy.

APARTMENT INVESTMENTS

Despite the trend just described toward owner-occupied multiple-dwelling units, there nonetheless will continue to be a very substantial market for traditional rental apartment projects and for rental townhouses. There is not only a solid portion of the population that will continue to desire rental units, but that portion will grow as the costs of ownership rise, and when mortgage money is scarce and costly. Because residential properties provide one of the basic needs of the population, namely *shelter,* the government has favored residential rental property owners by means of the tax laws. It will be recalled, for example, that such properties qualify for liberalized accelerated-depreciation methods, and to a lesser extent, liberalized depreciation-recapture provisions.

Types of Apartments

One classification of the various types of apartment projects is in the set of definitions used by the Institute of Real Estate Management of the National Association of Realtors:[3]

1. *High-rise elevator buildings:* This group is confined to elevator buildings of four stories or more.
2. *Low-rise:* Includes walk-up buildings, and elevator buildings of three stories or less.
3. *Garden-type:* A group of low-rise apartment buildings situated on a sizeable landscaped plot, under one management.

The appropriateness of a particular type of apartment project depends on local demands and local conditions; high-rise apartments, for example, are desirable in areas where there is a need for strict security, or land costs are extremely high. In some areas only low-rise and garden apartments are used, because

[3] *Income/Expense Analysis: Apartments, Condominiums, and Cooperatives* (1975 edition; Chicago: Institute of Real Estate Management, 1975), p. 160.

of local zoning requirements, or for aesthetic, or cost, or other reasons.

ACQUISITION OF RENTAL UNITS

In selecting an existing apartment project to acquire as an investment property, an analysis is first made (as described in previous chapters) of the present and future estimated cash flows for the project. The analysis starts with a market study to determine expected future rental income, and estimates are made of cash outflows for future operating expenses, debt service payments, and taxes.

The market-study format for an apartment project was given in Chapter 3. For that type of study, the community is examined in terms of population characteristics and growth patterns. A trade area analysis is undertaken, and an inventory made of competitive buildings. One reason for the importance of the market study is that it may help the investor to anticipate future conditions that could weaken the prospective demand for apartments within the project being considered for acquisition.

Apartment construction tends to come in bursts, such as in 1970 and in early 1971, often followed thereafter by a period of surplus apartments and high vacancy rates, as in some U.S. cities in late 1972 and in 1973. On top of this basic cycle that has been observed over many years is the recent development, described earlier, of families changing from apartment rental to apartment ownership. A residential market analysis must take account of such patterns. One can probably safely estimate, however, that important segments of the overall housing market will continue to require rental units, such as college students, military personnel on short-term assignments, large numbers of lower-income and middle-income families that are not prepared to take on real-estate ownership, and perhaps mobile executives and professional people.

Because apartment projects are income-producing investments (as contrasted with vacant land), the *gross income multiplier* (GIM) is widely used as one rough rule-of-thumb guide in determining an appropriate acquisition price. If, for example, the present annual gross income of an apartment project is $60,000, and the applicable GIM is 8.2, the market value estimate for the property would be $492,000 [$60,000 × 8.2]. This technique was described in detail in Chapter 3.

Financing Acquisition

The principal sources of mortgage funds for the acquisition of large-scale apartment projects are the life insurance companies; the mortgage trusts, one form of the real estate investment trusts; and, to a much lesser extent, the pension funds. FHA-insured single- and multiple-family project mortgages are participated in by these financial institutions, and also by the commercial banks, the mutual savings banks, and the savings and loan associations.

The seller of the residential property will, at times, provide first- or second-mortgage financing; or the seller may finance the buyer with a land contract; or he may sell the building only, and give the purchaser a long-term ground lease on the land that will be subordinated to the first mortgage on the building. The purchaser will, of course, seek to take over (assume) the seller's existing mortgage on the property when the existing interest rate is significantly lower than the market rate at the time of acquisition. In the same situation, a wrap-around mortgage may also be appropriate, as noted in previous chapters.

When the financial institutions have sufficient funds available, it is often possible for the apartment purchaser to obtain financing for a high portion of the purchase price. By combining a life-insurance first mortgage loan for, say, 75 per cent of the property's cost with second-mortgage financing from the seller, the purchaser can attain leverage approaching 90 per cent, or even higher. The same leverage may at times be achieved by having the financial institution purchase the land portion of the project and lease it (long-term) to the building purchaser; with the financial institution also providing first mortgage financing for the apartment building itself.

Equity participations. When mortgage money is in short supply, the *equity kicker* may be insisted upon by the mortgage lender; that is, a requirement is made that the equity investor make periodic payments to the mortgagee based upon the amount of the owner's periodic cash flow or income. Through the use of this requirement and other forms of equity interest demands, some large life insurance companies have managed to deny the owner-investor of much of his traditional cash flow and equity-build-up benefits.

Equity participations are also often required by insurance companies and REIT *lessors* under land sale-leaseback arrangements. The following description of the sale-leaseback of a garden apartment in St. Louis illustrates a common type of equity-participation requirement. In the following example it will be observed that the lessor will not only share in the gross income but also in the proceeds of any future refinancing; the land tenant also has the option to repurchase the land.[4]

GARDEN APARTMENTS IN ST. LOUIS

A REIT arranged a sale-leaseback for a Southwestern developer on a 284-unit garden apartment complex in St. Louis. The project had been completed for six months, with rentup proceeding at a healthy 40-unit per month rate. The REIT anticipated that the project would be fully occupied before the sale-leaseback was completed.

Following a $5.8 million first mortgage on the project by a commercial bank, the REIT committed to make an $850,000 land purchase-leaseback at a fixed rate of $10\frac{3}{4}$ per cent. In addition, the REIT would receive 15 per cent of gross income in excess of 95 per cent occupancy. The investor would also share in 15 per cent of the net proceeds of any future first mortgage refinancing. The lessee required a repurchase option exercisable from 20 to 25 years from the signing of the original lease. The repurchase price was set at $850,-000 plus three per cent per annum. Cash flow coverage was 175 per cent of the fixed rent.

Ownership Form

Because of the possibilities for using a high amount of leverage (which generates large interest-expense deductions), and because of large depreciation deductions (especially for the *first*

---

[4] "Have You Considered the Sale–Leaseback with Land?" *Professional Builder*, June, 1973, pp. 128–29. Such repurchase provisions should be carefully drawn to avoid an Internal Revenue Service interpretation that the arrangement resembles a mortgage.

user of the property), many apartment projects will generate low levels or even negative levels of taxable income. When this is expected to be the case, the investor should use an ownership form that permits period losses to be offset against his other income. The appropriate organizational forms for this situation include the general and limited partnership forms, and the individual ownership form, rather than the corporation, or the real estate investment trust. However, for projects looked to for substantial taxable income flows, the corporation or REIT form may be appropriate, depending upon the various strategy factors discussed in Chapter 8.

INCOME AND EXPENSE PATTERNS

As noted at the beginning of this chapter, when one invests in improved, income-producing property, as contrasted with vacant land, new income and expense patterns, as well as new risk/return considerations, become important investment factors. While vacant land generally represents a passive form of investment, income-producing property is usually an active form of investment, with substantial time and attention required of the investor. There are exceptions, of course, such as property rented to a top-quality tenant under a long-term *net* lease.

Apartment Income

The level of gross possible *rental income* (assuming full occupancy) for a particular apartment project will be determined, of course, by the level of competing apartment rent levels, the general demand level in the area, and (increasingly) the level of ownership costs for competing condominium apartments and townhouses. Other factors described in the next section as influencing the nature and level of operating expenses will also influence income levels, such as the age and quality of the apartment building, the tenants, the location of the building, and the lease provisions relating to the owner's responsibility for utilities, painting, and other expenses. Also important in rental income determination are any constraints on rent increases that are imposed by federal government price controls, and by local government rent controls.

The gross possible rental income will be reduced by the amount of income lost because of vacancies and bad debts, to determine the gross *actual* rental income for the apartment property in question. In areas of accelerated new apartment construction, it may take some years for the market to absorb the new rental units and for full occupancy to be reached. When new rival projects enter the area, the occupancy level of existing older apartment projects will suffer unless the older apartments have some comparative advantages in terms of location or facilities. In short, the vacancy rates for apartments are primarily tied to local supply as well as demand factors.

For some residential rental projects, *other rental income* provides a significant part of gross income. The principal sources of such income would include rents received for garage and parking facilities, and any rental income received from stores or offices located in the apartment building. *Miscellaneous income* is often generated by such sources as laundry and vending machines, maid services, signs on the building, and air-conditioning charges.

Apartment Expenses

Holding improved, income-producing property brings the burden of bookkeeping, cost-control, tax-planning, and maintenance, as well as such activities as credit and collection, the establishment of an insurance or risk-management program, advertising, and promotion. Accordingly, higher levels of costs, and new types of costs are incurred with developed properties, as compared with land investments. The various apartment ownership costs are discussed below under the categories of operating and non-operating expenses.

Operating expenses. Because of such factors as maintenance requirements, the provision of utilities, and the short-term leases that often attend investments in apartment projects, total operating expenses usually represent a relatively high percentage of gross income. The analysis of 91 newer elevator apartment buildings summarized in Table 3–2 indicated an average *expense ratio* (total operating expenses ÷ gross possible total income) of 48.5 per cent—on the average, almost 49 cents of every gross income dollar went to cover operating expenses. For the oldest 27 buildings in the same sample, the average expense ratio was 61 per cent.

Local *property taxes* usually represent the largest single operating expense, and in some urban areas these have reached as high as 30 per cent of gross possible income. Other major apartment expense items usually include *interior painting and decorating; interior and exterior maintenance and repairs; payroll expenses,* for example, payments for doormen, maids, elevator operators, telephone switchboard operators, and maintenance personnel; and *electricity.* For residential properties, *administrative expenses* are often significant amounts, in part because relatively short-term leases are usually involved. Such expenses are incurred for such things as credit and collection activities, advertising, legal and auditing services, and office supplies. Various *other operating expenses* include such things as property insurance, water, heating fuel, and miscellaneous supplies.

The level and nature of operating expenses will, of course, vary with the age of the building (as was discussed in Chapter 3), with the overall expense level typically rising as the building becomes older. The *location* of the building will also be a factor; with operating expenses generally being higher in urban areas. Other variables influencing expense levels will be: the *lease terms* relating to the tenant's responsibility for certain expense items such as electricity; the general *quality of the tenants* as regards treatment of the property and the rate of turnover; and, of course, the *nature of services and facilities provided* by the owner.

Non-operating expenses.   The nature and level of the non-operating expenses that represent financing costs, such as *interest payments and ground lease payments,* will depend on the basic terms of the financing arrangement made for the apartment project. While not classified as an expense, the periodic mortgage amortization payments (which also depend upon the financing arrangements) will represent a periodic cash outflow that will be included in a cash-flow investment analysis.

Another major non-operating expense is *depreciation.* The annual amount of this tax-deductible expense will be a function of the depreciable value of the apartment building, the depreciation method used, and the estimated remaining useful life. The Treasury Department's useful life guideline for residential properties is 40 years. As discussed previously, residential rental property receives favored tax treatment as regards depreciation methods and recapture requirements. The particular depreciation method allowed will depend on whether the investor is the first user of the property. For *new* residential rental properties, the owner may elect to use the double-declining-balance method of depreciation.

Planning and Control

An analysis of present and historical data on the income and expenses for a particular apartment project can be helpful in making the future cash flow projections, which in turn will be important in deciding whether or not to make an investment in the property. A careful analysis of such income and expense data can also be useful in measuring the operating efficiency of an apartment project, and useful for setting rental levels; that is, the data can be used for management planning and control, after the project has been acquired.

One measure of managerial *effectiveness* would be the level of the project's occupancy rate, as compared with the level of such rates for competing projects. Managerial *efficiency,* however, relates to the level of costs (inputs) incurred in relation to the space that is occupied (output). For a meaningful measure of efficiency, and hence of cost control, the expense data must be grouped in appropriate ways.

For management planning and control purposes it is useful to collect income and expense data over a given time period in accordance with these four categories:

1. Income and expenses (I & E) for the whole project.
2. I & E per room.
3. I & E per square foot of gross area.
4. I & E per square foot of rentable area.

The procedure simply calls for accumulating all of the income and expenses of the year (or other time period), by various basic types—for example, heating fuel, or supplies—and then dividing such amounts by the number of rooms, and by the number of total and leasable square feet in the apartment project.

The appendix to this chapter contains income and expense definitions, and guidelines on apartment-room counts and area measurements, that are provided by the Institute of Real Estate Management, of the National Association of Realtors.[5] Such definitions and guidelines are very helpful in making the income-expense analyses described above.

When the data have been accumulated for the project being analyzed, they can be compared with past years' figures for the same project (trend analysis), and they can be compared with data for other similar apartment projects. The Institute makes available composite income and expense data for periodically surveyed apartment projects.[6] Table 13–2 contains an example of grouped income and expense data for a hypothetical apartment project.

With apartment income and expense data such as in Table 13–2, the analyst not only has information that is useful for measuring and controlling management performance as described above, but also information that is useful for determining general rental levels, and for setting a rent schedule for individual apartments within the overall project.

Before leaving this subject it should be noted that the efficient use of a particular apartment project's space is sometimes measured by the *efficiency ratio,* as follows:

$$\text{Efficiency ratio (\%)} = \frac{\text{Rentable square feet}}{\text{Gross square feet}} \times 100$$

In the hypothetical apartment example in Table 13–2, the efficiency ratio would be 80 per cent [(120,000/150,000) × 100].

PLANNING HORIZON

The planned holding period (planning horizon) that is used in analyzing a proposed apartment investment will depend on the

[5] The present name of what was the National Association of Real Estate Boards.
[6] For example, see *Income/Expense Analysis: Apartments, Condominiums, and Cooperatives, op. cit.*

TABLE 13–2. Annual Income and Expense Data—Hypothetical
                        Apartment Project

Number of apartments: 150   Gross area of building: 150,000 square feet
Number of rentable rooms: 600   Rentable area of building: 120,000 square feet

			Income and Expenses		
	Total	Percentage of Gross Possible Income	per Room	per SF Gross Area	per SF Rentable Area
Gross Possible Income	*$360,000*	*100.0%*	*$600*	*$2.400*	*$3.000*
Gross Income, Actual	$342,000	95.0%	$570	$2.280	$2.850
less: Operating Expenses:					
Total payroll	27,000	7.5	45	0.180	0.225
Electricity	18,000	5.0	30	0.120	0.150
Gas	5,400	1.5	9	0.036	0.045
Water	3,600	1.0	6	0.024	0.030
Heating fuel	21,600	6.0	36	0.144	0.180
Management	14,400	4.0	24	0.096	0.120
Painting & decorating (int.)	10,800	3.0	18	0.072	0.090
Maintenance & repairs	14,400	4.0	24	0.096	0.120
Supplies	3,600	1.0	6	0.024	0.030
Services	5,400	1.5	9	0.036	0.045
Miscellaneous	5,400	1.5	9	0.036	0.045
Real estate taxes	50,400	14.0	84	0.336	0.420
Total Operating Expenses	180,000	50.0	300	1.200	1.500
Net Operating Income	$162,000	45.0%	$270	$1.080	$1.350

investment objectives of the prospective owner. Assuming that the investor is not seeking a quick turnover of the property, then the appropriate planning horizon may well be found to be in the 8-to-12–year range. As was discussed in Chapter 10, a large portion of the project's deductible interest and depreciation expenses will usually have been taken within the first ten years following acquisition; thereafter the bulk of the project's annual cash flows will probably be exposed to income taxes. In many cases, increased expenses are also incurred after eight or ten years for major repairs and appliance replacements.

For the investor seeking longer-term capital gains and income benefits, the planning horizon may be 20 years or more. In this situation the term of the mortgage loan, or the remaining useful life of the property may best serve as the planned holding period.

DISPOSITION OF APARTMENT PROJECTS

The various alternative means of disposing of real estate that were discussed in Chapter 11 would be applicable to the disposition of residential rental properties. If, for example, a substantial capital gain would be realized by the straight sale of a particular property, the owner may find it advantageous to sell on the installment basis, or to exchange the property for another real estate investment property. In the past few years, several apartment owners have disposed of their properties by converting them to condominiums, and thereupon selling the individual apartment units, or selling the project as a whole to a buyer who then markets the individual apartments.

The value of the apartment project at the time of disposition will be a function of the property's income in the year of disposition, and the annual income and cash flow amounts that are projected to be received in future years—beyond the date of disposition. Accordingly, the efficient design and management of a residential rental property will not only improve periodic returns to the investor during the holding period, but also improve the future resale value of the property.

RISK/RETURN ANALYSIS

It is difficult to make general statements regarding the level of rates of return from rental apartment investments. Not only is there a lack of available data for apartment investments, such as exist for common stock investments; but also the published studies of average apartment rental returns usually involve such built-in assumptions by the researcher as regard investors' tax rates, the amount of capital gains, and the amount of leverage. However, a survey of major real estate investors was made in the 1960's regarding the average after-tax returns on equity that were considered necessary by the investors to induce them to invest in various types of properties. The average *required* after-tax return for apartment investments was found to be 12.3 per cent; and 20.7 per cent was the average required rate for slum property.[7] The higher interest rates of the 1970's, and the correspondingly higher rates of return on bond investments, would presumably mean higher required returns on equity investments in apartments than those reflected in the 1966 study cited above.

While it is difficult to generalize about the overall level of returns from apartment investments, as noted above, and because of the many unique aspects of each apartment project, the *general nature* of the return should be understood. It seems clear, for example, that with the large depreciation deductions allowed for residential rental properties, and the high interest deductions attending most apartment investments, a high proportion of the investment return comes in the form of tax-shelter benefits. Such benefits are greatest when the depreciable value of the property is a high proportion of the total property value, and when high degrees of leverage are used.

Another major part of the investment return for many apartment projects is related to the cash proceeds of sale. Because of a variety of reasons, such as a rise in the cost of new construction or a general rise in land prices, many existing apartment projects have increased in market value over the years, rather than depre-

---

[7] R. Bruce Ricks, "Imputed Equity Returns on Real Estate Financed with Life Insurance Company Loans," *The Journal of Finance,* December, 1969, p. 934.

ciated in value—at the same time that outstanding mortgage loans are being paid down and equity interests are building up. Hence, significant gains have been realized on many apartment projects, which are taxed at the favorable capital gains tax rates except to the extent of recaptured depreciation. Even depreciation recapture is softened, however, for those residential rental properties that are held for more than eight years and four months.

In short, while most residential rental properties can be expected to generate some measure of periodic income and cash flows for owners, such properties are generally most attractive to investors in relatively high tax brackets who can take greatest advantage of the tax shelter and capital gains features of this form of investing.

Apartment Investment Risks

Many new apartment projects are started when the market demand is very strong, and boom conditions prevail (or are anticipated to prevail) in a particular city or town. In some cases the expected demand may not materialize because of a decision not to locate a major plant or other employment unit (such as a university) in the area, as was expected; or the existing boom conditions may simply turn out to be short-lived. The point to be made is that worsening local market conditions can make essentially *long-term* investments (such as apartment investments) go bad.

The risk of low occupancy rates (and rental income) that can arise from local economic conditions, can also arise from building obsolescence, or from a decline in the local neighborhood that prompts tenants to move elsewhere. The risk of not being able to recoup outlays for rapidly rising expenses, such as property taxes, labor costs, and heating fuel, is made greater when rent increases are constrained by long-term leases, by competitive conditions, or by government rent controls.

Many of the risks just described are tied to the fact that land that has been improved with a costly apartment project is fixed in its use for a lengthy time period—as contrasted with vacant land that can be turned to any one of a number of uses (within zoning and other constraints). Because the apartment project is essentially a long-lived investment property, a drop in current and prospective cash flow returns will have a negative impact upon the market value for the property itself that can lead to a significant loss when the property is sold or otherwise disposed of.

Minimizing risks.   Many authorities have pointed to the risks in rental apartment investing and caution is required, especially in periods when boom conditions exist that may prove to be only temporary.   Three steps that can be taken in relation to such risks are discussed below.

1. *Thorough market and feasibility studies.* These studies should measure as carefully as possible the expected future conditions relating to the local (and national) economy, present and potential competition, neighborhood patterns, prospective expenses (especially local property tax levels), future possible rent control, and the investor's own future tax situation.

2. *Advanced design.* The newly constructed apartment being considered for acquisition should be of advanced design. It should contain modern kitchen appliances, for example, and other features that are expected to become standard apartment features in future years. Perhaps a swimming pool or tennis court would be found desirable in terms of future needs. Advanced design helps to postpone obsolescence.

3. *Adjust analysis for risk.* When there is a relatively high degree of uncertainty regarding the level of future cash flows, the investor may wish to use one or more of the various risk-adjustment techniques. Five such techniques or approaches were discussed in Chapter 7, including *risk avoidance, sensitivity analysis, summation rate,* and *certainty equivalent* and *probability theory.* As additional tools for analyzing the impact of risks attending proposed apartment projects, the investor can estimate break-even occupancy rates and debt-service-coverage ratios, which were described in Chapter 9.

SUMMARY

Because of rising land and construction costs, there has been a trend toward multiple-family residential structures, and higher-density use of land for dwelling units.   In the past few years many of the multi-unit structures have become owner-occupied units because of the fast growth in the number of condominiums. There has continued to be a strong demand for rental apartments and townhouses, however, and the demand will increase as the costs of ownership rise, and when mortgage money is in short supply.

Assuming that funds are available in the market, it is often possible to obtain a high percentage of outside financing for the acquisition of an apartment project, by some combination of first and second mortgages, and a land sale–leaseback. The resulting high use of leverage together with the use of favorable depreciation tax deductions make this form of investment attractive to investors seeking tax-shelter benefits as well as capital gains.

Rental apartments also have some significant degree of investment risk because favorable future periodic income and capital gains are dependent upon the achievement (over the long run) of occupancy rates high enough to more than cover the relatively high level of periodic operating and non-operating expenses. The investment in an apartment project is an active form of investment because of the existence of a variety of management responsibilities. Such duties arise in part because of the relatively short-term leases involved in most apartment investments.

APPENDIX: APARTMENT BUILDING INCOME–EXPENSE ANALYSIS DATA FORM
(see pages 268–274)

This appendix contains a form used by apartment project owners to voluntarily report their income and expense experience for the benefit of other interested investors. The definitions and guidelines related to the income-expense form are also included.* An examination of the details of this material should provide insights into the nature of an apartment project investment.

The data actually reported by apartment owners are compiled and reported by the Institute of Real Estate Management. A sample of such composite data was presented in Chapter 3 (Table 3–2).

---

* The materials reproduced in this appendix are published by the Institute of Real Estate Management, and are used here with permission.

1975

INCOME/EXPENSE ANALYSIS - APARTMENTS, CONDOMINIUMS AND COOPERATIVES
(EXPERIENCE EXCHANGE)
INSTITUTE OF REAL ESTATE MANAGEMENT
155 East Superior Street • Chicago, Ill. 60611 • Phone: (312) 440-8600

PLEASE READ INSTRUCTIONS BEFORE STARTING

OPERATING RESULTS FOR THE YEAR 1975

FOR IREM USE

Permanent No.
City Code
Region
Chapter No.
M.A. No.
Building Type

INCOME

INSTRUCTION LINE		DOLLARS ONLY NO CENTS
1	APARTMENT RENTALS AT 100% (INCLUDE VALUE OF EMPLOYEE'S APT.)	$ .00
2	GARAGES AND PARKING	
	A) ENCLOSED GARAGES $	
	B) COVERED CARPORT	
	C) OPEN LOT PARKING	
	TOTAL GARAGES AND/OR PARKING	.00
3	STORES AT 100% OCCUPANCY	.00
4	OFFICES AT 100% OCCUPANCY	.00
5	**GROSS POSSIBLE RENTAL INCOME**	.00
6	MISCELLANEOUS (ELECTRICITY, MAID SERVICE, LAUNDRY, ETC.)	.00
7	**GROSS POSSIBLE TOTAL INCOME**	.00
8	LOSS DUE TO VACANCIES AND DELINQUENT RENTS	.00
9	**TOTAL ACTUAL COLLECTIONS**	.00

EXPENSES

INSTRUCTION LINE		DOLLARS ONLY NO CENTS
10	TOTAL PAYROLL EXPENSES (EXCEPT MANAGEMENT & PAINTING)	$ .00
11	SUPPLIES (JANITORIAL, LIGHT BULBS, UNIFORMS, ETC.)	.00
12	PAINTING AND DECORATING (INTERIOR ONLY, INCLUDE WAGES)	.00
13	MAINTENANCE AND REPAIRS (INTERIOR AND EXTERIOR)	.00
14	SERVICES (WINDOW WASH, EXTERMINATING, ETC., NOT MAINTENANCE)	.00
15	MISCELLANEOUS OPERATING EXPENSES (SEE EXPLANATION)	.00
16	ELECTRICITY	.00
17	WATER	.00
18	GAS (EXCLUDING HEATING FUEL)	.00
19	HEATING FUEL	.00
20	MANAGEMENT FEE (INCLUDE WAGES) $	
	LEASING FEE (INCLUDE WAGES) $	.00
	TOTAL BOTH	.00
21	OTHER ADMINISTRATIVE COSTS	.00
22	INSURANCE (EXCLUSIVE OF F.H.A. MORTGAGE AND EMPLOYEE GROUP INSURANCE)	.00
23	REAL ESTATE TAXES	.00
24	OTHER TAXES, FEES AND PERMITS, PERSONAL PROPERTY, FRANCHISE, ETC.	.00
	TOTAL ALL EXPENSES	$ .00
25	**NET OPERATING INCOME** (LINE 9 MINUS LINE 25)	$ .00
26		
27	TURNOVER NUMBER OF NEW TENANTS DURING THE YEAR (AFTER ONE FULL YEAR OF OCCUPANCY)	
28	ACTUAL CONSTRUCTION YEAR OF BUILDING	

BUILDING INFORMATION

Bldg. Name Or Code

City   State   Zip Code

Person To Contact

MAILING ADDRESS:

Managing Company

Address   State   Zip Code

City

Phone: Area

THIS FORM FOR FIRST-YEAR REPORTED BUILDINGS ONLY

RETURN THIS COPY

PLEASE ANSWER ALL QUESTIONS BELOW

A. HAVE YOU CHANGED YOUR TYPE OF HEATING SYSTEM DURING 1975? ☐ YES ☐ NO

B. HAVE YOU INCURRED EXTRAORDINARY EXPENSES FOR PAINTING & DECORATING (INTERIOR ONLY) DURING 1975? ☐ YES ☐ NO

C. HAVE YOU INCURRED EXTRAORDINARY EXPENSES FOR MAINTENANCE & REPAIRS (INTERIOR AND EXTERIOR) DURING 1975? ☐ YES ☐ NO

D. HAVE YOUR PREMIUMS FOR INSURANCE BEEN SUBSTANTIALLY ADJUSTED DURING 1975? ☐ YES ☐ NO

E. HAVE YOUR REAL ESTATE TAXES BEEN SUBSTANTIALLY ADJUSTED DURING 1975? ☐ YES ☐ NO

F. DID THIS BUILDING HAVE 12 FULL MONTHS OF OPERATION DURING 1975? ☐ YES ☐ NO

G. NAME OF LOCAL IREM CHAPTER:

PLEASE SEE OTHER SIDE →

IMPORTANT!!

REQUIRED BUILDING DATA —
FILL IN COMPLETELY

TYPE OF BUILDING
(check ONE only)
- (1) HIGH-RISE ELEVATOR
- (2) LOW-RISE UNDER 25 UNITS
- (3) LOW-RISE 25 OR MORE UNITS
- (4) GARDEN TYPE

TYPE OF OWNERSHIP
(check ONE only)
- (1) INVESTOR
- (2) F.H.A. OWNED
- (3) CO-OPERATIVE
- (4) CONDOMINIUM

LOCATION
(check ONE only)
- (1) CITY
- (2) SUBURBAN

HEATING FUEL
(check ONE only)
- (1) COAL
- (2) OIL
- (3) GAS
- (4) COMBINATION
- (5) ELECTRICITY
- (6) PURCHASED STEAM

INCLUDED IN RENT
(check ALL applicable)
- ELECTRICITY
- HEAT
- GAS - UTILITY
- AIR - COND.
- WINDOW - WASH
- WATER

FLOOR AREAS IN SQ. FT.
(Fill in)

GROSS FLOOR AREA OF ENTIRE BLDG. _____ Sq. Ft.

TOTAL RENTABLE FLOOR AREA OF:
- (A) APARTMENTS _____ Sq. Ft.
- (B) STORES _____ Sq. Ft.
- (C) OFFICES _____ Sq. Ft.
- (D) OTHER _____ Sq. Ft.

TOTAL RENTABLE AREA
(A+B+C+D, ABOVE) _____ Sq. Ft.

NUMBER OF PARKING SPACES
(Fill in)

- (A) ENCLOSED GARAGES
- (B) COVERED CARPORT
- (C) OPEN LOT PARKING

TOTAL SPACES
(A+B+C, ABOVE)

NOTE:
READ PAGE 5,
INSTRUCTIONS,
BEFORE COMPLETING
THIS SECTION

LIST NUMBER OF APTS. BY ROOM COUNT
(DO NOT INCLUDE STORES OR OFFICES)

NO. OF ROOMS	NO. OF UNFURNISHED APTS. (1)	NO. OF FURNISHED APTS. (2)
1		
1½		
2		
2½		
3		
3½		
4		
4½		
5		
5½		
6		
6½		
7		
7½		
8		
8½		
9		
9½		
TOTAL APTS.		
TOTAL NO. OF ROOMS		

INSTITUTE OF REAL ESTATE MANAGEMENT
of the National Association of Realtors®

EXPERIENCE EXCHANGE COMMITTEE   155 E. Superior Street, Chicago, Ill. 60611
Phone (312) 440-8600

HOW TO FILL OUT YOUR INCOME/EXPENSE ANALYSIS-APARTMENTS, CONDOMINIUMS AND COOPERATIVES DATA FORM

DO NOT REPORT ANY BUILDING OR GROUP OF BUILDINGS WITH LESS THAN
A TOTAL OF 12 RESIDENTIAL UNITS

DO NOT REPORT ANY BUILDING IF OFFICE OR STORE OCCUPANCY
REPRESENTS <u>MORE THAN 20 PERCENT</u> OF THE TOTAL RENTABLE AREA.

FRONT SIDE
OPERATING FIGURES

These explanations of the various captions should help you complete your report
with the minimum of difficulty. If you have any doubt where any expense item belongs, check it against these explanatory notes. The number beside each caption below refers to the item number on the reporting form on the left hand margin of the page.

FILL IN THE MAILING ADDRESS AND BUILDING INFORMATION IN THE LOWER LEFT CORNER BY
PLACING ONE LETTER OR NUMBER WITHIN THE VERTICAL SLASH MARKS. IF INFORMATION IS
ALREADY TYPED, UPDATE IF NECESSARY.

INCOME

(Round Out To Nearest Dollar - Do Not Use Cents)

NOTE: FOR ITEMS 1 THROUGH 9 BELOW BE SURE TO USE THE RENTAL RATES WHICH WERE IN EFFECT
THE YEAR FOR WHICH INCOME IS BEING REQUESTED.

1. <u>Apartment Rentals</u>: This figure should contain all apartment rents which could
have been collected, including employee apartments, if 100% of your building had
been occupied.

2. <u>Garages and Parking</u>: If there is a separate charge made for use of garage or parking area, report this in the appropriate category on either Line 2a, 2b or 2c.
THEN PLACE THE TOTAL OF THESE CHARGES IN THE SPACE PROVIDED (LABELED TOTAL GARAGES
AND/OR PARKING). If you include use of garage or parking area in the apartment
rent, reduce the apartment rental total on Line 1 by the portion applicable to
garages and parking and place this portion in the appropriate category on Line 2.

3.-4. <u>Stores and Offices</u>: Show the rental income you could have received from stores on
Line 3 and offices on Line 4 if both of these had been 100% occupied. If not applicable to your building omit these lines.

5. <u>Gross Possible Rental Income</u>: This is the total of Lines 1, 2, 3, and 4.

6. <u>Miscellaneous Other Income</u>: Report here all the income from gas and electricity
sold by the building to tenants, maid service, commissions from telephones, laundry
and vending machines, signs on the building and air-conditioning charges. Do NOT
include interest or dividend income.

7. <u>Gross Possible Total Income</u>: This is the total of Lines 5 and 6.

8. <u>Less Vacancies & Delinquent Rents</u>: Temporarily skip this line. Fill in Line 9
first, then come back to this line.

9. Total Actual Collections: On Line 9 show what you actually collected from all sources indicated on Lines 1 through 6 (including the rental value of apartments given to employees as part of their compensation), then subtract Line 9 from Line 7 (gross possible total income) and enter the difference on Line 8 as vacancies and delinquent rents.

EXPENSES

(Round Out To Nearest Dollar - Do Not Use Cents)

10. Total Payroll: Fill in amount paid janitors, doormen, maids, elevator operators, telephone switchboard operators, maintenance personnel, including market rental value of apartment, and payroll taxes and welfare benefits. Wages of administrative personnel and of painters shall be included in Nos. 12 & 20 below.

11. Supplies: On this line show all janitorial supplies, light bulbs, uniforms for employees and other such supplies which do not belong under painting, decorating, maintenance or repairs.

12. Painting & Decorating (interior): Include on this line the cost of all contracted labor, decorators on building payroll, and all materials and supplies used in the decorating of the interior of the building. Paint, wall-paper, brushes, wall-washing, and similar items belong in this category. Exterior painting should be included in maintenance and repairs on Line 13.

13. Maintenance & Repairs: This category is to account for all items of general maintenance and repairs, both interior and exterior. This includes landscaping costs, exterior painting or cleaning, elevator maintenance contracts, boiler inspection and repair contracts, air-conditioning service contracts; parts, small hand tools, fire extinguishers; plumbing, electrical, plastering, masonry, carpentry, heating, roofing or tuck pointing contractor's services unless such bills properly constitute a capital expenditure. Replacement of floor coverings, draperies, furnishings or light fixtures if not a capital expenditure also belongs in this category.

14. Services: This covers such contracted outside services as window washing, lobby directory, exterminating, rubbish removal, TV antenna service, but NOT services chargeable against the painting, decorating, maintenance or repair categories.

15. Miscellaneous Operating Expenses: This category is designed to include operating costs which do not fit under any other caption. Among such items might be damage to property of others not covered by insurance, directional signs, door lettering, etc. DO NOT use this category if any other caption may be used.

16. Electricity: This is a total figure and includes 100 per cent of your electrical expenses even if you bill some of it back to your tenants (electricity income is provided for above under miscellaneous income). It includes electricity for tenant and public areas, air-conditioning, elevators, laundry and other related purposes. If your building is electrically heated, do NOT report this here but on Line 19 below.

17. Water: Show all water costs including, if applicable in your community, sewerage charges. If other utility charges are billed to the water bill, give an estimate of each charge in its appropriate category.

18. Gas: Show here the cost of gas for utilities, i.e., cooking, air-conditioning, hot water, swimming pools, etc. Do NOT report the gas used for heating the building. This is reported on Line 19 below. If you receive a combined gas bill for heating and utilities, take your gas bill for the lowest summer month and multiply by 12 to determine what this item totals.

19. Heating Fuel: This figure should represent the cost of heating your building whether you use coal, gas, oil, electricity or any other fuel. Do NOT include the costs of ash removal or cost of gas, electricity, etc., used for cooking or hot water.

2

20. Management Fees: This figure should represent the agency fee and the salaries of personnel in the management office paid directly by the building owner. Also include leasing or rental fees paid in addition to management fees and any alteration supervisory charges paid by the owner to a managing agent. If renting, leasing, or renewal is charged, please show as a separate item.

21. Other Administrative Costs: This category includes the cost of all advertising, legal and auditing fees, dues in professional organizations, architectural or professional engineer's fees, telephone and building office expenses and office supplies paid by the owner.

22. Insurance: Include all one year charges for fire, liability, compensation, theft, boiler explosion, rent fidelity bonds and all insurance premiums except those paid to FHA for mortgage insurance or employee benefit plans. If the building's policies are paid on a three-year or five-year basis, pro-rate and include only one year's cost. If your buildings are under a favorable "blanket insurance coverage" at low rates, insert the typical market value rates.

23. Real Estate Taxes: This includes all local or state real estate taxes as well as any non-capitalized assessments. If your office does not pay this item, please ascertain figure from owner or County Treasurer's Office.

24. Other Taxes, Fees, & Permits: Show on this line any personal property taxes applicable to the building, franchise taxes, sign permit fees or any other tax necessary to the operation of the building. DO NOT INCLUDE any local, state, or federal income taxes paid by the ownership on profits derived from the operations.

    DO NOT INCLUDE UNDER ANY EXPENSE CATEGORY SUCH ITEMS AS GROUND RENT, CAPTIAL EXPENDITURES, MORTGAGE INTEREST OR AMORTIZATION, DEPRECIATION OR INCOME TAXES. THESE ARE NOT REFLECTIVE OF OPERATING EXPENSES.

25. Total All Expenses: Make sure the figures on Lines 10 through 24 add up correctly to the figure shown on Line 25.

26. Net Operating Income: Subtract the figure on Line 25 from that shown on Line 9 and show the difference on Line 26.

27. Turnover: The number of new tenants that came into the building during the year. If the building is new, the Turnover would begin after one full year of occupancy.

28. ACTUAL CONSTRUCTION YEAR OF BUILDING: THE DATE OF COMPLETION OF BUILDING WHEN TENANTS FIRST OCCUPIED BUILDING.

BACK SIDE
REQUIRED BUILDING DATA

TYPE OF BUILDING

High-Rise Elevator Buildings: This group is confined to elevator buildings which are four stories or more in height.

Low-Rise (under 25 units): Includes walk-up buildings and elevator buildings - 3 stories or less.

Low-Rise (25 units or more): Includes walk-up buildings and elevator buildings - 3 stories or less.

Garden-Type: We consider this to be a group of low-rise apartment buildings situated on a sizeable landscaped plot, under one management.

Square Foot Data: You are urged to supply the square foot data requested. This information will permit our report to show income and operating costs per sq. ft. as well as on a room count basis. If you are unable to report square foot data, this year, we will still accept your report.

3

Gross Floor Area of Entire Building: The Gross Square Feet of a building is the
sum of the areas at each floor level, including cellars, basements, mezzanines,
penthouses, corridors, lobbies, stores, offices, garages within the building, included within the principle outside faces of exterior walls, not including architectural setbacks or projections. Included are all stories or areas which have
floor surfaces with clear standing head room (6 feet 6 inches minimum) regardless
of their use. Where a ground level area, or part thereof within the principle
outside faces of the exterior walls is left unenclosed, the gross area of the unenclosed portion is to be considered as a part of the overall square footage of
the building. All unroofed areas and unenclosed roofed-over spaces, except as
defined above, are to be excluded from the area calculation.*

Rentable Floor Area: Rentable area shall be computed by measuring inside finish
of permanent outer building walls or from the glass line where at least 50% of the
outer building wall is glass. Rentable area shall also include all area within
outside walls less stairs, elevator shafts, flues, pipe shafts, vertical ducts,
air conditioning rooms, fan rooms, janitor closets, electrical closets, balconies--
and such other rooms not actually available to the tenant for his furnishings and
personnel--and their enclosing walls. No deductions shall be made for columns and
projections unnecessary to the building. **

EXAMPLE OF RENTABLE FLOOR AREA

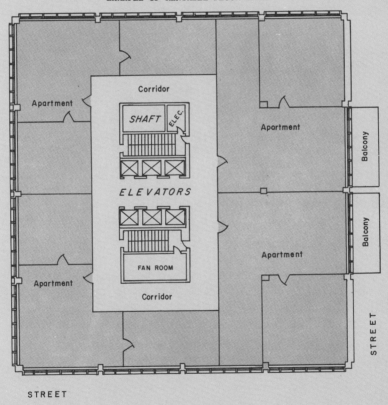

---

* Based upon a study made by The Real Estate Board of New York.

** Based upon the "American Standard" for measuring office areas as developed by
the Building Owners and Managers Association International.

4

NUMBER OF ROOMS

For uniform room count reporting, these principles are suggested: Rooms are counted the same as is usual in the industry (a living room - dining room - bedroom and kitchen are 4 rooms) -- with the following refinements:

Dining Room:
>   If dining room is combined with living room, count as one room, if less than 260 sq. feet - but 1½ rooms if more than 260 sq. feet.
>
>   Count breakfast room as a room, if it is more than 100 sq. feet, regardless of whether there is a separate dining room.

Kitchen:
>   If a regular, separate walk-in kitchen, count as a full room.
>
>   If a combined dining-kitchen area exists, count as follows:
>   Total area is 105 sq. feet or less. . .1 room
>   Total area is 105 to 140 sq. feet . . .1½ rooms
>   Total area is over 140 sq. feet . . . .2 rooms
>
>   If Pullman - or actually an integral part of living room, or so situated as to make most of the equipment visible in the living room, count as half room.

Other:
>   Bathrooms, porches, halls, clos   are not counted.

NUMBER OF APARTMENTS BY ROOM COUNT

Furnished Apartments: If 80 per cent or more of the apartments in the building which you are reporting are furnished, report the entire building as furnished.

Unfurnished Apartments: If 80 per cent or more of the apartments in the building which you are reporting are unfurnished, report the entire building as unfurnished.

If the building you are reporting is not within the ratios specified above for furnished or unfurnished do NOT report such building. It will improperly affect the interpretation of statistical data. Choose another building to report instead.

Age of the Building: Please check the appropriate year of construction for the building for first year reported buildings only.

If you have any questions as to the method of filling out the form, please do not hesitate to write or call the Experience Exchange Committee, Institute of Real Estate Management, 155 East Superior St., Chicago, Illinois 60611. Phone (312) 440-8600.

Start Now. It will take much less time than you think. Send in reports on all your buildings. Additional copies of the data form are available on request, or you can reproduce the data form on a copying machine in any quantity necessary to report all your buildings. Encourage others in your city to send in their Apartment Building statistics for a more meaningful sample.

EXPERIENCE EXCHANGE COMMITTEE

14

Shopping Center Investments

Shopping centers are one form of *commercial property*. While such other forms as the single retail store, and the property leased to such providers of services as tax-preparers or laundries, are prevalent, the current chapter considers only the shopping center, because of its importance and because most of the same investment principles and practices apply to the individual stores and service outlets.

Whereas apartments (as well as hotels and motels) call for direct, continuous, and active management and supervisory activities, and have relatively high fixed costs and high operating expense ratios, and usually have a relatively high rate of tenant turnover—the shopping center is a form of investment generally characterized by less active management responsibilities, relatively low operating expenses, and relatively low turnover of tenants. A distinction may also be made regarding the credit standing of tenants. A large percentage of rental income for most shopping centers comes from national retail chain stores having an AAA credit rating; example, that is, they have a net worth amounting to at least one million dollars.

The modern shopping center has become the dominant form of market place in this country. The major distinction between this form and the urban shopping areas and the once prevalent open market fairs is that the modern shopping center principally serves customers traveling to the shopping area by automobile. The shopping center form is generally characterized, therefore, by having a large paved parking area. The shopping center can further be characterized as a planned group or mix of retail and service units, generally with the entire center under one ownership and management.

The sharp rise in the use of automobiles for shopping and other purposes since World War II, and the burgeoning move to the suburbs, were the important factors contributing to the fast-rising number of shopping centers. The new centers have been located in the suburban areas were the automobile is the mode of transportation; where substantial purchasing power is located; and where land is usually less expensive than in the city—an important factor because of the need to provide large, free parking areas. In the megalopolis of the East Coast, where urban areas blend into suburban communities, many customers do travel by foot from nearby apartments, but the modern shopping center is still essentially the market place of the suburbs.

The Country Club Plaza in Kansas City that opened in 1920 was the first shopping center not based on public transportation, and having provision for automobile parking.[1] By 1955, there were some 1,000 shopping centers in the United States; and by 1973, there were an estimated 14,000 shopping centers in the U.S. and Canada, with about 800 to 1,000 being added yearly. In 1973, some 32 of Sears Roebuck's 33 new stores were opened in shopping centers, as were 38 of 40 stores opened by J. C. Penney.[2]

TYPES OF SHOPPING CENTERS

Three basic types of shopping centers have emerged; the *neighborhood center,* the *community center,* and the *regional center.* Generally the three types can be distinguished by their size.

[1] Homer Hoyt, *People, Profits, Places: A Blueprint for Retailing* (Washington, D.C.: National Retail Merchants Association, 1969), p. 28.
[2] *Wall Street Journal,* September 25, 1973.

Another distinguishing characteristic of the three types is the major, or key tenant that each type usually has:

Type of Center	*Key Tenant*
Neighborhood	Supermarket
Community	Junior-department store, or Variety store
Regional	Full-line department store

Some additional descriptive generalizations about the three shopping center types are presented in this section. In the material that follows in this chapter frequent reference will be made to the *gross leasable area* (GLA). This is the standard measurement used for the number of square feet (SF) of shopping-center floor space for which tenants pay rent. It includes (in addition to first floor space), basements, mezzanines, and upper floors. Not only does the number of GLA square feet become a measure for overall center size, but most rental payments are based on the number of square feet used by individual tenants; and square feet of GLA is used as the basis for financial and statistical analysis, as will be discussed later in this chapter.[3]

Neighborhood Center

The neighborhood center is the smallest type of shopping center and its function is to serve the daily living requirements of people in the immediate neighborhood. This type of center generally draws from an area having about 1,000 families. The neighborhood center provides for the sale of *convenience goods,* such as food and drugs; and *personal services,* such as laundry and dry cleaning, and beauty and barber shop services. The center is built around the supermarket, the largest space user; and the center usually has between 10 and 15 stores. The neighborhood shopping centers generally have a site size of between 4 and 10 acres, and the GLA of most such centers ranges from about 35,000 to about 75,000 SF. The typical neighborhood center will have

[3] In a financial analysis that compares shopping centers having basements with those having no basement, one must adjust for the fact that those with basements may have unrealistic GLA figures. It may be most appropriate to use first-floor areas only for such comparisons.

a GLA of about 50,000 SF (1.1 acres), of which about one-third (about 16,500 SF) will be used by the supermarket.

While there are many possible combinations of tenants in a neighborhood center, depending upon the immediate area's needs and upon the competitive situation, one real estate organization has cited the usual dozen tenants of a neighborhood center as follows: [4]

Supermarket	Family shoe store
Bakery	Drug store
Restaurant	Beauty shop
Variety store	Barber shop
Ladies' wear	Dry cleaners
Children's wear	Coin laundry

Community Center

In this medium-sized shopping center the major tenant is a *junior department store,* such as J. C. Penny, or a *variety store,* such as F. W. Woolworth or S. S. Kresge. The community center, in addition to convenience goods and personal services, provides some limited amounts of soft lines (wearing apparel) and hard goods (hardware and appliances).

The community center generally has a site size of between 10 and 25 acres, and about 15 to 40 stores, and draws trade from about 5,000 families. The GLA of most such centers ranges from about 120,000 to 200,000 SF, with the typical community center having about 150,000 SF, of which the major tenant will occupy about 30,000 SF.

The community centers typically have the kind of stores usually found in the neighborhood centers, such as the ubiquitous supermarket, and they often have as well the junior department store, and others such as medical or dental offices, jewelry stores, shoe repair shops, bakeries, and several apparel shops.

Regional Center

The largest shopping center type is the regional center, which provides one-stop shopping in depth, with full lines of soft

[4] *Cases in Shopping Center Valuation* (Chicago: American Institute of Real Estate Appraisers, 1964), p. 27.

wear and hard goods. The principal tenant is a full-line department store, such as Macy's or Marshall Field, with the larger
centers having more than one such store.

The size of the regional center site is at least 25 acres, and
this type of center has from 40 to 100 stores or more, and requires
at least 100,000 people from which to draw business. Most regional centers range in GLA from about 350,000 to 800,000 SF,
with the typical regional center having a GLA of about 400,000
SF, and its major tenant alone having over 100,000 SF. Several
regional centers in the United States have over one million square
feet.

The tenantry of the regional centers includes, in addition
to full-line department stores, large numbers (in relation to the
two other types of centers) of specialty stores, such as men's wear
stores, ladies' wear stores, ladies' shoe stores, card and gift shops,
sewing centers, candy and nut shops, and medical and financial
offices. A high proportion of the regional centers have one or
more bank offices among the tenantry. Table 14–1 summarizes
some of the distinctive features of the three types of shopping
centers just described.

Shopping Center Design

The site for a shopping center includes three principal components: the structures, the delivery areas (also used for trash
removal), and the shoppers' parking area. The neighborhood
center generally contains a row of stores some 300 to 400 feet
long, with delivery areas in the rear and customer parking in
front. For community centers and small regional centers, the
long row is used, or a U or L form with deliveries to the rear. All
of the types of centers just mentioned often have service stations,
banks, and sometimes restaurants as separate, free-standing structures in the center.

Perhaps the most important innovation in shopping center
design is the *enclosed mall,* which has been incorporated in many
regional shopping centers in recent years. Some early shopping
centers had open malls, that is, a pedestrian strip about 50 feet
wide with stores on both sides, facing each other. As early as
1956, Southdale in the Minneapolis area enclosed its mall to

provide weather-controlled comfort for shoppers; that has been
followed by many other conversions from open to enclosed malls,
and many new regional centers have incorporated the heated and
air-conditioned malls.[5]

On-site parking.   Because free, on-site customer parking is a major
attraction of the modern shopping center, adequate parking areas
become a key element in shopping center design.   The *parking
index* has become the standard yardstick of measuring parking
adequacy.   The parking index is the number of parking spaces
available per 1,000 square feet of gross leasable area.   An Urban
Land Institute study found that the median parking index was
6.8 for 109 sample regional centers, 6.3 for 120 community centers, and 6.4 for 124 neighborhood centers.[6]

[5] Homer Hoyt, *op. cit.*, p. 31.
[6] *The Dollars & Cents of Shopping Centers: 1972* (Washington, D.C.: Urban
Land Institute, 1972), p. 213.

TABLE 14–1.   General Characteristics of
Three Types of Shopping Centers

Type of Center	Site Size	Gross Leaseable Area
Neighborhood	4–10 acres	35,000–75,000 SF; Typical: 50,000 SF
Community	10–25 acres	120,000–200,000 SF; Typical: 150,000 SF
Regional	25$^+$ acres	350,000–800,000$^+$ SF (some 1,000,000$^+$ SF); Typical: 400,000 SF

FINANCING ACQUISITION

There are various alternative sources and methods of financing the acquisition of existing shopping centers that are generating favorable returns and are reasonably priced. The principal sources include life insurance companies, REIT's, and the seller. It is not uncommon to find shopping centers acquired for relatively small amounts of equity capital, and at times the purchaser is able to *mortgage out,* that is, finance the project without any of his own cash required.

The traditional real estate financing techniques, as discussed in general terms in previous chapters, are used in shopping-center financing, including the purchaser's assumption of the seller's first-mortgage financing; or the purchaser's new financing through a mortgage loan of his own; with the first mortgage financing often supplemented by a junior mortgage given to the seller or to a financial institution.

In addition to the traditional financing arragements, a sale–leaseback deal may be appropriate, with the purchaser of the shopping center arranging to sell the land to a financial institution and then lease it back; if additional financing is required,

Number of Stores	Major Tenant	Nature of Sales
10–15	Supermarket Typical: 16,500 SF	Convenience goods and personal services
15–40	Junior department store, or variety store Typical: 30,000 SF	Same as neighborhood center, plus limited amounts of soft lines and hard goods
40–100+	Full-line (major) department store Typical: 100,000 SF	One-stop shopping in depth

it may be desirable to sell and lease back the major tenant's building itself and perhaps the land thereunder as well. It is an increasingly popular arrangement, in newly constructed regional shopping center projects, for the department store land or building, or both, to be owned by the department store company even through the store is an integral part of the overall center.[7] Also, it is not uncommon for bank buildings and service station buildings located on land leased from the shopping center owner to be owned by the users of the buildings. Accordingly, in financing the acquisition of an existing center where such units are presently owned by the shopping center seller, it may be desirable as part of the financing arrangements to sell the buildings (with or without the land) to the present department store tenant and to the bank and service station tenants.

As discussed in the previous chapter, to obtain very high levels of financing by mortgages or sale–leaseback arangements with financial institutions, it may be necessary to give up equity participations which for shopping centers may well be tied to the future sales levels of the financed center, or of individually financed units.

OPERATING INCOME AND EXPENSES

As a first step in analyzing a shopping center property being considered for acquisition, input data relating to expected future income and expenses are required. In analyzing an existing property on which income and expense data are available for the past three to five years or more, the task becomes one of extrapolating past trends into the future, with adjustments for any expected major changes in the trading-area purchasing levels or in competitive conditions.

The income to the shopping center owner is provided by a relatively small number of tenants, that is, few in relation to an equal investment in, say, a rental apartment project. It will be

---

[7] Among some 109 regional centers studied in 1972, there were 34 centers in which one or more of the department store buildings in the center were not owned by the center. *The Dollars & Cents of Shopping Centers: 1972, op. cit.*, p. 201.

recalled that the neighborhood center, for example, generally has some 10 to 15 stores. The shopping center tenants are under leases having terms ranging up to 10 years or more. While an endless variety of lease arrangements are used, the income from the tenants is usually composed of the following elements: *minimum guaranteed yearly rent, overage rent, common-area charges,* and *escalation-clause payments.* The shopping center owner often receives some additional relatively minor amounts from non-tenant sources, such as from pay telephones, and vending machines. The basic forms of income received from tenants are now briefly described.

Rental income. Shopping center rental payments are normally based on some percentage of sales, with the tenant usually obligated to make some annual minimum rent payment.[8] Where the tenant's sales are high enough to more than cover the minimum rent, then *overage rent* will be paid. Assume, for example, a national chain supermarket using 20,000 SF of leased area in a neighborhood shopping center, pays 1.5 per cent of sales for rent, with a guaranteed annual minimum rent of $30,000. In this case, every dollar of annual sales above $2,000,000 would provide $1\frac{1}{2}¢$ in overage rent (also called *percentage rent*). The fixed and variable components of the total rent amounts relating to various sales levels are illustrated in Figure 14–1. With sales of $3 million, total rent would amount to $45,000.

The dollar amount of the annual rent from each shopping center tenant is tied, of course, to the number of square feet of GLA used by each tenant. In the just-cited example, the supermarket's minimum rent of $30,000 is $1.50 per SF for the 20,000 SF of gross leasable area. If the store's annual sales total $3 million, then the $45,000 rental payments for the year would be equivalent to $2.25 per square foot [$45,000 ÷ 20,000].

The wide range of rental levels that were paid by a sample of various types of shopping-center tenants is reflected in Table 14–2.

The fact that some businesses generate more sales per square

[8] Another common arrangement is for *straight-percentage rent;* that is, rentals are based on a percentage of sales without a minimum guaranteed rental amount.

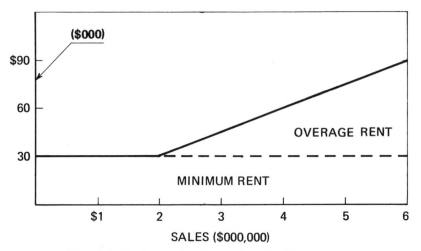

Fig. 14–1. Basic rental pattern, Shopping Center example.

foot than others accounts in large measure for the very wide range in rental rates as percentages of sales shown in Table 14–2. There are, however, other variables involved in the variations in the rents paid by different categories of tenants. As a general rule, major tenants in shopping centers pay lower rents than other tenants in the same centers. For example, in a neighborhood shopping center the supermarket and variety store will usually enjoy significantly lower per-square-foot rental rates than the smaller tenants in the same center—as reflected in the 1972 rent figures in Table 14–2. Some of the reasons for the favored status of the major tenant include:

1. The supermarket and variety store tenants are usually units of national chain stores, so their credit rating is superior to local "independent" merchants.
2. The large space occupied by the supermarket and variety store (together they often account for over one-half of the center's total GLA) mean lower construction cost per SF.
3. The crucial importance of the supermarket and variety store in terms of drawing business to the entire shopping center, and their own important contributions to total center rentals, place them in a relatively strong bargaining position.[9]

[9] This is especially true when the property is heavily leveraged and large debt-service payments must be met by the shopping-center owner. See: John Robert Foster, "Real Estate Financing and the Opportunity for Shopping Center Occupancy," *Land Economics,* August, 1968, pp. 319–29.

TABLE 14–2.   Median Total Rent Figures for Selected Types of Neighborhood Shopping Center Tenants

Tenant Classification	Total Rent as a Percent of Sales	Total Rent per SF	Other Charges per SF	Total Charges per SF
Supermarkets	1.35%	$1.60	$0.14	$1.74
Variety stores	4.94	1.37	0.13	1.50
Hardware	5.06	2.18	0.14	2.32
Ladies' wear	5.99	2.82	0.08	2.90
Bakeries	6.20	2.85	0.12	2.97
Cards & gifts	7.76	3.00	0.26	3.26
Flowers	8.01	3.43	0.09	3.52
Cleaners & dyers	9.15	2.86	0.19	3.05
Shoe repair	9.80	3.11	0.31	3.42
Coin laundries	19.14	2.78	0.14	2.92

Source: *The Dollars & Cents of Shopping Centers: 1972* (Washington, D. C.: Urban Land Institute, 1972), pp. 112–33. Data used with permission.

Other income from tenants. In addition to annual rent payments, shopping center tenants are usually required under their lease terms to contribute to so-called *common-area charges,* which are for expenses incurred by the owner in operating and maintaining the common areas of the center. The other principal source of income from the tenants relates to so-called *escalation clauses* that are commonly found in shopping center leases, whereby the tenants are required to make payments to the center owner that are tied to any escalation in the level of real estate taxes (and often property insurance premiums) during the life of the leases. As will be observed in Table 14–2, these other charges did not, in 1972, amount to much in relation to basic rent levels.

Forecasting income levels. Assuming that the acquisition of an existing shopping center is being considered, one starts with such given factors as: the *mix of tenants* operating the center's various shops and services; the *trading area* from which the center draws most of its customers; the *lease arrangements;* any as yet unused land representing *area for expansion;* and the various possible *competitive pressures.* Hence, to forecast future rental and other income for the existing center, as opposed to the proposed development of a new shopping center, one starts with certain constraints along with an accumulation of data on present and past income levels.

There may be various possibilities for improving the income level of a center, without changes occurring in the trading area, such as:

1. As leases expire, improve the tenant mix to increase the number of traditionally higher rental tenants—if this will not upset the complementary nature of the center's stores. It should be observed that the appropriate nature of individual stores, and the appropriate combination of stores, will depend on many variables, including the buying habits and desires of shoppers in the trading area, and of course any competitive shopping outlets.

2. The purchaser can help encourage the establishment of a *merchants association* for the center (or improve one if it already exists).[10] Such an association made up of the center's tenants can boost sales by appropriate joint promotional efforts and by agreements on the regulation of store hours, and other matters that have an impact on the overall image of the center.

3. The purchaser can seek to expand the number of stores in the center if the land and the market is available for more stores.

Assuming that such possible improvements as the above have been adjusted for—that is, that sales are maximized for the given buying needs of the trading area and the percentage thereof that is directed to the subject center, the forecast of future sales becomes based on an estimate of the potential future buying power of the trade area and whatever potential changes in the competitive situation. Because of the nature of shopping-center leases as described above, the amount of sales will determine the total rental income for a center having a given tenant mix.

Analyzing present and past sales. As a first step in projecting future shopping center sales (and then income), an analysis

---

[10] The 1972 study of the Urban Land Institute found that all of the 105 sample regional shopping centers had merchants associations; also 91 of 113 community centers had them, but only 58 of the 122 sample neighborhood centers. *The Dollars & Cents of Shopping Centers: 1972, op. cit.,* p. 211.

should be undertaken of the present and past sales of the center, if the prospective seller has not prepared and made available to prospective purchasers an adequate analysis. Most analyses would include the steps listed and discussed briefly below.

1. *Define the trading area.* Determine the geographical borders of the area in which the bulk of the shopping center's customers reside. The boundaries will be marked on street maps of the area.

2. *Determine the number of households within the trading area.* Census data and local planning commission data should be used, and where practical an actual house count should be used to determine the number of families residing in the trading area. The neighborhood shopping center trading area, for example, will usually be found to have at least from 1,000 to 2,000 families. From the public data mentioned above, plus annual data on the number of residential building permits issued, the number of trading-area households in each of the last three to five years can be determined.

3. *Compute the shopping center's dollar sales per family in the trading area for present and recent years.* This is accomplished by dividing the total center sales by the number of households found in the area.

Suppose, for example, that an analysis of a four-year-old shopping center being considered for purchase determines the following population and sales patterns from 1971 through 1974:

	Sales	Number of Households	Sales per Household
1971	$1,800,000	1,100	$1,636
1972	2,000,000	1,200	1,667
1973	2,300,000	1,350	1,704
1974	2,600,000	1,500	1,733
	Average annual growth rate		
	≈ 13%	≈ 10%	≈ 2%

The average annual growth rates shown in the above example can be found with the use of *Column 1* in the Appendix of this book. For example, to find the average annual growth rate in sales, one can proceed as follows:

$$\frac{1974 \ sales}{1971 \ sales} = \frac{\$2,600,000}{\$1,800,000} = 1.44$$

Using the *Compound Sum of $1 Columns,* for three years, one finds that the interest factor of 1.44 falls about midway between 12 and

14 per cent, so a sales increase from $1.8 million to $2.6 million represents an annual average compound growth rate of about 13 per cent.

    4. *Analyze the existing and recent competition for business within the trading area.* This analysis plus an analysis of existing traffic patterns in the area will supplement the data found on the trend of sales per household computed for the subject shopping center.

    5. *Estimate total disposable income of families in the trading area.* This can be done on the basis of home values in the trading area.

Projecting future sales. The first step in predicting future sales would be to estimate the number of households that will be in the trading area in future years and to estimate the amount of sales that the subject shopping center will obtain per household. A study of the trading area should indicate whether past growth will continue in the future at about the same rate or not. If there are several new large subdivisions or new apartment projects being planned or already under construction, the situation would, of course, be quite different from that of the area that has been completely developed.

    Whether or not one would expect a continuation of the sales-per-household patterns of recent years would be based on: (1) estimates of future changes in the disposable income levels for the trading area population—for example: Are significantly higher-priced homes being planned for the area?; (2) an analysis of future competition from planned new stores that would draw from the same trading area; and, of course, (3) an estimate of increased sales, if any, that could be expected by modifications in such things as the shopping center's tenant mix, and promotion efforts.

    Based on such an analysis, a projection for future sales can be made for each year of the planning horizon for the proposed center investment; and by applying the expected rental rates, the year-by-year rental income can be determined for use in the investment rate-of-return analysis.

    While the above paragraphs have described a market analysis approach that can be appropriately used in many situations, for many small neighborhood shopping centers the projections of sales and income can be done without such an elaborate analysis. Many a smaller shopping center (for example in suburban northern New Jersey) is located in a compact, fully developed community in which there are no open tracts of land available for the development of a new rival neighborhood shopping center. In such cases, past sales and income levels can often be expected to continue at about the same level, with adjustments for general inflationary growth in sales.

Operating expenses. The operating expenses of shopping centers are relatively low in relation to income, as compared with apartments and other management properties. Total operating expenses generally range from about 30 to 40 per cent of total receipts (the expense ratio) for shopping centers, against about 40 to 60 per cent for apartments. The major areas of expense reductions for shopping centers are utilities expenses which are paid by tenants rather than by the owner, and relatively low maintenance and management expenses.

The basic operating expense categories for shopping centers are indicated in Table 14–3, which shows the median income and expense figures for 124 neighborhood shopping centers surveyed in 1972 by the Urban Land Institute.

It will be observed that as for apartments, the largest single expense category for shopping centers is the real estate taxes. As noted previously, however, many shopping center leases have escalation clauses related to property taxes and insurance. The advertising and promotion expense for the shopping center owner is often at a relatively low level because of the advertising and promotion activities of individual tenants and of the merchants associations that exist in many centers. The principal distinction between the three types of centers, in terms of operating expenses, is that the maintenance expenses per square foot are, on the average, substantially higher for regional centers than for the other two types, because the regionals usually have more extensive common areas to maintain, such as the enclosed-mall areas; however, on the average, higher rent charges in regional centers offset the higher level of expenses of those centers.

When undertaking a comparative analysis of the operating expense levels of a shopping center being considered for acquisition with average expenses for other centers, it is not only desirable to compare the subject center with others of the same *type*, but also with others of the same general *age*. The older centers tend to have higher operating expenses as a percentage of operat-

TABLE 14-3. Median Operating Results, 124 Neighborhood Shopping Centers[a]

	Median $/SF of GLA	Percentage of Total Operating Receipts
Operating Receipts:		
Rent	$2.03	95.5%
Common area charges	0.08	3.6
Other charges	0.06	2.5
Total Operating Receipts	$2.16	100.0%
Operating Expenses:		
Building maintenance	$0.05	2.3%
Parking lot, mall, other public areas	0.10	4.2
Central utility systems	0.04	1.7
Advertising and promotion	0.03	1.0
Real estate taxes	0.28	13.3
Insurance	0.04	2.0
General and administrative	0.12	5.4
Total Operating Expenses	$0.69	30.0%
Operating Balance	$1.50	70.0%

[a]Because the data are medians, the details do not add to the totals; the percentage calculations are therefore only rough measures.
Source: *Dollars & Cents of Shopping Centers: 1972, op. cit.,* p. 98. Data used with permission.

ing receipts. The subject center should also be compared with other centers in the same general *geographical area,* for there can be sharp differences in expense levels in different parts of the country.

RISK/RETURN ANALYSIS

The non-operating expenses, including depreciation, interest, and taxes, tend to run in about the same patterns as for apartments;

on the average, loan-to-value ratios and depreciation patterns are similar, except that the guideline useful life for shopping centers is 50 years, against 40 years for apartments. Also, less liberal depreciation methods are allowed for shopping centers than for apartments.

There are very limited data available on investment returns for shopping centers; some studies have indicated, however, that in the 1960's, the income yields (net operating income divided by purchase price) from both types of investments tended to range from about 8 to about 10 per cent; and it is probable that the cash flow returns from both apartment and shopping center investments have been, on the average, in the same general range.

As discussed in the last section, however, operating expenses for shopping centers are generally lower than for apartments. Accordingly, for these two types of investments to have similar income yields, the *gross income multiplier* (GIM) would have to be higher, on average, for the shopping centers—which, in fact, is the case. A hypothetical example will illustrate these relationships.

	Apartment	Shopping center
Gross income	$100,000	$100,000
Less: Operating expenses	45,000	30,000
Net operating income	$ 55,000	$ 70,000
Purchase price	$650,000	$825,000
Income yield	8.5%	8.5%
Gross income multiplier	6.5×	8.25×

The nature of the returns to the equity investor are, in general, similar to the returns described in the last chapter for apartment investments. That is, while some measure of before-tax cash flow is generated by shopping center investments (obviously some centers will generate more than others), the high interest and depreciation charges, however, are typically the most important features of this kind of investment, as with apartments, meaning that much of the income is sheltered from taxes and tax losses are often generated. In short, the shopping center's periodic after-tax returns are relatively most attractive to investors with higher marginal tax rates. It will be recalled, however, that the

tax shelter features are somewhat better for apartment investments than for other properties because of the favored tax treatment accorded residential properties in the way of allowable depreciation methods.

The capital gains potential is another important aspect of
shopping center investments. The potential is greatest, of course,
for centers that are producing a substantially higher cash flow at
the time of sale than they were when originally purchased. Some
investors have also received significant gains in the form of rising
values of land (owned by the investor) located adjacent to the
shopping center. In fact, many large-scale investors attempt to
acquire a significant amount of land adjoining their shopping center property itself, and to hold it either for future sale as is, or
for later development with apartments and office buildings, which
would in turn add to the market value of the shopping center
itself.

Special Risks

As with other income properties the principal risk in shopping center investments is that of vacancies, which, for the presently successful shopping center, could be caused by a future drop
in the trading-area buying power. The substantial drop in buying
power can be created by lowered employment during major layoffs
or strikes, or by the closing of large employment centers. Because
continued sales will depend on continued employment in the
area (unless the center is selling mainly to retired people or to
vacationers), the risks are greatest for the shopping center located
in an area dependent for its prosperity on a few major employers.

Another, less severe, risk would be a gradual drop off in sales,
with the consequent reduction in overage rent. This could be
caused by a shift in the buying habits of those in the trading area,
which in turn is often caused by the development of a new competing shopping center, or a switch by a significant number of
shoppers from automobile to public transportation, or a lowered
willingness to drive long distances to shopping centers located
farther out from residential areas.

In the absence of drastic drops in the number of customers,
which is unlikely for most shopping centers in established com-

munities, there are many relatively attractive risk protection features of shopping center investments, such as:

1. Over half the rental income in most shopping centers comes from large firms having top credit ratings (either national or local chain stores).

2. In most shopping centers, the owner is protected by relatively long-term leases, in comparison with residential properties, with the minimum guaranteed rents usually adequate to at least cover the annual debt-service requirements.

3. The relatively low level of periodic operating expenses reduces the periodic cash flow requirements.

4. The investor–owner has inflation protection in two ways: rental income will increase as the price of merchandise increases, because of the overage rent provisions; and where escalation clauses exist, the shopping center tenants are required to pay for increases in property taxes and property insurance premiums.

5. Older, established shopping centers are generally not as likely to suffer physical obsolescence as some other real estate investment properties, and these centers are afforded further protection against new competition because new centers often will have higher construction and debt-service costs than existing centers. Further protection against new shopping center development is provided if no other large tracts are available for commercial development in the trading area.

Because of these various factors, the returns from shopping center investments are generally relatively stable and predictable. While many shopping centers can be acquired with relatively small amounts of cash in relation to the purchase price, these investment projects nonetheless represent major undertakings, and hence are not really as suited to the new small investor as residential properties, which can be invested in on a very small scale. However, for those in a position to undertake shopping center investments, there are some attractive risk/return features, as described in this chapter.

SUMMARY

Shopping centers rose in importance as a form of commercial property with the growing use of the automobile and the accompanying move of shoppers to the suburbs. The three size categories of shopping centers are the neighborhood, the community, and the regional centers.

The most common rental arrangement found for shopping centers has the tenant paying a specified annual minimum rent, plus a preset percentage of gross sales revenue referred to as *overage rent*. Because the total rent payments will therefore increase with rising sales levels, the investor is given some protection against inflation. Further protection is often provided in the form of escalation clauses, by which increases in specified expenses, such as property taxes, are passed on to the shopping center tenants.

The future periodic income and cash flow returns to the investor, and also the future value of a shopping center property, will depend on the buying power as well as the buying habits of families in the area served by the particular center. The risks of shopping center investing are tied to the same factors. Accordingly, before making a commitment to acquire a shopping center, the investor should make careful projections regarding future employment and disposable income in the trading area, as well as projections of future competition and buying habits in the area.

15

Motel

Investments

Motels arose, as did the shopping centers, with the widespread use of the automobile; and both types of enterprises have stressed free parking. Most of the early motels, which first appeared in the 1930's, were relatively small, with less than 30 units; they were usually located outside urban areas, and they were characterized by an absence of the extensive services and amenities offered by the urban hotels; for example, bell hop service, laundry service, room service, and evening entertainment.

Motels have, of course, tended over the years to become larger in size, and to offer more of the traditional hotel services, and have even entered urban areas, often under the label of *motor hotel* or *motor inn*. Because of these trends and the fact that many hotels have come to offer free parking, it has become increasingly difficult to clearly distinguish motels from hotels. While the number of *motels* has steadily increased since the 1930's, the number of *hotels* has actually declined, as shown in Table 15–1.

Because of motel competition, not only have the hotels as a group declined in number, but on the average hotels have suffered from lower occupancy rates than motels. The competition from motels has been strongest in the medium-sized cities, but the motels have also increasingly threatened the business of big-city hotels, most of which are over 40 years old and many of which are now situated in unattractive locations.

TABLE 15-1. Number of Hotels and Motels, 1939–1966

Year	Hotels	Motels[a]
1939	28,000	14,000
1948	30,000	26,000
1958	29,000	41,000
1963	23,000	42,000
1966[b]	22,000	45,000

[a] Includes motor courts.
[b] Estimated.
Source: Economic Factors and Case Studies in Hotel and Motel Valuation
(2nd ed.; Chicago: American Institute of Real Estate Appraisers, 1968), p. 2.

In this chapter we shall focus on investments in *motels* rather than on the traditional hotels; although as noted previously, several of the newer motels are very similar to the traditional urban hotels, both in size and in the extent of services provided to guests.

TYPES OF MOTELS

Most traveling is done for business (or government) purposes, or for personal reasons, including travel for pleasure during vacations and holidays, or because of critical events in private individual or family affairs.[1] These travel motives suggest the following categorization of motels, although there clearly will be overlaps.

Commercial motel. These cater to commercial travelers, including salesmen, businessmen, professional people, and others traveling for business appointments or for group meetings of various kinds. Such motels are usually located in or near the major centers of finance, business, and government, and tend to be large, with extensive services and facilities, including, of course, convention facilities.

Roadside motel. Motels of this type cater to highway trav-

[1] *Economic Factors and Case Studies in Hotel and Motel Valuation* (2nd ed.; Chicago: American Institute of Real Estate Appraisers, 1968), p. 7.

elers of various kinds such as tourists and salesmen. A large percentage of these motels are small, many having 20 units or less.

Resort motel. While motels of this type attract guests of various kinds, including a growing number of businessmen and others attending conventions in resort areas, they naturally cater principally to those on vacations or holidays. The larger resort motels usually provide extensive recreation facilities, as well as food, beverage, and entertainment facilities. Business is highly seasonal for most of these motels.

Another categorization of individual motels is by the extent of their relationship with other motels:

Chain motel. One investor owns several individual motels.

Franchised motel. The owner of the individual motel operates the business under a license from a franchisor, and for a licensing fee receives the use of the franchise name and services; the franchisee observing operating standards set by the franchisor.

Referral group motel. Some independent motels form together in loose associations with other motels for the benefits of common referral, of common directory listing, and of common identity.

Independent motel. Many motels continue to be owned and operated independently, with no group affiliation.

Motel Design

For many motels the most efficient land use calls for two-story construction, with units placed back to back as the traditional design, but with a recent trend toward double interior corridors. With three or more stories, maintenance costs are increased and elevators are required; in urban areas, however, because of higher land costs, high-rise motels become the most practical.

Because of the risk of obsolescence, as will be discussed later in this chapter, the most up-to-date architectural design and features are desirable for the construction of a new motel. A canteen center with vending machines and free ice, and recreational facilities including a swimming pool and playground area, are virtual necessities, as well as restaurants and other facilities for larger motels. Enough land should be acquired to provide for adequate room size (at least 12' × 24') and for adequate parking, recreational facilities, restaurant, and landscaped areas. It has been estimated that for large rooms and an attractive layout, the two-story motel should have as much as 1,000 SF of land per unit, for example, 2.3 acres for a 100-unit motel.[2]

Motel Location

While virtually all motels were at one time located close to highways to accommodate travelers en route to other destinations, the increasing use of motels by businessmen and others for more extended stays has expanded the range of attractive motel sites to include resort areas, places with tourist attractions, and even locations in the heart of the country's largest cities. Whatever the general type of location, *ease of access* and high *visibility* are two important considerations; with corner locations generally most suitable.[3]

MOTEL ACQUISITION AND FINANCING

The acquisition of an *existing motel*, as with other existing income-producing properties (as contrasted to the construction of a new structure), has the advantages attending property with an established image and clientele, trained personnel, and a recorded history of financial results. The fact that the existing property is offered for sale, on the other hand, could mean that the seller has an unfavorable forecast for the future of the property.

The usual sources of debt funds for financing income-producing real estate can be looked to for financing motel acquisitions; including, for example, life insurance companies, REIT's, the seller, and individual investors, with the usual financing instruments employed.

Because of the risks involved in motel investing, however, institutional lenders generally provide less liberal financing for motels than for most other real estate investment properties. A study by Ricks, of real estate financing by fifteen large life insur-

[2] Thomas H. Hall, III, "The Motor Hotel: Appraisals and Feasibility Studies," *The Appraisal Journal,* October, 1971, p. 568.
[3] *Ibid.,* p. 570.

TABLE 15–2. Life Insurance Company Financing for Selected Property Categories, Fourth Quarter, 1966[a]

Property Type	Loan-to-Value Ratio	Contract Interest Rate	Loan Maturity
Hotels & motels	65.9%	6.64%	16 years
Apartments—elevator	71.3	6.51	23
Shopping centers	69.8	6.37	20
Office buildings	70.8	6.36	20
All loans	70.0	6.42	20

[a]Fifteen large life insurance companies.
Source: R. Bruce Ricks, "Imputed Equity Returns on Real Estate Financed with Life Insurance Company Loans," *The Journal of Finance*, December, 1969, p. 925.

ance companies in the fourth quarter of 1966, indicated that on the average hotel and motel loans carried the highest interest rates, and had the shortest loan maturity of all of the eleven property categories considered. Aside from the institutional properties category, hotels and motels had the lowest loan-to-value ratio. Some sample comparative data from the study are shown in Table 15–2.

While financing is available for motel investments during periods when the financial institutions have loan funds, the investor should be prepared in many cases to make a relatively large cash down-payment, and to accept financing on relatively short-terms and at relatively high interest rates.

INCOME AND EXPENSE ANALYSIS

While the basic quantitative techniques discussed in previous chapters can be used in analyzing motel investment proposals, the nature of the input data requirements is somewhat unique, as compared with other real estate investment properties, because of the unusual income and expense patterns for motels.

The motel property investment probably represents more of a business operation than a passive real estate investment. The business aspects for many hotels involve the selling of food and beverages, as well as providing maid service for rooms. Being a business operation the motel investment brings such business-management burdens as promotion, accounting controls, personnel management, and purchasing policies. This aspect of the investment produces not only high operating expenses, but also daily management responsibilities for the investor, unless the owner engages professional third-party management. In the case of very large motels, an established motel chain may agree to manage the investor's individual motel, usually for a percentage of gross income or on some profit-sharing basis.

For the most part the discussion in this section will be concerned with the larger motels, of, say, from 50 to 100 units, or more. There still exist a large number of smaller motels, including several of 20 units or less, but these very often provide only a bare subsistence return to the owner–operator.

Motel Income

The bulk of motel revenue comes from two categories: (1) *room rents,* and (2) revenue from the sale of *food and beverages.* For many motels the food and beverage revenues account for 30 per cent or more of total revenue. Other sources of motel revenue are vending machine sales, and fees collected for telephone service. It should be noted, however, that for most hotels and motels, the often substantial telephone revenues fail to cover the costs of providing telephone service. An additional income source for many hotels, but for only a relatively few motels (except those motels located in urban centers), is in the leases of space to stores located on the property.

Projecting Future Income Levels

The customary manner of computing annual room sales revenue is as follows:

Annual room sales = *Average daily rate per occupied room*
× Number of rooms × 365
× Average annual occupancy percentage

For a *125-unit motel*, with an average room rate of $15.00, and a 72 per cent occupancy percentage, the annual room sales would amount to $492,750, as follows:

Annual room sales $= \$15.00 \times 125 \times 365 \times 0.72$
$= \$492,750$

The sales of food and beverages is usually found to be a rather consistent percentage of room sales; and to continue with the *125-unit motel* example, if the food and beverage (F&B) sales were found to be 79 per cent of room sales, they would total $389,273 [0.79 × $492,750]. If we further assume that telephone and other income runs 3.7 per cent of total gross revenue, then *other income* in this *125-unit motel* would total $33,889, computed as follows, where x = total revenue:

$$x = \$492,750 + \$389,273 + 0.037x$$
$$0.963x = \$882,023$$
$$x = \$915,912$$

Other income $= 0.037 \times \$915,912 = \$33,889$

Because food and beverage revenue and other income amounts are ordinarily tied directly or indirectly to the level of room sales, and the average room rate amount is usually predictable with some accuracy, the *future occupancy percentage* remains as the key variable in determining total revenue. In recent years motels have had average annual occupancy rates in the range of about 70 to 80 per cent, as compared with the lower average of about 60 to 70 per cent for hotels.[4] However, these figures will not necessarily hold in the future, and more importantly they only represent national averages.

For the individual motel, the forecasting of future occupancy rates for years into the future can be a most challenging task. Despite the uncertainties attending occupancy predictions, an analysis should be undertaken that not only takes account of past sales trends but also analyzes the supply and demand factors in the accommodations market in the country, in the region, and in the immediate location.

Many factors have been at work since World War II to foster

---

[4] *Economic Factors* . . . , *op. cit.,* pp. 10–11.

increased motel room sales. Such factors include a growing population, rising disposable incomes, lengthier paid vacation periods, improved roads and automobiles, and expanded air travel services and promotions. These factors and others have fostered a large increase in the number of pleasure travelers and the amounts spent per traveler. The motel sales levels have also benefited from the expanding number of individuals traveling for business or governmental purposes, and the expanding number of conventions.

The forecasting of future demand for the rooms of an individual motel requires an analysis of the types of travelers expected to be attracted, and the conditions that will affect the number of the expected types. As examples: for a motel principally serving highway travelers, an analysis will be made of expected traffic flows; and for the motel catering mainly to businessmen who are visiting local companies, an analysis will be made of the expected future activity levels of local business firms.

In response to the increased overall demand for accommodations, the number of motels (the supply) has increased. The individual considering the acquisition of a motel should make a careful review of other motels under construction in the local area and the probabilities that others will be added in the future. The recently experienced overbuilding and resulting low occupancy rates in the Orlando, Florida, area attests to the possibility that a strong demand for accommodations in a particular area can be overwhelmed by supply.

Motel Expenses

In the motel industry it is customary to treat receipts from occupied rooms, and from food and beverage revenues as sales, and to charge expenses directly relating to both categories to cost-of-sales accounts. This procedure yields gross operating income figures for the two separate sales areas that are useful for control purposes. The other operating expenses are then deducted to obtain a net operating income figure.[5]

---

[5] Many hotels keep a special uniform system of accounts that is not strictly observed here because of a desire for continuity with account titles used elsewhere in this book.

**TABLE 15-3. Sales and Expense Data for One Year,
Hypothetical 125-Unit Motel Example**

			Percentage of Gross Revenue
Room sales	$492,750		(53.8)
Food and beverage sales	389,273		(42.5)
Telephone & other income	33,889		(3.7)
Gross Revenue		$915,912	(100.0)
less: Cost of room sales	$139,219		(15.2)
Cost of F&B sales	313,242		(34.2)
Telephone expense	32,057		(3.5)
Total cost of sales		484,518	(52.9)
Gross Operating Income		$431,394	(47.1)
less: Administrative & general	$ 76,021		(8.3)
Advertising & promotion	28,393		(3.1)
Heat, light & power	32,057		(3.5)
Maintenance & repairs	37,552		(4.1)
Property tax	33,889		(3.7)
Insurance	4,580		(0.5)
Total operating expenses		212,492	(23.2)
Net Operating Income		$218,902	(23.9)

To illustrate the expense analysis, we expand our previous hypothetical *125-unit motel* example, by detailing the calculation of gross operating income and net operating income figures in Table 15-3.[6]

Operating expenses and cost of sales. The segregation of sales and cost of sales figures, as shown in Table 15-3, provides data that can be used to analyze the profitability of the two main sales

[6] The proportions of the various cost-of-sales and expense items in Table 15-3 conform approximately to the industry averages in 1966. See "Harris, Kerr, Forster & Co., 1966 Trends," contained in *Economic Factors . . . , op. cit.,* p. 68.

activities. The *gross profit margin percentage* can be found by using Equation 15–1;

$$\text{Gross profit margin (\%)} = \frac{\text{Gross revenue} - \text{Cost of sales}}{\text{Gross revenue}} \quad [15\text{--}1]$$

Applying Equation 15–1 to the 125-unit motel example, we obtain the gross profit margin percentages for total sales, room sales, and food and beverage sales, as follows:

$$\text{Gross profit margin (\%) (total)} = \frac{\$915,912 - \$484,518}{\$915,912} = 47.1\%$$

$$\text{Gross profit margin (\%) (rooms)} = \frac{\$492,750 - \$139,219}{\$492,750} = 71.8\%$$

$$\text{Gross profit margin (\%) (F\&B)} = \frac{\$389,273 - \$313,242}{\$389,273} = 19.5\%$$

The current profit margin percentages found for a specific motel being considered for acquisition should be compared with past years' margins and with the margins for other similar motels.

The expense ratio (cost of sales plus operating expenses/gross revenue) for the typical large motel having food services is relatively very high, as compared with other real estate investment properties. Cost of sales together with operating expenses amount to 76.1 per cent of gross revenue for the motel example analyzed in Table 15–3.

In addition to the cost of food and beverage purchases that will build up expense levels, there are the costs of relatively large staffs that are required to provide the extensive services of a motel. Also, relatively high administrative expenses are involved, as well as advertising, utilities, and the usual real estate taxes and insurance premiums. Motels also incur significant expenses for maintenance and repairs, to keep the rooms and facilities in attractive condition. Some motels will also have franchise fees as an additional deduction from revenues.

Non-operating expenses. The *interest costs* for motel financing, as noted previously, tend to be somewhat higher for motels than for other types of real estate. The usual real estate *depreciation* provisions apply to motel buildings, with the guideline useful life being 40 years for newly constructed buildings. Motel owners also have substantial deductions relating to the depreciation of furniture and equipment; and the opportunity to apply the investment tax credit to the purchase of new furniture and equipment. This latter tax benefit presently amounts to a credit against federal income taxes equal to ten per cent of the purchase price of qualifying personal property.[7]

It should be noted with regard to depreciation deductions, that the value of motel furniture and equipment as well as motel buildings will often suffer a significant decline because of a combination of physical depreciation and obsolescence, and provision should be made through maintenance outlays and through replacement reserves for updating motel property.

RISK/RETURN ANALYSIS

The returns and risks in motel investing are probably the highest of the principal types of developed real property investments. The 1966 study by Ricks, for example, of eleven categories of real estate properties determined that the average after-tax return on equity investments in motels was 11.42 per cent, almost two percentage points higher than the next highest figure of 9.53 per cent for elevator apartments.[8] Relatively high returns are made possible by the high level of gross income (rental rate) per occupied square foot compared with other income-producing properties. Accordingly, if occupancy can be kept at sufficiently high levels, and costs are controlled, the returns from this form of investment can be expected to be relatively high.

A distinction must be made, however, with respect to motel size. As noted previously, the very small motels often provide only a meager return to the owner–operator. Economies of scale and other benefits accrue to larger motels, with the minimum size requirement depending upon the individual motel's occupancy levels, the efficiency of operations, and the profit margins

---

[7] The details of the special tax depreciation provisions (including recapture provisions) for personal property are beyond the scope of this book.
[8] Ricks, *op. cit.*, p. 933.

obtained on food and beverage sales. The motel's periodic investment returns are often in the form of cash flows that are partly sheltered from taxes. The shelter is ordinarily not as substantial as with apartment investments because motels are subject to more restrictive depreciation expensing provisions, and motels are generally financed with lesser proportions of borrowed funds than apartments, with resulting lower interest expense deductions.

As a consequence of the patterns described above, the motel that is enjoying favorable occupancy levels would be of investment interest to those seeking income and cash flow returns, and not just to those investors seeking primarily tax savings.

Special Risks

The extremely *short-term nature of tenancy* exposes the motel to the risk of loss from a sudden drop in the occupancy rate, in addition to the risk of the more gradual changes experienced by other income-producing real estate. Not only is there a wide variety of factors that can cause either a sharp or gradual reduction in demand for motel space in a given locality, but the relative ease of entry for new, rival motels threatens the future outlook for existing motels.

General regional or national business conditions as well as changes in disposable income levels, and in the national fuel supply situation will tend to influence the overall level of motel industry returns. On the local level, there are any number of factors that can change the local motel supply–demand picture, including such obvious factors as a major change in traffic flow because of a new road by-passing an existing motel, and a drop in tourist or other business activity in the area served by the motel.

Because of the often sudden change in customer style preferences, motels face a high risk of *obsolescence,* that is, the risk of becoming outdated rather suddenly by the appearance of a newer motel having more fashionable features. The motel's vulnerability to obsolescence is compounded by the absence of long-term tenants, except for those occupying any stores that are located on the motel property.

One way motel investors (and those financing motels) seek to adjust for the risk element in motel investing is to finance a higher proportion of the capital needs with equity funds than is usual for other types of income-producing real estate. As noted previously, motels tend to have the lowest loan/value ratio of all of the major types of developed real estate property investments. The lower loan-to-value ratio brings a higher debt-service-coverage ratio, that is, the ratio of net operating income to debt service. A relatively high coverage ratio means, in effect, that there is room for a significant drop in net operating income before such income will be insufficient to cover the mortgage (debt service) payments.

Some other actions are at times helpful in adjusting for the risk of a reduction in occupancy levels, such as a policy of updating facilities to help forestall obsolescence. Some form of group affiliation as described earlier in the chapter may also be desirable in order to obtain the advantages of mutual referral and reservation service, as well as to receive the image benefits. The owner of several motels in diverse locations will further reduce the impact of a negative change in a particular locality— one benefit of *diversification*. A thorough analysis of future conditions that could influence occupancy levels should be undertaken by the prospective purchaser of a motel, as well as some form of *sensitivity analysis* to help gauge how sensitive the motel's profits and cash flows will be to future possible changes in occupancy rates.

Sensitivity Analysis

Because the various motel revenue components are usually tied directly to room revenues, the accounting profits and cash flows of motels are usually highly sensitive to changes in occupancy rates.[9] When high demand brings high occupancy rates, motel income and cash flows can be very attractive. When occupancy is at lower levels, income and cash flows are reduced and can become negative rather quickly because of the substantial fixed costs for motels. In recent years, however, most motels have

---

[9] While food and beverage sales are generally tied to room sales, they can decline suddenly because of competition from new restaurants, coffee shops, and bars in the area; or because of other reasons such as the withdrawal of the motel's liquor license.

been able to profitably operate with occupancy rates as low as
70 per cent, or even somewhat lower. Because of lower marginal
income per room, the new *economy motels* require higher average
occupancy percentages than do the more traditional motels.

A complete sensitivity analysis would entail the preparation
of investment profiles with year-by-year pro-forma income and
cash flow statements, and the various rate-of-return measures for
the motel under study, with each such profile based on a different
occupancy rate assumption. A less complete but still useful form
of sensitivity analysis would be to do a traditional break-even
analysis. Simplified illustrations of both techniques are presented
below, by continuing the large 125-unit motel example used
earlier in this chapter. For the following analyses, we assume
that the *125-unit motel* has the following:

1. The income and operating expense patterns discussed previously
   in this chapter, shown in the current rate column in Table 15-4.
2. A purchase price of $1,642,000.
3. The motel purchase will be financed with a 16-year, 9.5 per cent
   insurance company loan of $1,000,000 (61 per cent of the pur-
   chase price), with annual level payments of $124,035 each.
4. The following depreciation data:

	Value	Remaining Life	Method
Land	$ 200,000	–	–
Building	1,242,000	20 yr	St-L
Furniture & Equipment	200,000	10 yr	St-L

5. A corporation will hold the investment property, with the regular corporate tax rates applied to the motel's taxable income.
   Tax-loss carry-back and carry-forward benefits are ignored.

A complete analysis would include projections for each individual year of the proposed holding period and the calculation
of discounted cash flow rate-of-return figures. However, to simplify the exposition we shall use only the first year's operations,
and compute only those return measures related to that approach.

Table 15–4 contains the income and cash flow statements
(for the first year only) and financial ratios for the *125-unit motel*,
with data for the expected occupancy rate of 72 per cent—the

TABLE 15-4. Simplified Sensitivity Analysis—125-Unit Motel Example

	Occupancy Percentages		(Current Rate)	
	50%	60%	72%	80%
Room sales	$342,188	$410,625	$492,750	$ 547,500
Food & beverage sales	270,328	324,394	389,273	432,525
Telephone & other income	23,534	28,241	33,889	37,654
Gross Revenue	$636,050	$763,260	$915,912	$1,017,679
less: Cost of sales & tel. exp.	336,470	403,765	484,518	538,352
Gross Operating Income	$299,580	$359,495	$431,394	$ 479,327
less: Operating expenses	212,492	212,492	212,492	212,492
Net Operating Income	$ 87,088	$147,003	$218,902	$ 266,835
less: Depreciation expense	82,100	82,100	82,100	82,100
Interest expense	95,000	95,000	95,000	95,000
Taxable Income	($ 90,012)	($ 30,097)	$ 41,802	$ 89,735
less: Federal income tax (corp.)	0	0	8,696	29,573
Earnings After Tax	($ 90,012)	($ 30,097)	$ 33,106	$ 60,162
plus: Depreciation expense	82,100	82,100	82,100	82,100
less: Mortgage amortization	29,035	29,035	29,035	29,035
Cash Flow After Tax	($ 36,947)	$ 22,968	$ 86,171	$ 113,227
Cash Flow Before Tax	($ 36,947)	$ 22,968	$ 94,867	$ 142,800

Financial Analysis

Expense Ratio (COS + Operating expenses/Gross revenue)	86.3%	80.7%	76.1%	73.8%
Income Yield (NOI/Purchase price)	5.3%	9.0%	13.3%	16.3%
Return on Equity (EAT/Owners' eq.)	(neg.)	(neg.)	5.2%	9.4%
Pre-Tax Cash Yield (CFBT/Owners' eq.)	(neg.)	3.6%	14.8%	22.2%
After-Tax Cash Return (CFAT/ Owners' eq.)	(neg.)	3.6%	13.4%	17.6%
Cash Payback Period (Owners' eq./CFAT)	—	28.0 yr	7.5 yr	5.7 yr

assumption used earlier in the chapter; and with similar data for the motel under assumed occupancy rates of 50, 60, and 80 per cent. The room sales figures in the table are based on a continued assumption of an average rate of $15 per day per occupied room, and the food and beverage sales figures represent 79 per cent of room sales. The other income figure, and the various cost of sales, and operating expense amounts are based on the percentage of gross revenue shown in the previous Table 15–3.

Break-Even Analysis

If the motel's gross revenue and cost of sales are found to vary directly with changes in the occupancy rate, and the other cash outlays are fixed in amount, including the debt-service payment and operating expenses, then, as in the example at hand, one can calculate *the pre-tax cash flow break-even occupancy rate,* and prepare a break-even chart that will show the amount of cash flows (cash spendable income before taxes) that can be expected to be generated at various alternative occupancy rate levels. The break-even occupancy rate can be found wih Equation 15–2.[10]

[15–2]

$$\text{Break-even occupancy rate (pre-tax cash flow)} = \frac{Operating\ expenses + Debt\ service}{(Gross\ operating\ income/Occupancy\ \%)}$$

For the *125-unit motel,* we have:

$$\begin{aligned}
\text{Break-even occupancy rate (pre-tax cash flow)} &= \frac{\$212{,}492 + \$124{,}035}{(\$431{,}394/72)} \\
&= \frac{\$336{,}527}{\$5{,}992} \\
&= 56.2\%
\end{aligned}$$

At the 56.2 per cent occupancy level, the *125-unit motel* in question is generating enough marginal income (gross operating

[10] Equation 9–1 is an alternative formulation that can be used to find break-even occupancy.

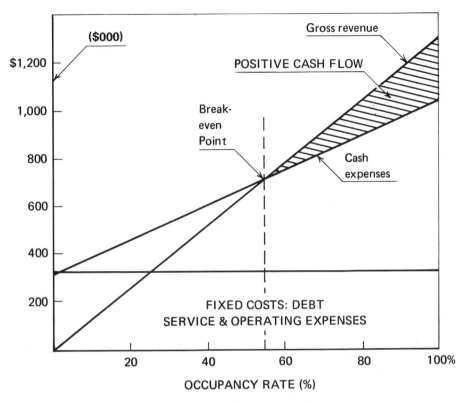

Fig. 15-1. Cash flow break-even chart, 125-Unit Motel example.

income) to just cover fixed costs (debt service plus operating expenses). For each additional percentage-point increase in the occupancy rate above the 56.2 per cent level, an additional $5,992 (marginal income) will be added to pre-tax cash flows. The break-even point of pre-tax cash flow can also be found by drawing a traditional break-even chart, as shown in Figure 15-1; the data for which are from Table 15-4.

SUMMARY

An investment in a motel is more in the nature of a business operation than a passive holding of property. In addition to the "sales" revenue from the rental of short-term living accommodations, many motels receive substantial revenue from the sale of food and beverages.

The need for substantial facilities and staff to provide competitive motel services results in a relatively high level of fixed expenses, and a high level of operating expenses, in relation to revenues. The high degree of *operating leverage* means that substantial investment returns are possible when high occupancy rates are achieved, and the risk of significant losses at low occupancy levels. The risk of low occupancy is present because of the short-term nature of tenancy, the possible oversupply of motel space in a given area, and because of a possible reduction in demand resulting from changes in traffic patterns, or for other reasons.

Because of the investment risks involved, debt financing for motels is usually provided on less favorable terms than for investments in other types of income-producing real property. The prospective motel investor can seek to assess the investment risks prior to making a purchase commitment by a careful study of present and potential future market conditions, a sensitivity analysis, and a break-even occupancy analysis.

V

Real Estate Development

16

Land Development

Thus far we have been concerned with investments in undeveloped land and in developed (existing) income-producing real property. Such investments were considered in relation to the investment goals of periodic income, cash flow, tax shelter, and price appreciation. In this final Part V, we shall be concerned with the development of real property; a form of investment that is undertaken with the objective of obtaining *entrepreneurial profits*.

NATURE OF REAL ESTATE DEVELOPMENT

The term *property development* refers to the making of improvements to an existing property (either land or developed property) by applying resources to the property. Such improvements are undertaken with the intention of obtaining a profit or gain by subsequently selling the improved property for a price that more than covers the outlays made by the investor for land acquisition and development costs.

It is apparent that the nature of this form of real estate investment is somewhat akin to a manufacturing or processing operation where value is added to raw materials; with the profit, if any, arising from the sale of the product at a value greater than the total cost of the raw material inputs and the value added thereto by the entrepreneur. The real estate developer, however, usually thinks in terms of a relatively few *projects,* rather than a continuous stream of *products.*

Real estate development involves much more than the placement of investment funds and property management; and it usually requires the full-time attention of the investor to see projects through to completion. The developer performs, in addition to a risk-taking function, the entrepreneurial activities of planning, scheduling, and controlling the use of cash and sundry physical and human resources. He becomes involved in the often complex facets of labor relations, engineering, architectural, legal, and accounting matters, among others; and, in land subdivision projects, he becomes heavily involved in selling and promotion activities.

As will be discussed later, the potential risks and returns from development activities can be substantial. While the individual promoter or building contractor has traditionally dominated the real estate development field, there has been in recent years an increasing number of large industrial corporations that have entered the field, either alone or in joint ventures with individual developers.

Real Estate Development Stages

The two basic categories, or stages of real estate development are: (1) *land development,* and (2) *building construction.* The first stage involves the preparation of land for the commencement of building construction work. Included in this category would be site preparation for an income-producing property such as an apartment building, or for any other planned construction on a particular site. Also included in the land development category would be *land subdivision,* that is, dividing a tract of land into lots for subsequent sale to those planning residential construction.

The second stage of real estate development noted above involves the actual construction of buildings on previously prepared construction sites. We would also include in this second category the remodeling, or rehabilitation of existing structures undertaken to obtain a profit from an increase in property value that is more than sufficient to cover the investment outlays.

The remainder of the present chapter focuses on the first stage only (land development), and the following chapter is concerned with the combination of the land development and construction stages. For the discussion in this chapter and the next we assume that the investor will sell the property upon completion of the development activities. In many cases the developer of an income-producing property will keep at least a partial long-term equity interest in the property, for goals other than entrepreneurial profit. The benefits received after project completion can be analyzed separately with the use of techniques described previously in this book.

THE LAND DEVELOPMENT PROCESS

In Chapter 12 we considered the type of real estate investment involving the acquisition of land with the strategy of reselling it at a later date in essentially unchanged form—whether the land is in the form of a developed lot or undeveloped acreage. We now consider the acquisition of land in the form of undeveloped acreage, that is, raw land, that the investor plans to develop prior to resale.

The land development steps can be delineated as: (1) land selection and acquisition, (2) site preparation, that is, developing land to the point where it is ready for the commencement of construction, and (3) sale of the developed land. While the investment steps just described would apply to any type of real estate property including commercial or industrial property as well as to the various kinds of residential properties, we shall focus in this chapter on the development of land for use as single-family dwelling lots, that is, *residential subdivision*. This is the most common form of land development as a separate investment form. That is, with other forms of property development the developer–promoter usually undertakes the actual construction as well as site preparation, as will be discussed in detail in the next chapter.

The subdivision of acreage into single-family residential lots can be undertaken for various kinds of residences, including, for example, suburban or urban homes, recreational homes or second homes, and retirement homes. Residential subdivisions can also vary in size, from 2 lots up to 1,000 lots or more. However, the basic investment principles discussed below are applicable to most types and sizes of residential subdivisions.

Site Survey

Before setting out to select a specific piece of land for subdivision purposes, the investor will ordinarily have a basic type of development in mind—that is, he will have a rather clear idea of the ultimate type of dwellings that will be placed on the land, and a general idea of the size of the operation. Prior to purchasing a specific piece of land, a thorough study will be made of the suitability of the land for the intended use. In the discussion that follows we shall assume that an investor plans to acquire land for use in developing lots that are to be sold as sites for second homes in a recreational area. A 100-lot subdivision of that type would typically require from 25 to 50 acres of land.

When seeking a tract of land for a second-home development project, certain location factors will be considered. It is generally advantageous for the site to be near a body of water, and preferably the tract will include some water frontage. The investor may also seek land that is located reasonably close to the urban area that will serve as the principal trade area for the project, say, within one or two hours' driving time. If the site is too close to the urban center, the land will be priced as suburban land and therefore be too costly for the intended second-home development plan. The second-home property site should also be far enough away from the city to offer a change-of-pace environment for urban buyers.

Other locational factors would include the availability of certain local area facilities and features that are not readily available in urban areas. In addition to bodies of water, such features might include mountains, golf courses, tennis courts, and horseback riding facilities. Attractive scenery and topography can be important; not only do they enhance the physical attractiveness of the property but if such natural features are favorable, then the land can be left in a relatively natural state, thereby reducing development costs. A study of the local property tax structure would be made. A low tax base is often found in rural areas that do not have to support expensive school systems and other metropolitan facilities.

The physical survey of the property being considered for acquisition will also include a check on the availability of local services for the future lot buyers' necessities—for example, grocery stores, and churches—and a review will be made of the availability of local labor, contractors, equipment, and materials necessary for the construction of streets and other improvements called for in the property development plan. Finally, the accessibility of the property is examined, with good all-weather roads being most desirable. After the physical survey, the developer will determine if there are any other features, such as local history, giving the property a charisma that can be used later in a sales campaign.

Assuming that the general physical features of the site being considered are favorable, a preliminary development map, or plat, will be made showing the planned layout of the lots. The layout (a form of land planning) would be designed in such a way as to maximize the overall value of the property in the form of lots. For example, for a tract having some ocean frontage, the land is often divided into: (1) a group of lots having ocean frontage, (2) another group having ocean views (but not frontage). and (3) a group of offshore lots. The development plan will have to conform to local zoning requirements relating to such things as minimum lot size and street and road construction specifications, and the plan will conform with local health department requirements regarding water supply and sewage disposal. State and local environmental-impact requirements will also have to be considered.

Revenue and Cost Projections

Upon a review of the positive and negative points discovered by means of the site survey, a judgment would be made as to whether the negative points can be overcome, and if so, at what cost. Estimates can then be made of project costs, including: (1) land costs, (2) development costs, and (3) the costs of the sales program. Some realistic sales estimates should be made independently of the cost figures, and if there is not a sufficient margin between expected revenues and projected costs, the particular property would be dropped from consideration.

The above paragraphs illustrate the general observation that a large part of the planning and study necessary for the typical residential subdivision project is done *prior to* purchasing a specific piece of property. If circumstances require haste in making an acquisition decision on the property being considered, and the preliminary study indicates a generally favorable project site, it may be necessary to either take a purchase option on the property or make a modest down-payment on the property, in order to keep it available while further study is undertaken. When a down-payment is made under such circumstances, a contract clause should be sought that frees the investor from any further liability in the event of non-purchase.

It will be noted that the site survey and economic projections in effect represent components of a preliminary *feasibility study*, which is an additional requirement for this type of investment, as contrasted with the investment in a developed property for which a *market study* is the basic requirement.

The expression *soft costs* refers to the often substantial costs incurred prior to actually making physical improvements to the land. The trend in recent years has been for the soft costs to become a larger percentage of total project costs, in part because of the increasing costs of complying with governmental requirements of various kinds. The rising level of soft costs makes it increasingly difficult to obtain desired amounts of debt financing for land development projects, because of the preference of lenders to provide funds for physical improvements.

Development Work

After the land has been acquired, the planning studies completed, the financing arranged, and the development plan approved by the local planning board or other agency, then the physical development work beings. The development would usually proceed in the following steps: (1) grading is undertaken for roads and for lots, (2) the lots and roads are staked out by a surveyor, (3) the water, sewer, and power lines are installed, (4) the roads and streets are constructed, and (5) planned recreational facilities are constructed, such as boat ramps, swimming pools, and picnic areas. On relatively large projects it may, of course, be prudent or necessary to develop the tract in stages, with the sales proceeds of the group of lots in each stage being used to help finance the development work for the next group of lots.

Sales Program

The sales program usually asumes a major or even primary role in the success of many subdivision projects. This type of real estate investment activity essentially involves buying land wholesale and selling it retail—in quantity. As contrasted to other types of land that will generate some interim income, such as working farm land, the developed residential lots will not be producing revenue while awaiting sale. In other words, after the subdivision work commences there will be no incoming revenue until the first lots are sold. If some lots can be sold before site preparation work is completed, this will, of course, help cash flows. Other aspects of lot sales that will influence overall project cash flows will be the interrelated decisions on selling prices and selling terms.

Selling terms. The land developer usually sells a lot for cash when the buyer plans to build a residence on the lot within a relatively short time after purchasing the land, as is usually the case in urban and suburban housing developments, and in some retirement-home developments. In such event the buyer may combine the cost of the land with the cost of constructing the residence when he seeks home mortgage financing; or the buyer may pay cash from his own savings, as is often the case with retired home buyers.

The vast majority, however, of second-home residential lots are sold to absentee buyers who usually make a small cash down-payment and cover the balance with a contract calling for uniform monthly payments over a 5-to-10-year period. Many subdividers have found that such sales terms not only help to improve the marketability of the lots, but also make higher prices possible. There are also tax advantages to selling property on the installment basis, as was discussed in an earlier chapter.

The installment sale is usually accomplished with the use of a *land contract,* by which the seller keeps title until all payments are made by the buyer. In most states, when the buyer defaults on his payments the contract is canceled and the buyer loses all previous payments and any claim to the property; however, he is not liable for the remainder of the contract amount outstanding. Because he retains title until all or substantially all of the payments have been made, the seller can mortgage his property interest under the land contract arrangement. A commonly employed alternative to the land contract arrangement is the taking by the seller of a purchase-money mortgage from the lot buyer.

DISCLOSURE REQUIREMENTS

There has been growing criticism among parts of the public relating to various aspects of land subdivisions that has resulted in increasing restrictions being placed on this form of real estate investment. First of all, there has been concern about the impact of the rapidly growing number of subdivisions on the local environment and ecology, especially where voters wish to retain the environment in as natural a state as possible. The result in many states, including for example Vermont and California, has been legislation that limits new developments to those considered to be unharmful to the local environment. These laws go beyond the traditional zoning ordinances and can cause substantial delays and extra costs for the developer seeking to conform to the various requirements.

Other areas of concern regarding land development activities are reflected in the increasingly demanding disclosure requirements relating to lot sales, as described below.

Sales Disclosure

In the past few years there has been a rising tide of buyer complaints about a variety of abuses in the sale of land, with many of the complaints coming from disappointed purchasers of lots who bought the land sight unseen. The problems relate principally to false impressions of the property that the buyer had at the time of purchase, sometimes resulting from false or misleading advertising promises, false promises by lot salesmen, failure to advise the buyer of key negative features of the property, or the failure of the developer, because of financial difficulty or otherwise, to complete promised recreational facilities.

In response to such buyer complaints, a series of increasingly strict disclosure requirements has been promulgated by a number of states and by the federal government. The state laws generally require the developer to file statements with government authorities and sometimes to give reports to prospective purchasers, with information on the actual state of the utilities and other development work, on the financial condition of the developer, and information on any negative features of the property. Some states further require that developers post a bond guaranteeing that roads and utilities installations will be completed.

The basic federal law is the Federal Housing Act of 1968; the Interstate Sales Full Disclosure Act, that requires registration of any lot sales that are part of a subdivision of at least fifty lots, when such sales are made through the mail or otherwise in interstate commerce. Registration is with the Department of Housing and Urban Development (HUD). In addition to the registration requirement, a printed property report must be furnished to the buyer prior to his signing a purchase agreement. During the period 1972 to 1974, the sales of over two hundred developments were suspended, and over $4 million in refunds were granted to buyers under the authority of the 1968 Act.[1]

Additional federal regulations apply to land offerings registered with HUD after December 1, 1973, that require extensive disclosure in property reports to prospective buyers, including information on any negative environmental conditions; and for larger subdivisions (with sales exceeding 300 lots, or $500,000), the developer is required to provide buyers with audited financial statements. Such governmental consumer protection requirements not only call for extra care on the part of the developer,

---

[1] *The Wall Street Journal*, January 24, 1974, p. 32.

but also result in outlays for the printing and other costs of compliance.

Financial Reporting

Before new accounting rules were promulgated in 1973, many land development companies recorded as immediate sales the full price of lots sold (less an allowance for bad debts), even when the lots were sold with as little as 1 or 2 per cent cash downpayments, and even though most land contracts are not enforceable, and despite the frequent lack of credit checks on buyers.[2] While sales and profits figures were included in financial reports prepared on the just-described accrual basis, many companies reported the same lot sales on the installment basis for tax purposes in order to defer the payment of taxes on profits from the sales. Under accounting guidelines for retail land sales issued in 1973, companies have the choice of using either the installment basis or the accrual basis for financial reporting purposes. In the latter case, however, *at least ten per cent* of the sales price must be received before a lot sale can be recorded as sales revenue.

When the note received from the lot buyer carries an interest rate that is unreasonably low in relation to existing market rates of interest, then under the same 1973 accounting rules mentioned above, the amount of sales revenue (and profits) recorded at the time the lot is sold must be adjusted downward.

Suppose, for example, a second-home lot is sold for $3,300, with a 10 per cent cash down-payment of $330, and the balance of $2,970 is to be financed over 5 years at 8 per cent interest, with 5 annual payments of $748.85. Assuming that the imputed market interest rate should be 12 per cent rather than 8 per cent, then with the use of interest tables, one can determine that 5 annual payments of $743.85 each would service a debt amounting to $2,682.[3] Accordingly, the real selling price of the lot would be considered to be $330 (the cash down-payment), plus $2,682 (the

---

[2] "Land-Sale Companies Refigure Their Books," *Business Week,* May 12, 1973, p. 78.

[3] The calculation would be as follows: $743.85 \times 3.605 = \$2,681.58$. The interest factor of 3.605 can be found in *Column 5,* in the Appendix at the back of the book.

market value of the note), or a total of $3,012, rather than the stated selling price of $3,300. While the sales revenues from the lot would be reduced by $288, the amount of recognized interest income would be increased by that same amount over the life of the note.

FINANCING LAND DEVELOPMENT

The typical features of the land development project make advantageous financing arrangements both very important, and very challenging to obtain. The land itself must be acquired, and even if the developer can finance the land acquisition with his own resources, the development costs, which may run to three or four times as much as the land itself, will have to be financed. Finally, if the developed individual lots are sold with very small cash down-payments, then the receivables must also be financed. This pattern results in what can be referred to as a *long cash cycle*. That is, the time between cash outlays and the ultimate cash inflows can extend for several years.

Land development financing generally is required not only for extended periods but in relatively large amounts, because developers tend to employ high leverage. That is, they tend to seek outside funds to finance the bulk of the cash requirements. At the same time, financing is often difficult to raise at a reasonable cost because the security involved is essentially raw land, and semi-finished or finished homesites that can remain non-income producing inventory assets, or the security is notes receivable (usually cancelable) signed by individual (often absentee) buyers whose credit standings have not always been carefully investigated.

Despite the fiancing difficulties, various methods and sources of financing have been found available for many development projects, some of which are now discussed.

Financing Land Acquisition

In many land development projects the cost of the raw land represents roughly only one-fifth of the sales value of the developed lots, and hence the developer may well be advised to finance that cost with his own resources. If the amount of land to be purchased is relatively large, the developer may be able to purchase one part of the land for immediate development and take options on the remaining desired tracts that can later be acquired with funds generated by the first lot sales.

In practice, however, many developers seek financing for part of the cost of the raw land. The usual source for this financing is the seller who may wish to sell on a deferred payment basis for tax purposes, or simply in order to consummate an advantageous sale. The term of the financing should be long enough to cover the period until the lots can be sold and the cash and notes received therefrom. The usual instrument of seller financing is the *blanket mortgage,* the terms of which release individual lots (parcels) from the mortgage as they are sold, at which time a preset portion of the mortgage debt would be paid down.

One variation of this seller-financing arrangement would be for the seller to retain title to the land until individual lots are sold, at which time title would be transferred, and the land seller would receive payment for a proportionate part of the overall selling price.

Financing Land Development Costs

The development costs, which as previously stated may run to three or four times the cost of the raw land, can be financed by a variety of methods and sources, usually by some combination thereof. A brief review follows of such financing arrangements.

Some financing will be provided by suppliers of materials, equipment and services who will ordinarily not require immediate cash payments. Another source will be cash received from lot buyers who make their purchases prior to the completion of improvements, and from the buyers of the first completed homesites. Any notes received from such early buyers can also be used as collateral for loans from institutional lenders; or the notes can perhaps be sold to individual investors.

Financial institutions such as commercial banks, mutual savings banks, REIT's, savings and loan associations, and insurance companies, as well as individual investors, may provide development financing either on a clean, or unsecured basis if the developer's credit standing is adequate, or by taking any assets as security that the developer can provide in addition to mortgages on the land and on completed lots.[4] Such other collateralized assets might include construction equipment, other buildings and equipment held by the developer, and savings accounts, certificates of deposit, and other such liquid assets.

Venture Capital

In addition to the use of the developer's own resources and debt financing sources, the developer may find it appropriate or perhaps necessary to raise additional *equity capital* by the sale of partnership interests or corporation shares, that is, venture capital. Outside investors may be solicited, or perhaps equity funds will be provided by contractors who will participate in the project's development work. While there are limitations on the extent to which REIT's can take direct short-term equity positions in land development projects, they and some other financial institutions can indirectly take equity interest through stock purchase warrants, or by other means.

TAX STRATEGY

For the type of land development activities described in this chapter, that is, the type that involves significant improvements to the land and the sale of large numbers of lots, the developer would be considered a dealer (rather than an investor) who is selling lots from inventory. Accordingly, the gains from lot sales would be taxable as ordinary income rather than as capital gains. If, however, the developer sells lots on the basis of a small cash down-payment he can usually qualify for reporting lot sales on the installment basis, and thereby defer payment of the bulk of the taxes payable on the profits from the sales.[5]

There is also some flexibility allowed the investor in timing

[4] Insurance companies and mutual savings banks are allowed to place a small percentage of total assets in otherwise unauthorized investments under so-called *basket provisions* in the regulatory acts.

[5] The various tax aspects of installment-basis reporting are discussed in Chapter 11.

the recognition of taxable income and losses from land development projects. For example, there are various allowable means of allocating raw land and land development costs to individual homesites.[6] In many cases, the developer may wish to allocate the maximum possible amount of project costs to the lots that are sold first, in order to reduce the amount of taxable income from those sales and thereby improve near-term cash flows.

Unless the developer has other income against which to offset interest and property tax expenses incurred prior to the sale of the lots, he may wish to capitalize these expenses and to allocate the maximum allowable amount thereof to the individual homesites to be sold first. It may also be possible to time the incurrence of period expenses, such as general administrative expenses, and advertising and selling expenses, so that they fall in periods when high levels of revenue are received from lot sales.

Capital Gains Treatment

For the investor who has owned a tract of land for at least five years and decides to sell part of his land in the form of lots, rather than sell the entire tract to a developer, there will be an opportunity for capital gains tax benefits, if the requirements of Section 1237 of the Internal Revenue Code are satisfied, as described below.

For the qualifying investor in the just-described situation, the profits from the sale of the first five lots would receive favorable capital gains treatment. In the year in which more than a cumulative total of five lots has been sold, the profits up to the amount of 5 per cent of the selling price of the lots in that year are treated as ordinary income, and the remainder of the profits, if any, are treated as capital gains. Selling expenses (e.g., brokerage commissions) up to 5 per cent of the selling price of the lots is deductible against the ordinary income amounts that may arise as described above.

As an example, suppose that in 1967, an investor purchased

---

[6] For a discussion of alternative allocation techniques, see Robert W. Sandison and Duane E. Waters, "Tax Planning for the Land Developer: Cost Allocations of Land and Improvements," *The Journal of Taxation,* August, 1972, pp. 80–86.

100 acres of farm land at $500 per acre, or a total of $50,000. He made no substantial improvements in the land. In 1973, the investor sold five 1-acre lots for $3,000 each, or a total of $15,000. The entire gain on the sale amounting to $12,500 [$15,000 − $2,500 = $12,500] will be subject to capital gains taxes. In 1974, the investor sold three lots for $3,500 each, or $10,500 total. Of the total profit (assuming zero selling expenses) of $9,000 [(3 × $3,500) − (3 × $500)], some $525, or 5 per cent of the selling price would be taxed as ordinary income, and the balance of $8,475 would be subject to capital gains taxation.

To qualify for the tax treatment described above, the seller must have: (1) not previously held the tract (or any part thereof) for sale to customers in the ordinary course of trade or business, (2) not held any other real property for sale to customers in the ordinary course of business, in the year of sale, (3) held the property for 5 years or more (unless it was acquired by inheritance or devise), and (4) made no substantial improvements in the property (e.g., street or utilities improvements). The last requirement listed is relaxed somewhat after the land is held for ten years.

ORGANIZATIONAL STRATEGY

The large, established land developers tend to use the corporate form for a variety of reasons, including the fund-raising advantages of that form and its limited liability feature.

The smaller, individual developer, however, should consider the various other ownership forms available and coordinate his organizational decision with the tax aspects of the development project to be undertaken. If, for example, the developer expects to have, say, two years of tax-deductible losses from the project before income is generated, then he may wish to use the individual proprietorship or partnership form during those years in order to offset project losses against his other income. He may later wish to convert ownership to the corporate form, if the corporate tax rates are significantly lower than his personal tax rates, and if limited liability becomes an important consideration.

The Subchapter S corporation may also be the appropriate legal vehicle for the just-mentioned type of developer. While this form is generally precluded for use in other forms of real estate investment, because it is not available for corporations receiving mainly passive income, such as rents, it would be available to land developers that otherwise qualify for its use.[7] If a Subchapter S corporation is successfully established, the organization can elect to be taxed as if it were a partnership, and therefore the developer can obtain the benefits of limited liability, and also offset the development project's losses against his other income.

RISK/RETURN ANALYSIS

The returns can be very high for the well-timed purchase of land that is acquired at a reasonable price, subdivided, and sold in favorable market conditions. In fact, the returns from successful land development projects are among the highest in the field of real estate investing. As will be discussed below, the risks are correspondingly high.

The form of return received for land development projects can be referred to as *entrepreneurial profit,* that is, a profit from a business activity, rather than from a passive investment. Because capital gains taxes generally do not apply to profits from the large-scale sale of lots, and because land itself cannot be depreciated for tax purposes, land development per se is not ordinarily considered a tax-sheltered investment. However, some period losses will usually be generated during the early years of a multi-year project; and the sale of lots on the installment basis will help defer tax payments.

Because land development projects of any size usually extend over a period of years, the future annual cash flows can be estimated, and an annual rate-of-return figure calculated with the use of the discounted cash flow model. In practice, however, a commonly-used method is to measure the amount of profit expected from the project *as a whole,* rather than on the traditional annual-return basis. Whether an annual return or project return measure is used, the return would usually be related to the amount of equity capital invested by the developer, rather than to the total capital invested in the project.

[7] The Subchapter S corporation is discussed further in Chapter 8.

Burning Sun Subdivision

The following hypothetical *Burning Sun Subdivision* example will illustrate the two just-described ways of measuring land development profits. To keep the illustration to a reasonable size, the facts will be simplified as much as possible. The facts are: 325 acres of land were purchased, including a mile and a half of waterfront property, at a total cost of $500,000. The developer used his own resources for the land purchase but borrowed the funds necessary to pay for all the development costs, detailed below. The land is to be divided into 850 recreational homesites that will be developed and sold *for cash* over the next 4 years. The total revenue expected to be obtained from the three categories of lots is approximately $2,800,000, as scheduled below.

Type of Lot	Number	Sale Price	Estimated Revenue
Waterfront	162	$6,800	$1,101,600
Waterview	246	3,450	848,700
Wood and other	442	1,925	850,850
			$2,801,150
Total	850	(approximately)	($2,800,000)

The land cost and the other estimated costs for all 4 years of the project are included in Table 16–1, which also indicates the overall expected pre-tax profit of $1,100,000.

A rough measure for the 4-year project as a whole would be obtained by dividing the pre-tax profit of $1.1 million by the developer's investment of $500,000. The result is a 220 per cent rate of return on equity investment, or an average pre-tax return of 55 per cent per year. When adjusting for total estimated federal income taxes of $501,000, the rough after-tax return would be 120 per cent for the entire project, and an average of 30 per cent per year. The annual federal income tax amounts are shown in Table 16–2.

For a more precise measure of the annual expected return from the project, the *annual* after-tax cash flows should be estimated, and the discounted rate of return determined. The pro-

TABLE 16–1. Estimated Revenue and Cost Data, All Four Years,
Burning Sun Subdivision

Sales, 850 lots		$2,800,000
less: Cost of sales:		
Land	$500,000	
Roads	175,000	
Other development costs	150,000	
Interest expense[a]	100,000	925,000
Gross Profit		$1,875,000
less: Period expenses:		
Administrative expense	$300,000	
Advertising expense	225,000	
Sales commissions	250,000	775,000
Pre-Tax Profit		$1,100,000

[a]Interest expense here is capitalized.

jected cash flow figures for *Burning Sun* are presented in Table 16–2. Based on those cash flows, the rate of return (annual basis) can be found to be 23.7 per cent.[8]

Special Risks

There are substantial risks in many land development projects that are associated with both the revenue side and the cost side. The failure of the market to absorb the lots within a reasonable time is of course the major risk, especially for developers having to carry the inventory of homesites with high-cost borrowed funds.

The failure of lots to sell as expected can arise from a local oversupply of lots. With many large corporations developing land into thousands of lots in California and elsewhere, the point of market saturation has no doubt been reached in some areas.

[8] The trial and error method for finding the discounted cash flow rate of return is described in Chapter 7.

The general level of demand for lots will drop during periods of economic recession, and in periods when money is tight and expensive. In the past some developers that successfully sold large numbers of lots subsequently suffered from large numbers of contract cancellations, because sales were made without adequate credit checks on buyers, or for other reasons.

Unexpected cost increases represent another practical risk for many land developments. Development outlays often turn out to be significantly higher than expected for such hard-cost items as recreational facilities. Some developments have failed because of land slides, unsatisfactory percolation (making required septic tank installations unfeasible), or other negative conditions that were unforseen by the developer at the time of land acquisition and early development work. Also adversely affecting many projects are higher than expected soft costs incurred for extensive planning studies, and government reports. Some projects have been subject to expensive delays or to extra construction expenses because of increasing demands for environmental safeguards, such as for costly sewage disposal systems. Delays in obtaining government approvals not only give rise to extra carrying costs, but subject a project to a possible adverse change in market conditions.

A further difficulty arising for some projects is the tendency to confuse cash flows with accounting revenues and costs, especially for developers selling on a deferred-payment basis. Some corporate developers have declared cash dividends based on high levels of project *earnings*, but later were forced to borrow funds to cover the dividend payments because of insufficient short-term *cash inflows* from their installment sales.

Because of the uncertainties attending land development projects, it is usually difficult to forecast future cash flows for a particular project. However, a careful projection of cash flows would be extremely important in minimizing the exposure to future insolvency. For each of the variables that are especially difficult to forecast, such as some construction costs, the cancellation rate on sales contracts, and even interest rates when funds are borrowed on a variable-rate basis, the investor can make three estimates (optimistic, pessimistic, and most likely), or use the other risk-adjustment techniques described in Chapter 7 of this book.

TABLE 16-2. Pro-Forma Income Statements, Cash Flow Projections—Burning Sun Subdivision

	Year—0	1	2	3	4
		Income and Expenses			
Sales (all cash)	—	$ 0	$ 0	$1,400,000	$1,400,000
less: Cost of sales:					
Land	—	0	0	250,000	250,000
Roads	—	0	0	87,500	87,500
Other development costs	—	0	0	75,000	75,000
Interest expense	—	0	0	100,000	0
Gross Profit	—	$ 0	$ 0	$ 887,500	$ 987,500
less: Period expenses:					
Administrative	—	75,000	75,000	75,000	75,000
Advertising	—	0	75,000	75,000	75,000
Sales Commissions	—	0	0	125,000	125,000
Taxable Income	—	($75,000)	($150,000)	$ 612,500	$ 712,500
less: Federal income taxes	—	0	0	172,500	328,500
Earnings After Tax	—	($75,000)	($150,000)	$ 440,000	$ 384,000

334

Cash Flow Projections

Cash Receipts:					
Sales (all cash)	—	$ 0	$ 0	$1,400,000	$1,400,000
Cash Disbursements:					
Land	$500,000	0	0	0	0
Roads	—	87,500	87,500	0	0
Other development costs	—	75,000	75,000	0	0
Interest expense	—	0	0	100,000	0
Administrative expenses	—	75,000	75,000	75,000	75,000
Advertising expenses	—	0	75,000	75,000	75,000
Sales commissions	—	0	0	125,000	125,000
Federal income taxes	—	0	0	172,500	328,500
Total Disbursements	$500,000	$237,500	$312,500	$ 547,500	$ 603,500
Net Cash Flow (before borrowing)	($500,000)	($237,500)	($312,500)	$ 852,500	$ 796,500
Borrowings	—	237,500	312,500	—	—
Repayment of borrowings	—	—	—	550,000	—
Net Cash Flow (after borrowing)	($500,000)	$ 0	$ 0	$ 302,500	$ 796,500

Careful forecasting together with a thorough investigation of the applicable governmental requirements are especially important steps for developers expecting to use relatively large amounts of borrowed funds. Another defensive measure to be employed whenever possible is that of diversification. Having land development projects underway in various geographical locations will help defend against adverse changes in market conditions and government environmental controls in one particular locality.

SUMMARY

Land development is a form of investment that requires more than the passive investment of funds and property management activities. It involves the entrepreneurial functions of planning, scheduling, and controlling various resources. It involves (in the case of residential subdivision projects) the acquisition of raw land and the production and sale of finished residential lots, and at times the design and construction of recreational facilities.

The extensive planning and study necessary for a subdivision project starts with a site survey, which is a study of the physical and other attributes of a particular tract of land that is being considered for a subdivision project. A preliminary development map is designed for the prospective site and revenue and cost projections are made for the project. When the appropriate site is selected, government approvals are received, and financing arrangements are made, then the physical development work commences, including grading, the installation of streets and utilities, and the construction of whatever recreational facilities.

The sales program is an important part of most land subdivision projects. It has been found that the marketing of sites for second homes is usually best accomplished by offering such sites for a small cash down-payment and a series of installment payments over a period of between five and ten years. The land contract or purchase-money mortgage can be used.

The profits from land development projects can be very high, as measured by the rate of return on owner's equity investment. The high returns in past years, however, have attracted some large corporations to this form of real estate investment activity, which in turn has resulted in market saturation in some areas. Additional risks are presented by the fast-growing number of regulations at all governmental levels regarding practically all phases of land development projects. Compliance with the many regulations can result in expensive delays and extra costs for the developer.

17

Property Development and Construction

At times the investor who develops a site for resale will decide to go on to the next step and construct houses or income-producing buildings on the site. This can occur when the developer considers it an attractive means of improving his cash flows or profits. Other investors undertake building construction as an integral part of a plan that was conceived when they originally acquired the land. It is this latter type of real estate investment project that we address in the present chapter.

The general nature and process of planning and executing a new real estate project that is designed to satisfy certain area needs will be the focus of our discussion. We assume that the investor plans to hold or to sell the completed project; that is, he is engaging in what is often referred to as *speculative building,* as contrasted to construction done under a cost-plus or other form of contract (*contract construction*).

NATURE OF DEVELOPMENT AND CONSTRUCTION

The land development and building construction process is an entrepreneurial activity that usually requires the full-time, *active* participation of the investor through various phases of activities starting with the planning phase, and ending with the marketing of the completed project. There are substantial benefits and risks associated with this form of real estate investing, and it is not generally considered an investment well suited to the unadventurous or the inexperienced investor. The benefits from property development and construction come principally in the form of profits from a favorable sale of the completed project, and from tax-shelter benefits received prior to completion.

Another generalization that can be made about property development and construction is that there is a high level of governmental intervention. In addition to the growing state and local land-use restrictions for environmental protection, there is a strong national government interest in residential construction activities. Hence, the developer generally spends an increasing amount of time studying and complying with a multitude of government regulations.

The property development and construction activity can cover a great variety of sizes and types of projects. One basic category includes income-producing properties varying from apartment houses to office buildings. It is this type of project that is emphasized in the present chapter. We first briefly discuss, however, another major category of projects, the development and construction of single-family residential units.

Homebuilding

In recent years there has been over 50,000 builders of homes in the United States. Their operations range from the building of a dozen or fewer structures a year, to the building of over 2,000 homes a year in large subdivisions, including PUD's (planned unit developments). Some developers have undertaken to construct whole towns.

The PUD's are developments incorporating various uses but developed as one unit, and they often have open-space and recreational areas for the common use of those residing in the development. Approval from local planning boards and other agencies would be sought for the overall development plan. In the past few years there has also been a growing number of new-town projects, which after receiving approval by the Housing and Urban Development Department can be financed with federal loan guarantees, under the 1970 New Communities Act.

The construction and sale of single-family homes can be profitable when the market is favorable, but unprofitable when market conditions turn around. In other words, there are pronounced cycles in this area of activity to which the investor–developer must adjust. When completed houses cannot be sold at reasonable prices because of a lack of mortgage money or for other reasons, the developer is left with an inventory that is costly to carry. The higher the interest costs, the higher the carrying costs. For example, the builder holding for 1 year, 10 unsold houses that cost an average of $50,000 each to build, will have $90,000 in interest charges alone, if he is paying 18 per cent per year to finance the $500,000 inventory.

The Development and Construction Process

The principal stages of the typical development and construction project involving an income-producing property would include:

1. Planning studies.
2. Land acquisition.
3. Land development (site preparation).
4. Building construction.
5. Rent-up period.
6. Property sale.

The order of the first two stages would be reversed when the investor holds title to a piece of vacant land prior to planning for its improvement; further, the order of the last two stages will be altered if the building is sold prior to its completion or prior to its becoming fully rented. The details of physical land development work and building construction work are beyond the scope of this book; rather the emphasis will be upon the planning stage, the means of financing the various stages, and upon the tax and other investment aspects of the development and construction process.

THE PLANNING PHASE

If the investor owns a piece of vacant land that he wishes to develop, the first planning study to be undertaken would be the *land-use study*. This study would be made to determine the highest and best use of the property. While some potential uses can be eliminated rather quickly because of the size, location, or other attributes of the property, an imaginative investigation of the remaining potential uses will determine the best alternative use, giving due consideration to the investor's experience and resources. The particular type of property development selected, for example, a neighborhood shopping center, will then become the subject of further studies, as described below.

If the investor does not hold a piece of land that is suitable for development he will usually have a general idea of the type of property development that he wishes to undertake, and will seek appropriate land after making *site surveys* of the most attractive available sites, as was discussed in the last chapter.

After a particular piece of property has been selected for further study, the local *market study* for the proposed new construction project becomes an extremely important next step. The value of the property upon completion, and hence the amount of profit or loss, will be determined by the ability to sell the residential homes or to lease the apartments or other income-producing properties that will be placed on the market by the investor. A thorough market study will also help to determine the design features of the building that will best meet the demands of potential future tenants. The general format for a typical real estate market study was described in Chapter 3.

A separate feasibility study will be required to determine the *engineering feasibility* of the planned construction, with respect to such things as foundation support, water supply, and sewage disposal. Also, a study will be made of the project's *legal feasibility* in terms of zoning for the type of buildings contemplated, and of other land-use restrictions imposed by local zoning boards and by local and state bodies governing the way land is to be developed.

A *financial feasibility* study will also be required, with projections of future revenue, costs, and cash flows. For this analysis and for other parts of the feasibility study, at least preliminary architectural drawings and specifications will be required, with cost estimates made for construction materials and labor.

The various planning studies such as those described above are not only a necessary step in successful project formulation, but they are also necessary for obtaining financing for the project. These studies and analyses call for substantial outlays of funds, and in recent years they have tended to assume a growing proportion of total project costs. The cause is usually the increasingly closer surveillance and more extensive requirements of government agencies concerned with land use, and the costs of delays in obtaining government approvals. The result is that some projects become financially unattractive that in former years would have been profitable.

FINANCING PROPERTY DEVELOPMENT AND CONSTRUCTION

Much of the success of a development and construction project will depend on the making of favorable financing arrangements for the various stages of the project as it progresses to completion. Financing costs become a major part of the investor's costs and many projects are highly leveraged. As one builder has stated: "The main raw material in any residential-construction project is money." [1] The variety of possible financing arrangements are practically infinite and we shall point to general financing patterns only in this section.

General Financing Patterns

Typical financing arrangements for an income-producing property such as an apartment house generally follow the develop-

[1] *The Wall Street Journal,* October 18, 1974, p. 20.

ment and construction stages listed previously. Assuming the equity investor finances the initial planning studies with his own funds (perhaps with the help of investment partners), the investor will then typically seek financing from outsiders for the following stages: land acquisition, land development, and building construction, and then permanent financing for the completed project. In general, each successive stage involves less risk and therefore less costly financing, and each step involves increasingly-longer-term financing.

Financing Land Acquisition

For many projects the investor's own equity funds will be used for the land acquisition, and creditor funds for the bulk of the development, construction, and permanent funds. When the investor's own funds are not sufficient to finance the total land cost, the cost may be financed by the land *seller* who will take back a *subordinated* money mortgage: the mortgagee–seller agrees to subordinate, that is, make inferior, his interest to that of future creditors who will finance the development and construction work. Alternatively, the investor–developer owning the land may sell the land to a financial institution or other investor and lease it back, thereby, in effect, financing the land cost.

Many other arrangements are possible. For example, the lender who provides the funds to finance land development will often provide part or all of the funds necessary for land acquisition. The investor may also finance land acquisition, as well as other project costs, with a combination of his own funds and those provided by other equity interest holders such as limited partners, as described in a later section of this chapter.

Permanent Financing

After the investor acquires the land for the project, he will usually present a loan package, containing the details of his planning studies, to a long-term real estate lender, such as a life insurance company or a real estate investment trust, or mutual savings bank or savings and loan association. The investor seeks from the financial institution a *commitment* to provide long-term, first-mortgage loan funds when the building is completed, or when it is completed *and* a specified percentage of space therein is leased. Obtaining the loan commitment is a key step for the investor, because without it he will usually have difficulty obtaining funds to finance the development and construction work, as described below.

Interim Financing

After the investor receives a permanent loan commitment he then will seek so-called interim financing; that is, a lender will be sought who will make a commitment to provide financing for the development and construction stages, with such funds to be made available in the form of *progress payments* as the work progresses. The interim lender, often a commercial bank or a real estate investment trust, will look to the permanent loan commitment as the future source of funds with which his own loans will be repaid, or *paid out* when the project is completed.

The interim financing often is provided in the form of two separate loans (the development and construction loans), and often two separate financial institutions or other lenders will be involved. The interim loans have intermediate-term maturities, usually less than three years, and will carry higher interest rates than the permanent financing because of the greater risk of loss associated with a partially completed project than with a completed building. During the development and construction stages there are a wide range of problems that can arise, from strikes, to materials shortages, to technical problems that were not anticipated in the planning stage. In recent years many interim lenders have tied their interest rates to a specified number of percentage points above the commercial banks' prime lending rate, which results in a variable, that is, changeable, interest rate.

A source of additional interim financing would be the credit provided by materials suppliers and by subcontractors. Also, of course, the investor may use equity funds, his own or his partners', to help cover the development and construction costs.

Gap commitment. When the permanent loan agreement specifies that part or all of the loan funds will not be released until a specified amount of the building space has been leased, the developer may be required by the interim lenders to obtain a gap commitment from another source. This commitment, for a fee, provides the developer with an agreement that funds will be provided to finance the period between the completion date of the building and the date when the full amount of the permanent loan funds will be made available. When gap loans are made they are secured by junior mortgages.

Level of Financing

The amount of the permanent loan agreed to by the long-term lender will determine, in turn, the amount of equity funds that will be required of the investor, and thereby the amount of leverage for the equity investor. The amount of loan funds provided ordinarily will *not* be a direct function of the costs expected to be incurred on the project; rather, the amount will be set as a percentage of the appraised value of the completed project, which in turn will be based primarily upon the amount of rental income expected to be generated by the project.

Because of this convention, it has at times been possible for the developer to obtain very high leverage, in some cases reaching 100 per cent (or even more) debt financing, which is referred to as *mortgaging out*. For a highly simplified example, suppose an apartment project is expected to have a total cost of $2 million, including land. It is forecasted that total annual rents will amount to $250,000, and the permanent lender capitalizes the rents at a 10 per cent rate to obtain an appraisal value of $2,500,000. If the life insurance lender is permitted by state regulation to lend up to 80 per cent of the appraised value; it could lend up to $2,000,000 [$2.5 million × 0.80]. If $2 million is loaned, the developer mortgages out with 100 per cent financing of his investment outlays. When the investor owns the project land, a purchase–leaseback thereof may also be made part of the financing arrangements.

It should be noted that the amount of permanent financing received, as well as the other terms of the loan agreement will not only be a function of the worthiness of the particular project, but will also depend on the general availability of loan funds, and the relative bargaining positions of the borrower and the lender. At times when money is scarce, as in recent years, the lender will often set stiff demands on the borrower before agreeing to provide a high percentage of the project's financing requirements. The demands may include a sharing of equity returns or cash flows generated by the project, the so-called *equity kickers*.

TAX AND OWNERSHIP STRATEGY

Because of the not unusual tendency for the developer–investor to take on projects that are very large in relation to the developer's own equity capital investment, the developer will often have to meet the demands by creditors for additional equity capital by offering equity participations to either the creditor institutions themselves, or to outside, so-called *venture capital suppliers*.

Raising venture capital becomes especially important in periods of tight money, and for projects having a relatively high level of *soft costs* incurred for planning studies and analyses, and of course for developers having relatively small amounts of capital available. There are a variety of ways of raising outside equity capital, including a joint venture with a financial institution or affiliate thereof), such as an insurance company or a real estate investment trust, or a joint venture with an industrial corporation. Equity funds can also be sought from individual investors through the sale of corporate shares or the sale of limited partnership interests (syndication). While the general aspects of these various forms of legal association were discussed in Chapter 8, there are some particular points regarding the raising of outside capital from individual investors that will be discussed in the following sections.

Equity Financing for Construction Costs

In many cases the developer will use his own equity funds together with financing from the land seller and the development-loan proceeds to finance land acquisition and site preparation. In this situation, the developer will then often seek venture capital funds to help finance the construction costs.

The vehicle often appropriate for raising equity construction funds is the limited partnership, usually referred to as a *syndicate,* with the developer being a general partner and the outside investors being limited partners. The general partner will offer management services to the partnership and often donate the land as his capital contribution, while the limited partners will contribute funds for construction that are needed to supplement the construction loan funds. For example, a project with a total cost of $6,000,000 might be financed as follows:

General partner	$ 200,000	(land cost)
Limited partners	1,800,000 ⎫	
Construction loan	4,000,000 ⎭	(construction costs)
Total financing	$6,000,000	

The general partner can achieve limited liability by establishing a corporation to hold the general partnership interest; the limited partners, of course, enjoy limited liability.[2] The general partner, in lieu of selling the land to the partnership, may lease the land to the partnership, in which case the partnership can deduct ground rent, whereas it could not deduct depreciation on the land if it held title thereto.

Limited partnership interests in the type of investment described above are attractive to many high-tax-bracket investors because construction losses can be deducted against their income received from other sources; and they also enjoy limited liability. In fact, in some cases, the limited partners' *entire* initial investment ($1,800,000 in the above number example) may, in effect, be deductible in the year the investment is made because of construction losses allocated to them during the first year of partnership operations. In such case the investment is said to be made in *soft dollars*. For investors in the 70 per cent tax bracket, the $1,800,000 investment becomes a *net* cash investment of only $540,000, after subtracting the tax-shelter benefit of $1,260,000 obtained by deducting $1,800,000 in construction losses.[3]

---

[2] A *nominee corporation* may be formed to hold the real property title during construction, to limit liability and for other benefits. For a good discussion on this point see Daniel S. Shapiro, "Tax Planning for Equity Financing by Real Estate Developers," *Taxes,* September, 1972, pp. 530–43. Also, (see pp. 537–8) note that certain tests must be met for the case where a corporation is the sole general partner.

The *deductible* construction costs can include real estate taxes and ground rents, if any; but the largest deductions during construction are usually for expenses associated with the construction loan, for example, interest, *points,* loan fees, and commitment fees. For some projects there will be other deductible period expenses, such as the costs of maintaining access roads, advertising expenses, and general administrative expenses. The deductions generated by these expenses are more advantageous to investors than depreciation deductions, because the latter are subject to recapture if the property is sold at a gain.

Starting in 1976, 50 per cent of the interest and property tax expenses incurred or paid during the construction of non-residential buildings will have to be capitalized (and amortized over six years), rather than be deductible as expenses in the years when the interest and taxes are incurred or paid. This new restriction is imposed by the Tax Reform Act of 1976. The same Act calls for 100 per cent capitalization of construction period interest and taxes for non-residential buildings in 1977; for residential buildings in 1978; and for low-income housing in 1982.

If the partnership continues to hold the building after completion, the project will many times continue to provide significant losses for the limited partners and cash flows for the developer-general partner, by the appropriate allocation of interest, *depreciation,* and other partnership expenses. With careful compliance with the tax-law requirements, the partnership losses can be allocated to the limited partners in amounts disproportionately high in relation to the amount of their capital contribution.[4] The Tax Reform Act of 1976 provides, however, that such special allocations can be set aside if they do not have *substantial economic effect.*

RISK/RETURN ANALYSIS

As with land development, the returns in the form of entrepreneurial profits can be very substantial from the construction and sale of real estate properties. The percentage return on the in-

[3] Limited partners cannot deduct losses in one year in excess of the amount of their capital contribution, except to the extent of their share of the partnership's *non-recourse liabilities;* that is, partnership liabilities for which no partner is personally liable.

[4] Daniel S. Shapiro, *op. cit.,* pp. 538–40.

vestor's equity investment can be very high because of the extreme leverage often possible with this form of investment. In times of plentiful loan funds the developer can often (as noted previously) even mortgage out by borrowing funds to cover the total investment outlays required by the project. While there is a paucity of data available on the dimension of development–construction profits, it has often been reported that many individuals have become millionaires by means of this form of investment activity.

For the developer–investor who has other income against which to offset construction losses there are significant tax-shelter benefits from this form of investment, and the various methods of disposing of the property upon completion can be considered as possible strategies for reducing the amount of tax on the investor's profit at the time of sale. However, when funds become scarce, the insurance company or other mortgagee may be able to insist upon a significant share of the traditional equity benefits, unless the developer is in an especially strong bargaining position.

Return Measures

As with land-development projects, it is often most practical to measure the absolute profit expected to be received from the development and construction project as a whole, rather than to attempt a careful measurement of the expected annual rate of return on investment, as is usually done with investments in already developed real estate properties. Furthermore, because the benefits from most construction projects are received over a relatively short period of time, the use of discounted cash flow techniques is not generally as appropriate as with the long-term investments in developed property. Discounted cash flow techniques would, however, become important if the development-construction project is expected to stretch out over a number of years.

The approach to estimating project profits would be to simply subtract total estimated costs from the estimated selling price. The estimated costs will include outlays for planning studies and professional fees, land costs, costs for land preparation, and building construction, as well as for the carrying costs, for example, interest, real estate taxes, and property insurance.

Estimated proceeds of sale. The figure to be used in the profit analysis for estimated selling price would be developed at least in part by considering the valuation approaches used by professional appraisers. For single-family homes, the valuation would be based mainly on the values of comparable homes in the area. For income-producing properties, the appraised value would depend primarily on the annual income that is anticipated from the building, and the gross income multiplier (GIM) or overall capitalization rate that is applied to the expected annual income, as was described in Chapter 3.

For a property expected to have, for example, gross rents of $800,000 per year (indefinitely), and a GIM of 10 is applied thereto, the estimated selling price would be $8 million. If, however, it is expected that during the first two years after completion, the rents will be only $500,000 and $700,000, respectively then the selling price may be estimated to be only $7,600,000, because of the $400,000 below-normal revenue during the rent-up period.

Special Risks

Offsetting the potential for very large profits from property development and construction activities is the high level of risk of loss. While there are the traditional business risks associated with this essentially entrepreneurial activity, there are also often very high financial risks. Both types of risk are accentuated for large-scale projects that require a lengthy period to take to completion, and hence have a long period of exposure to adverse changes.

Business risks. The business risks include both the possibilities of cost overruns and revenue short-falls. Development and construction costs are often difficult to anticipate and to control, especially for relatively large projects. During inflationary periods practically all labor and materials costs are likely to increase, and the cost of some individual inputs can rise dramatically when supply shortages develop. Other cost overruns can develop because of such things as unforeseen technical problems, lengthy strikes, overly optimistic cost estimates, and (increasingly) the extra costs and delays caused by environmental protection requirements.

The future selling price may be insufficient to cover the investment outlays, or there can be delays in the receipt of revenue because of the shortage of buyers able to finance acquisition, as sometimes occurs in the case of single-family homes. In the case of income-producing property, the selling price upon completion will be tied to the actual and estimated future rental income. Such rentals may be less than originally anticipated because of an oversupply of similar rental space at the time the completed property is placed on the market. Also, rent levels, may be kept at a low level by governmental price controls that are imposed from time to time.

Financial risks. The use of a high degree of leverage increases financial risk, that is, the risk of not being able to meet debt-service payments as they come due. Because of the key role played by debt financing in most real estate development and construction projects, the financial risks are often substantial.

The financing costs become the major carrying cost for the project while the building is under construction, and when the project is completed but yet unoccupied. A project that is carried for 3 years with debt funds averaging $10 million, will incur a total of $3 million in interest costs when the average annual interest rate is 10 per cent. When, as in recent years, the interest rate is variable (e.g., tied to the commercial banks' prime rate), and is rising during the construction stage, the impact on costs can be extremely adverse. On $10 million of borrowed funds, each increase of 1 per cent in the annual interest rate will add $100,000 to the annual carrying costs.

The large number of development and construction loan defaults experienced in 1974 reflects a combination of many of the business and financial risks described above.

Risk protection. While many future national and even local economic factors cannot, of course, be foreseen with precision, the developer should recognize that adverse conditions of some sort may well arise, especially with longer-term projects. Accordingly, certain defensive measures should be undertaken, such as making pessimistic estimates, as well as optimistic and most-likely estimates, when forecasting future income and expense figures. Also, sensitivity analysis should be undertaken to test the sensitivity of project risks and returns to possible adverse changes in project revenues and costs, including a possible future change in interest-rate levels.

The project risk will be reduced substantially when the developer–investor obtains advance commitments from principal future tenants, that is, prior to his undertaking the construction. Project risk will also be reduced by thorough planning studies, including a careful estimation of probable environmental protection requirements.

The developer also can expect to reduce overall risk through diversification, that is, by having a group of projects under way simultaneously that involve different types of properties and diverse locations. A defensive measure employed by most developers is to organize their projects in such a way that debt claims arising from a particular project will not result in judgments against their personal assets, and against their assets invested in unrelated projects.

The developer can of course be in a stronger position if he has substantial cash resources to draw on in case of need. This is a major advantage held by the large industrial corporations that invest in real estate; they are often in a position, for example, to wait out costly delays when projects take longer than expected to become fully rented at adequate rental levels. Some developers have also benefited in inflationary periods by having a significant portion of the total project investment in the form of land. The rise in land value may make the project profitable despite other difficulties that may arise.

SUMMARY

There are two principal categories of land development and building construction projects: (1) the single-family residential projects, ranging from one unit to large subdivisions; and the income-producing properties, ranging from apartment projects to warehouses. The principal stages involved (not always in the listed order) in the development and construction process include: planning studies, land acquisition, land development, building construction, rent-up period, and property sale. Extensive planning and scheduling are important aspects of major development and construction projects. The planning studies often include land-use studies, site surveys, market studies, and various feasibility studies.

Financing arrangements for development and construction projects assume great importance because most developers require extensive outside financing to successfully carry projects through the various stages to completion and sale. The size of the debt-service payments called for by mortgage financing, and the lease payments under sale–leaseback financing, will generally have a major impact on project risks and project returns.

The returns from development and construction projects can be extremely high in relation to the amount of equity capital invested by the developer. The returns from this form of investment come in the form of entrepreneurial profits at the time the property is sold, and in the form of tax-shelter benefits associated with tax losses generated during construction.

While potential returns are often very high, so also are the investment risks. The business risks include both possible cost overruns and the failure of the completed property to have the market value anticipated. Because most such investments are highly leveraged, the financial risk exists of being unable to meet debt-service payments as they come due.

Interest Tables

The tables in this Appendix (pages 355–368) are used with the permission of the American Institute of Real Estate Appraisers, and are found on pages 4, 20, 36, 52, 68, 84, 100, 116, 148, 150, 152, 154, 156, 158, 160, 162, 164, and 166 of *Ellwood Tables for Real Estate Appraising and Financing* (3rd ed.; Chicago: The American Institute of Real Estate Appraisers, 1970).

3 % **ANNUAL COMPOUND INTEREST TABLE** 3 %

EFFECTIVE RATE = 3%   BASE = 1.03

	1 AMOUNT OF I AT COMPOUND INTEREST $S^n = (1+i)^n$	2 ACCUMULATION OF I PER PERIOD $S_{\overline{n}|} = \dfrac{S^n - 1}{i}$	3 SINKING FUND FACTOR $1/S_{\overline{n}|} = \dfrac{i}{S^n - 1}$	4 PRES. VALUE REVERSION OF I $v^n = \dfrac{1}{S^n}$	5 PRESENT VALUE ORD. ANNUITY 1 PER PERIOD $a_{\overline{n}|} = \dfrac{1-v^n}{i}$	6 INSTALMENT TO AMORTIZE I $1/a_{\overline{n}|} = \dfrac{i}{1-v^n}$	n YEARS
1	1.030000	1.000000	1.000000	.970874	.970874	1.030000	1
2	1.060900	2.030000	.492611	.942596	1.913470	.522611	2
3	1.092727	3.090900	.323530	.915142	2.828611	.353530	3
4	1.125509	4.183627	.239027	.888487	3.717098	.269027	4
5	1.159274	5.309136	.188355	.862609	4.579707	.218355	5
6	1.194052	6.468410	.154598	.837484	5.417191	.184598	6
7	1.229874	7.662462	.130506	.813092	6.230283	.160506	7
8	1.266770	8.892336	.112456	.789409	7.019692	.142456	8
9	1.304773	10.159106	.098434	.766417	7.786109	.128434	9
10	1.343916	11.463879	.087231	.744094	8.530203	.117231	10
11	1.384234	12.807796	.078077	.722421	9.252624	.108077	11
12	1.425761	14.192030	.070462	.701380	9.954004	.100462	12
13	1.468534	15.617790	.064030	.680951	10.634955	.094030	13
14	1.512590	17.086324	.058526	.661118	11.296073	.088526	14
15	1.557967	18.598914	.053767	.641862	11.937935	.083767	15
16	1.604706	20.156881	.049611	.623167	12.561102	.079611	16
17	1.652848	21.761588	.045953	.605016	13.166118	.075953	17
18	1.702433	23.414435	.042709	.587395	13.753513	.072709	18
19	1.753506	25.116868	.039814	.570286	14.323799	.069814	19
20	1.806111	26.870374	.037216	.553676	14.877475	.067216	20
21	1.860295	28.676486	.034872	.537549	15.415024	.064872	21
22	1.916103	30.536780	.032747	.521893	15.936917	.062747	22
23	1.973587	32.452884	.030814	.506692	16.443608	.060814	23
24	2.032794	34.426470	.029047	.491934	16.935542	.059047	24
25	2.093778	36.459264	.027428	.477606	17.413148	.057428	25
26	2.156591	38.553042	.025938	.463695	17.876842	.055938	26
27	2.221289	40.709634	.024564	.450189	18.327031	.054564	27
28	2.287928	42.930923	.023293	.437077	18.764108	.053293	28
29	2.356566	45.218850	.022115	.424346	19.188455	.052115	29
30	2.427262	47.575410	.021019	.411987	19.600441	.051019	30
31	2.500080	50.002678	.019999	.399987	20.000428	.049999	31
32	2.575083	52.502759	.019047	.388337	20.388766	.049047	32
33	2.652335	55.077841	.018156	.377026	20.765792	.048156	33
34	2.731905	57.730177	.017322	.366045	21.131837	.047322	34
35	2.813862	60.462082	.016539	.355383	21.487220	.046539	25
36	2.898278	63.275944	.015804	.345032	21.832252	.045804	36
37	2.985227	66.174223	.015112	.334983	22.167235	.045112	37
38	3.074783	69.159449	.014459	.325226	22.492462	.044459	38
39	3.167027	72.234233	.013844	.315754	22.808215	.043844	39
40	3.262038	75.401260	.013262	.306557	23.114772	.043262	40
41	3.359899	78.663298	.012712	.297628	23.412400	.042712	41
42	3.460696	82.023196	.012192	.288959	23.701359	.042192	42
43	3.564517	85.483892	.011698	.280543	23.981902	.041698	43
44	3.671452	89.048409	.011230	.272372	24.254274	.041230	44
45	3.781596	92.719861	.010785	.264439	24.518713	.040785	45
46	3.895044	96.501457	.010363	.256737	24.775449	.040363	46
47	4.011895	100.396501	.009961	.249259	25.024708	.039961	47
48	4.132252	104.408396	.009578	.241999	25.266707	.039578	48
49	4.256219	108.540648	.009213	.234950	25.501657	.039213	49
50	4.383906	112.796867	.008865	.228107	25.729764	.038865	50
51	4.515423	117.180773	.008534	.221463	25.951227	.038534	51
52	4.650886	121.696197	.008217	.215013	26.166240	.038217	52
53	4.790412	126.347082	.007915	.208750	26.374990	.037915	53
54	4.934125	131.137495	.007626	.202670	26.577660	.037626	54
55	5.082149	136.071620	.007349	.196767	26.774428	.037349	55
56	5.234613	141.153768	.007084	.191036	26.965464	.037084	56
57	5.391651	146.388381	.006831	.185472	27.150936	.036831	57
58	5.553401	151.780033	.006588	.180070	27.331005	.036588	58
59	5.720003	157.333434	.006356	.174825	27.505831	.036356	59
60	5.891603	163.053437	.006133	.169733	27.675564	.036133	60

4% ANNUAL COMPOUND INTEREST TABLE 4%

EFFECTIVE RATE = 4%   BASE = 1.04

YEARS n	1 AMOUNT OF 1 AT COMPOUND INTEREST $S^n = (1+i)^n$	2 ACCUMULATION OF 1 PER PERIOD $S_{\overline{n}|} = \frac{S^n - 1}{i}$	3 SINKING FUND FACTOR $1/S_{\overline{n}|} = \frac{i}{S^n - 1}$	4 PRES. VALUE REVERSION OF 1 $v^n = \frac{1}{S^n}$	5 PRESENT VALUE ORD. ANNUITY 1 PER PERIOD $a_{\overline{n}|} = \frac{1 - v^n}{i}$	6 INSTALMENT TO AMORTIZE 1 $1/a_{\overline{n}|} = \frac{i}{1 - v^n}$	n YEARS
1	1.040000	1.000000	1.000000	.961538	.961538	1.040000	1
2	1.081600	2.040000	.490196	.924556	1.886095	.530196	2
3	1.124864	3.121600	.320349	.888996	2.775091	.360349	3
4	1.169859	4.246464	.235490	.854804	3.629895	.275490	4
5	1.216653	5.416323	.184627	.821927	4.451822	.224627	5
6	1.265319	6.632975	.150762	.790315	5.242137	.190762	6
7	1.315932	7.898294	.126610	.759918	6.002055	.166610	7
8	1.368569	9.214226	.108528	.730690	6.732745	.148528	8
9	1.423312	10.582795	.094493	.702587	7.435332	.134493	9
10	1.480244	12.006107	.083291	.675564	8.110896	.123291	10
11	1.539454	13.486351	.074149	.649581	8.760477	.114149	11
12	1.601032	15.025805	.066552	.624597	9.385074	.106552	12
13	1.665074	16.626838	.060144	.600574	9.985648	.100144	13
14	1.731676	18.291911	.054669	.577475	10.563123	.094669	14
15	1.800944	20.023588	.049941	.555265	11.118387	.089941	15
16	1.872981	21.824531	.045820	.533908	11.652296	.085820	16
17	1.947900	23.697512	.042199	.513373	12.165669	.082199	17
18	2.025817	25.645413	.038993	.493628	12.659297	.078993	18
19	2.106849	27.671229	.036139	.474642	13.133939	.076139	19
20	2.191123	29.778079	.033582	.456387	13.590326	.073582	20
21	2.278768	31.969202	.031280	.438834	14.029160	.071280	21
22	2.369919	34.247970	.029199	.421955	14.451115	.069199	22
23	2.464716	36.617889	.027309	.405726	14.856842	.067309	23
24	2.563304	39.082604	.025587	.390121	15.246963	.065587	24
25	2.665836	41.645908	.024012	.375117	15.622080	.064012	25
26	2.772470	44.311745	.022567	.360689	15.982769	.062567	26
27	2.883369	47.084214	.021239	.346817	16.329586	.061239	27
28	2.998703	49.967583	.020013	.333477	16.663063	.060013	28
29	3.118651	52.966286	.018880	.320651	16.983715	.058880	29
30	3.243398	56.084938	.017830	.308319	17.292033	.057830	30
31	3.373133	59.328335	.016855	.296460	17.588494	.056855	31
32	3.508059	62.701469	.015949	.285058	17.873551	.055949	32
33	3.648381	66.209527	.015104	.274094	18.147646	.055104	33
34	3.794316	69.857909	.014315	.263552	18.411198	.054315	34
35	3.946089	73.652225	.013577	.253415	18.664613	.053577	35
36	4.103933	77.598314	.012887	.243669	18.908282	.052887	36
37	4.268090	81.702246	.012240	.234297	19.142579	.052240	37
38	4.438813	85.970336	.011632	.225285	19.367864	.051632	38
39	4.616366	90.409150	.011061	.216621	19.584485	.051061	39
40	4.801021	95.025516	.010523	.208289	19.792774	.050523	40
41	4.993061	99.826536	.010017	.200278	19.993052	.050017	41
42	5.192784	104.819540	.009540	.192575	20.185627	.049540	42
43	5.400495	110.012382	.009090	.185168	20.370795	.049090	43
44	5.616515	115.412877	.008665	.178046	20.548841	.048665	44
45	5.841176	121.029392	.008262	.171198	20.720040	.048262	45
46	6.074823	126.870568	.007882	.164614	20.884654	.047882	46
47	6.317816	132.945390	.007522	.158283	21.042936	.047522	47
48	6.570528	139.263206	.007181	.152195	21.195131	.047181	48
49	6.833349	145.833734	.006857	.146341	21.341472	.046857	49
50	7.106683	152.667084	.006550	.140713	21.482185	.046550	50
51	7.390951	159.773767	.006259	.135301	21.617485	.046259	51
52	7.686589	167.164718	.005982	.130097	21.747582	.045982	52
53	7.994052	174.851306	.005719	.125093	21.872675	.045719	53
54	8.313814	182.845359	.005469	.120282	21.992957	.045469	54
55	8.646367	191.159173	.005231	.115656	22.108612	.045231	55
56	8.992222	199.805540	.005005	.111207	22.219819	.045005	56
57	9.351910	208.797761	.004789	.106930	22.326749	.044789	57
58	9.725987	218.149672	.004584	.102817	22.429567	.044584	58
59	10.115026	227.875659	.004388	.098863	22.528430	.044388	59
60	10.519627	237.990685	.004202	.095060	22.623490	.044202	60

5% ANNUAL COMPOUND INTEREST TABLE 5%

EFFECTIVE RATE = 5% BASE = 1.05

	1 AMOUNT OF 1 AT COMPOUND INTEREST $s^n = (1+i)^n$	2 ACCUMULATION OF 1 PER PERIOD $s_{\overline{n}|} = \dfrac{s^n-1}{i}$	3 SINKING FUND FACTOR $1 \cdot s_{\overline{n}|} = \dfrac{i}{s^n-1}$	4 PRES. VALUE REVERSION OF 1 $v^n = \dfrac{1}{s^n}$	5 PRESENT VALUE ORD. ANNUITY 1 PER PERIOD $a_{\overline{n}|} = \dfrac{1-v^n}{i}$	6 INSTALMENT TO AMORTIZE 1 $1 \cdot a_{\overline{n}|} = \dfrac{i}{1-v^n}$	n
YEARS							YEARS
1	1.050000	1.000000	1.000000	.952381	.952381	1.050000	1
2	1.102500	2.050000	.487805	.907029	1.859410	.537805	2
3	1.157625	3.152500	.317209	.863838	2.723248	.367209	3
4	1.215506	4.310125	.232012	.822702	3.545951	.282012	4
5	1.276282	5.525631	.180975	.783526	4.329477	.230975	5
6	1.340096	6.801913	.147017	.746215	5.075692	.197017	6
7	1.407100	8.142008	.122820	.710681	5.786373	.172820	7
8	1.477455	9.549109	.104722	.676839	6.463213	.154722	8
9	1.551328	11.026564	.090690	.644609	7.107822	.140690	9
10	1.628895	12.577893	.079505	.613913	7.721735	.129505	10
11	1.710339	14.206787	.070389	.584679	8.306414	.120389	11
12	1.795856	15.917127	.062825	.556837	8.863252	.112825	12
13	1.885649	17.712983	.056456	.530321	9.393573	.106456	13
14	1.979932	19.598632	.051024	.505068	9.898641	.101024	14
15	2.078928	21.578564	.046342	.481017	10.379658	.096342	15
16	2.182875	23.657492	.042270	.458112	10.837770	.092270	16
17	2.292018	25.840366	.038699	.436297	11.274066	.088699	17
18	2.406619	28.132385	.035546	.415521	11.689587	.085546	18
19	2.526950	30.539004	.032745	.395734	12.085321	.082745	19
20	2.653298	33.065954	.030243	.376889	12.462210	.080243	20
21	2.785963	35.719252	.027996	.358942	12.821153	.077996	21
22	2.925261	38.505214	.025971	.341850	13.163003	.075971	22
23	3.071524	41.430475	.024137	.325571	13.488574	.074137	23
24	3.225100	44.501999	.022471	.310068	13.798642	.072471	24
25	3.386355	47.727099	.020952	.295303	14.093945	.070952	25
26	3.555673	51.113454	.019564	.281241	14.375185	.069564	26
27	3.733456	54.669126	.018292	.267848	14.643034	.068292	27
28	3.920129	58.402583	.017123	.255094	14.898127	.067123	28
29	4.116136	62.322712	.016046	.242946	15.141074	.066046	29
30	4.321942	66.438848	.015051	.231377	15.372451	.065051	30
31	4.538039	70.760790	.014132	.220359	15.592811	.064132	31
32	4.764941	75.298829	.013280	.209866	15.802677	.063280	32
33	5.003189	80.063771	.012490	.199873	16.002549	.062490	33
34	5.253348	85.066959	.011755	.190355	16.192904	.061755	34
35	5.516015	90.320307	.011072	.181290	16.374194	.061072	35
36	5.791816	95.836323	.010434	.172657	16.546852	.060434	36
37	6.081407	101.628139	.009840	.164436	16.711287	.059840	37
38	6.385477	107.709546	.009284	.156605	16.867893	.059284	38
39	6.704751	114.095023	.008765	.149148	17.017041	.058765	39
40	7.039989	120.799774	.008278	.142046	17.159086	.058278	40
41	7.391988	127.839763	.007822	.135282	17.294368	.057822	41
42	7.761588	135.231751	.007395	.128840	17.423208	.057395	42
43	8.149667	142.993339	.006993	.122704	17.545912	.056993	43
44	8.557150	151.143006	.006616	.116861	17.662745	.056616	44
45	8.985008	159.700156	.006262	.111297	17.774070	.056262	45
46	9.434258	168.685164	.005928	.105997	17.880067	.055928	46
47	9.905971	178.119422	.005614	.100949	17.981016	.055614	47
48	10.401270	188.025393	.005318	.096142	18.077158	.055318	48
49	10.921333	198.426663	.005040	.091564	18.168722	.055040	49
50	11.467400	209.347996	.004777	.087204	18.255925	.054777	50
51	12.040770	220.815395	.004529	.083051	18.338977	.054529	51
52	12.642808	232.856165	.004294	.079096	18.418073	.054294	52
53	13.274949	245.498974	.004073	.075330	18.493403	.054073	53
54	13.938696	258.773922	.003864	.071743	18.565146	.053864	54
55	14.635631	272.712618	.003667	.068326	18.633472	.053667	55
56	15.367412	287.348249	.003480	.065073	18.698545	.053480	56
57	16.135783	302.715662	.003303	.061974	18.760519	.053303	57
58	16.942572	318.851445	.003136	.059023	18.819542	.053136	58
59	17.789701	335.794017	.002978	.056212	18.875754	.052978	59
60	18.679186	353.583718	.002828	.053536	18.929290	.052828	60

6% ANNUAL COMPOUND INTEREST TABLE 6%
EFFECTIVE RATE = 6%   BASE = 1.06

	1 AMOUNT OF 1 AT COMPOUND INTEREST $S^n = (1+i)^n$	2 ACCUMULATION OF 1 PER PERIOD $S_{\overline{n}|} = \frac{S^n - 1}{i}$	3 SINKING FUND FACTOR $1/S_{\overline{n}|} = \frac{i}{S^n - 1}$	4 PRES. VALUE REVERSION OF 1 $v^n = \frac{1}{S^n}$	5 PRESENT VALUE ORD. ANNUITY 1 PER PERIOD $a_{\overline{n}|} = \frac{1 - v^n}{i}$	6 INSTALMENT TO AMORTIZE 1 $1/a_{\overline{n}|} = \frac{i}{1 - v^n}$	n YEARS
1	1.060000	1.000000	1.000000	.943396	.943396	1.060000	1
2	1.123600	2.060000	.485437	.889996	1.833393	.545437	2
3	1.191016	3.183600	.314110	.839619	2.673012	.374110	3
4	1.262477	4.374616	.228591	.792094	3.465106	.288591	4
5	1.338226	5.637093	.177396	.747258	4.212364	.237396	5
6	1.418519	6.975319	.143363	.704961	4.917324	.203363	6
7	1.503630	8.393838	.119135	.665057	5.582381	.179135	7
8	1.593848	9.897468	.101036	.627412	6.209794	.161036	8
9	1.689479	11.491316	.087022	.591898	6.801692	.147022	9
10	1.790848	13.180795	.075868	.558395	7.360087	.135868	10
11	1.898299	14.971643	.066793	.526788	7.886875	.126793	11
12	2.012196	16.869941	.059277	.496969	8.383844	.119277	12
13	2.132928	18.882138	.052960	.468839	8.852683	.112960	13
14	2.260904	21.015066	.047585	.442301	9.294984	.107585	14
15	2.396558	23.275970	.042963	.417265	9.712249	.102963	15
16	2.540352	25.672528	.038952	.393646	10.105895	.098952	16
17	2.692773	28.212880	.035445	.371364	10.477260	.095445	17
18	2.854339	30.905653	.032357	.350344	10.827603	.092357	18
19	3.025600	33.759992	.029621	.330513	11.158116	.089621	19
20	3.207135	36.785591	.027185	.311805	11.469921	.087185	20
21	3.399564	39.992727	.025005	.294155	11.764077	.085005	21
22	3.603537	43.392290	.023046	.277505	12.041582	.083046	22
23	3.819750	46.995828	.021278	.261797	12.303379	.081278	23
24	4.048935	50.815577	.019679	.246979	12.550358	.079679	24
25	4.291871	54.864512	.018227	.232999	12.783356	.078227	25
26	4.549383	59.156383	.016904	.219810	13.003166	.076904	26
27	4.822346	63.705766	.015697	.207368	13.210534	.075697	27
28	5.111687	68.528112	.014593	.195630	13.406164	.074593	28
29	5.418388	73.639798	.013580	.184557	13.590721	.073580	29
30	5.743491	79.058186	.012649	.174110	13.764831	.072649	30
31	6.088101	84.801677	.011792	.164255	13.929086	.071792	31
32	6.453387	90.889778	.011002	.154957	14.084043	.071002	32
33	6.840590	97.343165	.010273	.146186	14.230230	.070273	33
34	7.251025	104.183755	.009598	.137912	14.368141	.069598	34
35	7.686087	111.434780	.008974	.130105	14.498246	.068974	35
36	8.147252	119.120867	.008395	.122741	14.620987	.068395	36
37	8.636087	127.268119	.007857	.115793	14.736780	.067857	37
38	9.154252	135.904206	.007358	.109239	14.846019	.067358	38
39	9.703507	145.058458	.006894	.103056	14.949075	.066894	39
40	10.285718	154.761966	.006462	.097222	15.046297	.066462	40
41	10.902861	165.047684	.006059	.091719	15.138016	.066059	41
42	11.557033	175.950545	.005683	.086527	15.224543	.065683	42
43	12.250455	187.507577	.005333	.081630	15.306173	.065333	43
44	12.985482	199.758032	.005006	.077009	15.383182	.065006	44
45	13.764611	212.743514	.004700	.072650	15.455832	.064700	45
46	14.590487	226.508125	.004415	.068538	15.524370	.064415	46
47	15.465917	241.098612	.004148	.064658	15.589028	.064148	47
48	16.393872	256.564529	.003898	.060998	15.650027	.063898	48
49	17.377504	272.958401	.003664	.057546	15.707572	.063664	49
50	18.420154	290.335905	.003444	.054288	15.761861	.063444	50
51	19.525364	308.756059	.003239	.051215	15.813076	.063239	51
52	20.696885	328.281422	.003046	.048316	15.861393	.063046	52
53	21.938698	348.978308	.002866	.045582	15.906974	.062866	53
54	23.255020	370.917006	.002696	.043001	15.949976	.062696	54
55	24.650322	394.172027	.002537	.040567	15.990543	.062537	55
56	26.129341	418.822348	.002388	.038271	16.028814	.062388	56
57	27.697101	444.951689	.002247	.036105	16.064919	.062247	57
58	29.358927	472.648790	.002116	.034061	16.098980	.062116	58
59	31.120463	502.007718	.001992	.032133	16.131113	.061992	59
60	32.987691	533.128181	.001876	.030314	16.161428	.061876	60

7% ANNUAL COMPOUND INTEREST TABLE 7%

EFFECTIVE RATE = 7%   BASE = 1.07

YEARS	1 AMOUNT OF I AT COMPOUND INTEREST $S^n = (1+i)^n$	2 ACCUMULATION OF I PER PERIOD $S_{\overline{n}} = \frac{S^n - 1}{i}$	3 SINKING FUND FACTOR $1/S_{\overline{n}} = \frac{i}{S^n - 1}$	4 PRES. VALUE REVERSION OF I $v^n = \frac{1}{S^n}$	5 PRESENT VALUE ORD. ANNUITY I PER PERIOD $a_{\overline{n}} = \frac{1-v^n}{i}$	6 INSTALMENT TO AMORTIZE I $1/a_{\overline{n}} = \frac{i}{1-v^n}$	n YEARS
1	1.070000	1.000000	1.000000	.934579	.934579	1.070000	1
2	1.144900	2.070000	.483092	.873439	1.808018	.553092	2
3	1.225043	3.214900	.311052	.816298	2.624316	.381052	3
4	1.310796	4.439943	.225228	.762895	3.387211	.295228	4
5	1.402552	5.750739	.173891	.712986	4.100197	.243891	5
6	1.500730	7.153291	.139796	.666342	4.766540	.209796	6
7	1.605781	8.654021	.115553	.622750	5.389289	.185553	7
8	1.718186	10.259803	.097468	.582009	5.971299	.167468	8
9	1.838459	11.977989	.083486	.543934	6.515232	.153486	9
10	1.967151	13.816448	.072378	.508349	7.023582	.142378	10
11	2.104852	15.783599	.063357	.475093	7.498674	.133357	11
12	2.252192	17.888451	.055902	.444012	7.942686	.125902	12
13	2.409845	20.140643	.049651	.414964	8.357651	.119651	13
14	2.578534	22.550488	.044345	.387817	8.745468	.114345	14
15	2.759032	25.129022	.039795	.362446	9.107914	.109795	15
16	2.952164	27.888054	.035858	.338735	9.446649	.105858	16
17	3.158815	30.840217	.032425	.316574	9.763223	.102425	17
18	3.379932	33.999033	.029413	.295864	10.059087	.099413	18
19	3.616528	37.378965	.026753	.276508	10.335595	.096753	19
20	3.869684	40.995492	.024393	.258419	10.594014	.094393	20
21	4.140562	44.865177	.022289	.241513	10.835527	.092289	21
22	4.430402	49.005739	.020406	.225713	11.061241	.090406	22
23	4.740530	53.436141	.018714	.210947	11.272187	.088714	23
24	5.072367	58.176671	.017189	.197147	11.469334	.087189	24
25	5.427433	63.249038	.015811	.184249	11.653583	.085811	25
26	5.807353	68.676470	.014561	.172195	11.825779	.084561	26
27	6.213868	74.483823	.013426	.160930	11.986709	.083426	27
28	6.648838	80.697691	.012392	.150402	12.137111	.082392	28
29	7.114257	87.346529	.011449	.140563	12.277674	.081449	29
30	7.612255	94.460786	.010586	.131367	12.409041	.080586	30
31	8.145113	102.073041	.009797	.122773	12.531814	.079797	31
32	8.715271	110.218154	.009073	.114741	12.646555	.079073	32
33	9.325340	118.933425	.008408	.107235	12.753790	.078408	33
34	9.978114	128.258765	.007797	.100219	12.854009	.077797	34
35	10.676581	138.236878	.007234	.093663	12.947672	.077234	35
36	11.423942	148.913460	.006715	.087535	13.035208	.076715	36
37	12.223618	160.337402	.006237	.081809	13.117017	.076237	37
38	13.079271	172.561020	.005795	.076457	13.193473	.075795	38
39	13.994820	185.640292	.005387	.071455	13.264928	.075387	39
40	14.974458	199.635112	.005009	.066780	13.331709	.075009	40
41	16.022670	214.609570	.004660	.062412	13.394120	.074660	41
42	17.144257	230.632240	.004336	.058329	13.452449	.074336	42
43	18.344355	247.776496	.004036	.054513	13.506962	.074036	43
44	19.628460	266.120851	.003758	.050946	13.557908	.073758	44
45	21.002452	285.749311	.003500	.047613	13.605522	.073500	45
46	22.472623	306.751763	.003260	.044499	13.650020	.073260	46
47	24.045707	329.224386	.003037	.041587	13.691608	.073037	47
48	25.728907	353.270093	.002831	.038867	13.730474	.072831	48
49	27.529930	378.998999	.002639	.036324	13.766799	.072639	49
50	29.457025	406.528929	.002460	.033948	13.800746	.072460	50
51	31.519017	435.985955	.002294	.031727	13.832473	.072294	51
52	33.725348	467.504971	.002139	.029651	13.862124	.072139	52
53	36.086122	501.230319	.001995	.027711	13.889836	.071995	53
54	38.612151	537.316442	.001861	.025899	13.915735	.071861	54
55	41.315001	575.928593	.001736	.024204	13.939939	.071736	55
56	44.207052	617.243594	.001620	.022621	13.962560	.071620	56
57	47.301545	661.450646	.001512	.021141	13.983701	.071512	57
58	50.612653	708.752191	.001411	.019758	14.003459	.071411	58
59	54.155539	759.364844	.001317	.018465	14.021924	.071317	59
60	57.946427	813.520383	.001229	.017257	14.039181	.071229	60

8% ANNUAL COMPOUND INTEREST TABLE 8%

EFFECTIVE RATE = 8%   BASE = 1.08

YEARS	1 AMOUNT OF I AT COMPOUND INTEREST $S^n = (1+i)^n$	2 ACCUMULATION OF I PER PERIOD $S_{\overline{n}|} = \frac{S^n - 1}{i}$	3 SINKING FUND FACTOR $1 \cdot S_{\overline{n}|} = \frac{i}{S^n - 1}$	4 PRES. VALUE REVERSION OF I $v^n = \frac{1}{S^n}$	5 PRESENT VALUE ORD. ANNUITY 1 PER PERIOD $a_{\overline{n}|} = \frac{1-v^n}{i}$	6 INSTALMENT TO AMORTIZE I $1/a_{\overline{n}|} = \frac{i}{1-v^n}$	n YEARS
1	1.080000	1.000000	1.000000	.925926	.925926	1.080000	1
2	1.166400	2.080000	.480769	.857339	1.783265	.560769	2
3	1.259712	3.246400	.308034	.793832	2.577097	.388034	3
4	1.360489	4.506112	.221921	.735030	3.312127	.301921	4
5	1.469328	5.866601	.170456	.680583	3.992710	.250456	5
6	1.586874	7.335929	.136315	.630170	4.622880	.216315	6
7	1.713824	8.922803	.112072	.583490	5.206370	.192072	7
8	1.850930	10.636628	.094015	.540269	5.746639	.174015	8
9	1.999005	12.487558	.080080	.500249	6.246888	.160080	9
10	2.158925	14.486562	.069029	.463193	6.710081	.149029	10
11	2.331639	16.645487	.060076	.428883	7.138964	.140076	11
12	2.518170	18.977126	.052695	.397114	7.536078	.132695	12
13	2.719624	21.495297	.046522	.367698	7.903776	.126522	13
14	2.937194	24.214920	.041297	.340461	8.244237	.121297	14
15	3.172169	27.152114	.036830	.315242	8.559479	.116830	15
16	3.425943	30.324283	.032977	.291890	8.851369	.112977	16
17	3.700018	33.750226	.029629	.270269	9.121638	.109629	17
18	3.996019	37.450244	.026702	.250249	9.371887	.106702	18
19	4.315701	41.446263	.024128	.231712	9.603599	.104128	19
20	4.660957	45.761964	.021852	.214548	9.818147	.101852	20
21	5.033834	50.422921	.019832	.198656	10.016803	.099832	21
22	5.436540	55.456755	.018032	.183941	10.200744	.098032	22
23	5.871464	60.893296	.016422	.170315	10.371059	.096422	23
24	6.341181	66.764759	.014978	.157699	10.528758	.094978	24
25	6.848475	73.105940	.013679	.146018	10.674776	.093679	25
26	7.396353	79.954415	.012507	.135202	10.809978	.092507	26
27	7.988061	87.350768	.011448	.125187	10.935165	.091448	27
28	8.627106	95.338830	.010489	.115914	11.051078	.090489	28
29	9.317275	103.965936	.009619	.107328	11.158406	.089619	29
30	10.062657	113.283211	.008827	.099377	11.257783	.088827	30
31	10.867669	123.345868	.008107	.092016	11.349799	.088107	31
32	11.737083	134.213537	.007451	.085200	11.434999	.087451	32
33	12.676050	145.950620	.006852	.078889	11.513888	.086852	33
34	13.690134	158.626670	.006304	.073045	11.586934	.086304	34
35	14.785344	172.316804	.005803	.067635	11.654568	.085803	35
36	15.968172	187.102148	.005345	.062625	11.717193	.085345	36
37	17.245626	203.070320	.004924	.057986	11.775179	.084924	37
38	18.625276	220.315945	.004539	.053690	11.828869	.084539	38
39	20.115298	238.941221	.004185	.049713	11.878582	.084185	39
40	21.724521	259.056519	.003860	.046031	11.924613	.083860	40
41	23.462483	280.781040	.003561	.042621	11.967235	.083561	41
42	25.339482	304.243523	.003287	.039464	12.006699	.083287	42
43	27.366640	329.583005	.003034	.036541	12.043240	.083034	43
44	29.555972	356.949646	.002802	.033834	12.077074	.082802	44
45	31.920449	386.505617	.002587	.031328	12.108401	.082587	45
46	34.474085	418.426067	.002390	.029007	12.137409	.082390	46
47	37.232012	452.900152	.002208	.026859	12.164267	.082208	47
48	40.210573	490.132164	.002040	.024869	12.189136	.082040	48
49	43.427419	530.342737	.001886	.023027	12.212163	.081886	49
50	46.901613	573.770156	.001743	.021321	12.233485	.081743	50
51	50.653742	620.671769	.001611	.019742	12.253227	.081611	51
52	54.706041	671.325510	.001490	.018280	12.271506	.081490	52
53	59.082524	726.031551	.001377	.016925	12.288432	.081377	53
54	63.809126	785.114075	.001274	.015672	12.304103	.081274	54
55	68.913856	848.923201	.001178	.014511	12.318614	.081178	55
56	74.426965	917.837058	.001090	.013436	12.332050	.081090	56
57	80.381122	992.264022	.001008	.012441	12.344491	.081008	57
58	86.811612	1072.645144	.000932	.011519	12.356010	.080932	58
59	93.756540	1159.456755	.000862	.010666	12.366676	.080862	59
60	101.257064	1253.213296	.000798	.009876	12.376552	.080798	60

9% **ANNUAL COMPOUND INTEREST TABLE** 9%

EFFECTIVE RATE = 9% BASE = 1.09

YEARS	1 AMOUNT OF I AT COMPOUND INTEREST $S^n = (1+i)^n$	2 ACCUMULATION OF I PER PERIOD $S_{\overline{n}|} = \frac{S^n - 1}{i}$	3 SINKING FUND FACTOR $1/S_{\overline{n}|} = \frac{i}{S^n - 1}$	4 PRES. VALUE REVERSION OF I $v^n = \frac{1}{S^n}$	5 PRESENT VALUE ORD. ANNUITY 1 PER PERIOD $a_{\overline{n}|} = \frac{1-v^n}{i}$	6 INSTALMENT TO AMORTIZE I $1/a_{\overline{n}|} = \frac{i}{1-v^n}$	n YEARS
1	1.090000	1.000000	1.000000	.917431	.917431	1.090000	1
2	1.188100	2.090000	.478469	.841680	1.759111	.568469	2
3	1.295029	3.278100	.305055	.772183	2.531295	.395055	3
4	1.411582	4.573129	.218669	.708425	3.239720	.308669	4
5	1.538624	5.984711	.167092	.649931	3.889651	.257092	5
6	1.667100	7.523335	.132920	.596267	4.485919	.222920	6
7	1.828039	9.200435	.108691	.547034	5.032953	.198691	7
8	1.992563	11.028474	.090674	.501866	5.534819	.180674	8
9	2.171893	13.021036	.076799	.460428	5.995247	.166799	9
10	2.367364	15.192930	.065820	.422411	6.417658	.155820	10
11	2.580426	17.560293	.056947	.387533	6.805191	.146947	11
12	2.812665	20.140720	.049651	.355535	7.160725	.139651	12
13	3.065805	22.953385	.043567	.326179	7.486904	.133567	13
14	3.341727	26.019189	.038433	.299246	7.786150	.128433	14
15	3.642482	29.360916	.034059	.274538	8.060688	.124059	15
16	3.970306	33.003399	.030300	.251870	8.312558	.120300	16
17	4.327633	36.973705	.027046	.231073	8.543631	.117046	17
18	4.717120	41.301338	.024212	.211994	8.755625	.114212	18
19	5.141661	46.018458	.021730	.194490	8.950115	.111730	19
20	5.604411	51.160120	.019546	.178431	9.128546	.109546	20
21	6.108808	56.764530	.017617	.163698	9.292244	.107617	21
22	6.658600	62.873338	.015905	.150182	9.442425	.105905	22
23	7.257874	69.531939	.014382	.137781	9.580207	.104382	23
24	7.911083	76.789813	.013023	.126405	9.706612	.103023	24
25	8.623081	84.700896	.011806	.115968	9.822580	.101806	25
26	9.399158	93.323977	.010715	.106393	9.928972	.100715	26
27	10.245082	102.723135	.009735	.097608	10.026580	.099735	27
28	11.167140	112.968217	.008852	.089548	10.116128	.098852	28
29	12.172182	124.135356	.008056	.082155	10.198283	.098056	29
30	13.267678	136.307539	.007336	.075371	10.273654	.097336	30
31	14.461770	149.575217	.006686	.069148	10.342802	.096686	31
32	15.763329	164.036987	.006096	.063438	10.406240	.096096	32
33	17.182028	179.800315	.005562	.058200	10.464441	.095562	33
34	18.728411	196.982344	.005077	.053395	10.517835	.095077	34
35	20.413968	215.710755	.004636	.048986	10.566821	.094636	35
36	22.251225	236.124723	.004235	.044941	10.611763	.094235	36
37	24.253835	258.375948	.003870	.041231	10.652993	.093870	37
38	26.436680	282.629783	.003538	.037826	10.690820	.093538	38
39	28.815982	309.066463	.003236	.034703	10.725523	.093236	39
40	31.409420	337.882445	.002960	.031838	10.757360	.092960	40
41	34.236268	369.291865	.002708	.029209	10.786569	.092708	41
42	37.317532	403.528133	.002478	.026797	10.813366	.092478	42
43	40.676110	440.845665	.002268	.024584	10.837951	.092268	43
44	44.336960	481.521775	.002077	.022555	10.860505	.092077	44
45	48.327286	525.858735	.001902	.020692	10.881197	.091902	45
46	52.676742	574.186021	.001742	.018984	10.900181	.091742	46
47	57.417649	626.862762	.001595	.017416	10.917597	.091595	47
48	62.585237	684.280411	.001461	.015978	10.933575	.091461	48
49	68.217908	746.865648	.001339	.014659	10.948234	.091339	49
50	74.357520	815.083556	.001227	.013449	10.961683	.091227	50
51	81.049697	889.441077	.001124	.012338	10.974021	.091124	51
52	88.344170	970.490773	.001030	.011319	10.985340	.091030	52
53	96.295145	1058.834943	.000944	.010385	10.995725	.090944	53
54	104.961708	1155.130088	.000866	.009527	11.005252	.090866	54
55	114.408262	1260.091796	.000794	.008741	11.013993	.090794	55
56	124.705005	1374.500057	.000728	.008019	11.022012	.090728	56
57	135.928456	1499.205063	.000667	.007357	11.029369	.090667	57
58	148.162017	1635.133518	.000612	.006749	11.036118	.090612	58
59	161.496598	1783.295535	.000561	.006192	11.042310	.090561	59
60	176.031292	1944.792133	.000514	.005681	11.047991	.090514	60

10%   ANNUAL COMPOUND INTEREST TABLE   10%

EFFECTIVE RATE = 10%   BASE = 1.10

	1 AMOUNT OF 1 AT COMPOUND INTEREST $s^n = (1+i)^n$	2 ACCUMULATION OF 1 PER PERIOD $s_{\overline{n}|} = \dfrac{s^n - 1}{i}$	3 SINKING FUND FACTOR $1/s_{\overline{n}|} = \dfrac{i}{s^n - 1}$	4 PRES. VALUE REVERSION OF 1 $v^n = \dfrac{1}{s^n}$	5 PRESENT VALUE ORD. ANNUITY 1 PER PERIOD $a_{\overline{n}|} = \dfrac{1 - v^n}{i}$	6 INSTALMENT TO AMORTIZE 1 $1/a_{\overline{n}|} = \dfrac{i}{1 - v^n}$	n YEARS
YEARS							
1	1.100000	1.000000	1.000000	.909091	.909091	1.100000	1
2	1.210000	2.100000	.476190	.826446	1.735537	.576190	2
3	1.331000	3.310000	.302115	.751315	2.486852	.402115	3
4	1.464100	4.641000	.215471	.683013	3.169865	.315471	4
5	1.610510	6.105100	.163797	.620921	3.790787	.263797	5
6	1.771561	7.715610	.129607	.564474	4.355261	.229607	6
7	1.948717	9.487171	.105405	.513158	4.868419	.205405	7
8	2.143589	11.435888	.087444	.466507	5.334926	.187444	8
9	2.357948	13.579477	.073641	.424098	5.759024	.173641	9
10	2.593742	15.937425	.062745	.385543	6.144567	.162745	10
11	2.853117	18.531167	.053963	.350494	6.495061	.153963	11
12	3.138428	21.384284	.046763	.318631	6.813692	.146763	12
13	3.452271	24.522712	.040779	.289664	7.103356	.140779	13
14	3.797498	27.974983	.035746	.263331	7.366687	.135746	14
15	4.177248	31.772482	.031474	.239392	7.606080	.131474	15
16	4.594973	35.949730	.027817	.217629	7.823709	.127817	16
17	5.054470	40.544703	.024664	.197845	8.021553	.124664	17
18	5.559917	45.599173	.021930	.179859	8.201412	.121930	18
19	6.115909	51.159090	.019547	.163508	8.364920	.119547	19
20	6.727500	57.274999	.017460	.148644	8.513564	.117460	20
21	7.400250	64.002499	.015624	.135131	8.648694	.115624	21
22	8.140275	71.402749	.014005	.122846	8.771540	.114005	22
23	8.954302	79.543024	.012572	.111678	8.883218	.112572	23
24	9.849733	88.497327	.011300	.101526	8.984744	.111300	24
25	10.834706	98.347059	.010168	.092296	9.077040	.110168	25
26	11.918177	109.181765	.009159	.083905	9.160945	.109159	26
27	13.109994	121.099942	.008258	.076278	9.237223	.108258	27
28	14.420994	134.209936	.007451	.069343	9.306567	.107451	28
29	15.863093	148.630930	.006728	.063039	9.369606	.106728	29
30	17.449402	164.494023	.006079	.057309	9.426914	.106079	30
31	19.194342	181.943425	.005496	.052099	9.479013	.105496	31
32	21.113777	201.137767	.004972	.047362	9.526376	.104972	32
33	23.225154	222.251544	.004499	.043057	9.569432	.104499	33
34	25.547670	245.476699	.004074	.039143	9.608575	.104074	34
35	28.102437	271.024368	.003690	.035584	9.644159	.103690	35
36	30.912681	299.126805	.003343	.032349	9.676508	.103343	36
37	34.003949	330.039486	.003030	.029408	9.705917	.103030	37
38	37.404343	364.043434	.002747	.026735	9.732651	.102747	38
39	41.144778	401.447778	.002491	.024304	9.756956	.102491	39
40	45.259256	442.592556	.002259	.022095	9.779051	.102259	40
41	49.785181	487.851811	.002050	.020086	9.799137	.102050	41
42	54.763699	537.636992	.001860	.018260	9.817397	.101860	42
43	60.240069	592.400692	.001688	.016600	9.833998	.101688	43
44	66.264076	652.640761	.001532	.015091	9.849089	.101532	44
45	72.890484	718.904837	.001391	.013719	9.862808	.101391	45
46	80.179532	791.795321	.001263	.012472	9.875280	.101263	46
47	88.197485	871.974853	.001147	.011338	9.886618	.101147	47
48	97.017234	960.172338	.001041	.010307	9.896926	.101041	48
49	106.718957	1057.189572	.000946	.009370	9.906296	.100946	49
50	117.390853	1163.908529	.000859	.008519	9.914814	.100859	50
51	129.129938	1281.299382	.000780	.007744	9.922559	.100780	51
52	142.042932	1410.429320	.000709	.007040	9.929599	.100709	52
53	156.247225	1552.472252	.000644	.006400	9.935999	.100644	53
54	171.871948	1708.719477	.000585	.005818	9.941817	.100585	54
55	189.059142	1880.591425	.000532	.005289	9.947106	.100532	55
56	207.965057	2069.650562	.000483	.004809	9.951915	.100483	56
57	228.761562	2277.615624	.000439	.004371	9.956286	.100439	57
58	251.637719	2506.377186	.000399	.003974	9.960260	.100399	58
59	276.801490	2758.014905	.000363	.003613	9.963873	.100363	59
60	304.481640	3034.816395	.000330	.003284	9.967157	.100330	60

12 × **ANNUAL** COMPOUND INTEREST TABLE 12 ×

EFFECTIVE RATE = 12%   BASE = 1.1200

	1 AMOUNT OF 1 AT COMPOUND INTEREST $S^n = (1 + i)^n$	2 ACCUMULATION OF 1 PER PERIOD $S_{\overline{n}} = \frac{S^n - 1}{i}$	3 SINKING FUND FACTOR $1/S_{\overline{n}} = \frac{i}{S^n - 1}$	4 PRES. VALUE REVERSION OF 1 $V^n = \frac{1}{S^n}$	5 PRESENT VALUE ORD. ANNUITY 1 PER PERIOD $a_{\overline{n}} = \frac{1 - V^n}{i}$	6 INSTALMENT TO AMORTIZE 1 $1/a_{\overline{n}} = \frac{i}{1 - V^n}$	n
YEARS							YEARS
1	1.120000	1.000000	1.000000	.892857	.892857	1.120000	1
2	1.254400	2.120000	.471698	.797194	1.690051	.591698	2
3	1.404928	3.374400	.296349	.711780	2.401831	.416349	3
4	1.573519	4.779328	.209234	.635518	3.037349	.329234	4
5	1.762342	6.352847	.157410	.567427	3.604776	.277410	5
6	1.973823	8.115189	.123226	.506631	4.111407	.243226	6
7	2.210681	10.089012	.099118	.452349	4.563757	.219118	7
8	2.475963	12.299693	.081303	.403883	4.967640	.201303	8
9	2.773079	14.775656	.067679	.360610	5.328250	.187679	9
10	3.105848	17.548735	.056984	.321973	5.650223	.176984	10
11	3.478550	20.654583	.048415	.287476	5.937699	.168415	11
12	3.895976	24.133133	.041437	.256675	6.194374	.161437	12
13	4.363493	28.029109	.035677	.229174	6.423548	.155677	13
14	4.887112	32.392602	.030871	.204620	6.628168	.150871	14
15	5.473566	37.279715	.026824	.182696	6.810864	.146824	15
16	6.130394	42.753280	.023390	.163122	6.973986	.143390	16
17	6.866041	48.883674	.020457	.145644	7.119630	.140457	17
18	7.689966	55.749715	.017937	.130040	7.249670	.137937	18
19	8.612762	63.439681	.015763	.116107	7.365777	.135763	19
20	9.646293	72.052442	.013879	.103667	7.469444	.133879	20
21	10.803848	81.698736	.012240	.092560	7.562003	.132240	21
22	12.100310	92.502584	.010811	.082643	7.644646	.130811	22
23	13.552347	104.602894	.009560	.073788	7.718434	.129560	23
24	15.178629	118.155241	.008463	.065882	7.784316	.128463	24
25	17.000064	133.333870	.007500	.058823	7.843139	.127500	25
26	19.040072	150.333934	.006652	.052521	7.895660	.126652	26
27	21.324881	169.374007	.005904	.046894	7.942554	.125904	27
28	23.883866	190.698887	.005244	.041869	7.984423	.125244	28
29	26.749930	214.582754	.004660	.037383	8.021806	.124660	29
30	29.959922	241.332684	.004144	.033378	8.055184	.124144	30
31	33.555113	271.292606	.003686	.029802	8.084986	.123686	31
32	37.581726	304.847719	.003280	.026609	8.111594	.123280	32
33	42.091533	342.429445	.002920	.023758	8.135352	.122920	33
34	47.142517	384.520979	.002601	.021212	8.156564	.122601	34
35	52.799620	431.663496	.002317	.018940	8.175504	.122317	35
36	59.135574	484.463116	.002064	.016910	8.192414	.122064	36
37	66.231843	543.598690	.001840	.015098	8.207513	.121840	37
38	74.179664	609.830532	.001640	.013481	8.220993	.121640	38
39	83.081224	684.010196	.001462	.012036	8.233030	.121462	39
40	93.050970	767.091420	.001304	.010747	8.243777	.121304	40
41	104.217087	860.142390	.001163	.009595	8.253372	.121163	41
42	116.723137	964.359477	.001037	.008567	8.261939	.121037	42
43	130.729914	1081.082614	.000925	.007649	8.269589	.120925	43
44	146.417503	1211.812527	.000825	.006830	8.276418	.120825	44
45	163.987604	1358.230031	.000736	.006098	8.282516	.120736	45
46	183.666116	1522.217634	.000657	.005445	8.287961	.120657	46
47	205.706050	1705.883750	.000586	.004861	8.292822	.120586	47
48	230.390776	1911.589800	.000523	.004340	8.297163	.120523	48
49	258.037669	2141.980576	.000467	.003875	8.301038	.120467	49
50	289.002189	2400.018245	.000417	.003460	8.304498	.120417	50
51	323.682452	2689.020434	.000372	.003089	8.307588	.120372	51
52	362.524346	3012.702886	.000332	.002758	8.310346	.120332	52
53	406.027268	3375.227233	.000296	.002463	8.312809	.120296	53
54	454.750540	3781.254500	.000264	.002199	8.315008	.120264	54
55	509.320605	4236.005040	.000236	.001963	8.316972	.120236	55
56	570.439077	4745.325645	.000211	.001753	8.318725	.120211	56
57	638.891767	5315.764723	.000188	.001565	8.320290	.120188	57
58	715.558779	5954.656489	.000168	.001398	8.321687	.120168	58
59	801.425832	6670.215267	.000150	.001248	8.322935	.120150	59
60	897.596932	7471.641099	.000134	.001114	8.324049	.120134	60

ANNUAL COMPOUND INTEREST TABLE 14%
EFFECTIVE RATE = 14%   BASE = 1.14

YEARS	1 AMOUNT OF 1 AT COMPOUND INTEREST $S^n=(1+i)^n$	2 ACCUMULATION OF 1 PER PERIOD $S_{\overline{n}|}=\frac{S^n-1}{i}$	3 SINKING FUND FACTOR $1/S_{\overline{n}|}=\frac{i}{S^n-1}$	4 PRES. VALUE REVERSION OF 1 $V^n=\frac{1}{S^n}$	5 PRESENT VALUE ORD. ANNUITY 1 PER PERIOD $a_{\overline{n}|}=\frac{1-V^n}{i}$	6 INSTALMENT TO AMORTIZE 1 $1/a_{\overline{n}|}=\frac{i}{1-V^n}$
1	1.140000	1.0000	1.000000	.877193	.877193	1.140000
2	1.299600	2.1400	.467290	.769468	1.646661	.607290
3	1.481544	3.4396	.290731	.674971	2.321623	.430731
4	1.688960	4.9211	.203205	.592080	2.913712	.343205
5	1.925415	6.6101	.151284	.519368	3.433080	.291284
6	2.194973	8.5355	.117158	.455587	3.888667	.257158
7	2.502269	10.7305	.093192	.399637	4.288304	.233192
8	2.852586	13.2328	.075570	.350559	4.638863	.215570
9	3.251949	16.0853	.062168	.307508	4.946371	.202168
10	3.707221	19.3373	.051714	.269744	5.216115	.191714
11	4.226232	23.0445	.043394	.236617	5.452732	.183394
12	4.817905	27.2707	.036669	.207559	5.660291	.176669
13	5.492411	32.0887	.031164	.182069	5.842360	.171164
14	6.261349	37.5811	.026609	.159710	6.002070	.166609
15	7.137938	43.8424	.022809	.140096	6.142166	.162809
16	8.137249	50.9804	.019615	.122892	6.265058	.159615
17	9.276464	59.1176	.016915	.107800	6.372858	.156915
18	10.575169	68.3941	.014621	.094561	6.467419	.154621
19	12.055693	78.9692	.012663	.082948	6.550367	.152663
20	13.743490	91.0249	.010986	.072762	6.623129	.150986
21	15.667578	104.7684	.009545	.063826	6.686955	.149545
22	17.861039	120.4360	.008303	.055988	6.742943	.148303
23	20.361585	138.2970	.007231	.049112	6.792055	.147231
24	23.212207	158.6586	.006303	.043081	6.835136	.146303
25	26.461916	181.8708	.005498	.037790	6.872926	.145498
26	30.166584	208.3327	.004800	.033149	6.906075	.144800
27	34.389906	238.4993	.004193	.029078	6.935153	.144193
28	39.204492	272.8892	.003665	.025507	6.960660	.143665
29	44.693121	312.0937	.003204	.022375	6.983035	.143204
30	50.950158	356.7868	.002803	.019627	7.002662	.142803

ANNUAL COMPOUND INTEREST TABLE 16%
EFFECTIVE RATE = 16%   BASE = 1.16

n YEARS	1 AMOUNT OF 1 AT COMPOUND INTEREST $S^n=(1+i)^n$	2 ACCUMULATION OF 1 PER PERIOD $S_{\overline{n}|}=\frac{S^n-1}{i}$	3 SINKING FUND FACTOR $1/S_{\overline{n}|}=\frac{i}{S^n-1}$	4 PRES. VALUE REVERSION OF 1 $V^n=\frac{1}{S^n}$	5 PRESENT VALUE ORD. ANNUITY 1 PER PERIOD $a_{\overline{n}|}=\frac{1-V^n}{i}$	6 INSTALMENT TO AMORTIZE 1 $1/a_{\overline{n}|}=\frac{i}{1-V^n}$
1	1.160000	1.0000	1.000000	.862068	.862068	1.160000
2	1.345600	2.1600	.462963	.743163	1.605231	.622963
3	1.560896	3.5056	.285257	.640658	2.245889	.445257
4	1.810639	5.0665	.197375	.552291	2.798180	.357375
5	2.100342	6.8771	.145409	.476113	3.274293	.305409
6	2.436396	8.9775	.111390	.410442	3.684735	.271390
7	2.826220	11.4139	.087613	.353829	4.038564	.247613
8	3.278415	14.2401	.070224	.305025	4.343589	.230224
9	3.802961	17.5185	.057083	.262953	4.606542	.217083
10	4.411435	21.3215	.046901	.226684	4.833226	.206901
11	5.117265	25.7329	.038861	.195417	5.028643	.198861
12	5.936027	30.8502	.032415	.168463	5.197106	.192415
13	6.885792	36.7862	.027184	.145227	5.342333	.187184
14	7.987518	43.6720	.022898	.125195	5.467528	.182898
15	9.265521	51.6595	.019358	.107927	5.575455	.179358
16	10.748005	60.9250	.016414	.093041	5.668496	.176414
17	12.467685	71.6730	.013952	.080207	5.748703	.173952
18	14.462515	84.1407	.011885	.069144	5.817847	.171885
19	16.776517	98.6032	.010142	.059607	5.877454	.170142
20	19.460760	115.3797	.008667	.051385	5.928839	.168667
21	22.574482	134.8405	.007416	.044298	5.973137	.167416
22	26.186399	157.4150	.006353	.038188	6.011325	.166353
23	30.376223	183.6014	.005447	.032920	6.044245	.165447
24	35.236418	213.9776	.004673	.028380	6.072625	.164673
25	40.874245	249.2140	.004013	.024465	6.097090	.164013
26	47.414124	290.0883	.003447	.021091	6.118181	.163447
27	55.000384	337.5024	.002963	.018182	6.136363	.162963
28	63.800446	392.5028	.002548	.015674	6.152037	.162548
29	74.008517	456.3032	.002192	.013512	6.165549	.162192
30	85.849880	530.3117	.001886	.011648	6.177197	.161886

ANNUAL COMPOUND INTEREST TABLE 18%
EFFECTIVE RATE = 18%   BASE = 1.18

YEARS	1 AMOUNT OF 1 AT COMPOUND INTEREST $S^n=(1+i)^n$	2 ACCUMULATION OF 1 PER PERIOD $S_{\overline{n}|}=\frac{S^n-1}{i}$	3 SINKING FUND FACTOR $1/S_{\overline{n}|}=\frac{i}{S^n-1}$	4 PRES. VALUE REVERSION OF 1 $V^n=\frac{1}{S^n}$	5 PRESENT VALUE ORD. ANNUITY 1 PER PERIOD $a_{\overline{n}|}=\frac{1-V^n}{i}$	6 INSTALMENT TO AMORTIZE 1 $1/a_{\overline{n}|}=\frac{i}{1-V^n}$
1	1.180000	1.0000	1.000000	.847458	.847458	1.180000
2	1.392400	2.1800	.458715	.718184	1.565642	.638715
3	1.643032	3.5724	.279923	.608631	2.174273	.459923
4	1.938778	5.2154	.191738	.515789	2.690062	.371738
5	2.287758	7.1542	.139778	.437109	3.127171	.319778
6	2.699554	9.4420	.105910	.370432	3.497603	.285910
7	3.185474	12.1415	.082362	.313925	3.811528	.262362
8	3.758859	15.3270	.065243	.266038	4.077566	.245243
9	4.435454	19.0859	.052395	.225456	4.303022	.232395
10	5.233836	23.5213	.042515	.191064	4.494086	.222515
11	6.175926	28.7551	.034776	.161919	4.656005	.214776
12	7.287593	34.9311	.028628	.137220	4.793225	.208628
13	8.599360	42.2187	.023686	.116288	4.909513	.203686
14	10.147244	50.8180	.019678	.098549	5.008062	.199678
15	11.973748	60.9653	.016403	.083516	5.091578	.196403
16	14.129023	72.9390	.013710	.070776	5.162354	.193710
17	16.672247	87.0680	.011485	.059980	5.222334	.191485
18	19.673251	103.7403	.009639	.050830	5.273164	.189639
19	23.214437	123.4135	.008103	.043077	5.316241	.188103
20	27.393035	146.6280	.006820	.036506	5.352747	.186820
21	32.323782	174.0210	.005746	.030937	5.383684	.185746
22	38.142063	206.3448	.004846	.026218	5.409902	.184846
23	45.007634	244.4869	.004090	.022218	5.432120	.184090
24	53.109008	289.4945	.003454	.018829	5.450949	.183454
25	62.668629	342.6035	.002919	.015957	5.466906	.182919
26	73.948983	405.2721	.002467	.013523	5.480429	.182467
27	87.259799	479.2211	.002087	.011460	5.491889	.182087
28	102.966563	566.4809	.001765	.009712	5.501601	.181765
29	121.500545	669.4475	.001494	.008230	5.509831	.181494
30	143.370643	790.9480	.001264	.006975	5.516806	.181264

ANNUAL COMPOUND INTEREST TABLE 20%
EFFECTIVE RATE = 20%   BASE = 1.20

1 AMOUNT OF 1 AT COMPOUND INTEREST $S^n=(1+i)^n$	2 ACCUMULATION OF 1 PER PERIOD $S_{\overline{n}|}=\frac{S^n-1}{i}$	3 SINKING FUND FACTOR $1/S_{\overline{n}|}=\frac{i}{S^n-1}$	4 PRES. VALUE REVERSION OF 1 $V^n=\frac{1}{S^n}$	5 PRESENT VALUE ORD. ANNUITY 1 PER PERIOD $a_{\overline{n}|}=\frac{1-V^n}{i}$	6 INSTALMENT TO AMORTIZE 1 $1/a_{\overline{n}|}=\frac{i}{1-V^n}$	n YEARS
1.200000	1.000000	1.000000	.833333	.833333	1.200000	1
1.440000	2.200000	.454545	.694444	1.527777	.654545	2
1.728000	3.640000	.274725	.578704	2.106481	.474725	3
2.073600	5.368000	.186289	.482253	2.588734	.386289	4
2.488320	7.441600	.134380	.401878	2.990612	.334380	5
2.985984	9.929920	.100706	.334898	3.325510	.300706	6
3.583181	12.915904	.077424	.279082	3.604592	.277424	7
4.299817	16.499085	.060609	.232568	3.837160	.260609	8
5.159780	20.798902	.048079	.193807	4.030967	.248079	9
6.191736	25.958682	.038523	.161506	4.192473	.238523	10
7.430083	32.150418	.031104	.134588	4.327061	.231104	11
8.916100	39.580501	.025265	.112157	4.439218	.225265	12
10.699320	48.496601	.020620	.093464	4.532682	.220620	13
12.839184	59.195921	.016893	.077887	4.610569	.216893	14
15.407021	72.035105	.013882	.064905	4.675474	.213882	15
18.488514	87.442126	.011436	.054088	4.729562	.211436	16
22.186217	105.930640	.009440	.045073	4.774635	.209440	17
26.623460	128.116857	.007805	.037561	4.812196	.207805	18
31.948153	154.740317	.006462	.031301	4.843497	.206462	19
38.337783	186.688470	.005357	.026085	4.869582	.205357	20
46.005340	225.026253	.004444	.021737	4.891319	.204444	21
55.206408	271.031593	.003690	.018114	4.909433	.203690	22
66.247690	326.238001	.003065	.015095	4.924528	.203065	23
79.497228	392.485691	.002548	.012579	4.937107	.202548	24
95.396675	471.982919	.002119	.010483	4.947590	.202119	25
114.476010	567.379594	.001762	.008735	4.956325	.201762	26
137.371212	681.855604	.001467	.007280	4.963605	.201467	27
164.845454	819.226816	.001221	.006066	4.969671	.201221	28
197.814545	984.072270	.001016	.005055	4.974726	.201016	29
237.377454	1181.886815	.000846	.004213	4.978939	.200846	30

ANNUAL COMPOUND INTEREST TABLE 22%

EFFECTIVE RATE = 22%   BASE = 1.22

YEARS n	1 AMOUNT OF 1 AT COMPOUND INTEREST $S^n = (1+i)^n$	2 ACCUMULATION OF 1 PER PERIOD $S_{\overline{n}|} = \frac{S^n-1}{i}$	3 SINKING FUND FACTOR $1/S_{\overline{n}|} = \frac{i}{S^n-1}$	4 PRES. VALUE REVERSION OF 1 $V^n = \frac{1}{S^n}$	5 PRESENT VALUE ORD. ANNUITY 1 PER PERIOD $a_{\overline{n}|} = \frac{1-V^n}{i}$	6 INSTALMENT TO AMORTIZE 1 $1/a_{\overline{n}|} = \frac{i}{1-V^n}$
1	1.220000	1.000000	1.000000	.819672	.819672	1.220000
2	1.488400	2.220000	.450450	.671862	1.491534	.670450
3	1.815848	3.708400	.269658	.550707	2.042241	.489658
4	2.215335	5.524248	.181020	.451399	2.493640	.401020
5	2.702708	7.739583	.129206	.369999	2.863639	.349206
6	3.297304	10.442291	.095764	.303278	3.166917	.315764
7	4.022711	13.739595	.072782	.248589	3.415506	.292782
8	4.907707	17.762306	.056299	.203761	3.619267	.276299
9	5.987402	22.670013	.044111	.167017	3.786284	.264111
10	7.304631	28.657415	.034895	.136899	3.923183	.254895
11	8.911649	35.962046	.027807	.112213	4.035396	.247807
12	10.872213	44.873695	.022285	.091978	4.127374	.242285
13	13.264099	55.745908	.017939	.075391	4.202765	.237939
14	16.182201	69.010007	.014491	.061796	4.264561	.234491
15	19.742285	85.192208	.011738	.050653	4.315214	.231738
16	24.085588	104.934493	.009530	.041519	4.356733	.229530
17	29.384417	129.020081	.007751	.034032	4.390765	.227751
18	35.848989	158.404498	.006313	.027895	4.418660	.226313
19	43.735766	194.253487	.005148	.022865	4.441525	.225148
20	53.357635	237.989253	.004202	.018741	4.460266	.224202
21	65.096315	291.346888	.003432	.015362	4.475628	.223432
22	79.417504	356.443203	.002805	.012592	4.488220	.222805
23	96.889355	435.860707	.002294	.010321	4.498541	.222294
24	118.205016	532.750062	.001877	.008460	4.507001	.221877
25	144.210119	650.955078	.001536	.006934	4.513935	.221536

ANNUAL COMPOUND INTEREST TABLE 24%

EFFECTIVE RATE = 24%   BASE = 1.24

n YEARS	1 AMOUNT OF 1 AT COMPOUND INTEREST $S^n = (1+i)^n$	2 ACCUMULATION OF 1 PER PERIOD $S_{\overline{n}|} = \frac{S^n-1}{i}$	3 SINKING FUND FACTOR $1/S_{\overline{n}|} = \frac{i}{S^n-1}$	4 PRES. VALUE REVERSION OF 1 $V^n = \frac{1}{S^n}$	5 PRESENT VALUE ORD. ANNUITY 1 PER PERIOD $a_{\overline{n}|} = \frac{1-V^n}{i}$	6 INSTALMENT TO AMORTIZE 1 $1/a_{\overline{n}|} = \frac{i}{1-V^n}$
1	1.240000	1.000000	1.000000	.806452	.806452	1.240000
2	1.537600	2.240000	.446429	.650364	1.456816	.686429
3	1.906624	3.777600	.264718	.524487	1.981303	.504718
4	2.364214	5.684224	.175926	.422974	2.404277	.415926
5	2.931625	8.048438	.124248	.341108	2.745385	.364248
6	3.635215	10.980063	.091074	.275087	3.020472	.331074
7	4.507666	14.615278	.068422	.221844	3.242316	.308422
8	5.589506	19.122944	.052293	.178907	3.421223	.292293
9	6.930988	24.712450	.040465	.144280	3.565503	.280465
10	8.594425	31.643438	.031602	.116354	3.681857	.271602
11	10.657087	40.237863	.024852	.093834	3.775691	.264852
12	13.214788	50.894950	.019648	.075673	3.851364	.259648
13	16.386337	64.109738	.015598	.061026	3.912390	.255598
14	20.319057	80.496075	.012423	.049215	3.961605	.252423
15	25.195631	100.815132	.009919	.039689	4.001294	.249919
16	31.242582	126.010763	.007936	.032008	4.033302	.247936
17	38.740802	157.253345	.006359	.025813	4.059115	.246359
18	48.038594	195.994147	.005102	.020817	4.079932	.245102
19	59.567857	244.032741	.004098	.016788	4.096720	.244098
20	73.864143	303.600598	.003294	.013538	4.110258	.243294
21	91.591537	377.464741	.002649	.010918	4.121176	.242649
22	113.573506	469.056278	.002132	.008805	4.129981	.242132
23	140.831147	582.629784	.001716	.007101	4.137082	.241716
24	174.630622	723.460931	.001382	.005726	4.142808	.241382
25	216.541971	898.091553	.001113	.004618	4.147426	.241113

ANNUAL COMPOUND INTEREST TABLE 26%

EFFECTIVE RATE = 26%   BASE = 1.26

	1 AMOUNT OF 1 AT COMPOUND INTEREST $S^n=(1+i)^n$	2 ACCUMULATION OF 1 PER PERIOD $S_{\overline{n}|}=\frac{S^n-1}{i}$	3 SINKING FUND FACTOR $1/S_{\overline{n}|}=\frac{i}{S^n-1}$	4 PRES. VALUE REVERSION OF 1 $V^n=\frac{1}{S^n}$	5 PRESENT VALUE ORD. ANNUITY 1 PER PERIOD $a_{\overline{n}|}=\frac{1-V^n}{i}$	6 INSTALMENT TO AMORTIZE 1 $1/a_{\overline{n}|}=\frac{i}{1-V^n}$
1	1.260000	1.000000	1.000000	.793651	.793651	1.260000
2	1.587600	2.260000	.442478	.629882	1.423533	.702478
3	2.000376	3.847600	.259902	.499906	1.923439	.519902
4	2.520474	5.847976	.170999	.396751	2.320190	.430999
5	3.175797	8.368450	.119496	.314882	2.635072	.379496
6	4.001504	11.544247	.086623	.249906	2.884978	.346623
7	5.041895	15.545751	.064326	.198338	3.083316	.324326
8	6.352788	20.587646	.048573	.157411	3.240727	.308573
9	8.004513	26.940434	.037119	.124930	3.365657	.297119
10	10.085686	34.944947	.028616	.099150	3.464807	.286616
11	12.707964	45.030633	.022207	.078691	3.543498	.282207
12	16.012035	57.738591	.017319	.062453	3.605951	.277319
13	20.175164	73.750632	.013559	.049566	3.655517	.273559
14	25.420706	93.925796	.010647	.039338	3.694855	.270647
15	32.030090	119.346502	.008379	.031221	3.726076	.268379
16	40.357913	151.376592	.006606	.024778	3.750854	.266606
17	50.850971	191.734505	.005216	.019665	3.770519	.265216
18	64.072223	242.585476	.004122	.015607	3.786126	.264122
19	80.731001	306.657699	.003261	.012387	3.798513	.263261
20	101.721061	387.388700	.002581	.009831	3.808344	.262581
21	128.168537	489.109761	.002045	.007802	3.816146	.262045
22	161.492356	617.278298	.001620	.006192	3.822338	.261620
23	203.480369	778.770654	.001284	.004914	3.827252	.261284
24	256.385265	982.251023	.001018	.003900	3.831152	.261018
25	323.045434	1238.636288	.000807	.003096	3.834248	.260807

ANNUAL COMPOUND INTEREST TABLE 28%

EFFECTIVE RATE = 28%   BASE = 1.28

n YEARS	1 AMOUNT OF 1 AT COMPOUND INTEREST $S^n=(1+i)^n$	2 ACCUMULATION OF 1 PER PERIOD $S_{\overline{n}|}=\frac{S^n-1}{i}$	3 SINKING FUND FACTOR $1/S_{\overline{n}|}=\frac{i}{S^n-1}$	4 PRES. VALUE REVERSION OF 1 $V^n=\frac{1}{S^n}$	5 PRESENT VALUE ORD. ANNUITY 1 PER PERIOD $a_{\overline{n}|}=\frac{1-V^n}{i}$	6 INSTALMENT TO AMORTIZE 1 $1/a_{\overline{n}|}=\frac{i}{1-V^n}$
1	1.280000	1.000000	1.000000	.781250	.781250	1.280000
2	1.638400	2.280000	.438596	.610352	1.391602	.718596
3	2.097152	3.918400	.255206	.476837	1.868439	.535206
4	2.684355	6.015552	.166236	.372529	2.240968	.446236
5	3.435974	8.699907	.114944	.291038	2.532006	.394944
6	4.398047	12.135881	.082400	.227374	2.759380	.362400
7	5.629499	16.533928	.060482	.177636	2.937016	.340482
8	7.205759	22.163427	.045119	.138778	3.075794	.325119
9	9.223372	29.369186	.034049	.108420	3.184214	.314049
10	11.805916	38.592558	.025912	.084703	3.268917	.305912
11	15.111573	50.398474	.019842	.066174	3.335091	.299842
12	19.342813	65.510047	.015265	.051699	3.386790	.295265
13	24.758801	84.852860	.011785	.040390	3.427180	.291785
14	31.691265	109.611661	.009123	.031554	3.458734	.289123
15	40.564819	141.302926	.007077	.024652	3.483386	.287077
16	51.922968	181.867745	.005499	.019259	3.502645	.285499
17	66.461400	233.790713	.004277	.015046	3.517691	.284277
18	85.070592	300.252113	.003331	.011755	3.529446	.283331
19	108.890357	385.322705	.002595	.009184	3.538630	.282595
20	139.379657	494.213062	.002023	.007175	3.545805	.282023
21	178.405961	633.592719	.001578	.005605	3.551410	.281578
22	228.359631	811.998680	.001232	.004379	3.555789	.281232
23	292.300327	1040.358311	.000961	.003421	3.559210	.280961
24	374.144419	1332.658638	.000750	.002673	3.561883	.280750
25	478.904856	1706.803057	.000586	.002088	3.563971	.280586

30ˣ   ANNUAL COMPOUND INTEREST TABLE   **30**ˣ

EFFECTIVE RATE = 30%　　　BASE = 1.30

	1 AMOUNT OF 1 AT COMPOUND INTEREST $S^n = (1+i)^n$	2 ACCUMULATION OF 1 PER PERIOD $S_{\overline{n}|} = \dfrac{S^n-1}{i}$	3 SINKING FUND FACTOR $1/S_{\overline{n}|} = \dfrac{i}{S^n-1}$	4 PRES. VALUE REVERSION OF 1 $V^n = \dfrac{1}{S^n}$	5 PRESENT VALUE ORD. ANNUITY 1 PER PERIOD $a_{\overline{n}|} = \dfrac{1-V^n}{i}$	6 INSTALMENT TO AMORTIZE 1 $1/a_{\overline{n}|} = \dfrac{i}{1-V^n}$	n
YEARS							YEARS
1	1.300000	1.000000	1.000000	.769231	.769231	1.300000	1
2	1.690000	2.300000	.434783	.591716	1.360941	.734783	2
3	2.197000	3.990000	.250627	.455166	1.816113	.550627	3
4	2.856100	6.187000	.161629	.350128	2.166241	.461629	4
5	3.712930	9.043100	.110582	.269329	2.435570	.410582	5
6	4.826809	12.756030	.078394	.207176	2.642746	.378394	6
7	6.274852	17.582839	.056874	.159366	2.802112	.356874	7
8	8.157307	23.857691	.041915	.122589	2.924701	.341915	8
9	10.604499	32.014998	.031235	.094300	3.019001	.331235	9
10	13.785849	42.619497	.023463	.072538	3.091539	.323463	10
11	17.921160	56.405346	.017729	.055799	3.147338	.317729	11
12	23.298085	74.326506	.013454	.042922	3.190260	.313454	12
13	30.287510	97.622591	.010244	.033017	3.223277	.310244	13
14	39.373763	127.910101	.007818	.025398	3.248675	.307818	14
15	51.185892	167.283864	.005978	.019537	3.268212	.305978	15
16	66.541660	218.469756	.004577	.015028	3.283240	.304577	16
17	86.504158	285.011416	.003509	.011560	3.294800	.303509	17
18	112.455405	371.515574	.002692	.008892	3.303692	.302692	18
19	146.192026	483.970979	.002066	.006840	3.310532	.302066	19
20	190.049634	630.163005	.001587	.005262	3.315794	.301587	20
21	247.064524	820.212639	.001219	.004048	3.319842	.301219	21
22	321.183882	1067.277163	.000937	.003113	3.322955	.300937	22
23	417.539046	1388.461054	.000720	.002395	3.325350	.300720	23
24	542.800760	1806.000091	.000554	.001842	3.327192	.300554	24
25	705.640988	2348.800851	.000426	.001417	3.328609	.300426	25

Index